101 Performance Projects
For Your **BMW**
3 Series 1982-2000

Wayne R. Dempsey

MOTORBOOKS

First published in 2006 by Motorbooks, an imprint of MBI Publishing Company, Galtier Plaza, Suite 200, 380 Jackson Street, St. Paul, MN 55101-3885 USA

MBI Publishing Company titles are also available at discounts in bulk quantity for industrial or sales-promotional use. For details write to Special Sales Manager at MBI Publishing Company, Galtier Plaza, Suite 200, 380 Jackson Street, St. Paul, MN 55101-3885 USA

ISBN-13: 978-0-7603-2695-4
ISBN-10: 0-7603-2695-9

Editor: Lindsay Hitch
Designer: Christopher Fayers

Printed in China

On the cover, main: Light, nimble, and designed with the driving enthusiast in mind, the 3 Series has rightly earned its reputation as one of the world's greatest driving sports sedans. The Motorsports models of the 3 Series have been designated as M3 models. The car in the foreground is an E30 M3, outfitted with a high-performance inline four-cylinder engine. The white E36 M3 is fitted with a high-performance version of BMW's legendary inline six-cylinder engine. *Les Bidrawn*

Inset: BMW camshafts are fragile and can easily break if not handled correctly. Using the method described in Project 11, you can safely remove the camshafts without the expensive factory removal tool.

On the title page: An original BMW lightweight M3 (LTW) turned track racer by Hans Kopecky off SSF Auto Parts.

On the back cover: A 1995 M3 on a rolling dynamometer. Engine modifications include a large-bore throttle body, cold air intake, Jim Conforti chip, Stromung exhaust, lightweight aluminum flywheel, 3.2-liter M3 clutch package, Schrick 256/264 camshafts, and 24-pound Ford Motorsports fuel injectors.

About the Author

Wayne R. Dempsey is the author of the highly successful books *101 Projects for Your Porsche 911* and *How to Rebuild and Modify Porsche 911 Engines*. Wayne earned both BS and MS degrees in mechanical engineering from the Massachusetts Institute of Technology, specializing in flexible manufacturing technology. His introduction to automobiles began when he raced with the MIT Solar Electric Vehicle Racing Team. Literally starting in their garages, Wayne and his partner, Tom Gould, founded Pelican Parts, an internet-based Porsche and BMW parts company. Wayne has written most of the technical articles featured on www.PelicanParts.com. Wayne's current BMW stable includes a 1992 318is, a 1993 325is, a 1995 325ic, a 1987 325e, a 1998 supercharged 528i sedan, and a 1999 528it wagon.

101 Projects Website

www.101Projects.com contains book updates, exclusive photos, a BMW 3 Series forum and BBS, links to sites for more information, and locations where you can purchase the parts and tools mentioned in this book.

CONTENTS

CONTENTS

ACKNOWLEDGMENTS

It's obvious that a book of this magnitude does not simply write itself, but needs a cooperative effort from many people in all walks of life. A lot of people have helped me with this book over the past four years and have joined in my enthusiastic vision of what I wanted it to be. First, I would like to thank my very patient wife, Nori; without her unending support and patience this project would never have gotten finished. Also, thanks to my two young children, Sean and Holly, to whom this book is dedicated. Special thanks to Lindsay Hitch, Jim Michels, Becky Pagel, Chris Fayers, and Carol Drotman for packaging my wordy content into a concise and usable format. Special thanks to Zack Miller for giving me more space to add more content, and for putting up with my occasionally irascible temper. Of course, no good acknowledgments section would be complete without a note of thanks to my parents, Meg and Ed Dempsey. In the beginning, I'm certain they thought I was headed for trouble, but somehow they managed to turn the tide, and this book is one of many accomplishments that they have been proud of over the years. Also very helpful were Peter Bodensteiner, Ward Myers, Hans Kopecky, Fletcher Benton, Jay Horak, Randy Leffingwell, Jim Goodroe, Josh Berman, Jared Fenton, Eli Sesma, Jay Linton, Rick Clewett, Chris Bethel, Steve Andersen, Alex Wong, Tom Gould, and a host of others who have given me help and encouragement with this great book.

DECIPHERING THE INFORMATION BOXES

At the beginning of each project you'll find a list of topics keyed to picture icons. This is a guide to assist you in having all the "right stuff" to complete the project. Most of the list is self-explanatory, but in case you're curious here is a breakdown:

 Time is a rough estimate for anyone with basic car and tool skills. If you don't know your open-end 15-millimeter from a Vise-Grip, you may want to add to the time estimate.

 Tab is a ballpark expense figure. Use it as a basic guideline, not as a firm figure.

Talent is represented by a mechanic icon. One mechanic means any warm body with the inkling to tinker can do the job. Two mechanics means the project requires some mechanical experience and ability. Three mechanics means you are comfortable working on more complex assemblies, such as top ends, clutches, or exhausts. Four mechanics implies you are well versed in wrenching. Perhaps you've even had some training. A project at this level could be attempted with the assistance of a more experienced mechanic. Five mechanics marks a job best left to the pros, but those who aspire to professional tuner status could press ahead.

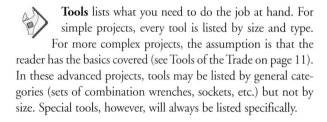 **Tools** lists what you need to do the job at hand. For simple projects, every tool is listed by size and type. For more complex projects, the assumption is that the reader has the basics covered (see Tools of the Trade on page 11). In these advanced projects, tools may be listed by general categories (sets of combination wrenches, sockets, etc.) but not by size. Special tools, however, will always be listed specifically.

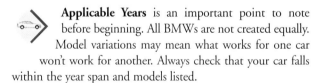 **Applicable Years** is an important point to note before beginning. All BMWs are not created equally. Model variations may mean what works for one car won't work for another. Always check that your car falls within the year span and models listed.

 Tinware lists the parts you will have to acquire to complete this project and directly relates to Tab.

 Tip lists a slick trick that will make the project easier. It might be a gem of knowledge that the shop manual doesn't include.

 Performance Gain is self-explanatory. What you get for your money is answered right here.

Complementary Modification will offer some trick bit and alterations to help you get the most out of the project. In some cases, these might be other projects that work well when performed with the current one.

INTRODUCTION

Since its introduction in 1975, the BMW 3 Series has earned a reputation as one of the world's greatest sports sedans. Not only has the 3 Series been improved and refined over the years to a state of near perfection, it has also garnered a huge, loyal following of people who love to drive these cars. BMW 3 Series owners tend to adore their cars and also enjoy restoring, modifying, and maintaining them to perfection. If you're one of these people, then this book was written especially for you.

Information is the key to success in any project or endeavor. Without the proper knowledge, you can make costly mistakes and waste your time as you trudge through the learning process. The projects in this book aim to eliminate any guesswork that you may have while working on your BMW. My motto has always been, "Let me make the mistakes and warn you about them, so you won't do the same." I've made many mistakes—and learned the hard way—the best and worst ways to repair, restore, and modify these cars. My lessons, as well as those learned by the expert mechanics I've consulted with, are compiled here for you.

Who am I? I am the owner of one of the largest BMW online parts retailers, www.PelicanParts.com. I designed and built Pelican Parts especially for the do-it-yourself (DIY) mechanics who love to work on their own cars—people just like me. Our website has hundreds of BMW technical articles that are the foundation for most of the projects in this book. If you like what you see in this book, you will definitely enjoy more of the same at our website, www.PelicanParts.com.

The projects in this book are written in a format and style that should empower anyone to work on his or her car. One of the principal drawbacks to owning a BMW is the high cost of maintaining it. You can literally save thousands of dollars in mechanics' costs simply by performing the work yourself. With this book, more people can get out working on their BMWs—it's too much fun not to! Plus, when you personally complete a job on your BMW, you get the added satisfaction of having done it yourself. Working on your own 3 Series can build an emotional attachment to your car that is common among BMW owners.

This book is divided into 11 sections, each focusing on a particular system of the BMW 3 Series. In an attempt to appeal to everyone, some of the projects are basic, while others are more advanced. Some of the projects are simply overviews of systems found on the 3 Series. For example, Project 22 covers supercharger installation and is simply meant to give you an inside look into what happens when you take your engine's performance to the next level.

Most projects follow a distinct how-to format. Step-by-step instructions explain how to perform the job, what tools to use, and what mistakes to avoid. The photos that accompany the projects tell a story of their own. I've included hints and tips throughout each project, so make sure to read all the text and photo captions before you start.

Beyond this book, I've also created a bonus CD-ROM that contains additional information and photos. The CD-ROM is available for purchase at www.101Projects.com, which also provides a discussion forum so that you can ask questions and get feedback regarding any of these projects. You can often find me—along with many other BMW experts—there, ready to share knowledge and exchange ideas.

Please don't be afraid to get this book dirty—take it with you underneath the car. Get it greasy. Compare the pictures in the book to your own car. Follow along, step by step, as you tear into each project. If this book gets dirty, then I will sleep well at night knowing that it's being put to good use.

While this book is a great guide for determining what upgrades and maintenance to perform on your BMW, it's not meant to be the only book for your car. I simply can't provide all the detailed diagrams, torque settings, and factory procedures that are documented in the original factory workshop manuals. Be sure to review the BMW 3 Series Resources section of this book for the best places to find additional technical information for the BMW 3 Series.

This book is not meant to be read from cover to cover but is designed to be flipped through so that you can get an idea of which projects interest you. I've structured the projects so that you can simply open up the book and start working on your car. I do recommend, however, that you read both Tools of the Trade and Project 1: Jacking up Your Car before you start working on any of the projects.

I have taken special care to ensure this book's index is useful and easy to navigate. The index contains words used within the projects as well as other common words related to each project. That way, if there are different names for a part or procedure, you can still locate it within the text. For example, shocks are listed as both "shock absorbers" and "inserts," as they are sometimes called.

Finally, remember that safety should be your **number one** concern. It's easy to get so involved with working on your 3 Series that you forget how vulnerable the human body can be. Have patience, and think about every action you take before you make it. Think ahead as to what might happen if you slip or if something breaks.

I hope you enjoy the book, as I have spent several years compiling and organizing this information so that it's easy to understand and follow. If you have any feedback or questions for me, you can contact me at www.101Projects.com. Enjoy!

BMW MODEL DESIGNATIONS

One of the most challenging aspects of discussing BMWs is making sense of the designations that BMW uses to name its cars. In general, BMW follows a pretty consistent pattern, but unfortunately, many confusing exceptions have occurred. To assist you in this regard, I've compiled a handy chart of nearly all of the BMW models and engines produced.

What does it mean when someone calls my car an E30? To start, BMW has labeled each chassis style with an engineering code. For example, the 1992–1999 3 Series cars are known as the E36 chassis group. The 3 Series cars of 1984–1992 are known as the E30 chassis group. I refer to these two chassis numbers throughout the book.

As the body styles changed over the years, BMW introduced a new designation with each radical change. Of course, there are confusing exceptions to this rule. One example is the 3 Series convertibles of 1992–1993. BMW didn't have the E36 convertible chassis ready yet, so they sold the E36 in the coupe and sedan form alongside the E30 convertible for those two years.

Here's a chart that indicates the most common chassis platforms:

Code	Description
114	1602 through 2002tii
118	1500, 1600, 1800, 1800tii
120	2000C/CS/CA
121	2000, 2000ti, 2000tilux
E3	2500 through 3.3Li and Bavaria
E6	1600, 1800, 2000 touring
E9	2500CS through 3.0 CSi
E12	5 Series cars from 1974 to 1981
E21	3 Series cars from 1976 to 1983
E23	7 Series cars from 1977 to 1986
E24	6 Series cars from 1976 to 1989
E26	M1
E28	5 Series cars from 1981 to 1987
E30	3 Series cars from 1984 to 1991 (1982–1983 E30 sold in Europe)
E31	8 Series cars from 1989 to 1997
E32	7 Series cars from 1986 to 1994
E34	5 Series cars from 1988 to 1995
E36	3 Series cars from 1992 to 1999 (3 Series compact through 2000)
E36/5	318ti
E36/7	Z3 roadster
E38	7 Series cars from 1994 to 2001
E39	5 Series cars from late 1995 to 2003
E46	3 Series cars from 1999 to 2005
E52	Z8 roadster
E53	X5 SAV
E60	5 Series from 2003
E63	6 Series coupes from 2004
E64	6 Series convertibles from 2004
E65	7 Series cars from 2002 (short wheelbase)
E66	7 Series cars from 2002 (long wheelbase)
E83	X3
E85	Z4 roadster
E87	1 Series from 2005
E90	3 Series from 2006

What do the letters on the back of the car mean? To add to the confusion, BMW has used a whole host of letters and numbers to designate differences between the different models in a series. For instance, "is" would mean "injected sports" model.

Here's a breakdown of the letters and what they mean. It's important to keep in mind that various BMWs use multiple combinations of these letters. However, these letters are the most common.

Ci	Fuel injected coupe. This designation is used on most modern BMWs
Csi	Fuel injected sports coupe
e	ETA model. Built by BMW as efficiency-minded cars during the 1980s with lower-revving engines having higher torque due to a shorter stroke
es	ETA: sports ETA model with sports package
i	Fuel injected
ic	Fuel injected cabriolet and convertible models
is	Fuel injected sports. Sports package with better suspension, sway bars, etc.
iT	Fuel injected touring. BMW's station wagon
iX	Fuel injected all-wheel drive
L	Luxury (before E32). Basically, a normal car fitted with full leather and all options (e.g., L6, L7)
L	Long wheelbase (from E32 on). Includes E38, E66, et al.
M	Motorsport: M3 and M5, for example. BMW's hot rod
Ti	Fuel injected touring compact
Tii	Fuel injected touring international. Used only on early cars

Okay, so what is the difference between a 525i and a 535i, or a 325i and a 328is? With the exception of the early cars (1600, 1800, 2002, etc.), BMW typically uses a three-digit numbering system to identify models. The first number refers to the series: 328is would belong to the 3 Series, while a 740iL would belong to the 7 Series. The last two numbers are typically the engine displacement, in liters, of a particular model. So, a 328is would refer to a 3 Series, fuel-injected 2.8-liter engine with the sports package. The 740iL would refer to a 7 Series, fuel-injected 4.0-liter engine with a luxury package.

Exceptions to these rules are plentiful. For example, the "is" specification, which refers to the sports package on the E30 cars, is also used to designate the two-door coupes on the E36 cars. All two-door coupes in the E36 lineup are called the "is" model.

Another strange exception occurred in 1996 with the introduction of the 328. In the previous year, BMW had offered two engines in the 3 Series line, the four-cylinder 1.8-liter engine (the 318) and the 2.5-liter six-cylinder engine (the 325). The 318 was offered as the basic model, while the 325 was the more luxurious model with a larger engine and more options installed as standard equipment. In 1996, the 328, with its larger 2.8-liter engine, became the upscale model; the basic model received a detuned version of the older 2.5-liter engine from the 325. However, BMW didn't want the 1996 basic model to have the same name as the 1995 luxury model, so it called the new basic model the 323, even though it had a 2.5-liter engine.

Exceptions like these have been common throughout the years, so keep in mind that the last two numbers of the model do not always mean actual engine displacement.

What are they talking about when they say my 325i has an M20? Usually BMW uses an M or S designation to identify its engines. The M engines are generally stock engines, while the S engines are the motorsport engines used in the M series of cars (just the opposite of what you'd think). In most cases, several different engines are used in a particular series; a 2.8, 3.5, and 4.0 are all available in the E34 5 Series.

Here is a breakdown of the various designations and engines. For each engine listed, there is usually a displacement code. For instance, an M20B27 would be an M20 engine with a 2.7-liter displacement.

These are old BMW engine codes that are no longer used:

M41	Four-cylinder 1.6-liter DIDTA carburetor
M42	Four-cylinder 1.8-liter DIDTA carburetor
M49	Six-cylinder 3.4-liter 24-valve motorsport twin cam
M60	Six-cylinder 2.0-liter and 2.3-liter carburetor or fuel injection
M68	Six-cylinder 2.5-liter and 2.8-liter carburetor
M69	Six-cylinder 3.2-liter fuel injection
M86	Six-cylinder 2.8-liter fuel injection (L-Jetronic)
M90	Six-cylinder 3.5-liter
M92	Four-cylinder 1.8-liter fuel injection (K-Jetronic)
M99	Four-cylinder 1.8-liter 2B4 carburetor
M102	Six-cylinder 3.2-liter turbocharged

These are the current BMW engine codes used today:

M10	Four-cylinder 1.8-liter or 2.0-liter SOHC, timing chain
M20	Six-cylinder 2.0-, 2.3-, 2.5-, or 2.7-liter SOHC, timing belt
M21	Six-cylinder 2.4-liter diesel SOHC, timing belt
M30	Six-cylinder 2.8-, 3.0-, 3.2-, or 3.4-liter SOHC, timing chain
M40	Four-cylinder 1.6- or 1.8-liter DOHC
M41	Four-cylinder 1.7-liter diesel
M42	Four-cylinder 1.8-liter DOHC
M44	Four-cylinder 1.9-liter DOHC
M50	Six-cylinder 2.0-, 2.3-, or 2.5-liter DOHC
M50TU	Six-cylinder 2.0-, 2.3-, or 2.5-liter DOHC, VANOS variable intake
M51	Six-cylinder 2.5-liter diesel
M52	Six-cylinder 2.0-, 2.3-, 2.5-, or 2.8-liter DOHC, VANOS variable intake
M52TU	Six-cylinder 2.5- and 3.0-liter DOHC, VANOS variable intake and exhaust
M54	Six-cylinder 2.5- and 3.0-liter DOHC, VANOS variable intake and exhaust
M56	Six-cylinder 2.5-liter DOHC, dual VANOS, SULEV (low emissions)
M60	Eight-cylinder 3.0- or 4.0-liter
M62	Eight-cylinder 3.5- or 4.4-liter
M70	12-cylinder 5.0-liter
M73	12-cylinder 5.4-liter
M88	Six-cylinder 3.5-liter, 24-valve motorsport engine (only BMW M1)
M88/3	Same as above, but for all other vehicles
S14	Four-cylinder 2.3-liter DOHC motorsport engine (only E30 M3)
S38	Six-cylinder 3.6- or 3.8-liter DOHC motorsport engine
S50	Six-cylinder 3.0- or 3.2-liter DOHC, dual VANOS motorsport engine (non-U.S. M3)
S50US	Six-cylinder 3.0- or 3.2-liter DOHC, single VANOS motorsport engine (U.S. M3)
S52	Six-cylinder 3.2-liter DOHC, dual VANOS motorsport engine
S54	Six-cylinder 3.2-liter DOHC, dual VANOS motorsport engine
S62	Eight-cylinder 5.0-liter quad cam, quad VANOS motorsport engine
S70	12-cylinder 5.6-liter motorsport engine

You can't ever have too much information, especially when working on an automobile. For the BMW 3 Series, there are a few really great technical resources that I refer to regularly when working on my own cars. Here's a brief breakdown of what I recommend:

PelicanParts.com—This website has a treasure-trove of technical articles, diagrams, hints, and a neat forum/BBS tied into this book. If you like the material presented in this book, then you'll love the increased detail and depth that

the PelicanParts.com website has to offer. In addition, Pelican Parts has the Internet's largest online parts catalog, complete with just about everything you could want or need for your BMW. You can even order "dealer-only" parts directly on the site, simply by typing the part number into the Pelican Parts search engine.

Bentley Manuals—This *101 Projects* book is written specifically to complement, and to be used in conjunction with, the Bentley workshop manuals. They are a reference bible for working on 3 Series cars, and I recommend that you do not pick up a wrench until you have one of these in hand. The Bentley manual contains all of the torque specs, parts information, electrical diagrams, and repair procedures that you would find in a typical factory workshop manual. I have purposely tried not to duplicate information that is already published in the Bentley manuals, instead saving room for material that is not specifically covered within them. These manuals are also available in a CD-ROM version with completely searchable text.

BMW 3 Series Enthusiast's Companion—Not to be confused with the *BMW Enthusiast's Companion*, this book is tailored specifically for the 3 Series. Although it's not a tech book, it does contain a thorough and complete history of the cars and the design theory that led to their development and refinement throughout the years. It specifically covers the early 3 Series up to and including the 2000 E46 3 Series models.

BMW Automobiles 1928–2001—This is a neat little spec book I found on eBay. There's no BMW part number, but the book covers all of the production car models and engines that BMW ever built. It's a really valuable resource filled with useful facts. For example, if you want to know, "How many E30 and E36 3 Series cars were built?" (Answer: 2,339,251 E30s from 1982 to 1994; and 2,745,773 E36s from 1990 to 2000.)

BMW Enthusiast's Companion—This book is similar to the BMW CCA CD-ROM set listed above. It's best described as *Roundel*'s greatest hits and contains a collection of great articles and tech tips pulled from the best minds of the BMW Car Club of America. Covering all models of BMW, the book offers valuable insights from basic maintenance to driving theory—all written by BMW owners for BMW drivers.

BMW ETK/TIS—This is the internal BMW parts catalog and factory manual system. While the parts system (ETK) is very well thought out, the technical information system (TIS) is very difficult to use or to derive any useful information from its pages. The factory manual information is only available through the TIS system and, as far as I know, it's only available from the dealers.

Electrical Troubleshooting Manual—This is a BMW factory manual that I happened to discover one day on eBay (BMW PN 01-00-1-468-774). It contains complete, comprehensive factory workshop electrical diagrams and pin-outs for the various connectors on the car. This manual is an absolute must if you are going to be troubleshooting electrical problems. The Bentley manuals also include comprehensive electrical diagrams, but given the choice, I prefer original factory documentation. At the time of this writing, the manual is currently out of print, but you may be able to find one at a used bookstore or on the Internet.

Haynes Repair Manual—I've never been a huge fan of the *Haynes* manuals, but I've purchased one for every car I've owned. They are excellent sources of information when compared to their overall cost (about $15). Keeping with the mantra that you can never have enough information, *Haynes* has sometimes been the only manual that had the one specific piece of information I was seeking.

Reader's Digest Complete Car Care Manual—As you're reading this, I'm sure that you're thinking that this must be a mistake. However, out of my extensive automotive book collection, I can honestly say that this book is my all-time favorite. Although it was last published in 1981, it contains some of the best illustrations, descriptions, and explanations of how all cars work. It's out of print, but you can find used copies on eBay. From A/C systems to automatic transmissions, this book explains the material so clearly and easily that even your Aunt Bertha will understand.

Roundel—The monthly magazine of the BMW Car Club of America (CCA) is archived on this CD-ROM set. Also published by Bentley, the set is a valuable collection of all of the articles that have appeared in the magazine over the past 30 years. There's a ton of good technical information inside, and it's a worthwhile addition to your collection. http://www. bmwcca.org/

We've all heard the clichés about having the right to tool for the job. Most of us have heard stories about a botched repair or wasted hours because somebody attempted to save a few dollars by putting off buying the right tool. Here's the nuts and bolts of it: Even though all good mechanics will admit that there is no substitute for the correct tool, they will also admit that no matter how many tools you have, you will never have every tool you need. I've learned that having just the right tool for the job can turn a five-hour problem into a five-minute fix. The more you work on your car—and the more you look at tool catalogs—you'll find that you'll cherish the art of buying and acquiring tools. But you need a good place to start. Here are some of my suggestions to get you on your way.

The Basic Tool Set

There are literally tens of thousands of tools available to perform an equal number of tasks. Fortunately, it's not likely you'll need all of them.

Everybody has to start somewhere, and for most people that means a small set or kit (often received as a gift). Sets are an excellent way to buy tools, since the discounts are pretty sizeable, compared to buying each tool individually. Aside from the cost, one of your primary considerations should be quality. The warranty and ease of replacement are other good considerations. It does no good if you have to mail your broken tool back to Taiwan for replacement, or if your tool truck guy doesn't come around at 2 a.m. on Sunday when you need him the most. Ultimately, the best bet is to buy tools that don't break, or to carry the spares you need.

Two of the best and most-economical places to purchase tools are Sears and Home Depot. They both offer good-quality tools, mostly American made, that seldom break. In addition, both the Sears Craftsman line and the Home Depot Husky line offer lifetime replacements. No matter how much damage is done to any tool you purchase from them, you can take it back and receive a replacement free of charge. Just be sure to purchase the specific brand that offers the warranty. For example, Sears sells both Craftsman tools and Sears-brand tools, but the latter is not covered under the lifetime replacement warranty.

The Craftsman and Husky lines are good-quality tools. It's human nature sometimes to cheap out and purchase tools sold for bargain-basement prices. These will usually follow the rule that "you get what you pay for." I advise that you stay away from tools made in Taiwan or China because the quality is often very questionable.

One exception to the foreign tool rule can apply to what I call "disposable" tools. Sometimes foreign-made socket sets that are cheaper than the American sets have socket walls that are much thinner than the American sets. The thinner walls allow these sockets to fit onto nuts that the American thick-walled sets might not. In cases like these, it is nice to have a set of these cheaper sockets around, although after three to four uses, they are sufficiently worn out and may need to be thrown away.

Your automotive tool set should include the following basic items:

Screwdrivers: You should have at least three flat-tip ($\frac{3}{32}$, $\frac{3}{16}$, and $\frac{5}{16}$) and two Phillips-tip (number 1 and number 2) screwdrivers. Inspect the tips of your screwdrivers to be sure that they are not bent, broken, or otherwise worn. A damaged screwdriver is a quick way to strip the head of a fastener, turning an otherwise simple repair into a nightmare. A ratcheting screwdriver is a useful tool as well, as it allows you to unscrew fasteners without removing the tip from the fastener.

Adjustable wrench: Many mechanics won't admit to actually owning an adjustable wrench (sometimes known as an adjustable crescent wrench) but usually have a couple hidden for lapses into laziness. Quality is of the utmost importance when choosing an adjustable wrench. Less-expensive wrenches have jaws that will stretch, mar, and otherwise fall apart when used; this is another way to damage a fastener and ruin your day. A good adjustable plumber's wrench can also come in handy when you need to remove large stubborn nuts.

Pliers: No tool set would be complete without a few sets of pliers. The three basic types are slip-joint, adjustable (sometimes called channel-lock), and needle-nose. The most important consideration when choosing pliers is the teeth. The teeth should be sharp—and they should stay sharp—as pliers are generally used under less-than-ideal circumstances. Again, don't cheap out on the pliers. The Vise-Grip brand is very good, and a set of multiple sizes will serve you well over many years.

Sockets and drivers: Aside from a variety of sizes, sockets come in either 12-point or six-point, with regular and deep versions. Twelve-point versions are more versatile, but six-point sockets are stronger and do less damage to fasteners. Socket drivers normally come in $\frac{1}{4}$-, $\frac{3}{8}$-, $\frac{1}{2}$-, $\frac{3}{4}$-, and 1-inch sizes. If I had a choice of only one driver size, it would be ⅜-inch. Not only is ⅜-inch ideal for torque applications on cars (up to about 60 ft-lb), but it also has the greatest number of available accessories. Your socket set should include a good ratchet (money well spent), a 2-inch extension, a 6-inch extension, and a universal joint.

The Sears Craftsman line used to offer a great 99-piece socket set for about $100 that was entirely metric, but I have not been able to find it lately. A complete metric set is a great starting point and will likely be the cornerstone of your collection. This set contains three socket ratchet drivers in three different sizes and the associated short and deep sockets. Also useful, a set of universal or swivel joints will allow you to reach difficult nuts. Start with the basic universal joint set, and then buy the kind with the built-in sockets when you need them.

A deep-socket metric set is useful as well. Again, Craftsman has a good-quality set. In general, if you find that you need an individual socket, it's wise to purchase a small set that has that size in it rather than purchase the individual socket.

Wrenches: The combination wrench is the backbone of any good automotive tool set. "Combination" means a wrench that is closed (boxed) at one end (like a socket) and open at the other end. There are other varieties available, such as double-open, double-boxed, deep-offset, and socket wrenches. Ideally, you'll need a range of 7- to 19-millimeter wrenches for starters (and an extra 10- and 13-millimeter will always come in handy). Recently, there have been a number of key innovations in wrench technology. Of these new tools, the GearWrenches are my favorite. These combination wrenches have very fine, reversible ratchets built in. They are useful in all circumstances, and I use the GearWrenches almost exclusively these days. I recommend the 12-piece all-metric set with the mini-reversible switch (see photo). This set retails for about $125.

Hammers: Sounds easy enough, but choosing a hammer is as complex as choosing any other tool. There are literally hundreds of different types of hammers, each in a variety of different sizes. There are ball-peen hammers, claw hammers, soft-blow hammers, nonmarring hammers, welding hammers, and picks, just to name a few. The hammer you need is the 16-ounce ball-peen. This is a great all-purpose hammer, but you may desire a 32-ounce ball-peen if you really need to hit something hard. Buying a hammer shouldn't be rocket science, but there are some precautions. Aside from the weight and the quality of the head, the handle is an important consideration. There are now a variety of different handles: wood, fiberglass, steel, and reinforced plastic. I prefer a hardwood, like oak, for ball-peen hammers, but all my hammers have different handles, based on how I want the blow to strike certain objects. Regardless of which handle you choose, make sure it will stay firmly attached to the head. A dislodged head will usually land on the hood or windshield of your car—or your face, if no cars are close by. You can soak wood handles in water to cause the wood to swell to the shape of the head bore. A rubber mallet is useful for removing parts without inflicting damage.

Allen/hex wrenches: Available as either a socket or Allen wrench, you will undoubtedly need a set of Allen/hex wrenches. There are many variations of this tool: socket-drive, T-handle, and multifunction. If you're only going to have one set, a basic right-angle Allen wrench set will give you the most versatility and serve you best. In my experience, having a spare 5- and 6-millimeter is a necessity, as they do wear out at the least opportune times. The next step up is the socket set that fits on the end of a ratchet driver. These are very useful for applying more torque when you need it.

Torx sockets/drivers: BMW loves Torx bolts and sockets. You will need a set of Torx sockets, a set of Torx screwdrivers, and a set of female Torx sockets to remove bolts like those found on the transmission. Don't shirk from purchasing these sets—you will definitely need them to work on your BMW.

Torque wrenches: No good mechanic or weekend warrior is complete without a torque wrench. The ultimate tool for assembly, the torque wrench measures and restricts the amount of torque applied to a fastener. This is of the utmost importance, since too little torque can result in a nut falling off, while too much torque can damage a valuable part. Make sure that you get a torque wrench with both English and metric measurements labeled on it. I recommend purchasing two wrenches: one for small increments (0–25 ft-lb) and one for larger tasks (above 25 ft-lb). Both Craftsman and Husky sell good-quality adjustable torque wrenches for about $65.

Electrical repair: You don't need a degree in physics to perform basic electrical repairs on cars, but you do need the right tools. At a minimum, you'll need a test light, wire-crimping pliers, wire strippers, an assortment of solder-less terminals, and a good multitester. Most parts stores carry inexpensive kits that are suitable for most jobs. Of course, a soldering iron is the correct way to make electrical repairs, but solder-less terminals are often more convenient. The automotive electronics company SUN manufactures a great handheld voltmeter, ammeter, tachometer, and dwell meter unit, any of which are available at most auto parts stores. Wiring diagrams for your specific model and year are also extremely valuable for troubleshooting electrical problems.

Hydraulic jack: Arguably the most important tool in your collection, it's wise not to cheap out on the hydraulic jack. Although good-quality jacks are often expensive, they are definitely worth it and will last a long, long time. Purchase a large jack with a very large lifting throw. Weight capacity is not as important as how high you can lift with the jack. Purchase a 3–5-ton jack with the highest lift that you can find. Typical costs for these are in the $150–400 range, but they are well worth it. The world's greatest floor jack is the

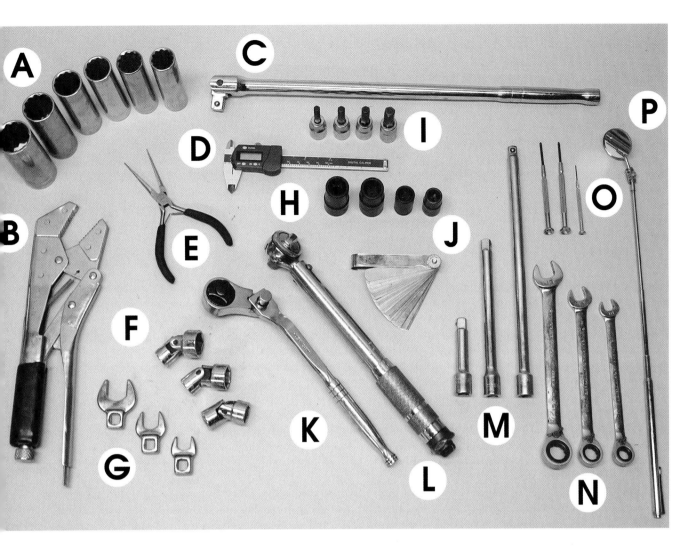

I've picked out some of the less commonplace tools for this photo. This is a collection of tools that you might not normally think to purchase, but I would consider them vital and use them on a daily basis: **A:** Deep socket metric sets are most useful for removing large fasteners. Eventually, you will need all the sockets in this set, so you might as well spring for them all at once. **B:** Locking pliers are sometimes called Vise-Grips and are very good multipurpose tools as long as they are not abused. Don't get lazy and use them instead of the proper tool for the job. **C:** Breaker bar. In conjunction with the deep socket set, you will need a tool that will give you the amount of torque you need to remove those troublesome fasteners. **D:** Digital calipers can measure just about anything. The price has dropped in the past few years, so you can pick up a decent-quality unit for not too much money. **E:** Needle-nose pliers are very handy for grabbing lost screws or nuts, or for simply installing small snap rings. Get a good-quality pair that won't bend or break. **F:** Swivel-foot sockets are great in hard-to-reach places, like the nuts on the intake manifolds. Depending on clearance, you can get away with a standard universal-joint adapter for your socket driver as well. **G:** Crowfoot wrenches are perfect for that one nut that you just can't get to. They are also good for removing hard-to-reach nuts on the exhaust manifold. **H:** Female Torx sockets are required for working on any BMW. The really strong nuts (like the ones that hold on the CV joints) are usually of this variety and require Torx sockets for removal. **I:** Hex wrench socket set. Most of us have the standard set of right-angle hex wrenches; however, the use of a socket driver increases your ability to get into tight places and apply greater torque. **J:** Feeler gauges are useful for setting valve clearances or checking the adjustment of your clutch. **K:** Flexible ratchet. I purchased this tool because it looked really cool, not because I could think of a unique purpose for it. However, it has become one of the most valuable tools in my collection. You don't realize the limitations of a standard ratchet until you've tried one of these. I have an equally useful one that bends forward as well. **L:** Torque wrench. This is a must-have tool in everyone's collection. Purchase a good-quality one, and make sure that its range covers the tasks that you need to accomplish. **M:** Extension sets for your ⅜-inch drive are most useful, but other sizes can also come in handy. Some nuts are just impossible to reach with a standard-length socket and ratchet. **N:** GearWrenches ratcheting wrenches are some of my favorite tools. Get the metric set with the tiny reversible lever on the end (shown in the photo). **O:** Mini screwdrivers. You don't know when you will need one, but when you do, they're tremendously useful. **P:** Inspection mirrors are useful when you just can't see into the rear of your engine compartment or around blind corners.

DK13HLQ from AC Hydraulics (see Photo 5 of Project 1). Also necessary are jack stands. I like to have two different sizes around so I can adjust the car to different heights. (See Project 1 for more details.)

Shop lamp: My favorite type of shop lamp is the 3-foot-long fluorescent handheld unit on a retractable cord. The spring-loaded cord winds back into the main housing, similar to a vacuum cleaner. The only disadvantage to this type of shop lamp is that you have to replace the entire lamp and cord assembly if you break a part of the assembly or accidentally run it over with your car (as has happened to me many times). A good alternative is the fluorescent handheld lamp without a retractable cord.

Stay away from the shop lamps that use a standard 60-watt incandescent light bulb. These get hot and can burn you under the car or, even worse, start fires if oil or gasoline accidentally drips on them. Stick with fluorescent lamps.

Shop halogen lamps are extremely high-powered lamps that come with adjustable stands and metal grille covers. Although these lamps get very hot, they give out a lot of light and are especially useful for lighting up engine compartments or the underside of the car.

Safety glasses: Anyone who has worked on cars for any length of time, or worked in a machine shop, knows the importance of wearing safety glasses whenever there is a chance that something might get in your eye. Never climb underneath the car without them. Always make sure that you have three or four pairs around. You will undoubtedly misplace them, and you want to make sure that you have plenty of spares so you don't avoid using them because you can't find them.

Miscellaneous: There are plenty of tools that fit into the miscellaneous category. Here are some that you should not be without: X-Acto or craft knife, small pick, tape measure, scissors, a set of good feeler gauges, a hack saw, a set of files, and an inspection mirror.

Throughout this book, I have recommended specific tools that are useful or required to perform a specific task. Examples include the Motive Products brake bleeder, the Peake Research R5 code reader tool, and many others. In most cases, you will need to purchase these tools (or similar ones) in order to complete the task.

The Advanced Collection

The upgraded tool set is simply an extension of the basic set. As you perform more tasks, your skills and needs will be further defined and you'll want to extend your investment to meet those needs. A greater range of sockets, wrenches, screwdrivers, and pliers will become increasingly helpful. You should also begin purchasing diagnostic tools.

Some popular tools you might be quick to add are snap ring pliers; socket-drive, Allen, stubby, and Torx wrench sets; and swivel sockets.

The Dremel tool and angle grinder are two of the most destructive yet useful tools for working on older cars (see Project 98). When bolts are rusted solid and there really aren't any alternatives, the grinding tools play an important role. No one should be without a Dremel tool, as it is most useful for cutting off small bolts and other pieces of metal that are difficult to reach. The Dremel tool with a flexible extension is particularly useful for reaching into tight places.

Everyone who works around the house probably has a good variable-speed electric hand drill. However, the drill bits are really the most important components of the drill. Make sure that you have a good, clean set of drill bits at all times. Bargain-basement drill bits are fine for drilling through wood, but when it comes to metal, you need the best quality you can get. Make sure to get a good-quality set; otherwise, you may end up hurting yourself or your car.

One tool that is not commonly used but can save you many hours is the electric impact wrench. This tool is similar to the air compressor impact wrenches that are used in automotive shops everywhere, except that it runs on ordinary 120-volt current. The impact wrench is useful for removing nuts that can't be secured and rotate when you try to remove them (like the shock tower nut in Project 60).

When serious engine problems are suspected, the tool most people turn to first is the compression tester, and for good reason. The compression tester will provide clues to such problems as bad rings, leaking valves, or even a hole in one of the pistons. A recent tool that is gaining more common acceptance is the leakdown tester. The leakdown tester works by pressurizing the cylinder and measuring how much pressure the cylinder loses over time. Although some people consider the leakdown tester to be a more precise measurement, it should be used in conjunction with the compression tester to gain a complete picture and better diagnosis of your engine (see Project 7).

SECTION ONE

Basics

This section is a good place to start in this book. If you've just purchased your 3 Series and it is lacking an owner's manual, the Basics section covers what you need to know. No special tools are required, and the projects in this section will give you a good idea of the format and tone of the rest of the book. If you've never worked on your BMW before, don't worry. These first few projects are very simple and provide a good introduction to your car.

BASICS

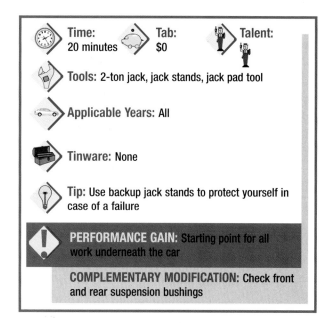

Time:
20 minutes

Tab:
$0

Talent:

Tools: 2-ton jack, jack stands, jack pad tool

Applicable Years: All

Tinware: None

Tip: Use backup jack stands to protect yourself in case of a failure

PERFORMANCE GAIN: Starting point for all work underneath the car

COMPLEMENTARY MODIFICATION: Check front and rear suspension bushings

About one-third of all tasks you need to perform on your BMW require the car to be raised off of the ground. Simple enough for the experienced mechanic, the procedure of lifting a 3,000-pound car can be a bit unnerving for the amateur.

First, let's talk a bit about safety. Haphazard use of a floor jack can result in some serious and costly damage to you or your car. Before you begin raising the car, make sure that the wheels of the car are blocked so it can't roll and that the car is on a level surface. It's wise to have your car in first gear and the parking brake on as well. Keep in mind that if you raise the rear of the car off the ground, the emergency brake no longer works (it works only on the two rearmost wheels of the car). If you place the car in park (automatic transmissions), it will only lock the rear wheels. Place a few 2x4 pieces of wood in front and in back of each wheel to make sure the car will not roll when you lift it off the ground. Always use a pair of jack stands at each end to support the car—not simply a floor jack. Even if you're only lifting the car up for a few minutes, place an emergency jack stand loosely underneath the transmission, engine, or rear differential just in case the floor jack fails.

I prefer to raise the E36 BMW with a BMW-specific jack pad. This special tool is available from PelicanParts.com and is placed in the factory jack holes on each side of the car. The ideal place for the rear jack stand to support is right underneath these jack pad inserts. Except for the emergency backup jack stand mentioned previously, I don't recommend that you place the jack stands underneath the engine, transmission, or differential, as this can lead to instability when raised up.

On the E36, begin by removing the jack pad insert covers with a flat-blade screwdriver. After the small plastic cover is removed, you can see into the jack pad socket. On the underside of the car, you may see a round plastic cover that is used as a locator for shop lifts. However, these might have already been removed or lost. Using a flat-blade screwdriver, pry out the plastic guide from underneath the car. The exposed hole and reinforced plate is the place to mount your jack stands. Remove the plastic locator first, as the jack stand will be unstable if you simply place it under the plastic locator and lower the car.

If you don't have a jack pad, place your floor jack in this reinforced area. Fit a rolled up newspaper in between the jack and the car to protect the undercarriage of your car. You may have difficulty placing your jack stands, because most of the reinforced area will be taken up by the floor jack.

If you're using the jack pad, center the pad surface in the jack lifting plate and raise the jack. It's perfectly okay if the car tilts while the wheels on the opposite side are still on the ground. Place the jack stand securely under the reinforced plate, and slowly lower the car. Again, I like to place newspaper between the jack stand and the car to avoid scratching or scraping the underside of the chassis.

If you are lifting the front of the car, place a jack stand under the front reinforced plate, lower the car onto the jack stand, and repeat for the opposite side of the car. If you are lifting the whole car off of the ground, place a jack stand under both the front and rear points, lower the car, and repeat for the other side. Likewise, if you are jacking up just the rear, place the jack stands under the rearmost reinforced points.

If you plan to raise just the rear of the car, there are a few methods. The most controversial one is to lift the entire car by the bottom of the rear differential. I know that shops have been doing this for ages with no reported damage to the differential or the mounts. Still, there are people out there who cringe when they hear this, and I suggest you avoid doing it. If you do need to quickly jack up your car by the differential, be sure to place a rolled up newspaper under the lifting pad of the jack to protect the underside.

Safety is of paramount importance. Never work under the car with it suspended simply by a jack—always use jack stands. As further insurance, always use a backup jack stand wherever you place your primary jack stands. One tiny flaw in the casting process can cause a jack stand to break, and the car could fall on top of you.

Once the car is up and supported on the jack stands, push on the car to see if it is stable. If the car moves at all, you do not have it properly supported. It is far better for the car to fall off the jack stands during this test than when you are underneath it. To be sure that it's stable, really try to

1 This BMW jack pad is a $30 tool from PelicanParts.com that fits in the factory jack receptacles and gives you a convenient method of safely raising the car. The car can be raised in small increments by jacking up one side, supporting it, and then doing the same on the other side. Repeat this procedure until the car is raised to the necessary height.

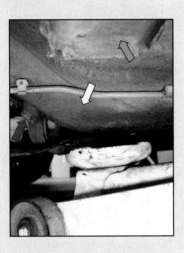

2 On both E30 and E36 BMWs, there is a large, stiff chassis rail that runs down the length of the chassis on each side of the car (yellow arrow). The front of this rail makes a perfect spot from which to lift the car. Placing the floor jack under this rail allows you to place a jack stand under the factory jack support area (green arrow, E30 shown) after the car has been raised. For reference, the red arrow points to the chassis mounting point for the front left A-arm, which is bolted to this long rail.

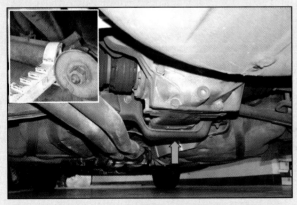

3 Jacking up the rear of the car can be easy if you have a long-reach jack. Place the jack under the rear support beam that runs the width of the car. The rear trailing arms are attached near this beam on either side of the car. Avoid lifting the car with the rear differential. Instead, lift the car from the large bracket that runs underneath the differential. With the car elevated, place jack stands under this wide beam as an alternative to the factory jack support areas (inset).

 4 The best place to support your E30 or E36 BMW with jack stands is under the factory jack support areas. These four spots, two on either side of the car, have either plastic bumpers (E36) or

square metal cups (E30) that act as locators for professional-style hydraulic lifts used at repair shops. Place four jack stands at equal height on either side of the car like this to create a stable platform for the car. Remove the plastic bumper guides on the E36 (inset, upper left) prior to placing the jack stands. On the E30, place the jack stands so they support the car without damaging the square metal cup.

5 After an extensive search for the world's most perfect jack, I found the DK13HLQ from AC Hydraulics. This is the best jack I have ever seen and is available at PelicanParts.com. This floor jack satisfies all my requirements and has more than earned its place in my garage. With a minimum height of only 80 millimeters (3.1 inches), it fits under any lowered BMW. In spite of the low minimum height, the jack has an unusually high lift of 735 millimeters (29 inches), enabling you to raise your car onto floor jacks in one swift motion. Combined with the easy-to-use lift foot pedal, this superior jack is perfect for any car enthusiast.

knock it off the jack stands. Set the floor jack underneath the engine or transmission while you're working as yet another backup support.

When you are ready to lower the car, be extremely careful of where you place the floor jack. You may not be able to easily remove the jack when the car is lowered, or the jack handle may crush or damage an oil line or tube on the way down. Proceed very slowly, and be aware that some floor jacks release very quickly. Be careful to place the car in gear, or to engage the parking brake, before you lower it. The car may roll once it's back on the ground.

BASICS

Time: 1 hour **Tab:** $30 **Talent:**

 Tools: 2-ton jack, jack stands, jack pad tool, 17-/19-millimeter and 13-millimeter socket and driver, filter wrench, screwdriver

 Applicable Years: All

 Tinware: Oil filter kit, 4–7 quarts of motor oil

 Tip: Have a 7-quart oil pan or bucket

 PERFORMANCE GAIN: Prolonged engine life and reliability

COMPLEMENTARY MODIFICATION: Install synthetic motor oil

Changing the engine oil frequently is perhaps the most important procedure you can do to maintain and prolong the life of your engine. With the better oils available today, the requirement for frequent changes is diminishing. Although BMW now recommends oil changes at greater intervals than in the past, I recommend that you change the oil at least every 5,000 miles. If you don't drive your car that often, change the oil at least once a year to keep it fresh.

Make sure you have everything required for the job. Nothing is more frustrating than emptying your oil, only to find out you don't have a replacement filter or enough oil. You will need an oil filter, a 13-millimeter socket (or large adjustable wrench), a roll of paper towels, a 7-quart or larger oil pan or bucket, and 4 to 7 quarts of oil. The E30 cars require between 3.5 and 4.2 quarts of oil, and the E36 cars require 5 quarts for four-cylinder engines and 6.0–6.5 quarts for six-cylinder engines. You'll also need a 17-millimeter or 19-millimeter socket to remove the drain plug from the bottom of the engine sump.

First, drive the car around so that the engine heats up to operating temperature. Empty your oil when it's hot; the heat makes the oil flow a lot easier, and more particles of metal and dirt will come out when the oil is emptied.

Park the car and place the oil pan or bucket underneath the oil tank. At the bottom of the engine sump is a plug for draining the oil. Remove this plug carefully, and have a very large oil pan—at least a 7-quart capacity—under it, with a drip pan under the bucket in case you underestimate. The oil will be very hot and will empty out extremely quickly, so be careful not to burn yourself (wear rubber gloves). There will be no time to

1 Remove the drain plug underneath the car. Depending on your engine type, it will be a 17-millimeter or 19-millimeter plug. Replace the small copper gasket underneath the plug each time, as it helps guard against oil leaks.

2 In the main photo, a long bolt secures the E36 metal oil filter housing (green arrow). Use a 13-millimeter socket and extension to loosen and remove the bolt. In the upper left, the late-model plastic housing cap requires a large wrench to remove it from the housing. Removing the top of the oil filter housing reveals the filter cartridge underneath (lower right).

3 When installing the new filter kit shown on the upper right, remove the small O-ring on the long bolt, as shown in the upper left. On the bottom right, you can see how the new filter housing O-ring fits around the top on cars with a metal canister lid. On the lower left side, you can see how the same O-ring fits around the late-model plastic canister lid.

4 The oil filter on the E30 cars is mounted on the right side of the engine. Unlike the E36 filter, it is a self-contained unit with a disposable metal housing. Grab a few paper towels, and place them underneath the filter when you unscrew it in order to catch excess oil as it leaks out of the engine and filter.

5 Fill your car with oil from the inlet in the top of the valve cover. If you're quick and skilled with the bottle, you can pour without spilling. However, most people use a funnel to prevent a mess.

grab more buckets or oil pans if you underestimate, so make sure that the one you choose is big enough.

While the oil is draining, remove the oil filter. Remove the filter with the oil pan still under the car because the oil filter is full of oil, which tends to drip out of the filter, into the engine, and out the drain hole.

On E30 cars, the filter is a complete unit with an outer metal housing. This filter should only be screwed on finger tight, but you may need a filter wrench to remove it. If the filter is really on tight, you may need to resort to more drastic measures. One sure-fire way to get the oil filter off is to

poke a long screwdriver through it and use the handle of the screwdriver for leverage. You can destroy the filter because you are going to install a new one. Be aware, though, that this method will cause oil to leak out of the filter into your engine compartment, so have some paper towels handy.

E36 cars use a cartridge-type filter within a metal oil filter housing. There is a cap on top of the housing that may require a 13-millimeter socket or a large adjustable wrench, depending on the year of your car. Remove the top, and underneath you will see the cartridge filter. Simply remove it from the oil filter housing. Have plenty of paper towels on hand, as oil will spill from the filter if you're not careful.

While the oil is draining, take the plug from the engine, and carefully clean it with a paper towel. When the plug is clean and all the oil has drained, replace it in the car with a new metal gasket. If you don't replace the gasket, the plug will leak oil. Torque the plug on E36 models to 25 N-m (18 ft-lb) for the 17-millimeter drain plug, or 60 N-m (44 ft-lb) for the 19-millimeter drain plug. On E30 cars, torque the drain plug to 33 N-m (24 ft-lb).

Head back into the engine compartment to install the new oil filter. For the E30 cars, install the oil filter with the seal wet—wipe a small bit of oil on a paper towel to make sure there is oil on the seal all the way around the filter. Screw on the filter snugly. No need to use the iron grip of death to tighten the oil filter, as it doesn't have a tendency to leak.

For the E36 cars, clean out the inside of the oil filter housing before installing the new oil filter cartridge. In your oil filter kit, you should also have two O-rings and a replacement copper gasket for the long bolt that attaches the top of the housing (early E36 cars). Replace the O-ring at the bottom of the long bolt, and also replace the large O-ring underneath the canister top. These two O-rings help to keep oil inside the filter when the engine is turned off. Leaving them off can lead to oil supply problems when you start your engine after it has been sitting for a while. Insert the new filter into the housing, and reinstall the long bolt and the canister top. Tighten the top of the canister to 25 N-m (18 ft-lb), or hand tighten if you have the larger, black plastic top.

Now it's time to fill up your BMW with motor oil. A lot of people aren't sure which motor oil to use in their cars. Traditionally, the characteristics of motor oil were linked closely to its weight. Heavier-weight oils protect well against heat; lighter-weight oils flow better in cold. In general, if you live in a cold climate, you should use 10W-40 or similar oil. This 10-weight oil behaves and protects against heat like a 40-weight oil. In warmer climates, you should use 20W-50 oil. This oil doesn't flow as well at the colder temperatures but gives an extra edge on the hotter end.

The question of whether to use synthetic or traditional "dinosaur" oil often comes up among car buffs. *Consumer Reports* (July 1996) ran an extensive test of the two types of oil, sampling many different brands. The testers installed rebuilt engines in 75 taxicabs and ran them through the harshest conditions on the streets of New York City. Placing different brands, weights, and formulations in the cars, they racked up

60,000 miles on the engines, tore them down, measured, and inspected the engine components for wear. The oil was changed at 3,000 miles in half of them, and the rest were changed at 6,000 miles. The results: Regardless of brand, synthetic or dino, weight, and oil change interval, there were no discernable differences in engine component wear in any of the engines. Their conclusion? Motor oils and the additives blended into them have improved so much over the years that frequent oil changes and expensive synthetics are no longer necessary.

Still, some people swear by synthetic oil. In practice, I don't recommend using synthetic oil in a car over 10 or 15 years old with old seals in the engine. There have been many documented cases in which synthetic oil has caused an otherwise dry car to start leaking. If you own an older BMW that doesn't have fresh seals in the engine, stick to the non-synthetics. However, if synthetic oil is the only type of oil that your engine has seen, stick with it.

Fill the oil tank from the oil filler hole in the top of the valve cover, located in the engine compartment. Add about 4 quarts to the engine, and check the dip stick (see Photo 1 of Project 7). Continue to add about ½ quart at a time and keep checking the dip stick. Fill it up until it reaches the top mark

of the dip stick, as the engine oil level will automatically lower when the oil filter fills up with oil. Put the oil filler cap back on the top of the valve cover; otherwise, you will end up with a messy engine compartment when you drive away.

Now, start up the engine with the hood open. The oil pressure light should stay on for a second or two and then go out. Hop out of the car and look at the engine compartment; then take a quick look underneath the car. Verify that there's no volume of oil seeping out of the engine. Next, take the car out for a drive and bring it up to operating temperature. Shut the car off, and then re-check the oil level. (Careful, the car will be hot.) At this point, I like to top the oil off at the top point on the dip stick. After the oil change is complete, be sure to dispose of the old oil at a respectable recycling station.

BMW cars have an internal oil lamp that needs to be reset when you perform your oil change. You can use a special tool to perform this reset, and the Peake Research R5 tool discussed in Project 28 also does the trick. There is another easy way to reset the oil and inspection dashboard lamps using a simple wire connected across some pins in the connector—more info on this at www.101Projects.com.

PROJECT 3   http://www.101projects.com/BMW/3.htm
Replacing the Air Filter

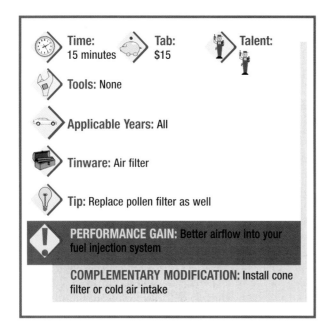

Time: 15 minutes

Tab: $15

Talent:

Tools: None

Applicable Years: All

Tinware: Air filter

Tip: Replace pollen filter as well

! PERFORMANCE GAIN: Better airflow into your fuel injection system

COMPLEMENTARY MODIFICATION: Install cone filter or cold air intake

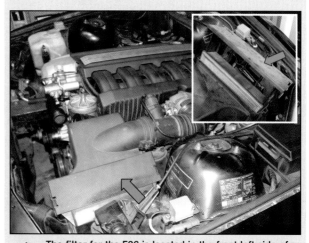

1 The filter for the E36 is located in the front left side of the engine compartment (green arrow). To remove the filter, simply pull up on the rectangular cover that holds the filter in place (photo inset).

Every 10,000 miles or so, you should change the air filter in your BMW. The air filter protects the fuel injection system and air intake system from dust and debris that can be sucked in under normal operation.

On E30 BMWs, the air filter is contained in a bubble-like housing located in the front left side of the engine

compartment. To remove the filter, merely lift the straps and pry up the cover.

On E36 cars, the filter is located in a similar spot, but it's mounted vertically. Simply pull up on the top cover, and the filter should come right out of its housing. Take a look

2 The K&N cone filter (shown here) is installed on an E30 325is. You can install one of these cone filters for a performance look. Filters are also available that fit inside the stock filter housing (photo inset).

inside the filter housing—often, leaves or dirt may have found their way in. Clean the housing out before installing the new filter.

For the BMW 3 Series there are basically two different types of air filters—the stock paper or cloth air filters, and aftermarket units. Aftermarket units utilize an oil-soaked fabric to achieve freer airflow. The bottleneck for airflow in the BMW engine is not necessarily the air filter. The primary advantage of the aftermarket units is that one will usually last the life of your car.

No matter what your friends tell you, aftermarket filters will not add significant horsepower to your engine. Many dynamometer tests have revealed that the freer-flowing air filters do not create horsepower out of thin air. If you install one of these filters into your car and swear there's more horsepower, you may be suffering from the placebo effect, perceiving significant gains in performance just because you added a so-called "performance part."

Aftermarket filters often do not filter as well as the factory units. Carefully research any aftermarket filter before you install it into your car. I prefer to use the stock OEM cloth/paper filters to ensure maximum filtering and protection. Whichever one you choose, make sure that it filters as well as or better than the original BMW specifications.

PROJECT 4
Replacing the Fuel Filter
http://www.101projects.com/BMW/4.htm

 Time: 1 hour　　 **Tab:** $15　　 **Talent:**

 Tools: Screwdriver, pliers, floor jack, and jack stands

 Applicable Years: All

 Tinware: Fuel filter

 Tip: Don't tackle this job with a full fuel tank

 PERFORMANCE GAIN: Cleaner running fuel system

COMPLEMENTARY MODIFICATION: Replace worn out or cracked rubber fuel lines

Replace the fuel filter in your BMW once a year or every 10,000 miles. It seems that, with today's odd blended fuels, it is not uncommon for dirt or grime in the gasoline to clog your tank.

Changing the fuel filter is not a job that I relish. It is almost guaranteed that you will spill at least some fuel on the ground and yourself as you swap out the fuel filter. Be sure to perform the replacement in a well-ventilated area—either outdoors or in your garage with a few large fans blowing air both in and out. Have a fire extinguisher handy, wear rubber gloves and eye protection, and have a few rolls of paper towels handy—you will need them.

The fuel level in the tank should be as low as possible, so drive around until the gas tank is almost empty in order to minimize problems before you start. First, jack the car up (see Project 1). I recommend that you only jack up the front of the car, and leave the rear on the ground to minimize any fuel flowing forward to the front of the car from the tank. The 3 Series BMWs have an intelligent design when it comes to fuel flow. The fuel pump is located in the top of the tank and can pump fuel out of the top as well. Why is this good? When you go to change the fuel filter, you can pull out the fuel pump relay, crank the starter a few times, and be assured that fuel isn't going to flow everywhere if you make a mistake. Some cars have a gravity-fed system that takes fuel out of the bottom of the tank. With these systems, you have to disconnect the line and clamp it very quickly or the entire tank of gas will empty out!

After the car is off of the ground, pull out the fuse for the fuel pump and crank the engine a few times. In general, this is fuse number 9 on E30 cars and fuse number 18 on E36 cars. Check your individual model prior to pulling the fuse (see the fuse box in Photo 1 of Project 82). Removing this fuse and turning over the starter/engine will reduce some of the fuel in the system. Unfortunately, you can't get all of it out, and some will spill when you disconnect the fuel filter. The filter itself will likely be full of fuel as well.

Now, crawl underneath the car. The location of the fuel filter has varied over the years from model to model. On the E36, the filter is located either on the left side of the car somewhat underneath the engine (early E36 cars) or in the middle of the car approximately under the left-side seat (late E36 cars). These later-style E36 cars have a protective cover that needs to be removed to access the filter. On most E30 cars, the filter is located near the left front wheel, roughly under the power steering reservoir, or in the rear, near the left rear wheel. To access the front location, you may wish to remove the left front road wheel for better access and visibility.

Next, disconnect the lines to the filter. I like to clamp the fuel line before disconnecting it to minimize the amount of fuel that will leak out. However, you have to be very careful clamping the line or you may damage it. A large C-clamp works well,

or you can use Vise-Grips, but only if you cover the jaws with several layers of duct tape to minimize the damage to the line. It's okay to squeeze the line closed tight, but you don't want to score, rip, or crack it with your clamping tools.

With both the inlet and the outlet to the fuel filter clamped, release the hose clamps on either side. Have a small pail or bucket handy to catch the excess fuel when you release the line. Sometimes the line will slip off, but most of the time it will require some coaxing. Use a small crescent wrench that fits nicely around the fuel pump inlet but is too small to fit around the fuel line. Wedge the wrench against the filter housing, and you should be able to pry off any stubborn fuel line. If all fails, and you simply cannot pull the line off of the filter, make a small ¼-inch cut along the length of the line and try again. Continue making cuts until you can remove the line. This will minimize the amount of line that you have to cut in order to get the filter off.

When the line is released, expect several ounces of gasoline to be coming your way. Be prepared with gloves, eye protection, paper towels, a bucket, and have the car located in a well-ventilated area. Take the filter out, put it in your bucket, and immediately take it and any leftover (or spilled) gasoline out of your garage.

Let the garage sit empty for 15–20 minutes before you re-enter; it will take that long for the fumes to clear. Then, simply reattach the new filter where the old one was. Make sure to observe the flow direction arrows on the filter and install it correctly (the arrows point in the direction of fuel flow, which is toward the engine). Tighten the clamps, but don't clamp them so tightly that you strip the clamp threads. When you restart the engine, do it outside of your garage in an open area and look under the car for any fuel leaks. If you see any leaks, turn off the car immediately, clean up the spilled fuel, and then chase down the source of the leaks.

1 While the location of the fuel filter has changed slightly across the various models, all fuel filters generally look the same (green arrow). This filter is located in the front of the car, near the steering rack. The photo inset shows what a brand new filter should look like right out of the box. Notice the directional arrows printed on the side of the filter. These arrows point in the direction of fuel flow (toward the engine).

Time: 1 hour

Tab: $10–30

Talent:

Tools: 8-millimeter Allen wrench, 19-millemeter socket for alternator bracket

Applicable Years: All

Tinware: Drive belt, A/C belt

Tip: Carry a spare main drive belt with you in case of failure

PERFORMANCE GAIN: No squeaky engine or water pump failure

COMPLEMENTARY MODIFICATION: Replace water pump and thermostat

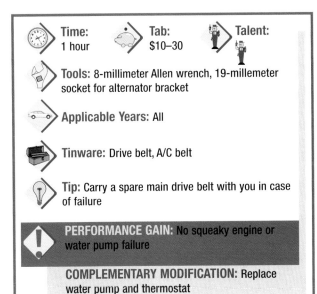
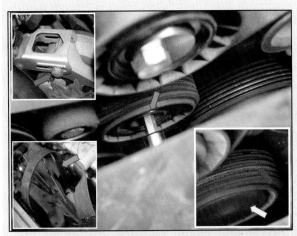

1 The green arrow shows the 8-millimeter Allen wrench you need in order to release tension from the tensioner pulley (E36). The red arrow shows the sort of cracking and belt wear you need to be concerned with. The yellow arrow points to the plastic cover that must be pried off in order to access the tensioner pulley. The purple arrow shows the older-style method of applying tension to the belt with the rack-and-pinion bracket. Finally, the blue arrow shows the ribbed belt being fitted around the fan.

2 These components are driven by the two rubber belts on a typical E36 six-cylinder engine. **A:** Fan/water pump (fan removed in the photo). **B:** A/C compressor. **C:** Tensioner for A/C belt. **D:** Main crankshaft pulley. **E:** Tensioner for main drive belt. **F:** Power steering pump. **G:** Idler pulley for alternator. **H:** Alternator

Checking and replacing the accessory drive belts is a simple, routine maintenance item. The belts are driven off of the crankshaft and power accessories such as the water pump, power steering pump, alternator, and air conditioning compressor. There are typically two belts on the car—one that powers the air conditioning compressor, and another that powers everything else. Check both periodically (every 3,000 miles or when you change your oil) and pay particular attention to the main belt. The car can run fine without the air conditioning belt installed.

Some early E30 cars use a standard V-belt design, while some later cars use what is known as a poly-ribbed belt (having many channels or ribs on the underside of the belt). The poly-ribbed belt setup utilizes a spring-loaded belt tensioner pulley that provides the proper tension for the belt at all times, making adjustment unnecessary. The traditional style V-belts need to be tensioned using standard clamps and tensioners. In particular, the alternator belt is tightened using a mini rack-and-pinion assembly (see Project 89).

When inspecting your belts, look for cracks (see red arrow in Photo 1). If you see any cracks at all, replace your belts immediately. The cracks usually occur on the inside of the belt (the surface that typically rides on the surface of the pulley). With poly-ribbed belts, this is the grooved surface. With V-belts, these are the surfaces on the legs of the "V."

The E36 cars use a poly-ribbed belt. Replacing poly-ribbed belts is a snap. The tensioners that hold the belt tight can be easily released using a socket and an 8-millimeter Allen wrench. Different tensioners turn different directions, so you may have to rotate the tensioner clockwise or counterclockwise,

depending on your particular car. This process is difficult to describe but very easy to do. First, pry off the small plastic cap that covers the tensioner. Then, place your tool into the tensioner and try rotating clockwise or counterclockwise—it will become immediately apparent how the tensioner releases the belt.

Removing the two belts is easy. Simply release the tension on the belt from the tensioner, and the belt should slide off. Then, you should be able to unwind the belt from the engine. Maneuver the belt around and through the fan; you do not need to remove the fan to swap out any of the belts.

Note: If your BMW has air conditioning, you will need to remove the A/C belt first, as it typically blocks the other belt. Another tip: If the A/C belt is worn and needs to be replaced, simply release the tension on it, and snip it with some large tin cutters to pull it out of the car.

Installing the new belt is easy. Simply slide most of the new belt onto the pulleys, release the tension on the tensioner, and slide the belt onto the tensioner. Make sure the belt is securely seated in all of the pulleys. Verify that the ribbed portion of the belt is set against the crankshaft pulley.

Replace any plastic caps you may have removed from the front of the tensioner pulleys. Now, start the car and peek in at the belts. Verify they are turning smoothly on all of the pulleys.

For engines with the older-style V-belts, the procedure is nearly identical, except for the tensioning. The alternator is mounted on a bracket that rotates and is used to keep tension on the belt. In addition, there is a small rack-and-pinion device on this bracket that allows you to crank up the tension on the belt. The first step in setting or releasing tension is to release the nut on the back of the bracket that keeps the whole assembly secure. Do not attempt to turn the geared bolt without first releasing the nut on the rear or you will most likely damage the teeth on the bracket. With the nut released, you can turn the geared bolt counterclockwise, releasing tension on the belt. Then, simply follow the rest of the steps outlined above for poly-ribbed belts, and you're on your way.

PROJECT 6
Washing Your Car

http://www.101projects.com/BMW/6.htm

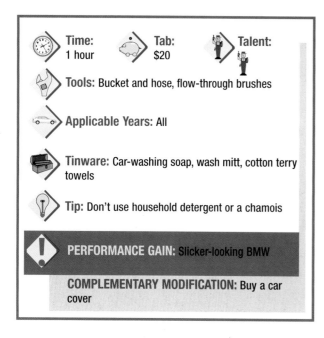

Time: 1 hour **Tab:** $20 **Talent:**

Tools: Bucket and hose, flow-through brushes

Applicable Years: All

Tinware: Car-washing soap, wash mitt, cotton terry towels

Tip: Don't use household detergent or a chamois

PERFORMANCE GAIN: Slicker-looking BMW

COMPLEMENTARY MODIFICATION: Buy a car cover

Washing your BMW is an art that includes reconditioning and protecting both the exterior paint and chrome, and the interior.

Before washing your car, determine exactly what it needs. If the car is simply dusty and has been sitting in the garage, you probably only need to wash it with plain water (no soap). Wet the car down, and use a wash mitt to remove any dust that might have settled on the car while inside the garage.

I don't recommend using a chamois to dry your car. The chamois can trap small particles of dirt in its porous material and can actually cause scratches in the surface of the paint when it's used to dry off the car. A really good alternative is

100 percent cotton terry towels. Make sure the towels have been washed at least once, and don't use a rinse or softener. The softener is an additive that can cause streaks, and it inhibits the towel's absorbency.

When washing the car, remember to get the valance and lower rocker panels. As these panels are closest to the ground, they tend to be the dirtiest. If your car suffers from more than simple dust accumulation, you will need to use a bit of car-washing soap. Don't use normal household soap or detergent, as this will remove the wax from the surface of the paint (normal detergents attack and remove oil-based wax). Car-washing soaps are very mild and shouldn't remove the layer of wax on your car.

Rinse the car completely with water from a hose, taking care not to spray the water in any areas where the seals may be cracking. If your BMW is a few years old, the overall watertight seal of the interior may not be as solid as desired. If your car does leak water, toss some towels inside the car near the windows or under the sunroof to make sure that you catch any water before it reaches the carpet and seats.

After the car is completely rinsed, start drying it immediately. It's best to dry off the car out of the reach of sunlight. Pull the car into the garage and dry it off in there. Removing the car from the sun helps to keep those ugly water spots from appearing.

To keep the paint free of scratches, make sure the towels are clean and free of debris. Handle the towels as if they were going to be used for surgery. Don't leave them outside, and if you drop them on the ground, don't use them again until they have been washed. Small particles of dirt trapped within the towels can cause nasty scratches in the paint. If you happen to encounter a water spot, use a section of a damp, clean terrycloth towel to gently rub it out.

When you are finished cleaning, it's time to tuck the car away. I recommend you use a good-quality cotton car cover if your car spends most of its life in the garage. The cover will protect it from dust accumulation and might help protect against items falling on the car or cats jumping on it. For cars stored outdoors, covers usually are not a great idea. They have a tendency to trap water, and the wind can make the cloth cover wear against the paint. If your car is not perfectly clean, the dirt particles trapped between the car and the cover have a tendency to scratch the paint.

One of the most interesting new products to hit the marketplace in recent years is the Mr. Clean car-washing system. I have used this on several of my cars, and I've been very pleased with the results. At about $25, the system combines a deionizing water filter with a soap sprayer and provides a quick and easy way to wash your car without having to dry it—and the deionized water doesn't leave ugly water spots. It's a very good product, although in practice I was not able to eliminate all of the water spots from the car. I recommend using the product along with a set of traditional towels to better dry the car.

Note: If you have an E36 BMW manufactured prior to July 1994, see Project 87 prior to washing your car.

1 The flow-through brushes from Carrand are some of the most innovative and time-saving products I've seen in recent years. These are the perfect car-washing tools for busy people. Simply hook up the brush to your hose, and water flows through as you clean. Add an automatic soap dispenser, and you can clean an absolutely filthy car in about 10 minutes. My personal favorite is the flow-through wheel-cleaning brush. It removes wheel dust and grime in about a minute. Used weekly, it's a great way to keep hard-to-remove grit and grime from building up on your wheels. The entire line of flow-through Carrand brushes can be found at www.PelicanParts.com.

Engine

The BMW engine is a robust, proven design. Remarkably, the basic design of the engines has remained relatively unchanged throughout the years. BMW has taken a good, reliable design and continually modified and improved it, making its inline six- and four-cylinder designs among the most reliable engines in any car. Still, there are components that wear out and need attention. This section will guide you through engine maintenance tasks and help you to evaluate what happens when you encounter the rare engine problem.

When to Rebuild

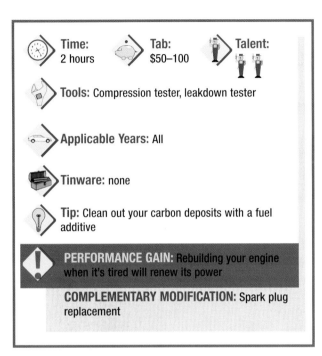

Time: 2 hours

Tab: $50–100

Talent:

Tools: Compression tester, leakdown tester

Applicable Years: All

Tinware: none

Tip: Clean out your carbon deposits with a fuel additive

PERFORMANCE GAIN: Rebuilding your engine when it's tired will renew its power

COMPLEMENTARY MODIFICATION: Spark plug replacement

When to rebuild? Indeed, this is a very common question, and one that is often not easily answered. Obviously, if the end of a rod is sticking out of your engine case, chances are it's time for a rebuild. However, with more subtle noises, broken pieces, and poor performance, the rebuild decision may not be crystal clear. In this project, I will provide some questions to ask yourself, and some answers to common myths, in an attempt to determine whether your engine needs to be rebuilt.

As with any serious medical condition, it's wise to get a second opinion with respect to BMW engine rebuilds. All too often, I have heard of unscrupulous (or overmeticulous) mechanics who have recommended, or even insisted on, a rebuild when not all of the signs pointed in that direction. Keep in mind that no matter how well-intentioned your mechanic may be, he may have a vested financial interest in seeing you rebuild your BMW engine. Of course, not knowing that you're armed with this book and prepared to do it yourself, he might recommend a full rebuild, which would guarantee about 40 hours of labor.

Always take your car to a second, independent mechanic and pay to have the car evaluated. Request a leakdown test on the engine (explained later in this project), and mention that you have a master mechanic friend waiting in the wings to rebuild the engine for you. The goal is to get an independent, unbiased, expert view of the condition of the engine. Many problems with BMW engines can be somewhat subtle and difficult for a novice to detect and decipher. In addition to

the hints, tips, procedures, and clues in the following sections, always get at least two expert opinions.

High-mileage engines

Each derivative of a BMW engine has its own quirks and problems. Most BMW engines are known for their longevity, but some are decidedly not. Just because your engine has a lot of miles on it doesn't mean that it's automatically time for a rebuild. With proper care and maintenance, some engines can easily last 250,000 miles or more. Of course, certain years have better track records than others, but the basic rules apply: If the engine was well cared for and not abused, it should last a long time and wear out gradually. In general, high mileage is not a true yardstick measurement of engine condition. The methods by which the car was operated and maintained during its life affect the condition of the engine much more than its total mileage.

High-mileage engines often show signs of their age in compression and leakdown tests, described later in this section. As the engine's age and mileage increases, the small tolerances within the engine slowly become larger. While this usually doesn't result in a catastrophic breakdown, high-mileage engines will gradually see performance degrade as the mileage increases. Such an engine may be referred to as "tired."

Stock engines almost always last longer than modified engines. Higher compression ratios and aftermarket turbos or superchargers generally place added stress on engines and make them wear out or fail quicker. Engines driven constantly on the track may especially show signs of wear. Race engines have such a typically short lifespan that their usage is typically tallied in hours run rather than miles traveled.

Failed smog tests

Out here in sunny California, we have one of the strictest emissions tests in the world. Cars are held up to standards that seem to get higher each year. Recently, the California Air Resource Board (CARB) instituted a dynamometer test whereby the wheels of a vehicle are placed on a roller and the car is tested for emissions at a specific speed. The test monitors the emissions for hydrocarbons, carbon monoxide, nitrogen oxides (NOx), and conditions that might produce smog. Unfortunately, as the tests get tougher and tougher to pass, more engines tend to fail. In some cases, the tests hold the cars to emissions standards they were never designed to meet.

Just because your car fails the smog test, don't assume its engine needs to be rebuilt. In fact, a recently rebuilt engine will most certainly fail the test if it hasn't been fully run in yet. To pass a smog test, make sure your car is running perfectly. Most of the time, a nonpassing car simply has its timing set incorrectly or has a fuel injection problem. Make sure all the fuel injection and ignition components are working 100 percent properly before you assume that the engine mechanicals may be suspect. A compression or leakdown test should be able to determine if your failure to pass a smog test was caused by internal engine wear.

Poor performance and poor gas mileage

When rings and valve guides begin to wear, the amount of burnt oil inside the engine increases and compression decreases. Both will have a negative impact on the power generated by your engine and result in poor performance and poor fuel economy. Burnt oil is a contaminant in the combustion chamber and will interfere with the combustion process. Lost compression will reduce your compression ratio and limit the power output of the engine.

However, there are plenty of other factors that can affect fuel economy and power. Most notably, the fuel injection system needs to be maintained in top shape to achieve the most power from the system. First eliminate both the fuel system and ignition system as a potential problem sources before you decide to rebuild. Also, try to isolate and fix other obscure problems: Improper suspension alignment can seriously reduce power, as can improper tire inflation. Brake problems (especially the emergency handbrake) can create significant drag. (See the related projects in this book for more information on fixing these problems.)

Strange engine noises

All internal combustion engines are designed to expand and contract as they heat and cool. As such, it is very difficult to diagnose strange engine noises that occur when the engine is cold, and unusual tapping or knocking noises are not uncommon when started stone cold. It's the strange noises made when the engine is warm and running that you need to watch out for. All engines tend to get noisier as they age, as clearances between the parts inside the engine become larger.

Engine noises are difficult to hear at times, as what may be a loud noise from one area of the engine may in fact be inaudible from another angle. Sometimes, while sitting inside the car, you will hear more of the lower-pitched noises, as the higher-pitched noises are filtered out by the car's insulation. Close your eyes when listening to the engine to eliminate potential distractions and concentrate on isolating the engine noises from one another.

An automotive stethoscope is useful for listening closely to the engine. This tool works best when placed against a solid piece of the engine. Local sounds from troubled components can be heard more clearly through the stethoscope because it helps to isolate outside noise. A long wooden dowel is a good alternative to the stethoscope, but be careful not to stick it too far into your ear, as intermittent engine vibrations may knock it too deep inside your ear. A piece of rubber vacuum hose will work also.

There are four basic types of noises that can come from the typical engine. Intermittent noises occur at irregular intervals in no reasonable pattern. For example, something may be rattling around inside one of the valve covers. There are noises that emanate with the crankshaft speed and occur once every revolution. Then there are valvetrain noises, which come and go once every two revolutions (on a four-stroke engine, the valvetrain operates at half the speed of the crankshaft). Such a noise would include the rockers and valve noise. This is probably the most common noise heard, and the fix for E30 cars may be to simply adjust the valves (see Project 21).

One common noise heard from a problem engine is a loud squeak when it's running. Such a noise can often be attributed to worn bearings on an alternator or power steering pump, or a worn-out drive belt. To test this theory in your car, take the belt off, run the engine for no more than 10 to 15 seconds, and see if the noise disappears. If it does, you know the problem is with the belt system.

There is a whole host of noises associated with problems such as rod knock, noisy valves, broken rings, chain tensioner failure, detonation, VANOS unit failures, and broken or pulled head or exhaust studs. Unfortunately, it's nearly impossible to accurately describe these noises in writing so that someone can diagnose them. Instead, take the car to your mechanic and have him listen to the engine. Engines can be loud and noisy, and if you haven't listened to a whole lot of them, your imagination can get the best of you. Listening to other finely tuned engines, perhaps in cars owned by your friends, will give you an idea of what a normal engine should sound like.

Oil consumption and smoking

As your engine ages, it will consume more oil. When the engine is brand-new, the clearances inside the engine are easily filled with a thin film of oil. As the surfaces wear, the clearances enlarge, and oil begins to slip by them. That oil then burns in the combustion chamber as it seeps past the valve guides and piston rings. The wider the clearances, the more oil will be burned away. Also, oils have different viscosities and burn at different rates. In general, thinner, lighter-weight oils tend to flow more easily past worn parts in the engine. Using heavier-weight oil in a tired engine may slightly reduce oil consumption.

In addition, excess clearances mean that the oil films that float the crankshaft bearings require more oil to work properly. Looser gap clearances between bearings mean that oil flows more easily around the bearing journals. More oil then is required to do the same task, with a corresponding drop in oil pressure and an increase in wear. This small drop in oil pressure can be spotted if you carefully take oil pressure readings over the life of the engine. In general, an increase in oil consumption, coupled with a decrease in oil pressure, is a sure-fire sign that the clearances in the engine have increased and the engine needs to be rebuilt. In addition, the presence of oil in the combustion chamber may have an adverse effect on the combustion process. Oil tends to lower the effective octane rating of the fuel mixture, thus making the engine a bit more prone to harmful detonation.

How much oil should your engine consume? One quart per 1,000 miles is what most manufacturers state "on the record." In my opinion, if your engine consumes any more oil than this, you have a problem. Consumption of 2 quarts per 1,000 miles is certainly cause for concern. If you're uncertain, check your owner's manual for information about how much oil your particular model and year should use.

There are three places where oil can be lost: past the piston rings, through the valve guides, or out the engine through oil leaks. If the car smokes excessively, there is significant oil being burned in the combustion chamber. Engines expand significantly when they run. Certain clearances that are designed for optimum performance at operating temperature are sometimes not ideal when the engine is cold. Oil seepage is considered normal when the engine is cold. For example, it's not uncommon for an engine to smoke when it's started, primarily because some oil seeped into the combustion chamber when the engine was cold. Smoke is not necessarily a sign that the engine needs to be rebuilt. However, significant smoke when the car is completely warmed up should be investigated.

What smoke should you look for? White smoke is typically caused by condensation in the engine and is generally harmless when present on startup. The exception to this rule is when steam or excessive white smoke exits from the tailpipe—in that case, you may have a leaking head gasket. Black smoke indicates a lot of unburned fuel in the combustion chamber, which may be a sign that the car is running too rich. In general, blue, sooty smoke is burning oil. If your engine emits a big puff of bluish smoke when pulling away from a stoplight, the rings are probably significantly worn.

Worn rings produce what is called "blowby." Just as oil can enter the combustion chamber, exhaust gases can be blown into the crankcase when the piston fires. Such blowby often comes out of the crankcase through the breather hoses and vents. On some cars, blowby funnels back into the air filter through the positive crankcase ventilation (PCV) valve.

Worn valve guides or valve seals can contribute to oil loss, although not as often as worn rings. Worn guides not only leak compression, but can also cause the valve heads to overheat and break off, because close valve guide clearances are necessary to properly cool the valve. Note that puffs of smoke on deceleration are usually a sign of worn guides and valve seals.

In addition to the oil burned naturally, your engine can lose a lot of oil due to leaks. Some oil leaks drip onto the exhaust pipes and are burned off by the high heat. As such, it may be difficult to gauge exactly how much oil is being burned by the engine and how much is being lost to oil leaks. Fortunately, once they are identified, many oil leaks can be repaired without tearing down and rebuilding the engine.

Reading spark plugs

The spark plug is the best indicator of what is going on inside the combustion chamber. You need to pull out all the spark plugs to perform compression and leakdown tests, so you might as well take a close look at them while they're out.

While today's modern fuels make plug reading much more difficult, you can still glean a lot of information from looking at them. A good, well-balanced engine will produce a plug that is dry and light brown. If the engine is running

1 When recording oil consumption, make regular notes of odometer and oil dip stick level readings. Also record exactly how much oil you add to the engine. A regular maintenance record can be extremely valuable in determining your engine's total oil consumption. The green arrow points to the oil dip stick, and the red photo points to the current oil level on the dip stick (inset).

2 Spark plugs can give you a quick snapshot of the inside of the combustion chamber. The spark plug on the left shows a finely tuned engine. Note the light brown color and lack of residue on the outside of the plug. The spark plug on the right shows an engine that is burning oil in the combustion chamber. This plug is wet with black, burned oil— a sign there is a problem with the rings or valve guides, and the engine needs to be rebuilt.

too rich, the plug will often be coated with a lot of extra carbon, and the rest of your combustion chamber probably looks the same. In an engine running too lean, the spark plug will have a powdery white coating on it, while the outer porcelain ring may appear burned.

When reading spark plugs, pay close attention to the white porcelain ring around the plug. This white area will give you an excellent background to inspect the color of the plug and determine how the combustion chamber looks inside.

If the plug is wet with oil, it indicates significant leakage into the combustion chamber past either the valve guides or the piston rings. This is generally a bad sign and an indicator that your compression test may yield unfavorable results.

Compression tests

The standard compression test measures the amount of pressure that builds up inside the combustion chamber when the engine is turned over. The typical compression tester is a pressure gauge attached by a short hose to a plug that screws into the spark plug hole. As the engine rotates, the compression gauge reads the maximum pressure exerted within the combustion chamber. The overall value can determine the condition of the rings or valves.

Before you start the compression test, set up the engine as follows: With the car cold, loosen the spark plugs with a spark plug socket and extension (see Project 8). Then tighten them very lightly. You want to test the engine when it's warm, yet if the spark plugs are very tight in the heads, you can damage the threads in the heads by removing them when the engine is hot. Loosen them a bit when the engine is cold to minimize damage. Although you might think that it's good practice to use anti-seize compound on the plug threads, one manufacturer, Porsche, specifically recommends against this, as anti-seize compound seems to interfere with the proper grounding of the plugs.

Warm the car up to operating temperature and then turn it off. Wait five minutes or so, as head temperatures tend to spike right after you turn the engine off. At that point, the engine's water pump has stopped, and the heat builds up with no way to dissipate. Removing the spark plugs right after turning off the engine can cause the threads in the aluminum to gall.

After about five minutes, remove the spark plugs from their holes. If you're working on an early car, simply disconnect the power line (+) from the ignition coil. If you're testing a car with the Motronic engine management system, remove the small square digital motor electronics (DME) relay that powers the system (check the fuse box). Doing this will disable the car's ignition system and prevent the spark plug wires from firing. Also remove the fuel pump relay at this time, if your car has one. You are going to be cranking the engine over several times, and you don't want raw fuel to be dumped into the system.

Recruit a helper so that you can watch the compression gauge while your helper cranks the engine. Attach a battery charger to your battery to avoid running it down. Don't fire the charger up to 50 amps, but instead leave it on about 10 amps, which should help the battery recover when it's not cranking. With the engine warm, install the compression tester in the spark plug hole. A bit of patience and skill are necessary to properly manipulate and screw in the compression tester—you don't want to cross-thread and damage the threads in the cylinder heads. With the compression tester installed, crank the engine over 12 to 16 times. Push the throttle all the way down with your foot to allow maximum airflow into the engine; if you don't, your compression readings will be off. The engine should make six to eight complete compression strokes (12 to 16 turns of the crankshaft). You can tell when the engine is on a compression stroke because the compression gauge will jump and show an increase when the cylinder is compressed. Carefully watch how the compression tester

gauge increases, and record the maximum value when you have completed the last compression stroke. The gauge will jump at first and then increase slowly until cranking the engine over more and more has no additional effect on the reading. Remove the compression tester, and repeat for each of the other cylinders.

What to do with the results? In general, compression tests are limited in what they can tell you, and different compression testers may give different readings. Cranking the engine faster (with a stronger battery or high-powered starter) may also skew readings. The most useful piece of information you can glean from them is how each cylinder compares to the others. All of the cylinders should give readings that are very close to each other, generally indicating an engine in good health. A good rule of thumb is that each cylinder should read a minimum of 85 percent of the value of the highest cylinder. If the highest reading is 150 psi, then the minimum acceptable reading would be about 128 psi.

Although this would be an acceptable figure, it is not necessarily ideal. All of the cylinders should be very close to each other (within 5–10 psi). On a newly assembled and run-in engine, compression numbers are usually within this range. As the engine ages and certain parts wear faster than others, one or more cylinders may experience more wear than the others, and this wear will show up in the compression tests. Needless to say, if all of your cylinders are in the 150-psi range and one cylinder is down around 120 psi, there is cause for concern. Strive to gather consistent readings across all the cylinders, without focusing on the actual values. If a reading is significantly off, go back and test that cylinder again to make sure that the measurement was not tainted by some sort of fluke, which is often the case.

What causes variations in compression tests, and why can't they be used as the final word on engine rebuilds? Several factors can affect the final pressure read by the tester. Engines running with very aggressive camshafts tend to give low compression readings, because there is significant overlap between the intake and exhaust strokes on the cam. During high-rpm engine operation, that overlap gives the engine more power. However, when turning the engine at low rpm, as with a compression test, the overlap causes some of the pressure in the combustion chamber to leak out before the valve is closed.

Altitude and temperature also affect the compression readings. The manufacturer's specifications are almost always stated at a specific altitude (14.7 psi at sea level, for example), and 59 degrees Fahrenheit. Both temperature and barometric pressure change with altitude, so you will need to adjust your measurements to accurately compare them with factory specifications. The accompanying chart provides conversion factors to compensate for changes in altitude.

A standard compression reading of 150 psi in Los Angeles (sea level) would measure significantly less in the surrounding mountains. For example, at an elevation of 6,000 feet, the expected reading would be 150 psi x 0.8359 = 125 psi. The cylinders would read low as compared to sea-level measurements, yet would be perfectly fine at this altitude.

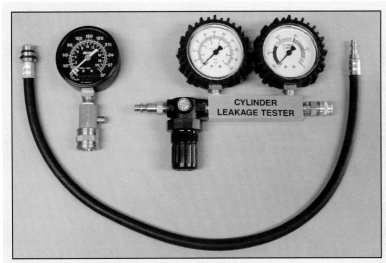

3 The compression tester (left) is useful primarily for comparing cylinders to one another. Most home mechanics lack either the leakdown test equipment (right) or the air compressor required to run a leakdown test. Most shops, however, have the equipment and will perform the leakdown test for a nominal fee. Leakage is typically measured in the volume of percentage lost. Good-running engines typically have leakage less than 10 percent. Engines with significant problems exhibit leakage of 30 percent or more. The leakdown test is very effective because it eliminates extraneous factors that might influence and skew the results of a compression test.

Compression Test Altitude Compensation Factors	
Altitude (feet)	Factor
500	0.987
1,500	0.960
2,500	0.933
3,500	0.907
4,500	0.880
5,500	0.853
6,500	0.826
7,500	0.800
8,500	0.773

Incorrectly adjusted valves can also alter compression test readings. If the valves do not open or close at the correct time, one cylinder may read vastly different from another. Make sure that your valves are adjusted properly prior to performing the test (E30 only). Along the same lines, premature camshaft wear can lead to variances in compression readings.

To determine if the rings are causing low compression readings, squirt approximately 1 tablespoon of standard 10W-30 engine oil into the cylinder. Crank the engine two or three times to spread the oil around inside the combustion chamber. Then retest the compression. If the readings shoot up significantly (45 psi or so), the problem is most likely with the piston rings seating to the cylinders. Squirting oil inside the combustion chamber in this manner allows the rings to temporarily seal more than they would if they were dry. If the compression readings do not change, then a leaky valve is the most likely culprit.

Leakdown testing

Without a doubt, the most comprehensive test you can perform on your engine is a leakdown test. While similar to the compression test, it eliminates nearly all extraneous variables that may alter the final compression readings in a typical compression test. In simple terms, the leakdown test pressurizes the cylinder and measures the amount of air that leaks out past either the rings or the valves, or through a gap between the heads and the cylinder.

The leakdown test equipment uses an external air compressor to pressurize the cylinder. The engine is held stationary, and the test is not dependent upon outside variables like cranking speed, altitude, temperature, or camshaft overlap. In fact, the leakdown test can be performed on nearly all engines, whether inside the car or not.

Unfortunately, leakdown test equipment is somewhat specialized, requires an air compressor, and is not exactly inexpensive. Most repair shops have a leakdown tester, but it's not common to find one in your neighbor's garage. Most shops will perform the leakdown test for a nominal fee. BMW engines generally don't require special leakdown adapters, so you can take your BMW to any good foreign-repair shop for the test.

Similar to the compression test, a leakdown test provides information on the condition of the rings and valves but from a slightly different perspective. The leak-down test can be performed on an engine that is not installed in the car; however, if the engine isn't warmed up, the test may not give accurate results.

For the leakdown test, begin by setting the engine to top dead center (TDC) on the compression stroke for the piston that you are checking. Make sure it's exactly at TDC, or the engine will begin to turn over as soon as you pressurize the cylinder. Both the intake and exhaust valves should be completely closed (at TDC); otherwise, air will immediately leak out of the cylinder. To make sure cylinder number 1 is at TDC, remove the distributor cap and rotate the engine clockwise until the rotor lines up with the small notch. If your car doesn't have a distributor cap, rotate the engine until the timing mark on the main pulley lines up with the corresponding mark on the crankcase. If the spark plug is installed in its hole, the engine should require quite a bit of effort to rotate to TDC. If the engine doesn't push back as you're rotating it, go around another 360 degrees and it should. The engine will be at TDC on the compression stroke.

4 Carbon deposits, like death and taxes, are a fact of life. Shown here is the inside of my E36 engine after about 78,000 miles on California gasoline. Although it looks quite ugly, you don't need to rebuild your engine to clean out your combustion chamber. Deposits can build up on the heads and get stuck on the valves, creating a stuck valve that may result in compression and performance loss. Before tearing open your engine, first clean up the carbon buildup in your combustion chamber. Of course, if your engine is relatively old and showing other signs of wear, a carbon-removal treatment will probably not solve your problems.

When you run the test, make sure the crank doesn't turn at all. Have an assistant hold the crank steady, or place a flywheel lock on the engine if it's out of the car. Connect the leakage tester to the engine in the same manner you would with a compression tester. Pump up the cylinder, and let the leakage tester measure the amount of air lost. The gauge should give readings in percentages. A newly rebuilt engine should have leakdown percentages of 3 to 5 percent. An engine in good running condition should show 10 percent or less. Numbers around 20 percent indicate some wear of the engine, but may still be adequate for good engine operation. Leakage around 30 percent indicates that problems are brewing and a rebuild may be necessary. Needless to say, a large leakage amount, such as 90 percent, indicates that there is a hole in the combustion chamber and the engine is probably not firing on this cylinder at all. Rotate the engine crankshaft clockwise 120 degrees when you're done and check the next cylinder in the firing order (180 degrees for four-cylinder cars). Repeat the process for each cylinder.

The leakdown test can pinpoint the exact problem in the engine. When the cylinder is compressed with air, you can usually hear where the air is releasing. Leakage past the intake valves can often be heard at the intake manifolds through the fuel injection. Exhaust valve leakage can sometimes be heard through the tailpipe. Leakage past the rings can sometimes be heard in the crankcase breather hoses.

While the leakdown test is probably the best indicator of engine condition, it shouldn't be the final word in your evaluation. Sometimes great-running engines, for one reason or another, do not do well on the leakdown tester. Remember that the leakdown tester does not test the engine when it's running—it only performs a static evaluation. Use the leakdown test as one indicator and back it up with other tests and observations.

Carbon deposits

Just about every engine I've seen torn open has had a significant layer of carbon buildup on the pistons and inside the heads and valves. Given today's ever-changing gasoline formulas, additional carbon buildup has become a problem in almost all engines.

Carbon deposits form naturally inside the combustion chamber as a by-product of the combustion process. Both engine oil and gasoline are hydrocarbons, so burning either of them results in a buildup of excess carbon deposits. These deposits are often caused by excessive oil burning in the combustion chamber, which is a sure sign that the engine needs a rebuild. In addition, a rich mixture setting can introduce more of the black soot that creates the carbon buildups in the engine. Short-trip driving and extended idling—not ideal running conditions for an engine—can also increase the buildup rate. While excess carbon deposits can be cleaned and removed without a complete overhaul, they are often yet another sign that something else in the engine needs attention (like rings or guides). Carbon deposits can cause the engine's valves to become shrouded and covered with carbon. In an opposite manner to porting and polishing the heads, the carbon buildup actually disrupts the flow of fuel mixture and can restrict the airflow into the combustion chamber.

As mentioned previously, worn valve guides or worn-out rings allow excess oil into the combustion chamber, which can vastly increase carbon buildup. Of course, the solution to this problem is a full rebuild, or, at the very least, a top-end valve job. How you drive your car can also affect deposit buildup. Short drives around town tend to increase carbon buildup, because slow-speed driving keeps the engine from heating up to normal operating temperatures. Fortunately, excess carbon deposits can be burned out by driving on the highway for an hour or so, because the combustion chamber heats up enough to burn away carbon deposits.

If your engine has been sitting for an extended period of time, try a gasoline additive in your fuel. Berryman B-12 Chemtool and Techron have good reputations for helping to dissolve and remove deposits. For the best results, take your BMW on a spirited drive for an hour or more along the freeway. Try to vary your rpm, but most importantly, keep them relatively high to raise cylinder head temperatures. The cleaning process combined with the heated cylinder heads, should eliminate any excess deposits. When you return from your drive, run the compression or leakdown test again, and you may be surprised at the improvement in the numbers!

The conclusion? Assessing the condition of your engine takes patience—you need to piece together the puzzle from the clues it provides you. Don't rely on a single test result or anomaly. Instead, take a big-picture approach to determine whether or not you need a rebuild.

Replacing Spark Plugs/Coils

⏱ **Time:** 1 hour	🐭 **Tab:** $15	🎎 **Talent:** 🎎🎎

🔧 **Tools:** Spark plug wrench

🚗 **Applicable Years:** All

🧰 **Tinware:** Spark plugs, plug wires (if required)

💡 **Tip:** Don't use anti-seize on the plugs when installing

⚠ **PERFORMANCE GAIN:** Cleaner, better-running engine

COMPLEMENTARY MODIFICATION: Replace valve cover gasket

Replacing the spark plugs and spark plug wires (where applicable) is a basic tune-up procedure for just about any car on the road. I recommend replacing the spark plugs every 10,000 miles or about once a year. You can probably go longer than that, but you never really know how long plugs will last, or you may forget to do it if you don't set up a yearly schedule.

On E36 six-cylinder engines, BMW eliminated the spark plug wires by integrating six small spark plug coils that sit on top of each spark plug. While this configuration may be a bit more expensive than the typical single-coil/single-capacitive discharge box configuration, it makes the car's ignition system more reliable by removing the spark plug wires, a component that frequently wear out and fails. It's a pretty cool setup not common on older cars. As manufacturing components have become increasingly inexpensive, ignition setups like these have become more common.

To prep the car, simply make sure the engine is cold. If you try to remove or install spark plugs in a hot car, the plugs may gum up or damage the relatively delicate threads in the aluminum cylinder head. Make sure the engine is cold or, at the bare minimum, only slightly warm to the touch.

Let's begin with six-cylinder cars. First, remove the top plastic covers from the engine (see Photo 1). These serve no mechanical purpose—they are there only for decoration and to prevent dust and debris from getting into the recesses of the engine. Underneath the left cover, you will see the six spark plug coils that sit on top of each of the plugs. You'll need to carefully remove each coil to gain access to the plugs. Using a screwdriver, release each connector from each coil.

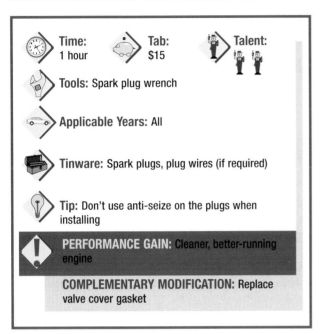

1 On the six-cylinder cars, there are two covers, a long thin one on the top of the car, and a wider one toward the left. On the two plastic covers, there will be two small, snap-in plugs on the top (inset). Carefully remove these plugs (don't drop them into the engine) with a small screwdriver, prying them up as you grab them. Underneath, you will find a nut that holds the cover onto the top of the engine. Remove the four nuts on these two covers, and they should slide up out of the way. The center cover was removed on this E36 six-cylinder engine.

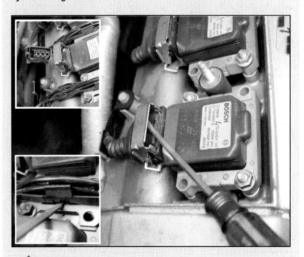

2 A metal retaining ring on the rear of each assembly fastens it to the coil. Once you lift up on the retaining clip, the connector should slide out of the coil (upper left). Carefully remove the connectors from each coil, taking care not to bend the wire harness too much. These wires are stiff and generally don't take kindly to being bent in multiple directions. To more easily maneuver the wires, detach the center clip that holds the wires that run through the center channel (lower left). Gently place the wires off to the side and out of the way, without bending them terribly.

3 If the valve cover seal leaks, the spark plug holes may completely fill up with oil. When you pull out the spark plug connector/coil combo, you may find it completely submerged in engine oil. Looking down the hole, you may not even be able to see the spark plug because the entire hole is filled up with oil (inset). This is actually quite common and doesn't seem to affect the performance of the engine. If you do find oil in your spark plug holes, go one step further and replace the valve cover gasket (Project 9). The replacement procedure is very simple once you remove the coils and should only take about 20 minutes longer, provided you have the correct gasket on hand.

4 In the photo inset, all four electrodes of this unusual spark plug have been eaten away (red arrow). This plug likely was improperly plated from the factory and, as it progressed through its life, the repeated sparking slowly ate away at the electrodes. A plug in this condition would misfire often (if it fired at all) and would generate poor performance for its particular cylinder. Surprisingly enough, none of the other spark plugs in this set exhibited this type of damage, leading me to believe it was defective from the manufacturer. On the right is a brand-new Bosch Platinum spark plug. Spark plugs have varied over the years as engines have changed slightly due to smog regulations. Get the proper spark plugs for your car (they are scaled by electrode type and heat range); otherwise, you may encounter ignition problems. Spark plugs are cheap— go with a brand name like Bosch or NGK and avoid the no-name brands. Measure the spark plug gap (if single electrode) with a spark plug gap tool before you install the plugs.

With the wires detached and placed slightly out of the way, you can remove the six coils. Each coil fastens to the valve cover using two screws. On two of the coils, there are two small ground straps that connect the coil to the cylinder head stud. Take note of these ground straps—they must be installed properly when you are finished, or the car may encounter ignition problems later on. Remove the two nuts that hold each coil to the valve cover. At this point, the coil assembly should easily pull off the engine.

The assembly has a small coil pack on one end and a spring-loaded spark plug connector on the opposite end. Simply remove the coil/plug assembly and place it off to the side. All of the coils are the same, so it doesn't matter which cylinder bank it came from—unless you are specifically trying to troubleshoot a bad coil fault code that was displayed by the main computer.

With the coil assembly removed, you should be able to look down the hole and see the spark plug hiding in there. If you find oil in your spark plug holes (see Photo 3), take some paper towels and soak up as much of the oil as possible before removing the spark plug. If you don't capture all of the excess oil, it will leak into the cylinder head through the spark plug hole once you remove the spark plug. Your car would then run quite sooty when you first start it up, and it may even foul the brand-new spark plugs you just installed!

Spark plug removal is easy; you just need the right spark plug wrench. I have one that I love—it's a spark plug socket with a rubber insert that catches the plug and also has a built-in swivel on the attachment end. These wrenches are readily available from a variety of sources and are especially useful when removing plugs in hard-to-reach places.

Using a breaker bar, grip the plug and turn it counter-clockwise until it is loose. Then pull out your spark plug wrench and grab the plug. When it comes out, inspect the spark plug closely. The spark plug is the best way to see what is going on inside your combustion chamber (see Project 7).

Install the new plugs using a torque wrench to measure the torque applied to the plug. The torque wrench is vital, as it will help you to keep from overtightening or undertightening the spark plugs. Make sure the plug is firmly seated in its spark plug socket—it is very easy to insert the plug into the head and have it cross-thread. This means the threads of the spark plug don't mesh properly with the ones in the head, instead choosing to cut their own path. This damages the threads on the head and, in extreme cases, may destroy the threads in the cylinder head entirely. You do not want this to happen. Proceed carefully and cautiously.

Install each plug into the cylinder heads without any anti-seize compound. Torque the spark plugs to 25 N-m (18.4 ft-lbs). One high-performance automotive manufacturer—Porsche—doesn't recommend using antiseize compound on spark plugs for any of its engines. The bulletin applies retroactively to all models with the theory that antiseize compound acts as an electrical insulator between the plug and the cylinder head. This insulation could be detrimental to the firing of the spark due to the loss of a good, consistent ground connection. Keeping these findings in mind, I make the same recommendations for BMW car owners—don't use anti-seize compound on the spark plugs.

With the new plugs installed and tightened to the correct torque, replace the coils—don't forget the small ground straps—and reattach the coil connectors. Snap the wires back into their center holders, and replace the top two plastic covers. When you're done, the engine should look back-to-normal again.

Changing plugs on the 318 four-cylinder cars, or the E30 cars, is a bit different and a bit easier. Start by removing the spark plug cover. There may be a handy little blue spark-plug-wire pull tool under the cover. Use it to remove the plug wires from the ends of the spark plugs. With the wires disconnected, remove the plugs and install the new plugs in a similar manner to the procedure for the E36 six-cylinder cars. Also, replace the spark plug wires every 30,000 miles, or whenever they look cracked or worn out.

PROJECT 9
http://www.101projects.com/BMW/9.htm
Replacing the Valve Cover Gasket

Troubled by oil leaks? The large (and long) valve cover gasket is a common site for oil leaks in BMW engines. Oil can leak out the side of the gasket into the engine compartment, or, in E36 cars, it can leak into the spark plug holes, causing a potential short circuit or annoying ignition problems. Thankfully, it's pretty easy to remove and replace the valve cover gasket on E30 cars since the cover just screws off (see Project 21). Six-cylinder E36 cars present more of a challenge. Begin by removing the ignition coils (see Project 8).

On E36 six-cylinder cars, with the coils removed, you can remove the top plastic cover on the wire harness box that straddles the intake manifold and valve cover. The lid on this box simply snaps off (see Project 30). With the lid removed, reach in and carefully pull the wire harnesses out of the way. At this point, you can remove the bolts that hold on the valve cover. Take careful note of which bolts have ground straps attached—and where they are—so you can replace them when you're ready to reassemble the valve cover.

Some of the bolts may be difficult to reach, in particular the one way in the back of the engine compartment, beneath

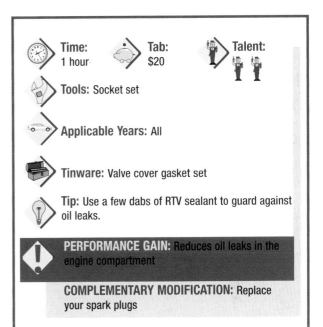

Time: 1 hour

Tab: $20

Talent:

Tools: Socket set

Applicable Years: All

Tinware: Valve cover gasket set

Tip: Use a few dabs of RTV sealant to guard against oil leaks.

PERFORMANCE GAIN: Reduces oil leaks in the engine compartment

COMPLEMENTARY MODIFICATION: Replace your spark plugs

1 The BMW factory manuals recommend adding some sealant to leak-prone sections of the cylinder head (green arrows). I used Permatex High-Temp RTV, and it worked very well for sealing these areas. Specifically, the factory manuals recommend adding sealant at the interface where the VANOS unit or front-mounting timing chain cover meet. They also recommend a bit of sealant at the rear of the cover.

2 Shown here is the installed valve cover gasket. The inset shows the gaskets that seal each spark plug hole. Worn gaskets may allow excess oil to leak into the spark plug holes (see Project 8). If you haven't replaced your spark plugs lately, now is a good time to do so.

the windshield wipers. A small ratchet will come in handy here. Once you have removed all of the bolts (15 in all for the six-cylinder engines), lightly tap the side of the valve cover with a rubber mallet to loosen it from its gasket. You should then be able to remove the valve cover.

Inspect the valve cover when it comes off. In particular, be careful with the baffle and seal on the inside. This seal does not appear to be a separate part, but it comes with the valve cover. It doesn't really do much—it just seals an air baffle to the valve cover. In any case, when you remove the valve cover, make sure you don't lose any rubber grommets or the flat washers that hold them in.

If you take your valve cover to a machine shop to be sandblasted, be sure to reassemble the bits and pieces in the proper order. Especially important are the rubber studs that hold the top plastic covers in place, as well as the baffle on the inside of the cover.

Prep the surfaces of the cylinder head and valve cover for the new seal by carefully cleaning all remnants of the old seal off of each of the mating surfaces. Be careful not to scratch any surfaces or drop bits of gasket into the engine.

Apply sealant (see Photo 1), and simply place the new gasket on the cylinder head. Place the two inner gaskets on the spark plugs holes in the center of the head. Finally, bolt down the cover, and reattach the nuts on the cover, replacing the rubber washers/bumpers under each one. Using a torque wrench, tighten the bolts to 10 N-m (89 in-lb). Reinstall the coils, reattach the wire harness, and replace the top plastic covers.

Machine Shop 101

Time: As long as it takes

Tab: $50–1,500

Talent: N/A

Tools: A good-quality machine shop

Applicable Years: All

Tinware: Valve guides, valve seats, new valves, if needed

Tip: Find a machinist that has time to answer your questions.

PERFORMANCE GAIN: Tightly machined parts for a better-running engine

COMPLEMENTARY MODIFICATION: Blueprint your engine

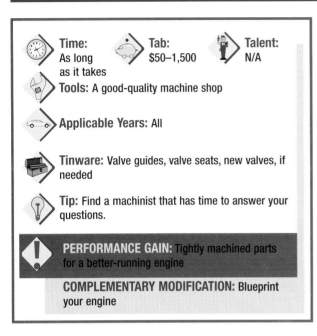

1 A bit better than sandblasting, the bead blaster is kinder to the surface of the metal. Paint, oil, dirt, and grime are no match for the bead blaster. Parts that are completely covered with grime exit the blaster looking like they came out of new BMW factory boxes. In order to properly assess the condition of cylinder heads, they must be completely cleaned in the bead blaster.

If you plan to have your engine rebuilt, or a top-end rebuild performed, you will probably need to take some of your parts to a machine shop. Some tasks require special, precise tools and knowledge that only a machine shop possesses. Most of the time, owners drop off their parts and then pick up magically rebuilt parts with no clue as to what really happened to them. This section aims to take some of the mystery out of what happens to your parts when you drop them off.

Machine shops are especially useful for their parts cleaning services. For less than $100, the shop will clean and bead blast sheet metal, flywheels, heads, body parts—just about anything you want. If you've ever sat in your garage with a piece of sandpaper and a block of wood, you will instantly recognize how much time and energy can be saved by having your parts blasted. If, for some reason, you can't use a blasting procedure (on engine cases or oil coolers, for example), most shops have advanced cleaning tanks that are similar to industrial-sized dishwashers for greasy, oil-soaked parts.

Cylinder head reconditioning is a popular procedure performed at the machine shop. This job generally can't be performed at home because the process requires too many specialized tools.

First, the valves and springs are separated from the head. The head is placed into a specialized spring compressor tool that compresses the valve spring, allowing for removal of the entire spring assembly. The valves can then be removed from the assembly. Finally, the head is either cleaned or blasted until it looks like it just came out of a brand-new BMW box.

2 Twenty-four valves look most impressive when they are laid out on the table like this. Each valve will be inspected and reconditioned to ensure proper sealing with the cylinder head.

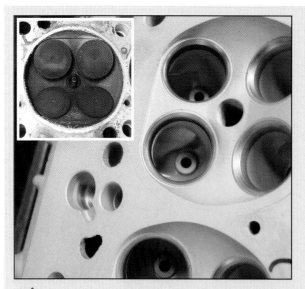

3 Cylinder heads look amazing after they have been cleaned and blasted. The inset shows what the combustion chamber looked like before blasting. Cleaning the head is essential to finding and fixing cracks (see Project 17).

4 The heads are machined on a special jig aligned to cut the valve seats to match the valves exactly. A special cutting tool cuts the angle of the seats, while the machine holds the heads aligned to the inner bore of the valve guide.

5 The tool used to grind the valve seats is made of special tool steel and is ground to reflect the desired profile and angle of the seats.

The heads are then inspected to see if they need new valve guides. In most cases, the guides will be worn beyond the recommended BMW specifications and need to be replaced. To quickly see if a guide is worn, the valve is inserted into the guide to see if it can wobble it back and forth. If it doesn't wobble, then a more precise small-bore gauge will be needed to accurately measure the guide.

If the guide is worn, it needs to be removed. Threads are tapped into the guide and a cap screw is screwed in. This screw gives the valve guide puller a grip to remove the valve from the head.

New guides are pressed into the head. Advances in valve guide technology have resulted in new materials with higher wear strengths. Newer guides may look different than the older ones and should last considerably longer. After the guides are pressed into the heads, they are reamed to ensure that the inner bore is within the proper specifications.

The heads contain valve seats, which are steel inserts pressed within the aluminum casting of the head. In most cases, it is not necessary to replace the seat in the head. The seat is machined in precise alignment with the new valve guide. A machine that aligns itself with the new guide cuts the seat at a specific angle so that the valve will seat and seal properly.

The valves themselves are machined as well to match the angles of the valve guides and valve seats. For a valve to be reused, it must still have a significant amount of material on both the outer edge and the valve stem itself. If not, the valve can no longer be used. In general, a valve can be used for one or two rebuilds before it will need to be replaced. Exhaust valves should only be used once, unless they are the more-expensive sodium-filled valves. The sodium-filled valves dissipate heat better than standard stainless-steel valves and thus are less vulnerable to the wear and tear of thermal shock that might affect a steel valve. The valves are set into a valve grinding tool and precisely ground to the angle that matches the angle on the valve seats.

As you can imagine, the machining of the valve, guide, and seat are precision processes that need to be aligned together. If a machine shop is sloppy, or its equipment is out of alignment, you might be in for trouble later on. In some cases, the cheapest machine shop might not do a quality job. Unfortunately, it's very difficult to check the tolerances on the valves after you get them back from the shop.

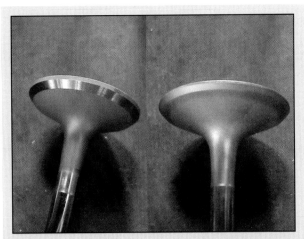

6 Valves can typically be reused if there is enough material on the edge for a regrind. The valve on the left is brand-new; the one on the right doesn't have enough material left on its edge for another regrind. Intake valves can often be reused without problems, but exhaust valves should only be used once, unless they are the more expensive sodium-filled valves. Sodium-filled exhaust valves dissipate heat much better than plain stainless-steel valves and thus have longer lives.

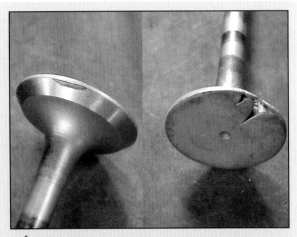

7 These two valves have seen better days. The valve on the left has been ground so thin its edge has cracked off. The valve on the right shows signs of getting too hot. If the seat and valve don't meet and mount perfectly, hot spots will build up, causing cracks like the ones in this valve.

8 If there is enough clearance left on the valve, it can be reground to match the valve seats. This process is performed on a special valve grinder that can be set to match the angle of the valve to the angle of the valve seat.

While you're there, also take your engine case in to be cleaned and checked. Be sure, however, that the case is not sandblasted, as sand may get caught in the tiny oil passages that feed various parts of the engine. The shop will check the engine case to ensure all the bearing surfaces are round and aligned with each other. If they are not, a procedure called "align boring" is performed. In many cases, machine shops will outsource align boring, because the necessary machines can be large and expensive. Align boring increases the outer diameter of the bearings to a specific size, while aligning all the bearing surfaces within the case. After the case is bored out, you must use oversized bearing sets instead of the standard sets.

Also take the crankshaft to the machine shop before using it in a rebuild. Magnafluxing is a common procedure associated with crankshaft inspection. This process exposes all the flaws in the crankshaft, affording detection of any microscopic cracks on the surface. Have your crankshaft Magnafluxed if you plan to reuse it.

Magnafluxing is a relatively simple process. The crankshaft is initially magnetized using a large circular magnet. The magnetic field is applied to the crankshaft at a 45-degree angle, so the process will detect cracks that run both parallel and perpendicular to the length of the crankshaft. The crankshaft is sprayed with a special liquid that has a magnetic powder suspended within the solution. This powder becomes trapped in any cracks present in the crankshaft. The crankshaft is then examined under an ultraviolet (black) light in total darkness. Under the black light, the cracks clearly show as bright lines in the surface. Crankshafts typically show failures at the points where the journal bearing meets a center flange.

After the crankshaft is tested, it is demagnetized and then washed in solvent to remove the Magnaflux material. Make sure the crankshaft is demagnetized; otherwise, the tiny bits of metal that inevitably find their way into your engine oil will stick to the crankshaft bearing journals.

It's also wise to get the crank polished. The bearing surfaces of the crank require a smooth surface in order to properly create a thin oil film to ride upon. If the surface is at all rough, it disrupts the flow of oil around the bearing. Polishing the crank keeps the oil flowing smoothly around the bearing surfaces and increases engine bearing life.

9 The Magnaflux process is quite interesting to watch. A crankshaft (or any metal object) is magnetized by the large electromagnetic coil shown on the left. Then, a magnetic powder that can only be seen in ultraviolet (UV) light is sprinkled on the crankshaft. The powder is then blown off the surfaces. It will find its way into any hidden cracks on the surface and can be seen when the UV light is shined on the crankshaft. The VW Type IV oil pump gear on the right has a crack near the base of one of the gear teeth. The crack shows up as a green line under the UV light (white arrow).

10 Your best asset in rebuilding your engine is a competent machinist. As chief technical writer for PelicanParts.com, I often ask my machinist for his opinion on engines I'm working on. Look for a machinist who doesn't mind answering your questions. Beware of machinists who insist they know what's best without explaining to you why. Very often, the cheapest machine shop isn't always the best bet, either. Try to find one that takes pride in its work. Ask around, as stories of bad shops spread easily from the mouths of disgruntled customers.

Additionally, the connecting rods need to be reconditioned at the machine shop. New wrist pin bushings should be placed at the rod's end. The procedure known as "resizing" ensures the size of the rod bearing that fits around the crankshaft is correct. Over the life of the engine, rods sometimes stretch, causing the rod bearing surface to become slightly out of round. In order to correct this problem, the rod cap is removed and a small amount of material is removed from the mating surface. The rod cap is then reattached to the rod, and the bearing surface is machined to original factory specifications. Removing a small amount of material from the smaller rod half is common and doesn't affect the strength or reliability of the rod.

Finally, it may be necessary to have your camshafts reground. Although most BMW engines don't exhibit large amounts of wear on the camshafts, some engines may require a regrind and polish close to original specifications. If the camshaft is at all pitted, it may be necessary to weld the pits, regrind the shaft, and retreat the metal to reharden the surface on the lobes of the cam.

Entrusting any or all of these tasks to a reputable machine shop will help ensure a long life for your engine.

PROJECT 11
Camshaft Replacement
http://www.101projects.com/BMW/11.htm

Time: 3 hours

Tab: None

Talent: ★★★

Tools: Camshaft alignment tool

Applicable Years: 1993–1999 E36

Tinware: New valve cover gasket

Tip: Have a friend help you keep the camshafts from rotating

! PERFORMANCE GAIN: M3 cams will give you more power and better response

COMPLEMENTARY MODIFICATION: Replace valve cover gasket, spark plugs

I recently had to tear down the top of my BMW 325is M50 engine to replace the head gasket (see Project 17). While performing this large task, I decided to perform a complete valve job on the cylinder head while I was at it—which required removing the camshafts from the cylinder head.

Piece of cake? Nope. BMW camshafts are not like those on other cars. The camshafts are very long and hollow, particularly on the six-cylinder cars. This makes them very prone to bending and cracking from adverse side loads placed on them during removal. After consulting the BMW factory documentation (and a few experts elsewhere), I discovered that a special BMW tool is required to safely remove the camshafts. "No problem," I thought. "I'll just purchase the tool and then rent it out through PelicanParts.com for others to use."

After further research, I learned the tool costs more than $1,400—and isn't even available for purchase at this time. Our

BMW dealer explained that the tool is custom-manufactured by one guy, in some small company, in the motherland of Germany. There would be an eight-month lead time for delivery of the tool, and even that wasn't guaranteed. In addition, I'd have had to buy two tools—one for the four-cylinder engines and an add-on adapter tool for the six-cylinder engines.

As chief technical writer for PelicanParts.com and a staunch defender of the do-it-yourself mechanic, I decided there had to be a way to do the job without using that specialized tool. I dove into research, inquiring with many shops and BMW owners as to how they removed camshafts. Just about everyone I spoke with told me they either took their car to the dealer, although one owner had the tool himself. "Hmm," I thought. "Not too promising." I even heard of one poor soul who took his 325is to a shop to have the camshafts professionally swapped out—and they still broke them. To add insult to injury, the shop managers told the fellow that they weren't responsible, and he had to buy new ones. I'll bet those dolts didn't even bother to check the BMW factory documentation (or even the Bentley manual) to find out the proper removal procedure.

I was determined to find a way to remove the camshafts without using the tool, and without breaking or damaging them. I'll spoil the suspense right now: I achieved successful removal and installation using a special technique I developed after studying the camshafts for many nights. Especially encouraging in this task was the tale of a fellow who'd seen a BMW racing crew carefully and quickly swap out camshafts in the pit—without the special tool. With this knowledge in hand, I had a feeling I would be able to figure out a way to do it, even though everyone else said not to try it. I figured, "What's the worst that will happen? I'll just break some camshafts." Ultimately, I want my readers and customers to know what works and what doesn't, without all the myths and hype.

Let me pause for a second, though, to say that BMW doesn't recommend that you use this method to remove

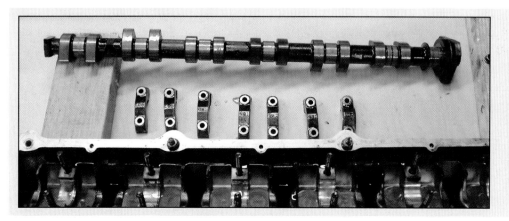

1 BMW camshafts are long and thin and prone to breaking. With that in mind, you must follow the removal procedure very carefully. Placing large loads on one end of the camshaft can cause it to break if it's constrained at the other end.

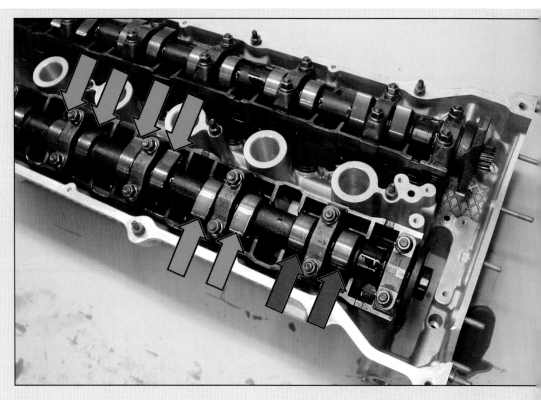

2 In this diagram, the camshaft is in its sweet spot and there are no forces acting on any of the lobes on the left side (green arrows). The valve springs are compressing heavily on the camshaft near cylinder number 1 (red arrows). By slowly removing the cap nuts on cylinder number 1, the camshaft can be safely removed.

the camshafts. If you don't do it correctly, you can break the camshafts. While this won't destroy the engine, you'll have to replace the very expensive camshafts—before you can run your car again. This would probably be the worst-case scenario. However, if you are careful and smart, and follow these directions and precautions precisely, you should be able to successfully remove the camshafts. (Note: I am not responsible if you use this method and you do end up breaking your camshafts.)

As noted before, the camshafts are hollow and very long. Camshafts are also hardened, which makes them very brittle and prone to cracking. They tend to break much easier than they bend, due to the hollow geometry combined with the metal-hardening process. If you place a force on one end of the camshaft and a force on the other end without adequately supporting the middle, you risk bending or breaking the camshaft. Thus, the key to safe removal is to balance the forces placed on it during the process.

Where do these forces come from? They come from valve spring preload. The camshaft can rotate, obviously, through 360 degrees of motion. At all times, there is at least one pair of camshaft lobes pressing down on valve lifters and compressing a pair of valve springs. Transmitted through the lifters, the springs place a tremendous force on the camshaft. Ordinarily, the bearing caps that lie between each camshaft lobe provide even support for the camshaft. However, if the camshaft is cocked, or if the force is not evenly distributed across the length of the camshaft, the camshaft will bend and break.

To understand what we need to do, I would first like to discuss how the factory tool works. The inset of Photo 4

shows drawings of the BMW factory tool. The tool shown in these drawings is only appropriate for the removal of camshafts on four-cylinder cars. The tool bolts onto the head near where the spark plugs are mounted. A handle on the tool then activates a set of rods that press down on each of the bearing caps that hold the camshaft to the head. At this point, with the tool in place, you can remove all of the nuts that hold the cam bearing caps in place. With the tool applying uniform pressure and force to each of the cam bearing caps (very important), you can release the rods slowly and let the camshaft rise off of the lower cam bearing surfaces. The tool applies even, uniform pressure across the entire camshaft during the removal process. When the camshaft lobes are no longer compressing the valve springs, then you can safely remove the camshaft, as it will have no more forces placed on it.

While this makes sense, understanding the problem is only the first step. You might think you could achieve the same results as the BMW tool by simply unscrewing all of the bearing caps uniformly. For example, each nut would be loosened a half turn until they were all removed. In theory, this seems like it would work very well. However, from my research, I found out this is almost a sure-fire way to break the camshafts. Simply removing the bearing cap nuts uniformly does not guarantee uniform pressure on the camshaft. I didn't seek the specifics, but I did hear there were quite a few camshafts broken using this method, so I quickly rejected it.

The problem lies with the tension placed on the camshaft by the valve springs. Reduce or remove this tension, and you should be able to safely remove the camshafts without

3 The camshaft tends to rotate from its sweet spot. For this reason, I recommend having an assistant on hand to hold the camshaft steady. This is not a task you can easily do by yourself; if you slip up, you will break the camshafts.

for cylinder number 1 should be slightly open (not fully open).

How can you tell if the valves for cylinders 2 through 6 are closed? Stick your pinky finger down behind the camshaft lobe, and try to rotate the camshaft lifter in its bore (see Photo 4). There will be a small clearance between the lifter and the camshaft when the valve is closed and no camshaft lobes are acting on the lifter. This will allow your finger to rotate the lifter in its bore.

A word of caution: The camshaft will be heavily spring-loaded because cylinder number 1 has two valves open and is compressing their valve springs. In addition, the cam lobes acting on cylinder number 1 will be cocked at an angle and can snap the camshaft into another position if it's not tightly held in place. For this reason, I strongly recommend that this be a "two-man" job. One holds the camshaft in place, while the second person removes it. If not, the camshaft can rotate while you're removing it, which may cause it to compress additional valve springs and break. Also, if

them breaking. How? Well, I came up with a bunch of ideas that I won't elaborate on here; see www.101Projects.com for those Rube Goldbergs. . . .

During normal operation, valves open and close. When the valves are closed, they do not place any load on the camshaft. So I got to thinking, "Is there a spot on the camshaft where only one set of valves is open at a particular time?" The answer is yes, and that is key to the removal technique here. The theory is that if only one set of valves is open, there are no forces or loads placed on the camshaft from any other lifters. Since each pair of cam lobes is supported by a single cam bearing cap in the center, slowly removing this bearing cap will leave equal pressure on both sides over a very small distance, making it virtually impossible to break the camshaft.

Without the cylinder head sitting in front of you, this technique can be hard to follow. Take a look at Photo 2. In this picture, the cam lobes for cylinder number 1 are shown with red arrows. The cam lobes for cylinders 2 through 6 are shown with green arrows. For the purpose of removing the camshaft, you want to rotate the camshaft using a wrench to grip the square end, as shown in Photo 3. If the head is out of the car, make sure it is supported on two small blocks of wood, so the opening valves won't try to lift the head off of your table from the opposite side.

Rotate the camshaft so the cam lobes for cylinder number 1 are acting on the valves for cylinder number 1. At this point, it doesn't matter whether you're working on the intake or exhaust side. There should be a point in the rotation where the cam lobes are acting on the valves for cylinder 1 and all of the other valves (2 through 6) are closed. At this point, the valves

you're feeling the lifters with your finger and the camshaft snaps back, you may end up crushing your finger. Trust me: it's a two-person job.

On my 1993 325is, I was able to find this sweet spot where there were no loads placed on the camshaft except for the valve springs from cylinder number 1. While all BMW 3 Series camshafts are similar, they may have different profiles and may not have this sweet spot. In that case, you need to find the spot closest to the sweet spot where the valves for cylinders 2 through 6 are barely compressed. I'm confident you will find one of these spots on your camshaft.

To remove the camshaft, simply rotate it into its sweet spot position and remove the cam bearing caps for cylinders 2 through 6. There should be no loads on the caps, and, after an initial loosening, you should be able to remove the nuts easily by hand. Make sure your assistant holds the camshaft securely and steadily so it doesn't slip. If it slips at this point, the lobes will try to compress the valve springs with no support on the camshaft, and it will surely break.

Turning your attention to cylinder number 1, slowly begin removing the bearing cap. Alternate between bolts, turning each one a quarter turn at a time to ensure both sides of the cam bearing cap receive equal pressure. The camshaft should slowly lift up as the valve springs pull the valves back into their seats in the head (see Photo 5). If the camshaft doesn't lift, give the bearing cap a very light tap with a small hammer. Continue until the bearing cap can be removed. The nuts will get very close to the end of their travel on the stud before you will be able to remove them by hand. This is normal. When the bearing cap is removed, there should be

4 To successfully remove the camshafts with the special BMW tool, there must first be no forces acting on five of the six camshaft lobes. You can check to see if there is any tension by placing your finger against the lifter (green arrow). You should be able to spin it slightly in its bore, indicating that there are no forces acting on the camshaft. Inset: The BMW factory tool is complicated, expensive, and generally only available from a BMW dealer (inset).

5 When you have verified there are no forces acting on the opposite end of the camshaft, slowly remove the nuts that hold down the bearing caps, alternating back and forth, turning each one a quarter turn. When the nuts are ready to come off (as in the photo), there should be very little force acting on the camshaft lobe.

nothing holding the camshaft to the head, and you can simply remove it from the head. (Just don't drop it.)

Alternate method: If you can't get to a point where all of the lifters for cylinders 2 through 6 can rotate in their bores, you'll need to slightly alter the previous procedure. Instead of removing the bearing caps for cylinders 2 through 6 all at once, use the following method: With the majority of the force on cylinder number 1 (at the camshaft sweet spot), remove the bearing caps for all cylinders by turning each nut counterclockwise one-quarter turn—and only one-quarter turn—before continuing to the next nut. Turn all of the screws one-quarter turn, and then repeat in the same order until all the bearing caps are loose. Because you have the camshaft oriented in the proper sweet spot, the force on any of the other lobes (2 through 6) should be minimal.

Installation of a camshaft is performed in the opposite manner of removal. Set the camshaft on the head so that the lobes for cylinders 2 through 6 are as far away from the lifters as possible. The lobes for cylinder number 1 should point down at an angle, and resting on the lifters. Begin tightening the bearing cap for cylinder number 1, one-quarter turn on each nut, alternating as you go. Constantly check the lifters as you tighten down the camshaft—they should be free to rotate in their bores if you have aligned them all correctly. If you used the alternate method detailed above, then reverse the alternate method for installation—tighten each nut of each bearing cap one-quarter turn, then repeat. Camshaft bearing caps should be tightened to 15 N-m (11 ft-lbs).

This procedure should work very well, particularly if the cylinder head is out of the car. You can perform this procedure if the engine is in the car, but it's quite a bit more difficult to navigate. One note of caution: If you do perform a camshaft swap with the engine in the car, don't accidentally tap your valves to your pistons. To be 100 percent safe, first turn your engine clockwise to top dead center (TDC) for cylinder number 1. Then, rotate the engine about 45 degrees clockwise to move all the pistons about halfway in their bores so they won't have any danger of touching the other pistons, no matter what you do.

For instructions on E30 camshaft removal (which is much easier), see www.101Projects.com/BMW/11.htm.

Intake Manifold Removal

 Time: 4 hours   **Tab:** $20   **Talent:** 👤👤👤👤

Tools: Socket set, screwdrivers, swivel sockets, needle-nose pliers

 Applicable Years: E36 six-cylinder cars

 Tinware: New rubber intake boot, intake manifold gaskets

 Tip: Take a lot of digital photos during the disassembly process

> ❗ **PERFORMANCE GAIN:** Allows you to tackle other projects, fix leaky manifold seals

COMPLEMENTARY MODIFICATION: Replace fuel injectors

1 Shown here is the air filter housing. The blue arrow points to the air intake channel that feeds the air filter. Remove the air filter housing and this channel by disconnecting it at the clips (orange arrows).

ENGINE

Let me start off by congratulating the BMW engineers for squeezing the E36 six-cylinder engine into an almost impossibly tight spot. It is quite a remarkable packaging job, considering they did it in the early 1990s when all they had were computers with 386 processors and rudimentary 2D CAD programs. Yet their success makes it a big pain for mechanics who work on these cars—it's a tight squeeze, and you have to remove a lot of stuff to remove the intake manifold.

The best way to learn how to remove the intake manifold is to carefully follow along with these pictures. This task includes one of the steps in the head gasket replacement (Project 17), so a number of other items have already been removed (fan, radiator, belts, etc.). If you're just pulling the intake manifold, you don't need to remove these other items.

For this project, I strongly recommend that you get a digital camera and take about a hundred photos of the disassembly process. If you have any questions as to how it was put together beforehand, you can easily refer back to the photos. As an additional resource, the companion CD-ROM to this book (available at www.101Projects.com) contains approximately 300 more photos of the manifold removal and installation process.

Before you begin, let the car sit for about six hours before working on it. The pressure in the fuel lines should

2 The throttle body and mass airflow sensor assembly are shown here. The two hoses located below that assembly need to be disconnected (orange arrow). Disconnect the electrical harness to the airflow sensor so you can move the sensor around easier (blue arrow). Disconnect the rubber boot from the sensor and the throttle body by releasing the clamps (yellow arrows). Check this boot carefully, as it often cracks and can cause erratic idling if it does. Disconnect the throttle body from the intake manifold (top two with the red arrows). At this point, you should be able to pull away the throttle body. Also, disconnect the vacuum hose that supplies the brake booster (green arrow), and detach the oil dip stick guide tube and the vent hose at the base of the dip stick.

3 Be careful of the throttle body cables when you detach the throttle body, as you don't want to twist or damage them. Also, do not disconnect the hoses that connect to the throttle body from underneath.

4 This photo shows a close-up of the fuel injector plugs after the harness has been removed. The valve cover breather hose (yellow arrow) must be disconnected. The rearmost intake manifold nuts (inset) can be difficult to get to, so I recommend using swivel sockets for this task (see Photo 2 of Project 49).

5 Disconnect the two fuel lines that circulate fuel through the injector rail. Carefully disconnect the clamps from the pipes that exit out of the bottom of the manifold (blue arrows). For S52/M52 engines, you may need special BMW tool 16-1-050 to release these fuel lines (purple arrows). There's also a clamp that holds the two metal lines underneath the manifold. Remove this clamp as well (look down the tunnel under the manifold for access). When reinstalling the manifold, the most frustrating attachment point was the bracket shown by the yellow arrow (remove this bolt after you have disconnected the fuel lines). A single bolt fastens the bottom of the manifold to this bracket, but getting that bolt threaded back into the hole was very difficult, because you can't see if the manifold is aligned with the bracket (misaligned in the photo). Use a small inspection mirror and an assistant to help you guide the bolt back into its proper place in the manifold. There's a similar bolt and bracket combination toward the front of the car.

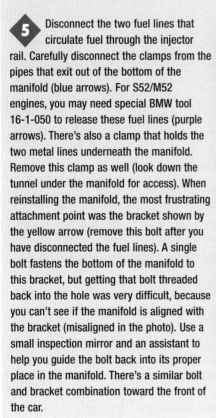

have dissipated somewhat, and the car should be stone cold while you're working on it. Disconnect the battery (see Project 84), as you will be working very close to the starter, which has live current running to it at all times. You will also be disconnecting fuel lines near this connection and you don't want to risk any sparks. Additionally, remove the gas cap from the gas tank to relieve any pressure that may have built up inside the tank from expanding fumes.

Since installation is simply the reverse of removal, just hook everything back up—but carefully inspect the intake boot for cracks prior to doing so. Consider replacing the intake boot while you're in there, as it may start to crack and break once you've disturbed it. Also, watch out for the lower rear manifold mounting bracket, as it can be very difficult to reattach (see Photo 4).

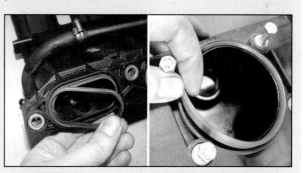

6 To remove the intake manifold, you need to remove the engine wire harness first and slide it out of the way. Start by unscrewing the main plugs (green arrows, lower right). Then, loosen the main wire junction box (blue arrow) by lifting up the rain tray under the wipers and removing the two small screws contained within (red arrow, upper right). Let the harness hang loose—you will need to push it out of the way when you lift out the manifold. Even more annoying than removing the wire harness, you need to disconnect a hose that is located underneath the manifold, inside the tunnel below the plastic manifold runners (yellow arrow). Reach in and disconnect the plastic clip on the hose. It was a tight squeeze for my hand, so you may need to ask someone with small hands for help. The purple arrow shows the fuel injector wire harness pushed off to the side.

7 With everything disconnected, the manifold should lift up out of the engine compartment but not without a fight. The manifold is tightly squeezed in between the cylinder head and the firewall (near the wipers). You will have to wrestle with it a bit to get it off the studs that attach it to the cylinder head. Double- and triple-check your connections to make sure you didn't forget to disconnect a hose or line.

8 While you have the intake manifold apart, you should replace a few important seals. The first is the throttle body seal, shown on the right. It seals the throttle body housing to the intake manifold. A leak in this gasket can cause poor running and an erratic idle. On the left, one of the manifold-to-head gaskets is shown. These gaskets can also cause erratic engine performance if there are leaks around them. If the seal is breached, it will create a vacuum leak, and the engine may suck in additional air on the intake stroke, altering the air/fuel mixture ratio for that particular cylinder.

ENGINE

 Time: 3 hours   **Tab:** $250 **Talent:** 🕺🕺🕺

 Tools: Chain tensioner tool, camshaft holding tool, flywheel lock tool

 Applicable Years: E36 (All) **Tinware:** None   **Tip:** Use the proper camshaft alignment tools

PERFORMANCE GAIN: Properly timed camshafts are vital to engine performance

COMPLEMENTARY MODIFICATION: Upgrade your camshafts

1 Since there are so many photos associated with this project, I have arranged them in assembly order with captions. Each caption covers a step in the assembly process. If you are simply replacing the VANOS unit, skip to Photo 11. First, make sure the engine is at top dead center (TDC). Then, install the TDC flywheel pin tool in the locking position to hold the flywheel steady (see Project 17). Lock the camshafts in place with the camshaft-locking tool (green arrow and photo inset) in order to properly align and time both the camshafts and the VANOS unit.

2 Prior to mounting the sprocket for the exhaust camshaft on the engine, verify that its teeth are not worn or damaged. Also inspect the mounting slots to see if there is any wear from having come loose in the past. Install the sprocket onto the exhaust camshaft. The mounting holes on the camshaft flange should be visible through the slots in the sprocket, and the holes should be biased toward the left side of the slots (red arrow). It may require some maneuvering to get the sprocket into its proper position. Normally, it takes multiple attempts to get it to look exactly like the photo.

3 Turn your attention to the lower chain tensioner, located on the lower part of the block on the right side of the car. Remove the tensioner by placing a socket on the end piece of the tensioner. Do not remove the tensioner block that is attached to the housing (not necessary). When the tensioner comes out, it is spring-loaded and will pop out when you release the tension with your socket and driver. Replace the tensioner with the proper tensioning tool. For now, simply hand tighten the tool—we don't need or want the chain tension to be super-tight right now. The tensioner tool (see photo inset) is used in place of the spring-loaded tensioner when timing the camshafts. Use BMW tool 11-3-390 for an early-style chain tensioner like the one in the photo, or BMW tool 11-4-20 if you have a later-style, updated tensioner. Use this tool, and do not rely solely on the spring-loaded tensioner, which does not provide enough tension when the engine is off to accurately time the camshafts. Use the tool, and get the accurate reading that your engine deserves. It is also a good time to replace the lower chain tensioner with an updated one from BMW (see Project 16).

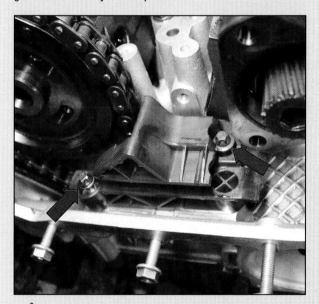

4 With the left sprocket in place, reinstall the center plastic chain guide and torque down the long bolts (10 N-m) that hold it in place (red arrows). Don't overtighten. The first time I did this, the long bolt was brittle and broke off in the cylinder head. I had to take the assembly apart again, fish out the bolt, and special order a new one (a three-day wait).

With the guide in place, reinstall the top chain tensioner. These tensioners sometimes fail, but there isn't a good method for testing them. Replace the tensioner if your engine has 80,000 miles on it or so. Tighten the bolts to 20 N-m (green arrows). Inspect the ramp for any significant wear or obvious deformation before you install it. The ramp should still be held in place by the two small hex keys that you inserted when you removed it. Do not release the tensioner yet.

ENGINE

49

7 The studs for the thrust washer and sprocket look very similar to the studs that mount the valve cover to the head, so don't mix them up. Compare yours carefully to photo to make sure that you have the right studs. There are two types of VANOS units—early and late. The early units do not have a plate spring, whereas the later units do. The plate spring fits over the intake camshaft thrust washer and requires slightly longer studs. This particular car does not have the spring plate.

6 Place the camshaft sensor cap onto the intake camshaft. This metal cap triggers the camshaft position sensor, which lets the engine know where the engine is in its four-cycle process. The camshaft position sensor (see Project 14) fits into the hole on the right side of this photo (blue arrow), and you can make out the small green O-ring to the lower right.

Install the thrust washer onto the intake camshaft. Use the special studs, and install it in the same configuration **8** it was in when removed. In this photo, you see the oil stain from the slots that surround the studs. Install this side facing you when you reinstall the thrust washer. Torque the studs to 20 N-m (14.7 ft-lbs).

9 Take the two intake sprockets and chain and attach them to the assembly. See the photo for the proper orientation of the two sprockets. The exhaust sprocket cup should face outward, and the intake sprocket cup should face inwards. Verify that both sprockets are correctly mounted, flush to the surfaces behind them. Install the intake sprocket with the flat side facing you (the VANOS unit). The collar of the intake sprocket faces and points to the camshaft. Align the two sprockets and chain so the slots are centered on both sprockets (see arrows). Soak the sprockets, gears, and chains in clean motor oil before you install them— these are sliding parts that need lubrication.

10 Install the thrust washer onto the intake camshaft and tighten the nuts. If you have the VANOS unit with a spring plate, install it first, before the thrust washer (not shown). Tighten the nuts to 10 N-m (7.3 ft-lbs). **Important:** With the nuts tight, the inside sprocket should be free to rotate back and forth about 20 degrees, along with the chain. When I assembled this engine, the sprocket and chain could not rotate. Some of the bolts and flanges were worn, and I had to replace them with new ones. The VANOS unit requires that this sandwich of parts be able to rotate smoothly. Verify this prior to proceeding. Install the four Torx screws onto the exhaust sprocket/camshaft assembly (left). Place them onto the sprocket and tighten them only **hand** tight. You will make adjustments later on, and these bolts are in place only to hold the exhaust camshaft in its proper position. Note: From this point on, these are the instructions to follow if you are simply replacing the VANOS unit and not resetting the cam timing.

11 The VANOS unit consists of a solenoid and a hydraulic gear that is activated when oil pressure is released into the unit by the solenoid. It's a rather simple device. Oil pressure pushes the gear on the unit out, and, as it moves outward, it rotates the small sliding camshaft sprockets, thus advancing the camshaft timing.

12 Test the VANOS unit by pulling out the gear plunger all the way. You should be able to pull on it with your hand and extend it from the housing (see arrow). If the unit still has oil in it, it will make a gurgling noise. Push the plunger back into the unit when you are finished.

13 Install a new seal onto the front of the cylinder head (see arrows). The seal should be made of a thin metal. BMW service manuals recommend silicone sealant around the left and right mounting points (alignment pins) for the front VANOS seal.

14 Now comes the tricky part: Rotate the front sprocket/chain assembly all the way clockwise to the right (toward the air cleaner). With the plunger of the VANOS unit pushed all the way back into its housing (this is important), place the VANOS unit on the cylinder head. The VANOS unit has inside gears that need to mesh with the gears on the sprocket. When you push the VANOS unit onto the cylinder head, it will not want to easily mesh with the gears on the sprocket. **Important:** the sprocket/chain assembly should still be rotated as far clockwise as possible.

15 With your fingers, rotate the spline shaft on the VANOS unit until you can engage one spline of the sprocket. Pushing forward on the VANOS unit, carefully rotate the sprocket/chain assembly counterclockwise. As you do this, the VANOS unit should slide in toward the cylinder head. Always ensure that the **first** suitable tooth combination between the sprocket and the VANOS unit engages.

16 Reinstall the main mounting bolt and engine lift ring. After tightening down the VANOS housing, clean up any squeeze-out from the silicone used to seal the unit to the cylinder head. With the sprockets properly installed, pull out the retaining pins on the top chain tensioner and reapply tension to the chain. The tensioner should spring back with some force and tighten the chain quickly. If it appears sluggish, or does not spring back, replace the tensioner before continuing. Next, tighten the tensioner tool for the lower chain tensioner to 1.3 N-m (1 ft-lb). This is such a small amount that you can use a hand-wheel ratchet to tighten the chain. Remove all slack in the chain prior to tightening the exhaust sprocket. Relying on the regular spring-loaded tensioner will not place enough tension on the chain to correctly tighten the sprocket.

17 With the lower tensioner tool still in place, tighten the four nuts on the exhaust sprocket (15 N-m, 11 ft-lbs). Reinstall the plugs on the outside of the VANOS cover. Remove the tensioner tool, and replace it with the real tensioner. Make sure the slot in the end of the tensioner is correctly aligned with the ramp on the inside of the engine (see Project 16). If the slot is not aligned with the chain ramp, the chain will rattle fiercely and may damage the engine.

18 Remove the camshaft holding tool from the rear of the engine. Also remove the flywheel locking tool. You're finished! The VANOS unit should be installed, the camshafts will be timed properly, and all you have left to do is connect the VANOS oil line, connect the VANOS electrical control line, reinstall the valve cover with a new seal, and reinstall the coils.

Camshaft Position Sensor Replacement

ENGINE

Time: 5 hours

Tab: $100

Talent: 🔧🔧🔧

Tools: 5-millimeter Allen wrench

Applicable Years: E36 (All)

Tinware: Camshaft position sensor (CPS), O-ring

Tip: If you're removing the manifold, replace some other hard-to-reach items

PERFORMANCE GAIN: Smooth-running engine

COMPLEMENTARY MODIFICATION: Replace crankshaft position sensor

---

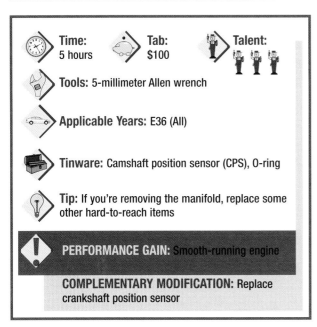

1 Shown here is the outside of the camshaft position sensor on a six-cylinder E36 engine. The inset shows a new O-ring installed into the head prior to sensor installation. Note the location of the VANOS oil line off to the right. The VANOS solenoid must be removed (Project 18) in order to reach the camshaft position sensor.

2 This photo shows the location of the camshaft position sensor on the E36 318 four-cylinder engine.

Your fuel injection computer (DME) may output a code that indicates a faulty camshaft position sensor (CPS). This important sensor tells the computer where the engine is in its rotation with respect to the combustion cycle. If the camshaft position sensor is not operating properly, your car will run very erratically.

Replacement of the sensor itself is quite easy. First, remove the VANOS solenoid to gain access to the sensor (see Photo 2 of Project 18). Then, using a 5-millimeter Allen wrench, remove the sensor's retaining bolt. The sensor should pull out of its location in the cylinder head. That's the easy part. The tough part is disconnecting the electrical connectors located underneath the intake manifold. If you have really skinny hands, you may be able to reach under the manifold and disconnect it. However, I had to first remove the intake manifold (see Project 12).

Alternatively, you may be able to reach in there once you disconnect and remove the oil filter housing. The housing attaches to the engine block with six bolts, but to access them you have to remove the alternator and alternator mounting bracket. Use a new gasket when you reinstall it. Even though this is a pain, it is much easier than removing the entire intake manifold. Now that you have a clear path, use a new O-ring when you install the new camshaft position sensor.

If you are doing a number of projects that require access under the intake manifold, I recommend removing it. While you have access, you can replace the knock sensors (Photo 22 of Project 17), the VANOS oil line (Project 18), the crankshaft position sensor (Project 15), and a host of other hoses and sensors that are normally hidden underneath the intake manifold.

3 This photo shows the location of the camshaft position sensor on the E36 six-cylinder engine. As you can see, access to the electrical connector underneath the intake manifold is very difficult. Removing the oil filter housing will help, but you will still need long, skinny arms to reach in there and disconnect the harness. It may be easier to remove the intake manifold, particularly if you plan to replace other items such as the knock sensors.

Crankshaft Position Sensor Replacement

ENGINE

The crankshaft position sensor is very important to proper engine operation. If it fails or works intermittently, the engine will either barely run or not start at all. Fortunately, the engine's main computer (DME) will indicate whether or not there are problems with the crankshaft position sensor. (See Project 28 for more details on reading fuel injection error codes.)

The sensor itself is easy to reach and replace. On some models, however, the wire harness that connects the sensor to the rest of the car is hidden underneath the intake manifold. Remove the intake manifold to replace the sensor. Or, you may be able to access it by reaching underneath the manifold—if you have skinny arms—by removing the oil filter housing first. Either way, getting to the harness connector is not easy.

To replace the sensor, unscrew the 5-millimeter Allen bolt that attaches the sensor to the engine case. The sensor will always be mounted facing the toothed degree wheel attached to the front of the crankshaft. Depending upon which car you have, you may need to remove the radiator fan (see Project 34).

Wire harness routing varies widely from car to car. On the E36 six-cylinder models, the harness is routed through a plastic cover and then underneath the intake manifold. Disconnect the wire harness from the engine, and replace the sensor. Be sure to route the new harness along the same path as the old harness.

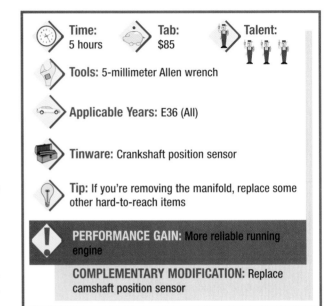

Time: 5 hours

Tab: $85

Talent:

Tools: 5-millimeter Allen wrench

Applicable Years: E36 (All)

Tinware: Crankshaft position sensor

Tip: If you're removing the manifold, replace some other hard-to-reach items

PERFORMANCE GAIN: More reliable running engine

COMPLEMENTARY MODIFICATION: Replace camshaft position sensor

On some E30 cars (1984–1987) 325e/s models, there are two sensors that read the toothed crankshaft wheel. When replacing these, double-check that you don't accidentally switch the two sensor plugs. They should be color-coded to match their receptacle plugs.

1 The crankshaft position sensor (orange arrow) is relatively easy to get to. However, like the camshaft position sensor, the wire harness connection is hidden underneath the intake manifold. Remove the intake manifold to replace the sensor; or, if you have skinny arms, you may be able to reach in there if you remove the oil filter housing first. The wire harness is integrated into an upper plastic guide (green arrow). The wire disappears beneath the VANOS solenoid and the intake manifold (blue arrow).

PROJECT 16

http://www.101projects.com/BMW/16.htm

Lower Chain Tensioner Replacement

Time: 30 minutes

Tab: $100

Talent: 🔧🔧

Tools: 32-millimeter deep socket

Applicable Years: E36 (All)

Tinware: New chain tensioner, new sealing ring

Tip: Use the later-style chain tensioner as an upgrade

PERFORMANCE GAIN: No more noisy chains

COMPLEMENTARY MODIFICATION: Replace upper VANOS chain tensioner

The BMW inline engines are driven by a chain that links the timing of the camshafts to the rotation of the crankshaft. Sometimes, the tensioner grows weak and begins to fail, causing the engine to give off an annoying rattle on deceleration. This rattle grows louder as time passes and may become more noticeable at slow speeds. While many people misdiagnose this problem as a failing VANOS unit (see Project 13), it's more likely to be a failing lower chain tensioner. This may occur in high-mileage or even some low-mileage engines; it doesn't seem to be uniformly related to the total number of miles driven.

BMW redesigned the tensioner in later years of the E36 and offers an upgraded tensioner that can be used in place of the older one. Thus, replacing the chain tensioner, which is a very easy process, typically solves the problem of the noisy chain.

Using a 32-millimeter deep socket, carefully remove the chain tensioner from the lower front of the cylinder head. Place a rag or paper towel under the tensioner to catch any excess oil that may leak from the engine. When removing the tensioner, proceed slowly, as it is under tension when you release it.

Installation is as simple as removal. Place a new sealing ring on the tensioner, and insert the tensioner into its hole in the cylinder head. At this point, the two small fingers on the tensioner should line up with a mating ridge on the chain guide inside the cylinder head. If this doesn't happen, you will have a very noisy, rattling engine when you start it up. To guide the installation of the chain tensioner, stick your finger in the hole in the cylinder head so you can feel the ridge on the chain guide. Hand tighten the tensioner to start, and then

use a torque wrench to tighten the tensioner to 50 N-m (37 ft-lbs) for the early-style tensioner and 40 N-m (30 ft-lbs) for the new-style tensioner. Use a new aluminum sealing ring between the tensioner and the engine block when reinstalling the tensioner.

When you start up your engine, listen carefully—it should run very quietly. If the noise is worse, however, then you probably didn't align the tensioner properly with the chain guide. If that's the case, remove the tensioner and reposition it. If the engine still makes noise, the problem may lie with the upper chain tensioner (also known as the VANOS chain tensioner) or the VANOS unit itself. In that case, see Project 13.

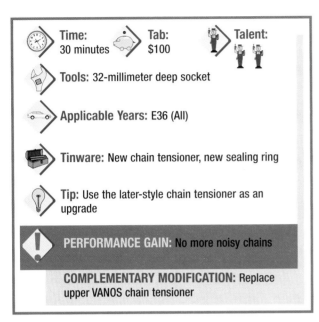

1 Shown here is the removal of the chain tensioner from the bottom of the E36 six-cylinder engines. This early-style tensioner has an inner piece and an outer shell (still attached to the cylinder head—orange arrow). When you reinstall the chain tensioner, make sure the groove in the tensioner fits precisely into the mating groove on the inside chain guide. If these two parts don't line up, you will have a lot of chain noise when you first start up the engine.

2 Shown here is the upgraded one-piece tensioner (11-31-1-405-081). This is a good upgrade, as the early units had a tendency to wear out. The inset photo shows the older-style chain tensioner for the E36 six-cylinder engines.

Head Gasket Replacement

ENGINE

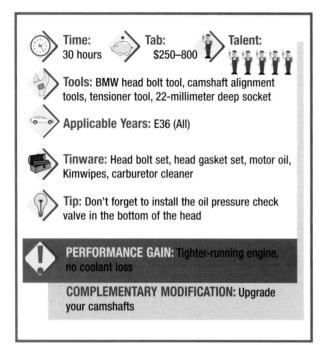

Time: 30 hours

Tab: $250–800

Talent: 🏋🏋🏋🏋🏋

Tools: BMW head bolt tool, camshaft alignment tools, tensioner tool, 22-millimeter deep socket

Applicable Years: E36 (All)

Tinware: Head bolt set, head gasket set, motor oil, Kimwipes, carburetor cleaner

Tip: Don't forget to install the oil pressure check valve in the bottom of the head

PERFORMANCE GAIN: Tighter-running engine, no coolant loss

COMPLEMENTARY MODIFICATION: Upgrade your camshafts

BMW engines are known for weak cooling systems. It's not uncommon to have a water pump fail or a thermostat get stuck, which can result in engine overheating. The car then typically runs fine for a few hundred miles after overheating, but it eventually begins to leak coolant and ultimately requires a complex head gasket replacement.

This project incorporates steps and procedures from many other projects. Here are the tasks that you need to perform prior to the specific steps outlined below:

Jack up the car (Project 1). Raise the front of the car to gain access to the coolant drain plug on the engine block, as well as the engine oil drain plug.

Empty engine oil (Project 2). Drain out the oil that has been contaminated with engine coolant.

Remove coolant (Project 33). Empty the coolant from the system prior to removing the cylinder head.

Remove radiator and fan (Project 34). Remove the fan to gain access to the front of the engine. Also, remove and flush the radiator, and replace the hoses.

Remove drive belts (Project 5). You will need to remove the belts in order to gain access to the water pump.

Remove water pump (Project 35). You should remove the water pump in order to clean it out or replace it with an upgraded unit.

Spark plugs (Project 8). Remove the ignition coils from the head, and remove the spark plugs.

Valve cover gasket (Project 9). Remove the valve cover to access the head bolts.

Camshaft removal (Project 11). It's possible to replace the head gasket without removing the camshafts. However, you should have the head resurfaced by a machine shop, and this process requires that you remove the camshafts.

Intake manifold removal (Project 12). The intake manifold covers a lot of items in the engine compartment and is attached to the cylinder head, so it needs to be removed.

VANOS installation/cam timing (Project 13). To remove the cylinder head, you must first remove the VANOS unit. To reinstall the head, you need to retime the camshafts and properly adjust the VANOS unit.

Cam sensor replacement (Project 14). Remove this sensor from the cylinder head and have a new one handy.

Crankshaft sensor replacement (Project 15). This sensor is only accessible with the intake manifold off, so it might be a good time to replace it.

Tensioner update (Project 16). Remove the lower chain tensioner to loosen the chain on the camshafts and upgrade to the new style if applicable.

VANOS oil line replacement (Project 18). Disconnect the VANOS oil line prior to removal of the head.

Machine shop 101 (Project 10). Send your cylinder head out to a machine shop that will resurface it and check for cracks.

The remainder of this project is presented step by step in the accompanying photos and captions.

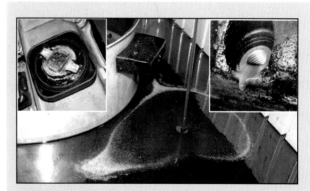

1 If you see this kind of mess with your car, you know you're in trouble. This is a perfect example of oil mixed with coolant due to a head gasket leak. The light-colored milky texture of contaminated oil is a sure sign of head gasket problems. For a quick analysis, remove the oil filler cap and compare it to the photo (upper left). Also take note if steam comes out of your tailpipe. Some condensation is normal upon startup, but if it continues well after the car is warmed up, you have a problem. Of course, the first clue is that your low coolant warning lamp will turn on, even after filling the reservoir multiple times.

2 More carnage can be seen under the valve covers. The underside of the valve cover is coated with a mixture of coolant and oil. At this point, we've emptied the oil and coolant, and removed the fan, radiator, drive belts, water pump, spark plugs, and valve cover.

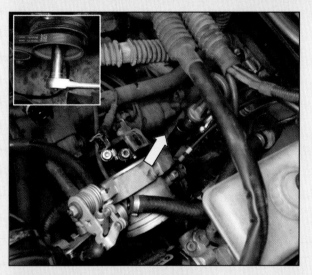

3 Before you remove the cylinder head, lock the engine at top dead center (TDC) for cylinder number 1 to accurately time the camshafts when you reassemble the engine. There is a special tool that needs to be inserted into a hole in the engine block, which then mates with a corresponding hole in the flywheel (photo 4). The intake manifold has been removed in this photo (see Project 12), and the yellow arrow indicates the general area where the tool needs to be inserted. You can rotate the engine's crankshaft by placing a 22-millimeter deep socket on the front pulley and rotating clockwise (photo inset). Install the camshaft alignment tool (see Project 13). If your camshaft alignment tool doesn't seem to fit, your car may have had the camshaft timing tweaked as part of a BMW service campaign to correct an uneven idle (affected engines built up to August 1992). Loosen the tool to allow it to fit in this situation.

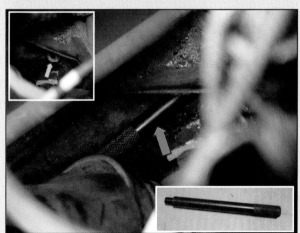

4 Here's a close-up of the spot in the engine case where you insert the flywheel locking tool. Your car should have a small blue plug that covers the hole (inset photo). The flywheel locking tool itself is a long, thin rod with a smaller insert tip on its end (inset, lower right). Insert this tool into the engine block and rotate the crankshaft pulley until the pin fits into the matching hole on the back side of the flywheel.

5 At TDC for cylinder number 1, the exhaust camshaft sprocket should have a small arrow that points upward, perpendicular to the plane of the head gasket. Double-check this if you're trying to find TDC when you're turning the engine over by hand.

6 Also check the front crankshaft pulley itself. The line by the yellow arrow will match up with the boss in the engine block (blue arrow) when the engine is at TDC for cylinder number 1 and cylinder number 6. Check the arrow on the exhaust camshaft sprocket shown in Photo 5—it should only pointing upward, not downward, when the engine is at TDC for cylinder number 1.

7 Shown here is the front of the VANOS unit prior to removal. The VANOS unit advances the camshaft timing at higher rpm, which translates into better engine performance while driving. Undo the nuts that attach the unit to the cylinder head. The cable for the crankshaft sensor (see also Project 15) is integrated with a small plastic cable guide that ties into the studs that also hold the thermostat housing and the VANOS housing (yellow arrows). Remove the thermostat in order to remove the VANOS unit.

8 With everything disconnected, you can now remove the VANOS unit. Disconnect the VANOS oil line (blue arrow), and disconnect the electrical connection to the VANOS solenoid, as indicated by the green arrow (see Project 18). Remove the unit from the front of the cylinder head and place it aside on your workbench. Push the upper VANOS chain tensioner down and lock it in place with small pins (red arrow). You can use a small Allen key as shown, or even large paper clips will do.

9 Remove the sprocket assemblies from the front of each camshaft (see Project 13). Use a zip tie or some wire to secure the timing chain (blue arrow)—you don't want this to fall into the recesses of the engine when you remove the cylinder head.

10 Remove the cylinder head bolts with a special BMW Torx deep socket tool (11-2-250). The bolts will be tight and difficult to remove, but if your tool is in good condition, you should have no problems removing all of them (14 total for six-cylinder engines). The bolts are hidden underneath the camshafts, so you will have to maneuver your tool past the camshafts to reach them.

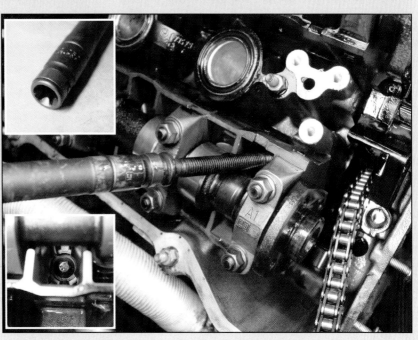

11 Remove the camshaft position sensor (see photos in Project 14) and disconnect the last remaining connections to the cylinder head. The small electrical connections pull out after releasing the small spring wire retainer. Don't forget the hose attached to the rear of the cylinder head that supplies the heater core (inset). Also disconnect and loosen the exhaust manifold (see Project 49).

12 With everything disconnected, the cylinder head should be loose on the engine block. Tap it with a rubber mallet and it should start to lift off of the block. If it doesn't budge, then chances are that you forgot to disconnect something that is holding it down. It's not uncommon to forget to remove a cylinder head bolt. Count the cylinder head bolts and make sure that you have 14 of them prior to your removal attempt (six-cylinder engines). As the head begins to lift off of the engine block, tilt it slightly toward the exhaust manifold and grab the timing chain. Tie off the timing chain with some wire or a zip tie so it will not fall into the recesses of the engine block.

13 Shown here is the head is coming off of the engine. Untie the timing chain from the top of the head, and secure it at the top of the engine block (blue arrow). Triple-check that everything attached to the head is now disconnected. The cylinder head is very heavy, and the angle for lifting while you're standing in front of it is very challenging. I do not recommend lifting the head off the car by yourself—get someone to help you lift the rearmost part of the head. If you attempt to lift the head off of the engine and something catches on your way up, it will be difficult to put it back down again without crushing or potentially damaging something.

14 Since you are removing the cylinder head from the engine, I recommend that you take it to a machine shop for evaluation and reconditioning (see Photo 17). Prior to taking it to the shop, you can remove the camshafts. Most machine shops won't have the specific knowledge or the BMW factory tool to remove the camshafts safely. You can remove them yourself without the tool by following Project 11. Be careful, though—if you don't proceed cautiously, you can bend and break the camshafts. In this photo, the long, thin BMW E36 six-cylinder camshaft has been removed from the cylinder head.

15 BMW calls this the camshaft bearing ledge; it keeps the hydraulic lifters in place and also supports and provides lubrication to the camshafts as they are running. The inset photo shows the hydraulic lifters in place. When you lift the bearing ledge out of the head, the lifters will fall out of their respective bores. Pay close attention to each lifter's location—you'll need to replace each lifter into its original bore to reduce wear on the bearing ledge and camshafts.

17 After the head is off the car, take it to your machine shop. Have the shop remove all the valves and clean it up in the bead blaster and parts washer. When the head is clean, problems like the one shown in this photo are easier to see. This particular head has a rather nasty crack in it (red arrows). Left undiscovered, this problem would have caused the replacement head gasket to fail shortly after it was installed, as coolant would have leaked around this crack. The moral of the story is that if you are doing all the work to get your cylinder head off the engine, take it to a machine shop to be inspected and freshened up.

16 Here's a close-up of the bearing ledge with the hydraulic lifters. When removing the bearing ledge, I quickly put the hydraulic lifters back into their bores so there's no chance of misplacing or inserting any into the wrong bore. Also, keep the intake and exhaust bearing ledges separate. Although they look similar, they are very different and cannot be interchanged. With the lifters removed, clean out any sludge in the recesses of the bearing ledge. Flip the bearing ledges upside down and drop in each of the lifters. Don't accidentally turn the bearing ledge around so the lifter that should go in one end actually goes in the other end. Take the entire assembly, with the lifters, and store it in a safe place, covered in plastic.

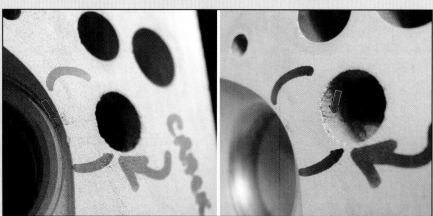

18 The repair process is not too difficult for an experienced machinist. The area around the crack is machined out so no traces of the crack remain. After the head is preheated in an oven to several hundred degrees, the aluminum is welded and the area is filled with replacement aluminum material. Finally, the area is reground and the mating surface machined flat. In this photo, it's difficult to see any remaining traces of the machine work, other than a few grinding scratches on the inside of the combustion chamber.

19 This is what the freshened head looks like after it has returned from the machine shop. All the valves have been measured, ground, and lapped to the valve seat. The crack has been repaired, and the entire mating surface has been machined flat. Don't forget to reinstall the oil pressure check valve on the bottom of the cylinder head. If you forget this piece, you will have engine oil pressure problems. Nothing is worse than buttoning up your entire engine—only to look over at your workbench and see this tiny check valve still sitting there.

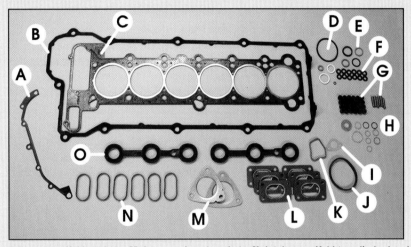

20 A typical cylinder head gasket set. Depending on the make or model of your car, you might have one or two small sealing rings or O-rings left over. Don't be alarmed, as this is somewhat normal. **A:** Front VANOS seal (metal). **B:** Valve cover gasket. **C:** Cylinder head gasket. **D:** Oil filter housing O-ring (small O-ring for oil filter too). **E:** Camshaft position sensor O-ring. **F:** Fuel injector O-rings. **G:** Valve seals and protective boots. **H:** Assorted copper and aluminum sealing rings. **I:** Rear heater core hose fitting seal. **J:** Intake manifold to throttle body seal. **K:** Thermostat housing seal. **L:** Exhaust manifold gaskets. **M:** Lower exhaust gaskets. **N:** Intake manifold to cylinder head seals. **O:** Spark plug hole seals. Additional sealing rings and O-rings: oil filter set (one tiny black O-ring, one big black O-ring, three small crush gaskets), VANOS oil line sealing rings (four), and VANOS solenoid O-ring.

21 Before mounting the cylinder head back onto the engine, clean up the engine block and pistons a bit. Using a plastic cleaning wheel attached to an electric drill, carefully brush off the dirt and debris from the cylinder head mating surface on the engine

block. Do not drop any gasket material or debris into the oil or cooling ducts on the surface. First, remove the larger chunks of gasket material with a razor blade, but be sure not to scratch the mating surface. Try to get it as clean as possible. Do not spill any oil or debris into the threaded holes in the engine block where the cylinder head bolts attach. These must be kept perfectly clean, or you will not achieve the proper torque settings for the head bolts. If oil or dirt does get into these holes, clean them out with brake cleaner and lint-free cloths. To clean the tops of the pistons, remove the flywheel lock and rotate the engine until each piston is at the top of the engine block surface (inset, upper right). Then clean each one with the drill and brush. When you're done, go over each surface with alcohol and a lint-free cloth to ensure the surface is as clean as possible, and to help prevent dirt from contaminating your head gasket.

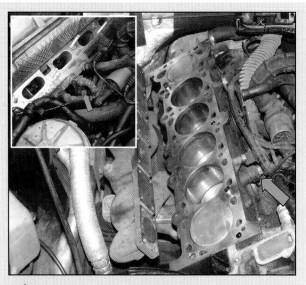

22 If your car displayed fuel injection trouble codes prior to the head gasket problem, now would be a good time to revisit them (see Project 28 and Project 29 for instructions on reading the fault codes). There are a few sensors that are best accessed and replaced when the intake manifold has been removed, including the cam position sensor (see Project 14), the crankshaft position sensor (see Project 15), and the two knock sensors. This photo shows the knock sensor for cylinders 1 through 3. If you have had problems with your car knocking, or the computer has shown you a fault code for one of the two knock sensors, replace them now. They are impossible to replace with the intake manifold in place.

23 Clean each lifter carefully with a lint-free cloth. I recommend using Kimwipes, which I discovered while working in clean rooms, building satellites. You can find them at PelicanParts.com. They are perfect for cleaning intricate engine parts where you don't want paper fibers or debris contaminating tiny oil passages. When each lifter is clean, dip it in fresh motor oil. Use whatever motor oil you plan to use when you refill the car. Press down on the inside of the lifter while it's submerged so that you can clean out the internal passages as well as possible. (This car had its entire oil system contaminated with coolant, so it was especially important to clean everything.) Failure to do this carefully may result in what is known as a noisy lifter—one that doesn't completely engage. This can lead to degradation in engine performance.

24 Carefully clean the inside of each lifter bore with lint-free Kimwipes. Use isopropyl alcohol or brake cleaner if there is any gunk or grime you can't remove with elbow grease alone. Soak each lifter in oil prior to putting it back into the bearing ledge. Be liberal with the engine oil, as the oil supply to the engine will be sparse when you first start it up.

25 With the bearing ledge and lifters liberally coated in engine oil, tip the cylinder head on its side and insert the lifters into the head. Make sure none of the lifters fall out of the ledge as you reinstall it onto the cylinder head. Carefully balance the head on its side while holding the bearing ledge with one hand (you should be able to do this alone). Install the intake ledge on the intake side, and the exhaust ledge on the exhaust side. When the first ledge is placed onto the head, keep it in place by installing two camshaft bearing caps on either end—when you go to install the second bearing ledge, the first one won't fall out.

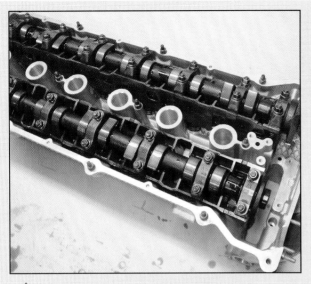

26 This photo shows the head with the camshafts installed. This installation process is tricky and can easily break the camshafts. See Project 11 for more information on removing and installing the camshafts.

27 Install the head sensors back into their respective ports with new sealing rings. If these were to leak after you start the engine, it would be necessary to remove the intake manifold again. Insert a new O-ring into the cam sensor hole. Double-check that you have properly installed the oil pressure check valve that seats into the bottom of the cylinder head (see Photo 19). If you forget to install it, you will have to tear down and remove the head all over again or you will forever have oil pressure problems with your engine.

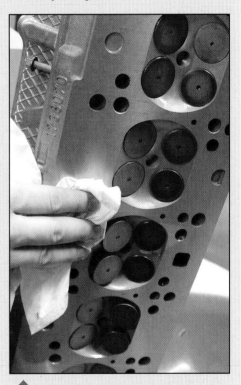

28 Install the flange for the heater core hose onto the rear of the cylinder head. Don't forget to reattach this hose when you reinstall the head on the engine block. Use a new gasket for this flange.

29 Clean the surface of the head and the engine block with brake cleaner and lint-free Kimwipes. If you didn't have the cylinder head resurfaced at a machine shop (recommended), make sure that any residue from the old head gasket has been removed. The head needs to be perfectly clean in order to maintain a proper seal. Don't skimp on the cleaning process—it is of paramount importance.

30 When the engine block is clean enough to eat off of, lay the new head gasket on the block. For machined cylinder heads, there is a 0.3-millimeter-thicker gasket available to compensate for the reduced material thickness on the head. If you don't use this gasket, the head will be slightly closer to the pistons, and the engine will have a slightly higher compression ratio. In most cases, using the standard thickness gasket is fine (you have to buy the thicker gasket separately, as it is more expensive than the standard thickness gasket and is not included in gasket sets). Before you install the cylinder head, remove the flywheel lock and rotate the engine about 30 degrees, moving all the pistons off the top of the engine block. Doing this prevents the valves from touching the tops of the pistons when you install the cylinder head and time the cams. This step is very important, so don't forget or skip it.

31 Each cylinder head bolt has a special washer that goes underneath it. Use only the special washers—don't substitute them with others. Lining the washer up with the hole can be tricky. I use a long screwdriver to help with this. Place the washer on the screwdriver. Then place the screwdriver in the hole, while holding the washer. Then let go of the washer, and it should fall down right over the hole.

32 Placing the head back on the engine block is a two-person job. As one person lowers the head, the other must thread the timing chain up through the front of the cylinder head. Do not let it drop into the recesses of the engine, as it can be difficult to fish out and align with the lower crankshaft sprocket. Once the chain is through the front of the head, tie it up with a zip tie or some wire. In this photo, the head carefully rests on top of the engine block as we manipulate the chain. After the chain is secured, move the head and locate it onto the top of the head gasket.

33 Tighten the head bolts with a calibrated torque wrench. The cylinder head bolts are a stretch-bolt design, which means they deform when tightened to their desired torque setting and should only be tightened once. If you find that you've forgotten to install something or made some other mistake and need to remove the cylinder head again, you must use new cylinder head bolts, since the ones that have already been tightened are no longer any good. After you tighten the cylinder head bolts, install and tighten the two small Torx bolts that attach the head to the front timing chain cover (holes shown by blue arrows on the right).

34 Shown here is the tightening order for the cylinder head bolts. Start with the first one and work your way out to number 14. The cylinder head bolts are tightened using a special process. The bolts are tightened to a specific value, and then they are turned a number of additional degrees (typically 90 degrees). This ensures a more accurate value for tightening the bolts. For the cylinder head, torque each of the bolts up to 80 percent of the jointing torque value, following the order in this photo. Then go back in the same order and torque them up to the final jointing torque. After that, turn the torque wrench through the specified torque angle. You can find the specifications for each of the E36 engines at www.101Projects.com.

35 With the cylinder head attached to the engine block, you can now time the camshafts. First, align the camshafts at TDC and install the camshaft alignment tool (BMW tool 11-3-240). The two dots on the camshafts should face upward. Only after the camshafts have been properly aligned at TDC, move the crankshaft back to TDC and reinstall the flywheel lock pin. You are now ready to set the camshaft timing (see Project 13).

37 With the camshafts properly timed and the camshaft tool removed, add the engine oil. I prefer to add the oil at this point because I can pour it all over the camshafts and lifters to ensure that they are properly lubricated when I start the engine. When you've completed the installation and are ready to start it up, pull out the fuel injection computer (DME) relay and let the engine turn over a few times to build up oil pressure. On this particular car, I encountered a sticky lifter problem, which resulted in a "clack-clack-clack" noise when the car started up. This is normal in the first few minutes after the head gasket replacement. If the sticky lifter problem doesn't go away, then I recommend changing your oil to a thinner viscosity. On this car, the sticky lifter refused to go away until I emptied the oil and replaced it with Mobil-1 synthetic. If the engine was highly contaminated with coolant, try changing the oil three times within the first 50 miles to flush any remnants of the coolant out of the system.

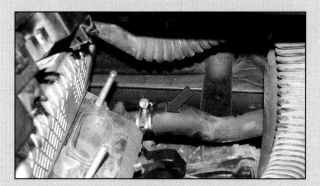

36 Don't forget to attach the heater core hose to the rear of the cylinder head. If you don't attach this hose, the coolant will spill all over the ground, and you will sit there wondering what you forgot to connect.

VANOS Oil Line and Solenoid Replacement

ENGINE

🕐 **Time:** 5 hours

🚗 **Tab:** $35

👨 **Talent:** 👨👨👨

🔧 **Tools:** 32-millimeter wrench, 19-millemeter socket

🚗 **Applicable Years:** E36 six-cylinder with VANOS

🧰 **Tinware:** New VANOS oil line, four sealing rings

💡 **Tip:** If you're removing the manifold, replace some other hard-to-reach items

⚠️ **PERFORMANCE GAIN:** No more messy oil leaks on the top of your engine

COMPLEMENTARY MODIFICATION: Replace crankshaft sensor, camshaft position sensor

---

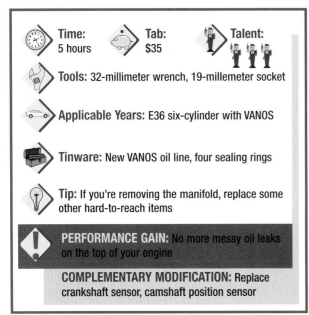

1 This photo shows the two ends of the VANOS oil supply line. On the left, you see the point where it mounts to the VANOS unit. On the right, the line snakes down under the intake manifold and mounts just behind the oil filter housing (yellow arrow). As you can see, the oil line has been leaking and is wet with oil. When installing the new line, use new sealing rings at both ends (green arrows). If you reuse the old sealing rings, they may end up leaking.

The later-model E36 six-cylinder engines have a mechanism that allows for variable advancing of the camshaft timing. The VANOS unit (Variable Onckenwellen Steuerung) is an electromechanical unit that uses a hydraulic piston to accelerate the camshaft timing at higher rpm. This unit is controlled electronically by a solenoid connected to the engine management system (DME).

The VANOS unit is hydraulically operated using pressurized oil from the engine. As such, the oil line that feeds the VANOS unit often begins to leak from age. It's very common for this line to weep oil and leak it on top of the engine. To replace it, you will need to remove the intake manifold first in order to gain access (see Project 12). Once the manifold is off,

removal of the line is as easy as disconnecting the two banjo bolts on each end and removing and replacing the line. Use new aluminum sealing rings when you install the new line.

Also accessible is the VANOS unit solenoid. This unit is responsible for actuating a valve that opens and allows pressurized oil to flow into the VANOS unit. To remove and replace this solenoid, you will also need to remove the intake manifold, as the electrical connector for the solenoid is hidden under the manifold. Be sure to use a new O-ring on the VANOS solenoid when you install its replacement.

2 This photo shows the removal of the VANOS unit solenoid. The solenoid opens a valve that allows oil into the VANOS unit, which then advances the camshaft timing. Use a 32-millimeter wrench to loosen the solenoid from the VANOS unit housing. The inset on the lower left shows the inside of the solenoid. Use a new O-ring when reinstalling the solenoid. The inset on the lower right shows the valve in the VANOS unit that the solenoid opens. The light blue arrow at the top shows the camshaft position sensor (Project 14). The VANOS solenoid must be removed in order to install the camshaft position sensor into the cylinder head.

Oil Pan Gasket Replacement

Time: 5 hours

Tab: $15

Talent: 🔧🔧🔧

Tools: Socket set

Applicable Years: All

Tinware: Oil pan gasket, new mounting bolts

Tip: Tack weld the oil pump nut while you're in there

PERFORMANCE GAIN: No more messy oil leaks, smoother-running engine with no vacuum leaks

COMPLEMENTARY MODIFICATION: Replace motor mounts, steering rack, rod bearings, and weld oil pump nut

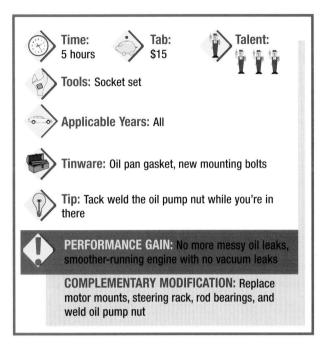

1 Begin the removal process by removing all of the small bolts that hold the oil pan to the bottom of the engine.

2 Depending on which engine you have, there may be a supplemental cover in the rear that needs to be removed. This oil pan for a 1984 318i is more involved than most other 3 Series models. The 318i has a lower cover that fits over the bottom of the flywheel and a two-piece oil pan design with a separate lower cover that needs to be removed. Most 3 Series engines have a one-piece oil pan that covers the entire lower part of the engine.

Most BMW inline engines feature a large open sump design that allows major engine overhauls and repairs without removing the engine from the car. In particular, you can replace rod bearings and the lower oil pump nut quite easily (see Project 24). However, in order to access the engine internals, you will need to remove the lower oil sump.

Unfortunately, the gasket on the oil sump often leaks with age. Replacement is not too difficult, but you do have to remove the entire front suspension to be able to remove the oil pan. Begin by jacking up the car (Project 1), and then remove the front two road wheels. Next, remove the lower suspension components. Depending upon which engine and chassis you have, the components you must remove may vary. In general, you will need to remove the following: lower crossbrace (X-brace) if installed (Project 66), left and right A-arms (Project 59), front axle support bar and motor mounts (Project 59), front sway bar (Project 59), and steering rack (Project 59).

When you remove the front axle support bar, you will also be removing the motor mounts. This means that the engine will need support to keep it from falling out of the car. If you let the engine hang without support, you may damage the transmission—and create a dangerous situation. To keep the engine suspended, use an engine support bar that spans the strut towers (see www.101Projects.com for recommended vendors). As an alternative, I've seen pictures of a makeshift engine support bar—a thick 4x4 from a lumber yard that spans across the two strut towers with an eye hook that attaches to the center engine hook. This works as well, but a manufactured

3 With the lower oil pan removed on this E30 318i, you can see the oil pump (blue arrow), the sump pickup screen (yellow arrow), and the oil pump chain (green arrow). Remove the upper oil pan (purple arrow). Replace the motor mounts if they are worn (see Project 25), as they should be very easy to access (red arrow). You also may want to weld in the oil pump nut (see Project 24).

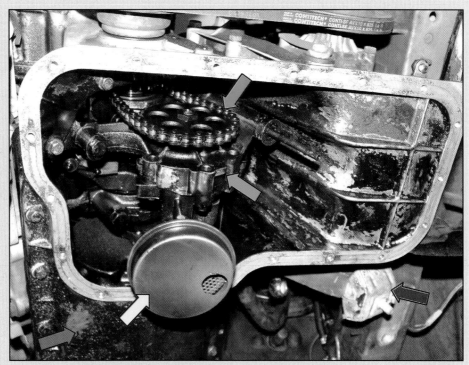

4 Here's the lower oil pan with a new gasket on top. Prior to installation back into the car, thoroughly clean the entire sump of any grime or sludge that may have collected. Also clean any residual gasket material from the sump/gasket surface, or you may end up with a leaky seam.

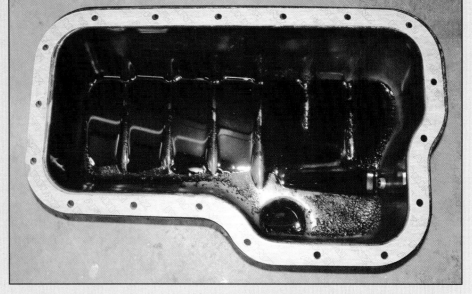

metal engine support is ideal. Also, if you have very tall jack stands, you can support the engine from the motor mount arms (which I did for this project). Place a jack stand under the front of the transmission for backup support if you go this route.

With the front suspension removed, you should have clear access to the bottom engine sump. Don't forget to empty the oil from the engine (Project 2), or you will have a sudden mess on your hands when you drop the oil pan. Remove the small screws that hold the engine sump to the bottom of the engine case. On E36 six-cylinder engines, two of the bolts in the rear of the pan are somewhat hidden; there

are two access holes for these bolts. With the small bolts removed, slide the pan off of the bottom of the engine. If the pan resists, tap it with a rubber mallet to break the seal of the gasket. Watch out for the oil pump pickup and sprocket near the front—they hang down into the pan.

After you've done your work in the bottom of the engine (welding the oil pump nut or replacing the rod bearings as detailed in Project 24), clean the mating surface of the engine block with gasket remover. Then place the new gasket on the sump and reinstall it. Bolt up the suspension and you're finished. You may want to have the wheels realigned, as dropping the suspension can affect alignment settings.

E30 Timing Belt Replacement

Replacing the rubber timing belt is one of the most important maintenance tasks for the six-cylinder E30 engine. As the engine ages and mileage climbs, an old, worn-out timing belt may break, causing catastrophic engine damage. A broken timing belt typically causes the valves to hit the tops of the pistons, bending the valves and/or destroying the pistons. A broken timing belt can indeed lead to the complete destruction of the engine.

To avoid this fate, replace the timing belt every 60,000 miles or every four years. If you live in a dry climate (like Arizona), or if you don't drive your car often, then I recommend replacing the belt more often. In dry climates, belts can become brittle and worn much more quickly. If your car sits for long periods of time, the belts take on the bends and shapes of the pulleys while the car is parked. Both circumstances increase the likelihood of belt failure.

Jack the car up to gain easier access to the crankshaft pulley and lower radiator hoses; it will also be easier to empty the coolant. Be sure to place the transmission in neutral so you can turn the engine more easily. Also remove the spark

 Time: 6 hours

 Tab: $180

 Talent: 👨👨👨

Tools: T-50 Torx socket, 3-millimeter Allen wrench, 22-millimeter deep socket

Applicable Years: E30 six-cylinder

Tinware: Timing belt, tensioner, radiator hoses, camshaft seals, red Loctite

Tip: Replace the camshaft seals while you have access to them

PERFORMANCE GAIN: Engine longevity

COMPLEMENTARY MODIFICATION: Water pump and thermostat replacement

ENGINE

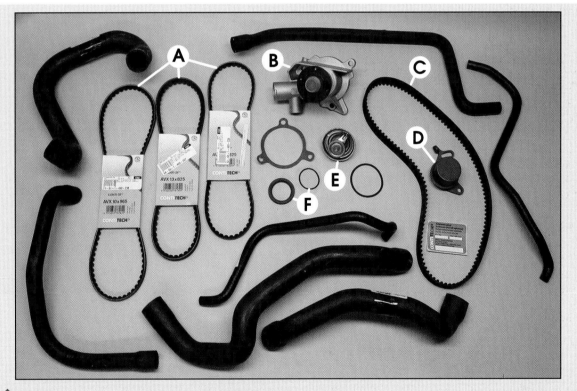

1 Shown here are the items included with the E30 timing belt kit available from PelicanParts.com and a few other items I recommend replacing. In addition to a complete set of radiator and coolant hoses, this photo shows: **A:** Air conditioning, alternator, and power steering belt. **B:** Water pump. **C:** Timing belt. **D:** Timing belt tensioner. **E:** Thermostat. **F:** Camshaft seal and O-ring. A complete coolant hose set is shown here as well.

2 This photo shows the engine compartment of a 1987 E30 325e engine compartment. Although not required when changing the E30 timing belt, I recommend that you also adjust the valves. I have removed the valve covers in this photo for that purpose, but their removal is not required to replace the timing belt. Although you could probably replace the timing belt with the radiator in place (yellow arrow), I do not recommend it. Removal is a snap and makes the job a whole lot easier. Begin by disconnecting the upper radiator hose (blue arrow) and the radiator overflow hose (red arrow).

3 With a large bucket and paper towels handy, remove the plug on the bottom of the radiator and disconnect the lower radiator hose (yellow arrow). If you wish to replace all of the coolant (recommended), pull out the plug on the engine block and remove the coolant from the block. Dispose of the coolant properly—it is toxic to children and small animals. Also verify that the engine is cold. When you disconnect the lower hose, you will spill some of the coolant, and you don't want to burn yourself.

4 With the radiator hoses removed, turn your attention to the radiator mounts, on the left and right sides of the radiator. Remove these mounts with a 10-millimeter socket (blue arrow). Inspect the mounts when you remove them; in most cases the rubber will be deteriorated and require replacement (yellow arrow). The photo inset shows the radiator coolant temperature sensor that also must be removed prior to pulling out the radiator.

plugs, as this will make it far easier to turn the engine—and to recognize any interference problems when you install the new timing belt.

Although it's not necessary, it's wise to inspect and/or replace the water pump and thermostat at this time (see Project 35). As a rule, replace the water pump every second time you replace the timing belt.

E30 cars manufactured in 1986 and later years should have a tensioner marked with "Z 127." If your tensioner does not have this code, replace it with one that does. This tensioner design replaced an earlier, potentially faulty, design.

Follow the procedure documented in the photos for detailed instructions on removing the timing belt and camshaft sprocket. Reinstall the tensioner before you install the new belt. To reinstall the tensioner, compress the spring as far as you can, and then temporarily tighten the adjustable tensioner bolt (green arrow, Photo 12). When you install the new timing belt, place it on the engine, working counterclockwise,

5 Shown here is the front of the engine after the radiator has been removed. At this point, the fan and fan pulley have been removed (see Project 34 for removal instructions). The belts have also been cut off with shears (you should replace them anyway). The yellow arrow shows the front of the distributor cap. The green arrow points to the air conditioning compressor. The blue arrow shows the alternator. The red arrow points to the water pump pulley. The orange arrow shows the main crankshaft pulley, and the purple arrow points to the power steering pump.

6 Here's a close-up of the alternator and its supporting brackets. You need to remove this bracket in order to remove the timing belt

cover. First, loosen the rear alternator bolt, indicated by the green arrow. Do not turn the front alternator pinion bolt until the rear nut is loosened. With the bolts loose, remove the nut that holds the bracket to the timing belt cover (yellow arrow) and swing the bracket out of the way. It's also a good time to remove the crankshaft sensor—simply pull it out of its bracket.

7 Now remove the distributor cap, which is held on with three small bolts. With the cap removed, you can remove the distributor rotor. Use a 3-millimeter Allen wrench or driver for this task. Replace the cap and rotor with new ones when replacing the timing belt.

starting from the crankshaft sprocket. Slip the belt over the intermediate shaft sprocket, around the tensioner, and over the camshaft sprocket. Now, loosen both bolts on the tensioner to apply tension to the timing belt. Verify that the timing marks for TDC on the camshaft sprocket match up with the notch on the cylinder head (see Photo 10). With a socket on the crankshaft pulley, carefully rotate the engine clockwise through two complete revolutions (720 degrees). Verify that the timing mark on the camshaft pulley is in place again. Torque the upper and lower tensioner mounting bolts to 22 N-m (16 ft-lbs).

With the tensioner in place, reinstall the crankshaft pulley and lower timing belt cover. Recheck that the camshaft sprocket is aligned with the cylinder head when the vibration damper or toothed timing wheel O/T mark is aligned with the lower timing belt cover. If not, remove the damper and lower timing belt cover and reposition the belt. Reinstall the front pulley, applying red Loctite to the six mounting bolts.

When you're finished, reinstall the radiator and bleed the cooling system as described in Project 33.

ENGINE

8 At this point, you should be able to remove the few small bolts that hold on the upper timing belt cover. The cover will slide off, and you should see the upper part of the timing belt. The red arrow indicates the camshaft timing sprocket, while the green arrow indicates the timing belt tensioner. If you plan to replace the camshaft seals (recommended), skip ahead to Photo 14, but loosen up the Torx bolt on the camshaft sprocket before you remove the timing belt. If you accidentally rotate the camshaft when the belt is off, you may bend the valves by pushing them into the pistons.

9 Place a deep 22-millimeter socket on the center of the crankshaft pulley and rotate the engine until it reaches top dead center (TDC) for cylinder number 1. At TDC for cylinder number 1, the O/T mark on the crankshaft pulley timing wheel or vibration damper (green arrow) will line up with the line on the lower timing belt cover (yellow arrow). In addition, the mark on the camshaft sprocket should line up with the mark on the cylinder head. Since this is a four-stroke engine, the TDC setting in the photo may also indicate that the engine is at overlap TDC for cylinder number 6. Check the camshaft sprocket to make sure (see Photo 10).

10 When setting the timing, it's very important to verify that the engine is set at top dead center (TDC) for cylinder number 1, indicated by the marking on the crankshaft and the camshaft sprocket as pictured. The green arrow shows the thin line on the sprocket that must match the corresponding mark on the cylinder head (yellow arrow). These two marks should line up, along with the mark in Photo 9. Only when these marks are aligned should you remove the timing belt.

11 The front pulley (also called the three-in-one pulley) is held on with six bolts (green arrow) that can be nearly impossible to see without a mirror. Remove these bolts prior to removing the front pulley. Use a 22-millimeter deep socket and a breaker bar to hold the crankshaft steady while you loosen and remove the bolts with a socket driver. After you get the bolts off, you should be able to pull the front pulley off of the crankshaft. Behind this pulley is a vibration damper (a mini-flywheel) that is also pulled off of the crankshaft (a toothed timing wheel is behind the pulley on later cars). You may need to employ extensive wiggling or a rubber mallet to budge the damper/timing wheel from its home position. With the pulley and damper/timing wheel removed, you can now remove the lower timing belt cover.

72

12 This collection of photos shows the removal of the timing belt tensioner. Mark the location of the main tensioner bolt (the one that fits through the slot) so you can approximate its location when you reinstall it. Using a wrench, remove the bolt that holds the tensioner, timing belt cover, and alternator bracket (inset, upper left). Then remove the main adjustment bolt for the tensioner (green arrow, lower left inset). With the bolts removed, you should be able to remove the tensioner and tensioner spring.

13 It's easy to slide out the timing belt once the lower cover has been removed and the tensioner has been disconnected. This photo shows the crankshaft pulley at the bottom and the intermediate shaft pulley off to the right.

14 I recommend you remove the camshaft sprocket so you can replace the two seals located behind it. These seals tend to deteriorate with age and cause leaks. Replace them when you have relatively easy access to them. Remove the camshaft sprocket with a T-50 Torx socket. Use a screwdriver propped up against the cylinder head to gently hold the sprocket in place while you remove the Torx bolt. Don't allow the camshaft to turn, as you could cause the valves to accidentally hit the pistons.

15 Shown here are the two camshaft seals that I recommend replacing while you have access to them. There's a small O-ring that fits into the cylinder head (green arrow) and a spring-seal that fits around the rotating end of the camshaft (red arrow). Replacement of these seals is similar to the replacement of the flywheel seal (see Project 44).

73

E30 Valve Adjustment

ENGINE

Time: 2 hours

Tab: $180

Talent:

Tools: 10-millimeter wrench, BMW spring-loaded valve-adjustment tool, feeler gauges, 22-millimeter deep socket

Applicable Years: E30 (All)

Tinware: New valve gasket cover

Tip: A stiff piece of wire works just as well as the BMW spring-loaded valve-adjustment tool

PERFORMANCE GAIN: More power, better gas mileage, quieter engine

COMPLEMENTARY MODIFICATION: Replace spark plugs

Adjusting the valves is one of the most common maintenance tasks required for the BMW E30, and should be done about every 10,000 miles. If valve clearances are too tight, the valves might not close all the way and the engine will not obtain optimum performance. Likewise, if the clearances are too loose, the valves will not open all the way; in addition to poor performance, you would have a very noisy valvetrain.

Before adjusting the valves, make sure the engine is stone cold. Although BMW provides specifications for adjusting the valves when the engine is warm, doing so may result in inaccurate settings. Don't start the engine for four hours before adjusting the valves; letting it sit overnight is even better. First step is to remove the valve cover. On the E30 cars, this is usually an easy process, although inevitably one or two brackets or components may get in the way (see Photo 1). While removing the cover, check the condition of the rear grounding strap. While some may look okay at first glance, in many cases they are frayed and about to break. Also count all the washers and nuts as you remove them—it's easy to drop one into the recesses of the cylinder head without realizing it. Remove the spark plugs when performing a valve adjustment. They probably need replacing anyway, and their absence makes it far easier to turn the engine over. You may need a socket extension to reach all of the plugs (see Project 8).

After the valve cover is removed, set the engine at top dead center (TDC) for piston number 1 (see Project 20). You can rotate the engine by placing a 22-millimeter deep socket on the crankshaft pulley nut and turning the engine clockwise. A note of caution: Make sure that the transmission

1 Shown here is the top valve cover of the six-cylinder E30 engine. To access the valves underneath, remove the cover by removing the eight screws that fix it to the top of the cylinder head. Depending on which model car you have, you may have to remove a secondary bracket or two in order to gain enough clearance to remove the cover.

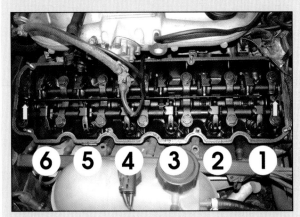

2 The valve cover has been removed from the top of the engine. The six rocker arms at the top of the photo control the opening and closing of the intake valves, while the rockers at the bottom control the exhaust valves. Valves are adjusted in pairs, intake and exhaust, at the same time. The numbers on the drawing indicate the cylinder numbers for the six-cylinder engine; the four-cylinder engine is similar, but without the number five and six cylinders. Begin by placing the engine at top dead center (TDC), and then adjust the valves in sequence according to the firing order (1-5-3-6-2-4 for the six-cylinder, and 1-3-4-2 for the four-cylinder). Before you close up the cylinder head, check the condition of the oiling tube fittings, which have a tendency to loosen up. Use a flare-nut wrench (see Project 56, Photo 2) to make sure these fittings are snug (yellow arrows).

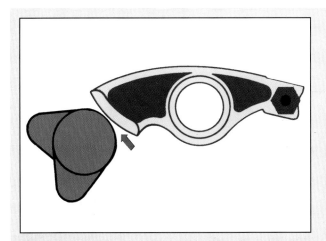

3 This diagram shows the correlation between the rocker arm and the camshaft when the valves are in position to be adjusted. The pair of valves for a cylinder is adjusted when the lobe of the camshaft points downward from the rockers and the valves are closed. This is easy to see when the valve cover is off and the rockers are exposed. At top dead center for cylinder number one, the camshaft lobes for the intake and exhaust camshafts will point downward, away from the rocker arm. The red arrow indicates the clearance that needs to be adjusted.

4 The actual valve adjustment is very easy on these cars. Using a 10-millimeter wrench (yellow arrow), loosen up the retaining nut (green arrow). Insert the spring-loaded valve adjustment tool (red arrow) into the small hole in the eccentric adjuster (blue arrow). Rotate the eccentric adjuster so there is a large clearance between the valve and the adjuster. Insert the feeler gauge (orange arrow) between the adjuster and the valve stem. Pull back on the spring-loaded tool to close the gap. Finally, tighten the 10-millimeter retaining bolt into place.

is in neutral and the parking brake is on before rotating the engine.

You will adjust the intake and exhaust valves for a particular cylinder when they are both closed, which occurs when the lobes on the camshaft are pointing downward, away from the rocker arm. At this point, you should be able to move the rocker arm with your fingers and feel a slight click as you rotate the rocker back and forth ever so slightly. This click, or slack, in the rocker is the clearance you are adjusting (see Photo 3).

When the engine is at TDC for piston number 1, adjust the valves for that cylinder. Both the intake and exhaust valves can be adjusted at the same time. For each valve, loosen the 10-millimeter retaining nut around the eccentric adjuster. Now, place the valve adjustment feeler gauge tool in between the valve and the adjuster (see table for values). Using a stiff piece of wire or the BMW spring-loaded adjustment tool (BMW tool 11-3-070), apply light pressure to the adjuster (see Photo 4). Then tighten the retaining nut. Lightly coat the feeler gauge blade with engine oil to ease the adjustment process. Recheck the clearance after you tighten the nut, as the clearance has a tendency to change slightly when the retaining nut is retightened.

Now, rotate the engine crankshaft 120 degrees using the fan pulley if you have a six-cylinder engine, or 180 degrees if you have a four-cylinder. The next valve in the sequence should be ready to be adjusted. For the six-cylinder engines, the adjustment order corresponds to the firing order of the engine, 1-5-3-6-2-4. For the four-cylinder engines, the firing order is 1-3-4-2.

When you are finished, rotate the engine back to TDC for cylinder number 1. Go back through the rotation procedure and check the clearance of all the valves using the feeler gauge. If any feel too tight or too loose, repeat the adjustment procedure for that valve.

When the whole process is complete, replace the valve cover and tighten the nuts to about 15 N-m (11 ft-lbs) in a criss-cross pattern, starting from the inside four nuts. Use a three-step process to tighten the nuts: hand tight, snug tight, final torque. Use a new valve cover gasket, and don't forget to install the washers underneath the nuts. Also, be aware that the fuel injection harness may get in the way of the valve cover—bolting down the cover with the harness trapped inside creates a rather large leak. Following a successful valve adjustment procedure, you should feel a significant increase in power and hear a significant decrease in valvetrain noise.

	Six-cylinder	Four-cylinder
Adjustment when engine is cold (coolant temp below 95ºF/35ºC)	0.25 millimeter (0.010 inch)	0.20 millimeter (0.008 inch)
Adjustment when engine is warm (coolant temp above 176ºF/80ºC)	0.30 millimeter (0.012 inch)	0.25 millimeter (0.010 inch)
Cylinder firing order	1-5-3-6-2-4	1-3-4-2
Crankshaft rotation between adjustments	1/3 turn (120º)	1/2 turn (180º)

ENGINE

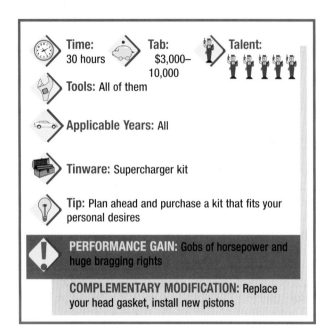

Time: 30 hours

Tab: $3,000–10,000

Talent: ★★★★★

Tools: All of them

Applicable Years: All

Tinware: Supercharger kit

Tip: Plan ahead and purchase a kit that fits your personal desires

PERFORMANCE GAIN: Gobs of horsepower and huge bragging rights

COMPLEMENTARY MODIFICATION: Replace your head gasket, install new pistons

A lot of people think that turbocharging and supercharging are the holy grails of power increases. While it's true you can extract a large amount of power from them, people incorrectly assume that any aftermarket supercharger tossed on a BMW engine will instantly generate heaps of horsepower. As

with any good, reliable means of generating horsepower, the addition of a turbocharger or supercharger needs to be carefully coordinated with your engine's design and your desired performance characteristics.

It's important to take a few moments to talk about turbocharging and supercharging, or "forced induction" as it is known. A forced-induction engine has some assistance in filling the combustion chamber with air/fuel mixture. On a normally aspirated engine, the maximum manifold pressure is very close to atmospheric pressure (14.7 psi at sea level). On a forced-induction engine, the turbocharger or supercharger increases manifold pressure to a level above 14.7 psi. The result is a denser air/fuel mixture in the combustion chamber, and thus more power.

The turbocharger and supercharger are very similar in principle. Both use a compressor/blower to increase the overall pressure of gases inserted into the combustion chamber (cold side). This increase in pressure results in an air/fuel mixture that is more compressed than normal, thereby generating a more powerful piston stroke. Because of the higher density of the mixture, forced induction allows you to create a smaller-displacement engine with the same energy output that as a normally aspirated, larger-displacement engine.

What about reliability? Factory-designed forced-induction engines (like the factory BMW M12 race motors installed in

1 Here's a shot of the Downing Atlanta supercharger kit installed in a 318ti. These compact cars are very light and nimble, and create quite a performance machine when you bump up the horsepower with one of these kits. Because of its size, this twin-screw supercharger kit requires a lot of custom parts, including a new intake manifold. It's a tough squeeze, but the twin-screw Eaton supercharger fits under the hood. The system incorporates an auxiliary fuel pressure regulator (AFPR) that is boost sensitive and raises the pressure in the fuel rail—each time an injector cycles, an appropriate additional amount of fuel is matched with the greater charge of air. It is a simple but elegant solution to the fuel management issue.

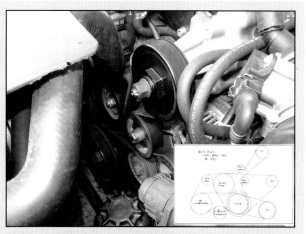

2 The bypass valve is a semi-unique feature of the Downing Atlanta kit. This little device acts as a vacuum-operated actuator attached to a simple butterfly valve. Since the valve is normally closed, it requires vacuum to hold it open. Vacuum is present in the intake manifold at idle and even at steady throttle or highway cruising. When boost is demanded (by depressing the accelerator), the condition in the manifold changes from vacuum to pressure, the bypass valve snaps shut, and boost is instantly sent to the intake runners instead of looping back into the system (the path of least resistance). The bypass valve can also be a valuable diagnostic tool. By fixing the valve in the open position with a piece of wire or a zip tie, the engine can function as naturally aspirated. This eliminates boost, as well as the boost signal that is sent to the auxiliary fuel pressure regulator (AFPR). If a particular drivability problem is still present, the supercharger system can then be eliminated as a contributing factor.

3 The supercharger from the Downing Atlanta kit is driven by the main crankshaft. A few new idlers and tensioners allow the belt to snake around the front of the car and around the supercharger pulley. When installing your kit, make sure all the brackets are tight and the belt is not slightly twisted. If there is an axial load placed on the shaft of the supercharger, it can prematurely wear out the bearings on this very expensive unit. An axial load is a pushing or pulling force on the pulley shaft while it's turning.

4 Here are the primary pieces contained in the Downing Atlanta supercharger kit. **A:** K&N air filter. **B:** Throttle cable. **C:** Intake manifold gaskets. **D:** Intake elbow. **E:** Auxiliary fuel pressure regulator (AFPR). **F:** Drive belt. **G:** Bypass valve. **H:** New intake manifold. **I:** Eaton supercharger. **J:** Drive belt idler pulleys. **K:** Intake adapter. **L:** Intake manifold elbow. **M:** Hose clamps. **N:** Mounting brackets. **O:** Fuel and vacuum hose. **P:** Mounting brackets. **Q:** Radiator hose. (Additional mounting hardware and screws not shown.)

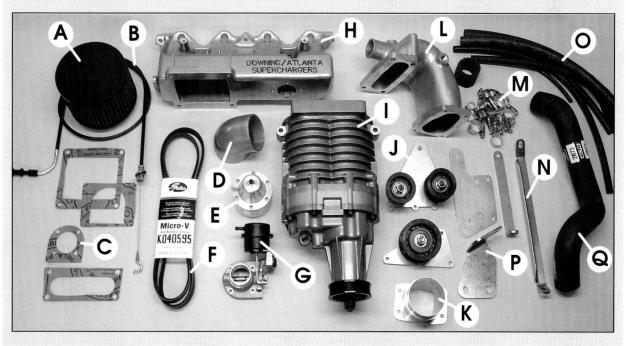

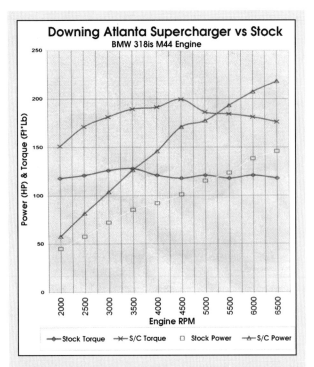

Downing Atlanta Supercharger vs Stock
BMW 318is M44 Engine

Legend: Stock Torque · S/C Torque · Stock Power · S/C Power

5 This graph shows clearly why Downing Atlanta's supercharger kits are so popular. They take the mild-mannered BMW four-cylinder inline engines and turn them into monsters. When combined with a lightweight chassis like the 318ti, the combination makes for a powerful and nimble track car with all the benefits of BMW handling and performance.

the 1980s Formula 1 cars) are specially designed to accommodate the additional stresses placed on them by the added boost. Engines like these are designed from the ground up and usually have very low compression ratios to compensate for the added pressures when the car is operating under full boost. On the flip side, bolting on a turbocharger or supercharger to a stock engine will result in more wear and tear on the engine. If you plan to install a forced-induction system on your stock engine, you must plan on purchasing only high-octane fuel. The increased compression in the cylinders also increases the likelihood of detonation, which can destroy your engine very quickly.

How they work

The supercharger is powered by a pulley that attaches to the crankshaft. As the engine's rpm increases, outside air is compressed and mixed with fuel and discharged into the intake system. There are three common types of superchargers: impeller (centrifugal), twin rotating screws (screw-type), and counter-rotating rotors (Roots-type). As the engine spins faster, the boost from the supercharger will increase. Boost is the measurement of the increase in pressure in the intake charge over normal outside atmospheric levels. Typical boost levels for a street BMW range from 6 to 9 psi. The typical supercharger experiences peak revolutions of about 15,000

rpm for the screw-type, and up to about 40,000 rpm for centrifugal-type superchargers.

The turbocharger unit drives its compressor from the excess exhaust given off by the engine. Although the back pressure on the exhaust may rob a small amount of power from the engine, the boost from the turbo is generally thought of as free boost. The turbocharger unit is very similar in operation to a centrifugal supercharger, with the exception that it is driven off of the exhaust gases versus a pulley attached to the crankshaft. Typical peak revolutions of turbos can range anywhere from 75,000 all the way up to 150,000 rpm.

Head-to-head comparison
Power and efficiency
Whereas the turbo runs off of the exhaust system, a supercharger takes power from the engine crankshaft to run the blower. All things being equal, superchargers sap more power overhead (40–50 horsepower to spin the blower at full boost) from the engine to run the compressor than turbochargers. Turbos, however, are not without horsepower cost—the back pressure from the turbo and restrictions from the convoluted exhaust piping act to reduce horsepower. However, these losses are minimal when compared to the horsepower cost of driving a supercharger off the crankshaft. The bottom line is that if you're looking to squeeze the maximum amount of power out of a specific displacement (as you would if you were running in certain club racer classes), turbocharger systems win hands down over superchargers.

Power lag
Reduction of lag is the top reason why superchargers are preferred over turbochargers for street cars. Since the turbocharger is spooled up by the exhaust gases from the engine, it doesn't achieve significant boost levels until the engine's rpm reaches a certain level. This means little or no boost in the lower rpm range. When the boost finally kicks in, it can be an unsettling experience, as the car rockets off as soon as you reach an rpm level that produces boost. This power surge can also place additional stresses on stock drivetrain and suspension components. There are several things you can do to reduce turbo lag (described further in this project), but these fixes sacrifice top-end power. A supercharger, on the other hand, connects directly to the crankshaft and spins and creates boost at all times. The screw-type and Roots-type superchargers are able to create significant boost levels at low rpm, so there's typically not much lag. Whereas a turbocharger has power that instantly comes online at about 3,000 or 4,000 rpm, the supercharger has a nice, even boost curve that generates excellent power off of the line.

Reliability
Turbocharger systems are somewhat complex, and thus are considered less reliable than superchargers. In addition, all of the turbo system components work with exhaust gases, which creates additional heat stress and wear on the system. When you first shut off a car with a turbo system, the temperatures

ENGINE

can spike inside the turbo and you can experience problems with the impeller bearings being cooked by this high heat (some people install turbo timers that let the engine run at idle and cool down for a minute or so before shutting off). Turbochargers spin at much higher rpm than superchargers; thus, the bearings inside tend to wear out much faster. Many turbo system exhaust components are handmade, and as such, weld seams often crack with age.

Heat

The turbocharger system is powered by hot exhaust gases, which tend to inadvertently heat up the intake mixture charge. Hot air expands and becomes less dense, so this heating effect works against the compressing action of the turbocharger. Cooler air means a higher air/fuel mixture density, which is the whole point of installing a forced-induction system. To solve this problem, most turbos require an intercooler, which increases the complexity and cost of the system. Hot air is cycled through a large intercooler, cooling the air before it goes into the intake manifold. The cooler air helps to reduce detonation and also increases the density of the air/fuel mixture. Just about all the intercoolers I've seen on the 3 Series cars have been installed in the front bumper—not a simple task. In addition to the heat gathered from the exhaust gases, the intake air temperature increases when the air is compressed. All turbochargers should be run with an intercooler, and most superchargers can also benefit from the use of an intercooler as well.

Installation and tuning

Superchargers in general are very easy to install. Many bolt-on kits exist that can be installed over a weekend, and BMW inline engines have plenty of room in the engine compartment. Supercharger kits often require only a few modifications to the fuel system or a new fuel injection mapping chip for the DME to get the engine up and running well. On the other hand, most turbo installations involve complex routing of exhaust pipes, oil lines, and other components, many of which must be modified to fit properly. Intercoolers are typically difficult to fit in the front bumper of the 3 Series cars. Although turbo systems can be made to run with the stock fuel and ignition systems (DME), in order to extract the most power out of a turbocharger system, you should run the engine with an engine management system (see Project 23).

Cost

In general, both types of systems can be expensive, costing anywhere from $3,000 for a basic kit up to $10,000 for a complete setup and installation. Since the turbo systems are more complicated, they tend to be slightly more expensive, particularly when you add the cost of a front-mounted intercooler. Another consideration is the cost of installation. Most supercharger installations are relatively straightforward, as you only need to modify the left side of the engine bay and the intake system. Installation of a turbo setup is much trickier (and a bit more expensive) due to the effort involved with

6 Shown here is a VF-Engineering supercharger kit for an E36 M3. The supercharger is a Vortech centrifugal unit and uses CNC brackets with plastic-molded ducting for a factory-installed look. Proprietary engine management software tuned by GIAC is flashed into the DME to reprogram it for the increased power. The small size of the supercharger unit allows you to utilize the stock intake manifold. With a kit like this, you can achieve an impressive 347 horsepower and 292 ft-lbs of torque at 6,750 rpm.

routing and installing the exhaust pipes. Despite what many manufacturers may say, turbo kits are almost never a straight bolt-on installation. The pipes and brackets are almost always hand-made and often require some tweaking to fit.

Power output and streetability

Turbochargers and superchargers can both produce significant power gains, although turbochargers can squeeze more total power out of the system due to the fact that they run off free energy from the exhaust system. Because the turbocharger units operate at very high rpm, they can produce very high levels of boost in the upper rpm range and deliver much more peak horsepower at these levels. However, most people don't drive their cars at peak rpm on the street. Most of the driving is done in the lower rpm bands, where superchargers have the power advantage. If you want to drive around town with more power off of the line, then a supercharger kit is probably the best choice. If you are going to be racing the car on a track or you want maximum top-end power on the highway, then a turbocharger will allow you to squeeze the most power out of your engine.

Superchargers

There are two types of superchargers that are commonly installed onto BMW inline engines: centrifugal and screw-type. Of the two, the centrifugal supercharger is most like a turbocharger, with the exception that a belt connected to the engine's crankshaft drives it. Centrifugal superchargers compress air using a spinning impeller. With centrifugal superchargers, you can often swap out impeller sizes and change the drive pulley to customize the boost curve for your particular needs. Centrifugal superchargers are typically set to generate their peak boost at or near engine redline. In general, they develop more of their boost at higher rpm and offer less boost on the low end of the rpm range. Paxton, Powerdyne, ProCharger, and Vortech all manufacture quality centrifugal superchargers.

Screw-type superchargers are an improvement on the design of the older Roots-type supercharger. A twin-screw mechanism geared off the front pulley compresses air as it moves between the two screw blades. These are also often called positive-displacement units because they move a fixed amount of air per revolution. This design creates good compression at lower rpm, resulting in a significant increase in power from idle all the way through the rest of the power range. Drag racers who want instant boost off the line typically go with the screw-type supercharger. One problem with the screw-type, however, is that it takes up significantly more space than a centrifugal supercharger. With BMW four-cylinder engines like the 318i, this is not a huge problem, as there is extra room in the engine compartment for the intake manifold adapters (see Photo 1). Downing Atlanta makes an excellent supercharger kit that utilizes a screw-type blower to extract more than 200 horsepower from a stock four-cylinder engine. Other manufacturers of screw-type superchargers include Kenne Belle, Eaton, and Whipple.

Turbocharger systems

Many people incorrectly think a larger turbocharger alone will generate more boost and horsepower. In reality, this is not necessarily true. A larger forced-induction unit must also accompany other important changes in the engine. Maximum boost pressure is limited by a pressure relief valve called a "wastegate." The wastegate acts to release exhaust gas pressure, slowing the turbine so the engine doesn't suffer from too much boost being applied. Installing a larger turbocharger without making adjustments to the wastegate will result in no increase in maximum boost levels.

How does the size of the turbocharger affect performance? The numeric digits used to describe turbos (K24, K26, K27, etc.) usually correspond to the actual size of the exhaust fan wheel inside the turbocharger (called the "hot side"). In addition, there is the wheel on the intake ("cold side") that compresses the air to create the actual boost. Changing the sizes of the two wheels alters the overall personality of the turbocharger and can be used to tailor the turbo response to your specific application.

For example, a small turbine wheel in the exhaust, combined with a small impeller wheel on the compressor side, will spin the turbo up quickly and generate a quick throttle response, but it will also tend to drop off power on the top end. A small turbine in the exhaust with a large blower will generate a good compromise between throttle response and top-end power. To obtain the best top-end performance, a large turbo wheel can be combined with a large blower wheel. The down side is that throttle response will suffer in the lower rpm range.

Installing a smaller turbine wheel in the exhaust means that it will spin up much faster than a larger one. The ideal turbo configuration for everyday street driving is to have a smaller turbine on the hot side and a larger blower turbine on the cold side. This particular configuration is a good compromise between low-end throttle response and high-end power. The down side to this configuration is that it takes a certain level of exhaust pressure at a minimum rpm to spin up the exhaust (hot side) turbine to the point that it can begin to impact the intake pressures. This is what is commonly known as "turbo lag." In a race engine, turbo lag is not typically a major issue, since the transmission gearing and overall setup of the engine are usually designed to operate within a narrow power band high in the rpm range.

How do you improve performance? Swapping the turbocharger with one that has a different ratio between the wheels can change your turbo engine's characteristics. There are numerous options for turbochargers, and each one changes the performance characteristics differently than the next. Do some research and ask others who have installed various units on their BMWs before you spend a large amount of money on a new turbocharger. Adding an intercooler, or upgrading your existing one, will also increase the overall performance. Simply dialing in more boost from the turbocharger (by changing the wastegate relief valve setting) can give you an immediate performance improvement. Also, increasing the compression in the engine will give you more low-end power. However, these approaches can be extremely hazardous to your engine. Severe detonation from poor-quality gas can cause pistons to overheat, and the engine can literally blow itself apart. For more information on turbocharging, see the book *Turbochargers* by Hugh MacInnes or *Maximum Boost* by Corky Bell.

How much boost?

This age-old question is answered with the old saying, "There's no such thing as a free lunch." How much boost you run on your forced-induction system depends upon a wide variety of factors.

What type of induction is it? As mentioned, turbo systems come to full boost capability and then bleed off excess with a wastegate. While this creates great power in the upper rpm range, it also means you're running at highly boosted levels for extended periods of time. A centrifugal supercharger only reaches maximum boost at the highest rpm, and then only for a few seconds. So, you can run much higher peak boost levels on a centrifugal supercharger than you can with a turbo or screw-type supercharger system.

Which fuel octane? Running a boosted engine puts a lot of stress on the internals of the engine, as you are pushing more and more power through the drivetrain. However, the real killer for these engines is detonation. If the octane is too low and the compression of the engine too high, the fuel will explode prematurely, resulting in what is commonly known as "engine knocking," or "detonation." When the mixture in the combustion chamber burns, it increases the pressure in the cylinder and pushes down on the piston. When detonation occurs, the piston is still rising and compressing the mixture.

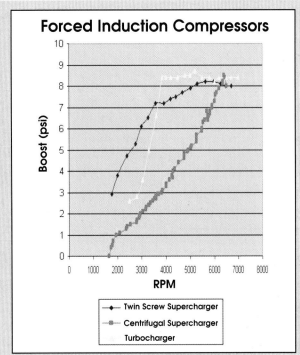

Forced Induction Compressors

Legend:
- Twin Screw Supercharger
- Centrifugal Supercharger
- Turbocharger

7 Shown here is a turbocharger setup installed on an E36. The Turbonetics turbocharger unit is mounted on the left side of the engine compartment, with the exhaust from the engine feeding it from underneath. The BMW inline engines do not lend themselves to turbo installations, as the intake and exhaust are separated by the bulk of the engine. Routing the exhaust to the turbocharger is typically complicated. The fundamental components of the BMW inline six-cylinder engine are very strong and withstand some pretty high boost levels. A stock M3 engine (S52) with a properly tuned turbocharger system has run 11.11 seconds in the quarter-mile at 129 miles per hour and 22.05 psi boost. I wouldn't suggest running that much boost around town, but for a stock engine, those are impressive numbers.

8 Note the different boost levels between a centrifugal supercharger, a twin-screw supercharger, and a turbocharger system. As you can see, the twin-screw generates more boost per rpm than the centrifugal unit. The turbocharger graph shows low boost levels until about 3,500 rpm, where it rockets up to full boost in a hurry. *Steve Andersen*

Thus, when ignition occurs, the pressure builds and has no release. The pressure pushes down on the piston as it's rising, creating a tremendous amount of pressure that has nowhere to go. Unchecked, detonation will destroy pistons and blow out head gaskets. It's the number one killer of forced-induction engines. To prevent destruction, reduce your boost levels so that the engine no longer detonates. The engine management system (DME) normally adjusts timing and ignition in response to signals received from the knock sensor to reduce detonation in the cylinders. However, running really high amounts of boost with lower octane fuel can overwhelm the stock system and confuse it. The bottom line is that the higher the boost you wish to run, the higher the octane of fuel you will have to buy. If you want to head to the drag strip and run all out with as much boost as you possibly can, be prepared to buy race fuel with octane ratings in the 105–110 range.

What is the air/fuel mixture? When you install a forced-induction system onto an engine, you increase the amount of air injected into the combustion chamber. Most of the time, this will cause the air/fuel mixture to become lean. You must compensate by increasing the amount of fuel that is combined with the air, since that air is now compressed and thus more dense. According to modern fuel injection theory, combustion achieves its maximum efficiency at an air/fuel ratio of 14.67:1. Although this ratio may be optimal for good fuel economy, it's not best for maximizing power. On a normally aspirated engine at full throttle, maximum power is achieved with an air/fuel ratio set from about 14.2:1 to 14.3:1. On boosted engines, this maximum power ratio is closer to the range of 12.2:1 to 12.4:1. If your boosted engine is running too lean, it will increase the likelihood of detonation and also will increase the operating temperature of the cylinder head. It's very important to make sure that your engine is running on the rich side. I recommend running an aftermarket air/fuel mixture gauge to monitor and protect against the engine running lean.

What modifications have been done to the DME? The DME (digital motor electronics) controls the ignition and air/fuel ratio injected into the engine. Installing a forced-induction system is such a major change to the engine that it's difficult to adapt the computer to correctly compensate for the compressed intake charge. The Downing Atlanta supercharger kit uses an auxiliary fuel pressure regulator that increases fuel pressure in direct relation to the amount of boost the supercharger is outputting. This is a simple yet clever way to adjust the fuel mixture without having to reprogram any chips or sensors.

What is the compression ratio? Engines that start with a high compression ratio (like the 1996–1999 E36 M3 at 10.5:1) cannot be boosted as much as engines with lower

9 Even early cars can benefit from turbocharging. This early 3 Series four-cylinder uses the Bosch CIS system and a small turbocharger to compress the air intake mixture. With a little bit of ingenuity, a system like this can create quite a bit of horsepower.

10 Shown here is a boost gauge is mounted on the driver's side A-pillar. I recommend installing one of these in your car if you're running a forced-induction system. A boost gauge provides a snapshot of the health of the induction system and will alert you to boost levels that may be too high.

ratios. To properly integrate forced induction, the engine should be designed from the ground up with forced induction in mind. The higher compression ratios of the M3 (and the 328 with 10.2:1) don't naturally lend themselves to forced-induction kits. In general, forced-induction engines are blueprinted to have a very low compression ratio (like the venerable Porsche 911 Turbo with 7.0:1). The bottom line is you can generate more horsepower by maximizing boost from the turbo than you can with higher compression. If you run higher compression, you will be forced to run with less boost at the higher end to avoid destroying the engine. Thus, you want to design the engine to have low compression, so that you can run higher boost at higher rpm and generate more horsepower. You can lower the compression ratio by a variety of methods, such as adding a thicker head gasket, installing lower-compression custom-made pistons, etc.

How old is the engine? Bearings and clearances wear out over years of use. Most companies that sell superchargers don't recommend installing them on a tired engine. The chances you will blow out your head gasket increase as the engine gets older. Increasing the overall compression inside the combustion chamber increases the wear and tear on all the parts in the drivetrain.

The bottom line? There are a few rules of thumb when it comes to running forced-induction engines. The following table gives you a broad outline of what maximum boost levels you can run for a variety of compression ratios:

Boost Level	Compression Ratio
8 psi	10.5:1
9–10 psi	10.0:1
11–12 psi	9.5:1
13–14 psi	9.0:1
15–18 psi	8.5:1
*running on 91 octane with a BMW inline engine	

Conclusions

Which forced-induction unit you install really depends upon your overall goals, which should include ease of installation and budget limitations. If you ask 10 different enthusiasts what their preferences are, you will get 10 completely different answers. There are those who are turbo fans, and there are others who are die-hard supercharger recruits. Obviously, this project can only scratch the surface of what's involved in designing and implementing a turbocharger or supercharger system.

Some closing remarks regarding the relative performance of these two systems: If you want a drag car with lots of power off of the line, you should probably go with a supercharger system. It will give you boost at low rpm and a predictable power curve. If you're looking for top speed on the Autobahn, where you want to squeeze out all the power you can, I recommend a turbocharger system. It will give you maximum power at the higher end of your rpm range. With most supercharger systems, you will achieve maximum boost only when you're at redline. With a turbocharger, you will have nearly full boost all the way from about 3,000 to 4,000 rpm to redline.

If you like to feel the rush of power and want the ability to create gobs of peak horsepower, go with a turbocharger. Turbo systems are also considered to be more flexible in that they can often be designed to fit most owners' requirements, while superchargers can be a bit more limited.

If you want your car to feel somewhat stock with a big push on the high-end, then go with a centrifugal supercharger. If you just want more even power across the entire rpm range, then install a positive-displacement (twin-screw) supercharger.

In terms of installation ease, the supercharger systems win by a mile. Turbocharger systems can be made to perform better, but they generally require more time, money, and installation effort to achieve this end.

Engine Management Systems

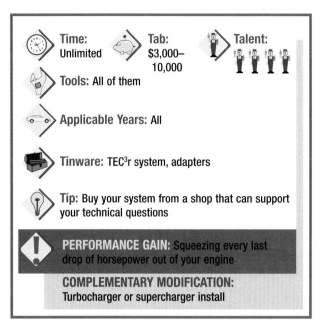

Time: Unlimited

Tab: $3,000–10,000

Talent:

Tools: All of them

Applicable Years: All

Tinware: TEC³r system, adapters

Tip: Buy your system from a shop that can support your technical questions

PERFORMANCE GAIN: Squeezing every last drop of horsepower out of your engine

COMPLEMENTARY MODIFICATION: Turbocharger or supercharger install

The Motronic system (also called the digital motor electronics, or DME) is hands down the best overall fuel injection system when you consider price and performance. Ignition timing and fuel delivery are controlled by a digital map recorded in a removable chip within the main engine management (DME) computer. The computer takes input from a variety of sensors on the engine—cylinder head temperature, altitude (ambient air pressure), crank angle, throttle position, exhaust gas oxygen (mixture), ambient air temperature, and mass airflow—and adjusts engine functions accordingly. The DME chip is programmed by the factory with a map of certain performance parameters (mostly conservative, so the engine will react well under a host of varying conditions). Major changes to the engine (including different camshafts, exhaust, etc.) require an updated map to take full advantage of these modifications. Failure to update the Motronic system when significantly altering your engine may actually result in decreased performance, as the original system is finely tuned to supply the correct timing and fuel injection values only for a stock engine configuration.

Each factory Motronic system is matched directly to a specific engine configuration. Because of the proprietary nature of the Motronic system, there aren't many changes you can perform without updating the DME chip. To gain the maximum benefit from engine modifications, either upgrade the DME chip or install a programmable aftermarket engine management system.

Similar to the Motronic system, there are several complete aftermarket engine management systems that integrate fuel delivery and ignition system control. Electromotive and

Motec manufacture two of the most popular systems for BMWs, although the market is expanding with many more choices as well. While these systems will squeeze the maximum performance out of your engine, they are not for the faint of heart, are technically challenging, and cost a pretty penny. They are without a doubt the most flexible of any fuel/ignition systems and will enable you to extract every ounce of power from your engine if you spend the time tweaking the system. Most are programmable from a laptop computer and can even interact with your computer both ways, giving you performance data and feedback from the engine as you run it through its paces. These systems cost anywhere from $3,000 to $10,000; however, they are usable on nearly any size BMW engine in any configuration.

With the option of complete engine control, total power optimization becomes a reality. The latest engine management system from Electromotive is the TEC³r (Total Engine Control, Version 3), shown in Photo 1. This single-plug system costs about $2,500. It is far more advanced than previous versions and offers almost unlimited flexibility in designing your fuel and ignition systems.

The TEC³r system has a proportional air-to-fuel ratio table that allows you to systematically control the mixture from idle to full throttle. According to modern fuel injection theory, fuel and air combustion achieves its maximum efficiency at a ratio of 14.67:1. Although this ratio may be optimal for good fuel economy, it's not best for maximizing power. On a normally aspirated engine at full throttle, maximum power is achieved with an air/fuel ratio set at about 13.8:1 to 14.0:1. On boosted engines, this maximum power ratio is closer to the range of 12.2:1 to 12.4:1. Using the variable fuel ratio characteristics of the TEC³r, you can create one set of programs for the track, where fuel delivery and optimum performance are critical, and another set for the street, where maximum fuel efficiency is desired. Because the TEC³r system senses engine load via a manifold absolute pressure sensor, the system can determine whether you're cruising on the highway or driving on the track. One single program can also be designed for both applications.

The system consists of a separate electronic control unit (ECU) and ignition coil packs. These coil packs, or direct-fire units (DFUs), deliver a full-charge spark up to 15,000 rpm. For a BMW inline six-cylinder engine, use a three-coil assembly. Each coil fires a spark for two cylinders that are opposite from each other in the firing order. By using a separate ignition coil for each pair of companion cylinders, the time available to recharge the coils increases by a factor of three (on the six-cylinder BMW engine). This configuration produces full spark energy while delivering spark duration up to 2 milliseconds at 6,000 rpm. This duration is more than 10 times

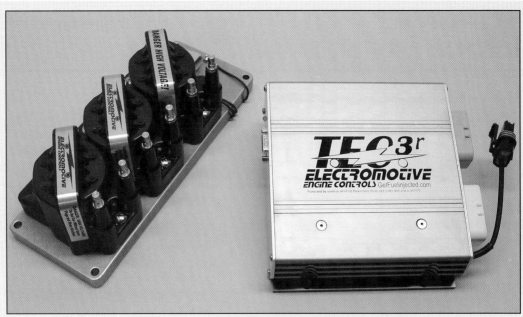

1 The TEC³r engine management system consists of the ECU and coil packs. Previous versions integrated these two components. Mount the coil pack in the engine compartment, relatively close to the spark plugs. Mount the ECU near the cockpit for easy access.

longer than most capacitive discharge units and directly translates into better combustion and more power. For coil-on-plug engines, like the BMW E36 inline engine, stock ignition coils can be used in place of the DFU.

Each coil pack is wired into two cylinders that are opposite of each other in the firing order (1 and 6, 5 and 2, 3 and 4). The ignition portion of the TEC³r system is wired so that the companion cylinders fire at the same time. Each coil fires a plug on the compression stroke for one cylinder and on the exhaust stroke for the companion cylinder. This produces what is known as a "waste spark" on the exhaust stroke of the companion cylinder. The cylinder that has compressed the air/fuel mixture receives a higher voltage spark than its companion cylinder, because the mixture creates an environment around the spark plug that offers a more conductive path. The majority of spark energy is delivered to the compressed cylinder. A small amount of spark voltage is directed to the cylinder on its exhaust stroke. This waste spark has no effect at all on the performance of the engine. Direct connection from the coil to each of the cylinders eliminates sending the spark through the distributor cap and rotor (on early cars), which can cause cross-firing and other distributor-related performance problems. In addition, computer-controlled custom advance/retard curves eliminate any mechanical problems that may occur with centrifugal or vacuum timing adjustment.

The TEC³r ECU is dynamically programmed with easy-to-use software that comes with the system. The Tuning Wizard in WinTec 3.0 software allows you to create an instant engine profile in just a few steps (see Photo 2). By inputting all the parameters of your engine, you can start with a good base profile from which to make modifications. Mapped programs download to the ECU via a computer serial cable and can be updated, changed, or restored at any time. The base programs can be tweaked to get about 90

percent of the full power potential out of the engine. To achieve the final 10 percent, you'll have to perform extensive track testing or run your engine on a dyno.

The TEC³r system works by sampling the values from sensors in the engine and comparing them to various tables that control fuel delivery and ignition timing. These sensors consist of the following:

- Oxygen sensor: measures the air/fuel mixture by measuring the exhaust gases
- Manifold absolute pressure sensor: measures pressure, while compensating for altitude changes; you can also substitute a mass airflow sensor instead of the MAP.
- Knock sensor: detects and measures detonation caused by poor fuels or too much timing advance
- Crank angle sensor: measures rpm and crank location
- Throttle position sensor: measures position for idle control and how quickly the pedal is depressed for fuel enrichments (or deceleration cut-off)
- Cam angle sensor: detects cam timing for true sequential mode fuel injection
- Coolant sensor: measures engine temperature for warm-up enrichments
- Manifold air temperature sensor: measures air temperature entering the engine for mixture compensation
- Idle speed control: controls idle speed for warm up and air conditioner

These sensors work in conjunction to measure and create a picture of the engine conditions at any one point in time. The ECU takes the sensor readings and translates them into formulas for delivering fuel and firing sparks. Using advanced data-logging features, the sensor readings and the results of the ECU changes are recorded, snapping a picture of all the engine functions at any point. The data can be recalled for

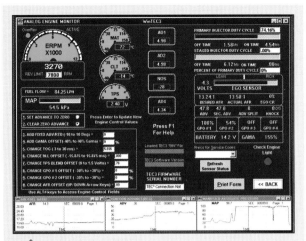

2 This screen shot from the TEC³r programming utility WinTec shows the real-time logging capability of the system. Other capabilities include a real-time monitoring screen, a 3D ignition advance graph, and a quick update table used to alter fuel ratio mappings.

analysis and used as a reference for future programming of the ECU.

The TEC³r operates in either phased sequential or true sequential mode. Phased sequential means the fuel injectors are activated multiple times per crankshaft cycle—once on an open valve and once on a closed valve. Early versions of the Motronic system were designed as phased injection systems. The fuel injectors on one-half of the engine would all open and close together. They share the same wiring harness and are electrically controlled as a group. True sequential injection means that each injector is activated in close coordination with that cylinder's ignition cycle. Fuel squirts out of the injector in precise coordination with the opening and closing of the intake valve. Fuel is never injected into the cylinder head when the valve is closed. The TEC³r, operating in true sequential mode, injects fuel only when the intake valve is open, which smoothes out the engine idle and creates a cleaner-running engine. At higher rpm, phased sequential and true sequential modes show virtually identical performance, as the injectors are firing almost continuously.

Another advantage to the TEC³r system is its flexibility; it can be used on just about any engine. Its ability to run engines up to 12 cylinders means it can be moved from one engine to another as you upgrade. It's a very worthwile investment that can grow with you even if you upgrade your engine or your car.

Pushing the limits of ultra-high performance, the TEC³r also has four general output parameters (GPO) that can be controlled by any number of engine conditions. For instance, the system can automatically turn on cooling fans or open electric thermostats if the engine temperature or rpm increases past a certain threshold, or provide the driver with a custom-designed shift light on the dashboard. In what

could be the ultimate performance system, the TEC³r can control a variable turbo boost valve coupled with a knock sensor. This would allow you to run the maximum possible boost on a turbo or supercharged engine while actively monitoring and correcting for detonation. The engine management system can control this boost pressure, engine timing, and a host of other variables to achieve the highest possible boost without inflicting collateral damage. This system would be able to dynamically compensate for any octane fuel—automatically adjusting the timing and air/fuel ratio to squeeze the most power out of the engine.

The TEC³r system can run in an open- or closed-loop configuration with respect to air/fuel mixture measurement. Open-loop mode is useful for racers who run leaded race fuels that cannot be used in conjunction with an oxygen sensor. In this mode, the system reads measurements from its sensors, and then compares the readings to its internal program maps. Spark and fuel mixture are controlled using these maps, without correcting for changes that would normally be measured by the oxygen sensor.

The TEC³r is also able to self-diagnose problems with the engine's sensors. The ECU has a check engine warning lamp that indicates if any of the engine's sensors are producing faulty signals. The error codes isolate the exact problem and can be quickly downloaded from the ECU to diagnose the problem.

The TEC³r is not specifically designed for the BMW and thus requires some adaptation to fit BMW engines. Sias Tuning manufactures a plug-and-play adapter kit that allows you to slide in the TEC³r unit in place of a Motronic DME, and replace the mass airflow (MAF) sensor with a manifold air pressure (MAP) sensor. The Sias Tuning kit is a good starting point for entry into the world of engine management. However, the plug-and-play adapter is somewhat limited in scope, because it uses all of the GPOs (general-purpose outputs) to control the various components of the car. The big advantage to an adapter like this is that you can simply reinstall the stock DME unit if you need to have the car checked for emissions. I recommend starting with an adapter kit. Then, if you seriously modify the engine, you can upgrade the engine's sensors and create a specific wiring harness for the system.

Why invest in one of these systems if you haven't significantly modified your engine? Because they are really neat to play with, and you can custom design your own fuel and ignition maps. You probably won't squeeze out any more horsepower than you would with a good aftermarket performance chip, but you will have fun playing around with the unit. On the other hand, if you want to design the ultimate engine, you need to install some type of engine management system. With a system like this, you can design and build any engine combination you want. Whether you desire a supercharged, boosted engine, or a super-high-compression-ratio engine that runs on pump gas, the engine management system will be able to control and optimize it. The possibilities are truly endless and unbounded.

Rod Bearings and Oil Pump Nut Replacement

ENGINE

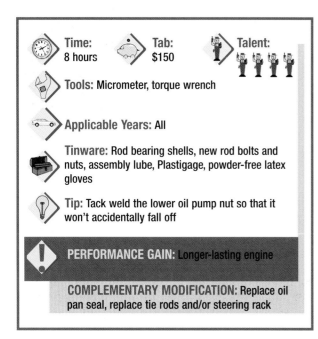

Time: 8 hours

Tab: $150

Talent:

Tools: Micrometer, torque wrench

Applicable Years: All

Tinware: Rod bearing shells, new rod bolts and nuts, assembly lube, Plastigage, powder-free latex gloves

Tip: Tack weld the lower oil pump nut so that it won't accidentally fall off

PERFORMANCE GAIN: Longer-lasting engine

COMPLEMENTARY MODIFICATION: Replace oil pan seal, replace tie rods and/or steering rack

The connecting rod bearings in BMW engines transmit 100 percent of the load from combustion to the crankshaft. As a result, the bearing surfaces do not wear evenly. The side of the bearing facing opposite the piston tends to get the most wear, because the rod pushes on it with a huge amount of force when the cylinder fires. On the opposite side of the power stroke, the same rod pulls the piston and rod assembly back toward the crankshaft, creating wear on the opposite side. These push-pull forces on the crankshaft bearings are exactly opposite each other and create wear patterns on opposite sides of the bearing journals. BMW connecting rods, like the crankshaft itself, are robust parts. Rods typically become damaged when a more basic problem, like low oil pressure, caused by high heat or simply low oil levels, causes the rod bearings to run dry. The rod bearing journals are some of the last components to receive oil, and thus are often the first to run dry when the engine oil level runs low. The result is catastrophic failure, as the rod itself crushes and squeezes the rod bearings against the crankshaft.

If your engine has suffered from a loss of oil pressure, the first thing I recommend you do is replace your rod bearings. They are the one component most likely to be damaged by low oil pressure and the one component that, if worn, will result in complete engine failure. When most people think of bearings, they think of ball bearings like you would find in the wheel of a bicycle. The rod bearings are very different; they are basically a strip of curved metal that an oil film floats on. When the engine is running perfectly, the connecting rod bearing never touches the crankshaft, as thin oil molecules are suspended between the bearing and the crankshaft. The only time they might touch under normal circumstances is when you first start up the engine and there's not much oil pressure built up yet.

If your engine runs low on oil pressure, the crankshaft will ride on the actual metal bearing strip with no thin film in between. This accelerates the rod bearing wear significantly, causing the bearings to overheat and disintegrate in a matter of minutes. If the engine hasn't seized and you've driven the car with the low oil pressure lamp on for even a short while, you should bite the bullet and replace the rod bearings as soon as possible. A catastrophic drop in oil pressure might be caused by hitting a large rock on the freeway that punctures the bottom of your oil sump, or having the oil pump nut come loose on your E36 six-cylinder engine (more on this later).

Rod bearing replacement is generally straightforward. The toughest part of the procedure is getting to the bearings themselves. On the E30 and E36, this involves removing the front suspension, front axle support bar, steering rack (Project 59), and lower sump oil pan (Project 19). Once all of this equipment is out of the way, you have ready access to the rod bearings.

Begin by rotating the engine so you can reach the rod bolts. The rod bolts can be accessed in the following sequence: 1 and 6, 3 and 4, and 2 and 5. Turn the crankshaft over so each pair moves to its lowest position. Use a socket and driver on the front crankshaft pulley nut (see Photo 3 of

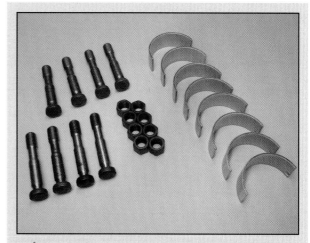

1 A complete rod bearing replacement kit for a four-cylinder 318i contains eight bearing shells, eight rod bolts, and eight rod nuts. Don't ever reuse rod bolts—they are stretch bolts and are only designed to be tightened once. Be sure to purchase the correct size rod bearings, as they need to match the size of your crankshaft (see Photo 3).

2 You can access the rod bearings relatively easily after you remove a bunch of other items (front axle support bar, steering rack, lower oil pan cover). Although it may seem difficult to reach the rod bearings, having access to them in this manner means that you won't have to remove the engine and tear it down as on many other cars. This is a view of the crankshaft and connecting rods from underneath the engine. The red arrow points to a rod nut. The yellow arrow indicates the back side of a piston. The green arrow shows a bolt that holds a cap for the crankshaft bearings. The blue arrow on the left shows the engine flywheel. The purple arrow points to the bottom half of the engine oil dip stick. Crankshafts are marked with various colored paint, depending upon tolerances (in this case a red mark, shown here by the orange arrow).

Project 17). Remove the two rod bolts from each of the two rods, and gently pull off the rod end cap. If it sticks on the end of the rod, tap it lightly with a very small hammer. With the cap removed, gently push the other rod half up into the engine until the rod can clear the crankshaft journal. Place a small strip of cardboard against the surface of the crankshaft—you don't want to scratch the delicate polished surface of the crankshaft with the edge of the rod.

Inspect the rod bearings when you remove them. They should be a dull grey, with no indications of wear or discoloration. If they are shiny, if you see brass-colored metal, or if the bearings are missing chunks or pieces, they are surely worn and need to be replaced.

Replacement rod bearings must be matched to the crank. If you use a crankshaft that has had rod journals reground, you will have to use oversized rod bearings. Measure the rod journals on the crank before you order any replacement rod bearings.

Using a clean-room wipe and isopropyl alcohol, carefully clean each rod bearing (see Photo 4). Install each bearing into the rod cap and rod half. Depending upon which engine you have, there may be upper and lower bearing shell halves (blue for the top side and red for the lower side near the rod cap). Using a clean-room wipe and isopropyl alcohol, clean all oil and residue off of the new rod bolts and nuts. Then install the new rod bolts into the cap. Apply a generous, but even, layer of assembly lube to the rod bearing. Spread the assembly lube across the rod bearing with your finger while wearing powder-free latex gloves. If you don't wear gloves, wash your hands first with nonpumice soft soap and make sure they are clean of any dirt or debris. Lubricate both bearing halves, and wipe a small amount around the sides of the big end of the rod to help lubricate any side contact the rod and crankshaft might see before adequate oil pressure is achieved.

3 If you remove the crankshaft from the car, you have the luxury of using a regular-sized micrometer to measure the rod bearing journals. If maneuvering inside the lower part of the BMW engine, you may have to experiment with various micrometers and dial calipers in order to measure the journals accurately.

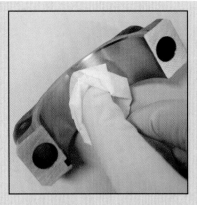

4 Perhaps the most important task in the assembly process may very well be proper cleaning. Clean as much of the rod and bearing cap as possible with brake or carburetor cleaner. Gently wipe the surface of the bearing with a clean-room wipe and alcohol, and also wipe the bearing journal of the rod. Wipe down the crankshaft rod bearing surface, and double-check that there is no dirt anywhere on the assembly.

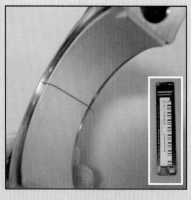

5 Use Plastigage to measure the clearance between the rod bearing and the crankshaft. Lay the wax out across the bearing surface as shown here. After tightening the rod nuts and bolts to their final torque values (using only old rod bolts and nuts), the wax will flatten out. Compare the width of the wax to the measurement scale enclosed with the Plastigage to obtain an accurate reading of the clearances. For most engines, the specified value should read between 0.020 and 0.055 millimeter.

Each rod is stamped with a unique number, and rods and their matching caps must be kept together. Make sure the numbers stamped in the rod butt up against each other. If you have the cap aligned correctly, with the numbers lining up, the rod bearing tangs located on the edge of each bearing will also butt up against each other. Double-check that you have properly lubed all the bearings and lined up the rods with their matching caps before you begin to torque the rod nuts to their final values.

Rod nuts and bolts are one-time-use parts designed to be tightened to their torque values only once. Always use new rod bolts and nuts when replacing your rod bearings. When tightening the rod bolts, carefully follow the torque values and use a calibrated torque wrench. Rod bolt torque values vary considerably; see www.101Projects.com for a listing of torque values and tightening procedures. Most procedures involve tightening the rod bolt to a specific torque value, and then further tightening the bolt a certain number of degrees.

With the new bearings installed, follow BMW's engine break-in instructions. Disconnect the fuel or DME relay, and allow the car to build oil pressure by turning over the starter in 10-second increments. Repeat this step at least three times to build oil pressure in the engine. Breaking in an engine involves all of the parts in the engine beginning to wear together and finding their groove. Close-tolerance parts actually wear and machine themselves into proper alignment with their counterparts over time. For the first 1,200 miles, do not exceed engine rpm of 5,500 or road speed of 105 miles per hour.

Interestingly enough, there is a factory recall notice (SI B 11 04 04) that dictates rod bearing replacement on the E46 M3 with the S54B32 engine, produced from February 12, 2001, through May 22, 2003. The original bearings in these engines were prone to failure if the engines were driven at high rpm for extended periods of time (exactly what you'd expect to do to an M3). The design of the S54 motor is very similar to the earlier inline six-cylinders, and the rod bearing replacement procedure is the same. The factory recall involves replacing the bearings and an update to the factory engine management software (DME) to restrict the top rpm when the car is in lower gears.

Oil pump nut

A relatively new failure mode is occurring on some six-cylinder BMW engines, like the ones used in the E36 series. The oil pump gear attaches to the engine crank by a chain and a sprocket held on with a small reverse-thread nut. There have been many recent reports of this nut coming loose and falling off the sprocket. As a result, the sprocket becomes loose and can separate from the oil pump, leading to zero oil pressure in the engine. This can be catastrophic to the rod bearings, which are typically the first components to fail.

It hasn't been determined what causes this loosening of the nut. Some people I've spoken to seem to believe the odds of it falling off may be increased by aggressive driving and go so far as to suggest it happens when the chassis of the car is spun around on the pavement (like at the race track). Whatever the cause, this very serious problem seems to be affecting many more cars as they age and are driven harder and harder. The problem doesn't seem to correlate to mileage, as many lower-mileage cars appear to have been affected as well (cars with less than 50,000 miles on the odometer).

To solve this problem, remove the lower oil pan and secure the nut in place so that it will not fall out. The one fail-safe trick to secure the nut is to tack weld it to the sprocket. Once welded, that nut is not going to come off under almost any circumstance. Other people have run safety wire through the nut, applied Loctite, and deformed the inner edge of the nut with a punch. If you don't weld it, at least replace the nut with a new one (part number 11-41-1-735-137). Keep in mind that this nut is reverse threaded, so to remove it, you need to turn it clockwise.

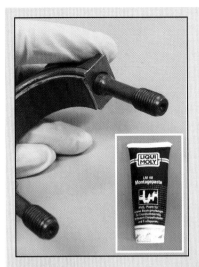

6 Wearing a powder-free latex glove, use your finger to gently spread a thin layer of assembly lube on the inside surface of each bearing. Don't gob it on, but spread it evenly across the bearing surface. I prefer to use LiquiMoly assembly lube, as it doesn't run as much as others I've tried.

7 Don't mix and match the rod end caps. There are numbers stamped on them to keep them properly oriented with respect to the rods. The edges with numbers on them should line up when bolting the rods together. The rods in your BMW engine may vary slightly from those shown here.

8 Here's a close-up shot of the underside of the piston (yellow arrow). The blue arrow shows the connecting rod. On the side of the rod there should be a paint mark indicating which size bearing fits the rod. The inset shows a worn-out rod bearing. This bearing was run in an engine that ran low on oil pressure. As a result, the crank and bearings rode on each other, resulting in significant wear as the crank and bearings experienced direct metal-to-metal contact. *Inset: Jacques Weingartz*

9 The dreaded oil pump nut (red arrow) is a reverse-thread nut known to back out unexpectedly, resulting in the sprocket falling off of the oil pump shaft. This will cause an immediate drop in oil pressure and quite possibly complete destruction of the engine. Tack weld the nut to the sprocket so it won't fall off. You can always use a Dremel tool later on if you need to replace the sprocket or the chain. The upper inset photo shows the splined shaft of the oil pump that the sprocket mates to. The lower inset photo shows the inside teeth of the sprocket. The nut may be loose and the car will run fine for thousands of miles, as the chain tends to keep the sprocket roughly in place on the oil pump shaft.

ENGINE

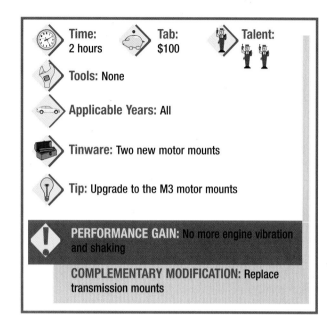

Time: 2 hours

Tab: $100

Talent: ♟♟

Tools: None

Applicable Years: All

Tinware: Two new motor mounts

Tip: Upgrade to the M3 motor mounts

! PERFORMANCE GAIN: No more engine vibration and shaking

COMPLEMENTARY MODIFICATION: Replace transmission mounts

The BMW 3 Series engine mounts commonly deteriorate with age. The rubber within the mounts becomes old and brittle, and fails to isolate the drivetrain from the rest of the chassis.

Old, worn-out motor and transmission mounts can cause shifting problems, because the drivetrain is no longer firmly held in its position. Two signs of this failure mode are: the gearshift knob jerks backward under hard acceleration, or selecting gears becomes difficult during cornering. Cracks in the rubber of the mounts are a visible indicator that the motor mounts need to be replaced. The rubber will deteriorate over the years and need to be replaced even if the car has relatively few miles on it.

On 1987 and older E30 cars, there is a major problem related to broken motor mounts. Because of a faulty design in the radiator hose layout, extreme flexing of the engine, due to worn out motor mounts, can cause the power steering pump pulley to cut through one of the radiator hoses. There have been many reports of this, particularly on the track while cornering, where the car ends up spinning out in a pool of its own coolant from the sliced hose. In 1988, BMW rerouted the hose and solved this problem, but for the 1987 and earlier cars, it's very important to make sure the motor mounts are in top condition.

There are many different mounts you can use in place of the stock mounts for your car. The stock E28 5 Series mounts from the larger 3.5 six-cylinder engines work as a good, beefy, OEM replacement. For my own cars, I prefer the E36 motor mounts. They are a bit beefier and stiffer than stock mounts and are direct bolt-on replacements. The E36 cabriolet motor mounts have an upper metal cap that helps to enforce and stabilize the motor mount (like the tranny mount enforcers discussed in Project 38). Although I haven't used these mounts in a non-cabriolet, I suspect they would add stiffness, particularly because of the cap. You can also purchase a set of solid performance mounts, although they are very expensive and may give too harsh a ride for a street car. Stick with OEM mounts if you drive on the street most of the time.

Replacing the mounts couldn't be easier. Jack up the front of the car, and support it on jack stands (see Project 1). Working on one side of the car at a time, remove the top and bottom bolts that hold in the motor mount. Then, using your floor jack, lift up that side of the engine. You can place your floor jack under the sump to lift the engine. When you have enough clearance, swap out the mount with a new one. Be sure to line up the small notch on the motor mount with the notch on the chassis (similar to the notch in the transmission mounts; see Project 38). Also be sure to install the motor mounts right-side up rather than upside-down (see Photo 2). Then, tighten the nuts on each motor mount, lower the car, and you're done!

1 The new motor mount shown on the left is for a 1984 E30 318i. The new motor mount on the right is the later-style one used on nearly all E36 cars. The mounts have two studs embedded in them. These studs fit through holes in the engine mount support and the lower front axle support bar.

The best products ...

A CLASSIC COMBINATION

2 On the left is a typical E36 motor mount (purple arrow). The orange arrow indicates the lower mount nut. The inset photo shows the top of the mount, inside the top side of the engine mount arm. On the right is a motor mount installed on a 318i (green arrow). The blue arrow indicates the lower motor mount stud and nut. The yellow arrow points to a metal heat shield that insulates the motor mount from the exhaust manifold. Don't forget to reinstall this plate when you replace the mount. The inset photo captures a worst-case scenario—a motor mount that broke and sheared off during an autocross event. *C M Isar*

PROJECT 26   http://www.101projects.com/BMW/26.htm
Installing a Performance Intake System

There's been a lot of talk on Internet chat boards lately about cold air intake (CAI) systems. Some manufacturers swear up and down that there's hidden horsepower in the intake system. Other so-called "experts" claim it's total bunk—a myth easily circulated in the age of the Internet. I believe that the truth lies somewhere in between. On some BMW models, a properly engineered cold air intake kit can effectively cool the intake charge entering into the cylinders. Why do you want this in the first place? Cooler air decreases the likelihood of engine detonation and, theoretically, since cooler air is denser air and denser air has more oxygen molecules to use in the combustion process, cooler air should correspond to an increase in horsepower.

First of all, the stock BMW E36 intake system is already a cold air intake system. It sucks air from the outside, and insulates this intake from the heat generated by the engine. But it doesn't work too well in the area of airflow restriction. The stock system is somewhat restrictive and makes the air work its way around in order to enter the engine. Aftermarket performance intakes serve two purposes: first, to better inject colder air directly into the intake system, and second, to reduce the restrictions inherent in the stock system.

Just how much horsepower can you expect to gain? It all depends on your particular BMW model and which kit you

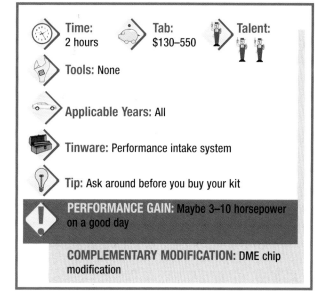

Time: 2 hours

Tab: $130–550

Talent: 👤👤

Tools: None

Applicable Years: All

Tinware: Performance intake system

Tip: Ask around before you buy your kit

PERFORMANCE GAIN: Maybe 3–10 horsepower on a good day

COMPLEMENTARY MODIFICATION: DME chip modification

use. A poorly designed kit used with an aftermarket air filter may actually create more restriction in the intake and cause a decrease in horsepower. In addition, an intake system that leaks because it was poorly installed will also decrease performance. I have seen dyno tests where an intake system has

1 The Dinan cold air intake assembly funnels cool air from an inlet hole in the spoiler and channels it up into the engine. It's an expensive, high-quality system manufactured out of carbon fiber and currently certified to meet California emissions requirements (CARB). In addition, Dinan is sanctioned by BMW, and the dealer can install this unit if you'd like (about 1.5 hours labor). If you have installed the European ellipsoid headlamps (see Project 94), you might have to modify the brackets in the kit to make it fit properly.

done nothing or has even reduced horsepower. Then again, I have also seen tests where significant gains of about 10 horsepower were recorded.

The bottom line is that a performance intake system is typically an expensive aftermarket add-on that may increase your horsepower only slightly. Some kits cost over $500, which translates into a very high dollar-per-horsepower ratio. Some other kits are less expensive and incorporate reusable aftermarket filters. While I'm not a huge fan of reusable filters, as they tend to filter fewer particles than the stock ones (see Project 3), there can be cost savings in the long run by eliminating the need to replace them so often.

Perhaps the only thing that most people agree on is that a performance intake system will give you a much better engine growl at higher revs. I'm personally a huge fan of growling noises, so this would be a plus for me if I were making the decision to install one of these systems. For those of you who prefer a quieter engine, you might be slightly annoyed at the new music your engine is playing.

There are two distinct types of systems available on the market. The short ram system is located in the top of the engine compartment and uses a heat shield to block heat from the engine. The filters are easy to change on this type of system. The other is typically referred to as a "cold air intake" and uses long tubes that connect the intake to inlets in the front bumper. The second type of system capitalizes on the air pressure available at the front bumper, although the filter is difficult to reach for changing or cleaning. Also, if your intake is low to the ground, you must be very careful not to go through deep puddles; otherwise, water may get sucked up into your engine intake (hydrolocking your engine).

There are literally hundreds of manufacturers of these products, from the large tuning companies to people selling homemade kits on eBay. If you install one of these on your car, do your research first and stick with a well-known manufacturer. I've heard good recommendations from people who run kits available from Dinan, East Coast Induction Systems, Cosmos Racing, and Advanced Flow Engineering.

SECTION THREE

Fuel Injection

Without a doubt, the fuel injection system can be one of the most finicky systems on your BMW to diagnose and troubleshoot. While one can write volumes on fuel injection systems, this section focuses on the Motronic engine management system, and identifying common problems and potential pitfalls of fuel injection. Read through these projects to identify and solve problems with your own fuel injection system.

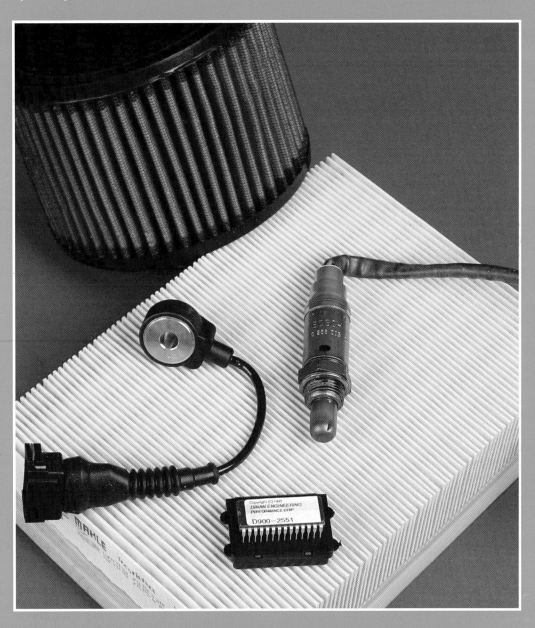

Replacing the Oxygen Sensor

FUEL INJECTION

The oxygen sensor (also called an O_2 sensor) is a critical component in modern fuel injection systems. A finely tuned fuel injection system with an oxygen sensor can maintain an air/fuel ratio within a tolerance of 0.02 percent. Keeping the engine at the stoichiometric level (14.67:1 air/fuel ratio) helps the engine generate the most power with the least amount of emissions.

The oxygen sensor is located in the engine's exhaust system and monitors the oxygen content of the exhaust gases. The amount of oxygen in the exhaust varies according to the air/fuel ratio of the fuel injection system. The oxygen sensor sends a small voltage signal to the electronic control unit (ECU) of the fuel injection system. The ECU makes constant adjustments in fuel delivery according to the oxygen sensor's signal in order to maintain the optimum air/fuel ratio.

There are a few signs that your oxygen sensor may be failing. It is difficult to diagnose problems with the sensor unless all other components in the fuel injection system have been checked and are determined to be operating correctly. Some symptoms of a failed oxygen sensor system include: irregular idle during warm-up, irregular idle with warm engine, engine not accelerating/engine backfiring, poor engine performance, high fuel consumption, weak driving performance, carbon monoxide (CO) concentration too high or too low at idle, and the check engine light illuminated.

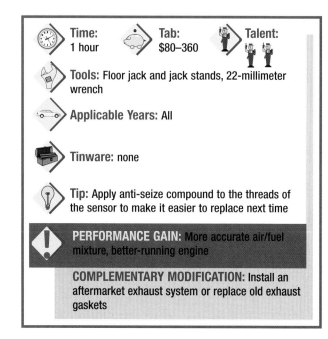

Time: 1 hour

Tab: $80–360

Talent: 👤👤

Tools: Floor jack and jack stands, 22-millimeter wrench

Applicable Years: All

Tinware: none

Tip: Apply anti-seize compound to the threads of the sensor to make it easier to replace next time

PERFORMANCE GAIN: More accurate air/fuel mixture, better-running engine

COMPLEMENTARY MODIFICATION: Install an aftermarket exhaust system or replace old exhaust gaskets

If the oxygen sensor is not working, the car will run very poorly and will output a lot of harmful emissions. On most BMWs, the engine's computer provides a warning signal that lights up the check engine lamp if the signal received by the computer is out of its normal range. (For more on fuel injection codes, see Projects 28 and 29.)

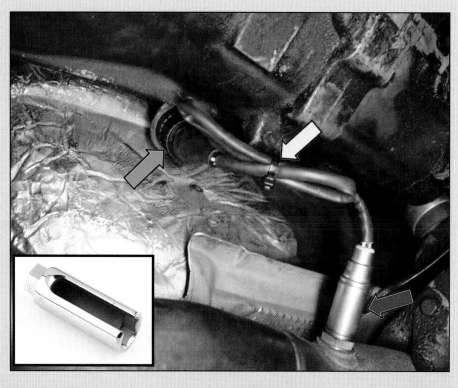

1 Shown here is a typical oxygen sensor for E36 six-cylinder cars (red arrow). The small black connector, shown by the green arrow, attaches the sensor to the wire harness and can easily be removed by twisting it counter-clockwise. I have often found that new O_2 sensors come with the correct plug, but the cables are way too long. If this is the case, secure the cable with a nylon zip-tie, as shown by the yellow arrow. Make sure the cable is not located anywhere near any exhaust components—you don't want to melt the cable to the O_2 sensor. The photo inset shows the special tool that is required to remove the sensor from hard-to-reach places (available from PelicanParts.com).

If you disconnect the oxygen sensor and ground it to the chassis, the ECU will think that the car is running lean (not enough fuel) and will try to richen the mixture. At the other extreme, if you disconnect the oxygen sensor and replace it with a small AA battery that supplies 1.5 volts, the ECU will think that the car is running rich and attempt to adjust the mixture to be leaner.

Needless to say, troubleshooting the complete fuel injection system is beyond this project's scope. If you suspect the oxygen sensor may be causing fuel injection problems, replace it. As a rule of thumb, I recommend that you replace the sensor every 30,000 miles. The oxygen sensor is located on the exhaust manifold and/or exhaust pipes that lead to the muffler. The location, and even the number of sensors, varies from model year to model year, but each sensor is typically easy to reach and remove.

First, jack up the car to access the sensor (see Project 1). Then, using a 22-millimeter wrench, remove the sensor from the exhaust pipe. On the E36 318, the sensor is much more difficult to reach; you may have to use a special deep

socket with a slit cut in the side to remove it (see photo). Rotate the electrical plug for the O_2 sensor counterclockwise to remove it. New O_2 sensors should have the same exact plug and be ready to attach to your car. On early E36 3 Series cars, the plug is located toward the right side of the rear of the transmission. From 1996 on, E36 models are equipped with multiple O_2 sensors. There's one right in front and another right behind each catalytic converter (a total of four on the six-cylinder cars). On the E30 cars, the O_2 sensor is located toward the engine on the lower part of the exhaust manifold. When you remove the O_2 sensor, you will probably find it coated with black soot. This is normal for an old, worn-out sensor.

Install the new sensor snug tight; or, if you have the proper slit tool and a torque wrench, tighten it to 55 N-m (40 ft-lbs). Carefully apply anti-seize compound to the threads of the plug before you install it, but make sure the anti-seize doesn't get into any of the slits on the head of the sensor. Check the sensor first, as new sensors sometimes come with anti-seize already on the threads.

PROJECT 28

http://www.101projects.com/BMW/28.htm

Reading BMW Fuel Injection Fault Codes

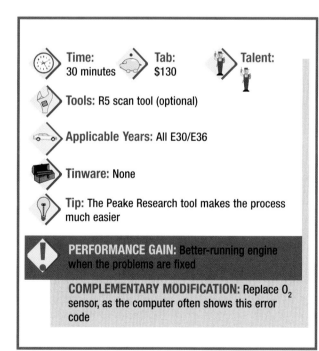

Time: 30 minutes

Tab: $130

Talent:

Tools: R5 scan tool (optional)

Applicable Years: All E30/E36

Tinware: None

Tip: The Peake Research tool makes the process much easier

PERFORMANCE GAIN: Better-running engine when the problems are fixed

COMPLEMENTARY MODIFICATION: Replace O_2 sensor, as the computer often shows this error code

All BMW models from 1984 on use the sophisticated Bosch Motronic engine management system. The Motronic system—also called the digital motor electronics, or DME—is hands down the best overall fuel injection system available, when you consider price and performance. A digital map—recorded in a removable chip within the main

fuel injection (DME) computer—controls ignition timing and fuel delivery. The computer takes input from a variety of sensors to monitor cylinder head temperature, altitude (ambient air pressure), crank angle, throttle position, exhaust gas oxygen (mixture), ambient air temperature, and mass airflow. The factory programs the DME chip with certain performance characteristics (mostly conservative) so the engine reacts well under a range of conditions.

As with any electronic device, components can fail, triggering problems with the system. The BMW Motronic system reacts to these failures and indicates them to the driver so they can be fixed. However, if one of the computer's sensors is not working properly, the computer may not successfully identify the current state of the engine and may not choose the appropriate fuel mixture or timing advance level. When this happens, the fuel mileage drops, engine performance suffers, emissions increase, and the car typically illuminates the check engine light.

In order to identify the faulty sensor and fix the problem, you will need to find out which error code is being triggered by the computer. Pre-1995 BMWs are equipped with what is known as "OBD-I" (onboard diagnostics level I). Starting in 1996, BMWs were equipped with a more advanced version called OBD-II (see Project 29), which was mandated by the U.S. government in order to standardize automotive repair and diagnostics.

The OBD system monitors and checks all of the fuel injection sensors and systems in the vehicle, and turns on the check engine lamp if it finds a problem or irregularity with one of them. The computer lodges a diagnostic trouble code (DTC) in the main computer until it is read and reset. Disconnecting the battery does not reset the codes—they need to be manually reset.

For BMWs equipped with OBD-I, you can read the codes using a system that is built into the car. For OBD-II-compliant cars (1996 and later), the codes can only be read using a scan tool (more on this later). To read codes for an OBD-I car, turn the ignition key on (but do not start the engine) and press the gas pedal to the floor five times within a period of five seconds. If timed right, the check engine lamp will light up for five seconds, then blink off, then blink on for 2.5 seconds, and then go off for another 2.5 seconds. After this, the computer will report all the trouble fault codes stored in your car.

The codes are given in short flashes of the check engine light, followed by short pauses. The codes are all four-digit numbers. For example, the trouble fault code for the battery voltage level is 1231. This would show up flashing as "flash, pause, flash, flash, pause, flash, flash, flash, pause, flash." Have a pen and paper handy, as the codes flash faster than you might think.

If there is more than one fault code stored, each code will be separated by a pause of 2.5 seconds. When there are no more codes, the computer will give the code "1000," which is one short flash, and the light will remain off. Then the check engine light will flash a half-second and then turn off.

1 BMW 3 Series cars have a large 20-pin connector (green arrow) that the R5 tool uses to interface with the DME computer. Once the ignition is turned on, simply plug the tool into the socket—it can only go into the socket one way. When you are done reading the codes, you can reset them using the R5 tool. Press the select button until you see "cE" on the display, and then press go. You can also use the tool to reset the oil service lamp and the inspection lamps that light up on some earlier BMWs.

To replay the codes, turn the ignition key off and on again, and repeat the procedure with the gas pedal (five times within five seconds).

The table below lists all the possible fault codes you can read by using this method:

Code	Error	Notes/Corrective Action
1000	End of output, no more fault codes	This code marks the end of the stream of error codes and tells you the computer has finished showing them to you.
1444	No more faults	This code confirms that all faults have been fixed. Required to erase the computer's memory.
1211	DME Motronic computer fault	Rarely seen, this code indicates a problem with the DME computer. Most problems result in a dead computer that cannot give out codes. If the code does appear, start and rerun the test for about one minute. If the code reappears, chances are you need to replace the DME computer.
1215	Mass airflow sensor fault	The mass airflow sensor measures the amount of air that is drawn into the engine. (Note: A big hole in one of your fuel injection intake boots may cause the car to stall and generate this code.)
1216	Throttle position switch fault	Later-model Motronic systems use a potentiometer (pot) to measure throttle position and adjust fuel levels appropriately. If the pot is not giving off the proper values, it will produce this code.
1218	DME computer output, group one	These two codes can be generated when there is a ground fault short circuit from B+ at one of the two DME output amplifier stages. This code is not
1219	DME computer output, group two	typically seen alone and is usually generated with a host of other codes. Possible problems may be O_2 sensor heater relay, fuel evap system problem, EKP relay, ignition coil problem, faulty idle speed actuator, etc. If you get this code, disconnect the DME and let it sit for 15 minutes, then recheck the codes. If it persists and no other problems are found, then it is probably an internal DME problem. If the code goes away, ignore it and call it an intermittent error.

Code	Description	Details
1221	Oxygen sensor (primary)	The O_2 sensor measures the amount of oxygen in the exhaust. This code is generated if the sensor is unplugged or broken. Sensor values are read when the engine is warmer than 70°C and should be within 0.02 and 0.85 volts. Negative values indicate the sensor needs to be replaced, while slow fluctuation indicates the sensor is clogged with soot. Cars with catalytic converters that have been removed may push this code.
1212	Oxygen sensor(secondary)	
1222	Oxygen sensor lean/rich detect (primary)	If the signal from the O_2 sensor indicates a very lean or very rich mixture for more than 10 seconds, the computer generates this code. It could mean a faulty O_2 sensor or a problem with another component.
1213	Oxygen sensor lean/rich detect (secondary)	
1223	Coolant temperature sensor	Measures the temperature of the coolant inside the engine block. Used to determine if the engine is warm or cold. Check the wiring and the expected resistance value of the sensor.
1224	Intake air temperature sensor	Measures the temperature of air entering the engine's fuel injection system and adjusts the mixture accordingly. Colder air is denser than warmer air and needs to be compensated for.
1225	Knock sensor number 1	The knock sensor detects preignition that can damage the engine. If the knock sensor is triggered, it will back off the timing of the car, reducing the pinging. A fault is generated if there is an open circuit, a ground fault, or multiple signals that don't correspond to proper engine operation.
1226	Knock sensor number 2	
1231	Battery voltage/DME relay monitor	Monitors the condition of the battery and charging system, and produces a fault if a component goes out of specification or fails.
1232	Throttle idle position switch	On older Motronic systems, this switch was used along with the wide-open position switch as a primitive throttle position switch.
1233	Throttle wide-open switch	See above.
1234	Speedometer A signal	This code is generated when the engine is under load, over 2,500 rpm, and no discernable speedometer signal can be detected for more than 10 seconds. Check the wiring harness and instrument console.
1237	A/C compressor cutoff	The compressor is automatically turned off when accelerating from low speed under full throttle. This code indicates a fault in the cut-out circuit or its wiring.
1241	Mass airflow sensor	Codes 1241 and 2241 can be incorrectly generated on 1992 and later models. The actual fault is a malfunctioning idle air valve and the need for an updated EPROM. (See BMW bulletins for more details.)
1242	A/C compressor signal	This code is generated if there is a ground fault (short circuit) or if the system detects that the compressor unit is disconnected.
1243	Crankshaft position sensor	This code is triggered when the crank angle sensor is disconnected or a signal is generated that is not accurate when compared to the other engine sensors.
1244	Camshaft position sensor	Displayed when the signal from the camshaft pulse generator is out of spec or absent. May indicate a problem with the injector side of the DME output stage.
1245	AEGS intervention, electronic transmission	Many BMWs are equipped with electronic transmissions. If the transmission encounters a major problem, it will generate an emergency message, and your on-board computer should show "transmission emergency program." Ignition timing will retard when this program runs.
1247	Ignition secondary monitor	
1251	Fuel injector number 1 (single or group)	Check the injector or injector group for proper wire harness connectivity. Also check the injectors for a clear, wide stream pattern. Code 1283 (fuel injector output stage) may also be triggered in conjunction with this code.
1252	Fuel injector number 2 (single or group)	
1253	Fuel injector number 3	
1254	Fuel injector number 4	
1255	Fuel injector number 5	
1256	Fuel injector number 6	
1261	Fuel pump relay control	This code is generated when there is a break or ground fault in the circuitry associated with the DME fuel pump relay. Check pin number 3 of the DME or the output stage in the DME (DME version M1.3 only).

1262	Idle speed control	This shows up if the idle speed actuator shows a ground fault, or if the car stalls from an idle above 600 rpm.
1263	Fuel tank evaporative system (EVAP)	The fuel tank evaporative system has a purge control valve that generates this code if there is a short circuit or open connection (DME version M1.3 only).
1264	Oxygen sensor heating element	This code is triggered if there is an open circuit or a short within the oxygen heating element circuit. Check the O_2 heating element relay and the air pump relay. Also indicates a potentially faulty O_2 sensor.
1265	Check engine lamp	If the lamp in the dashboard burns out or shorts to ground, then this code is generated.
1266	VANOS system	Check the wiring or the relay associated with the VANOS system (variable camshaft adjustment).
1267	Air pump relay control	Check the air pump relay and wiring (where applicable).
1271	Ignition coil number 1	An open circuit or ground fault in the ignition wiring has occurred with an ignition coil. Place a timing light on the ignition wires and check for a signal. Also check the wires for faults, and check the spark plugs too.
1271	Ignition coil number 2	
1271	Ignition coil number 3	
1271	Ignition coil number 4	
1271	Ignition coil number 5	
1271	Ignition coil number 6	
1281	DME memory unit supply	This indicates a fault with the internal memory of the DME computer, sometimes caused by low battery voltage. Delete the codes and disconnect the DME for 15 minutes. Reconnect, let the car idle for five minutes, then drive over 30 miles per hour for more than five minutes. Recheck. If the code occurs again, the DME is faulty and should be replaced.
1282	Fault code memory	This code occurs when the DME generates a set of conflicting codes. Disconnect the DME for 15 minutes, reconnect, then simulate a fault code, like unplugging the airflow sensor or idle actuator. If the code reoccurs, you will need to replace the DME.
1283	Fuel injector output stage	This code is generated when there is a short circuit or open connection between the wiring from the DME to an injector or injector stage.
1284	Knock control test pulse	The ECU periodically checks the knock sensor circuitry by sending a test pulse through the system. This code indicates that a test was performed, but no pulse was registered. Check the wiring and knock sensors.

When you have finished reading the codes, reset the computer and clear out the codes. Make sure that the last code (1000) has occurred, and then press down on the gas pedal for more than 10 seconds to clear the memory of the DME. Repeat the fault code reading process, and the computer should generate code "1444," which means that there are no faults stored.

Wire harnesses are a major source of fault codes. As cars get older, their wiring harnesses have a habit of becoming what is known as "work hardened." The wires becomes brittle and often break inside their plastic sheaths. Only by testing the continuity of the wires end-to-end will you be able to determine whether the wire is broken or not.

For cars manufactured starting in 1996, BMW uses the industry standard OBD-II method of monitoring the fuel injection system. OBD-II cars cannot be checked using the gas pedal method previously described but instead must be checked using a code scanner or an ODB-II interface tool

(see Project 29). I like to use the Peake Research R5/FCX fault code tool, available from a variety of sources including PelicanParts.com. This tool is compatible with most BMWs built from 1987 to 2000. It displays all the engine fault codes and also has the ability to reset the oil service lamp. This tool works with both OBD-I and OBD-II cars. I like to use it on pre-1996 cars, as it is much easier to read the codes with this tool than it is using the gas pedal method.

With the tool plugged in (see photo), it will spin the LED lights for a few moments and then prompt you with a menu. Hit the select button on the tool until you read the letters "Fc," which stands for fault codes. Click go on the tool, and it will read the codes one by one from the computer. Note that the codes that show up on the tool are unique to this tool. You need a copy of the tool's operating manual in order to decode the proper codes for your car. For a list of troubleshooting tips and info on the tool, please see the 101Projects.com website.

Monitoring OBD-II Systems

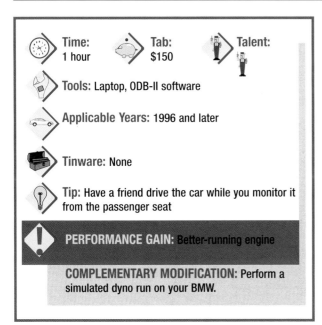

Time: 1 hour

Tab: $150

Talent:

Tools: Laptop, ODB-II software

Applicable Years: 1996 and later

Tinware: None

Tip: Have a friend drive the car while you monitor it from the passenger seat

PERFORMANCE GAIN: Better-running engine

COMPLEMENTARY MODIFICATION: Perform a simulated dyno run on your BMW.

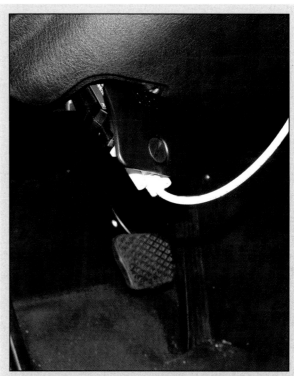

The OBD-II port is located near the driver's footwell, on the lower left side. Flip open the cover, pull off the plastic connector cover, and plug in the adapter. Run the cable over the steering wheel and plug it into your laptop, which can rest on the passenger's seat.

In 1996, automotive manufacturers began equipping all new cars with the second generation of the federally mandated onboard emissions diagnostic system called OBD-II. An earlier version, called OBD-I, is implemented on Bosch Motronic-equipped BMWs through 1995 but is not as advanced or easy to tap into as OBD-II. (For more information on fuel injection fault codes of the OBD-I system, see Project 28.) The OBD-II system was developed primarily to combat emissions problems by quickly and easily identifying failed components of the fuel injection system.

In the past, it was prohibitively expensive to purchase the equipment required to read and process information from the OBD-II interface. However, scanning tools and software have come down significantly in price, enabling just about any home mechanic to read, record, and monitor the entire fuel injection system. There are many scanner tools available today, and quite a few allow you to monitor the OBD-II interface on a laptop computer or even a PocketPC. These scan tools save time and money by allowing you to diagnose potential problems without repeatedly taking your car in to a mechanic or dealer. I have heard people gripe about how today's modern cars have become so complex that the average do-it-yourself mechanic can't figure out what's wrong with the car. I disagree. OBD-II cars are much easier to diagnose and repair than earlier models, primarily because the computer will tell you exactly what is wrong, taking the guesswork out of complicated troubleshooting.

For my own garage, I chose the laptop-based software from AutoEnginuity, available from a variety of sources, including PelicanParts.com. The package comes complete with an OBD-II adapter, a serial cable, and software to install on a Windows-equipped laptop computer. Installation and setup are as simple as plugging a cable into your BMW's OBD-II port.

In addition to the full capabilities of the OBD-II scanning software, the AutoEnginuity package includes a tool call SpeedTracer. This utility allows me to estimate various performance characteristics of my BMW by monitoring the sensor output from the OBD-II computer. In real time, the software acquires the engine's rpm, the car's speed in miles per hour, and the ambient temperature. Mixing that with known characteristics of the car from preconfigured profiles stored within the software, the computer can accurately estimate performance characteristics like horsepower and torque. Using the real-time monitors, the software can measure quarter-mile times and speeds, as well as 0–60 mile-per-hour performance. All stock OBD-II-compliant BMW cars are already profiled in the software. In addition, you can enter compensation variables into the software (e.g., temperature, humidity, altitude) to help correct the horsepower

FUEL INJECTION

99

FUEL INJECTION

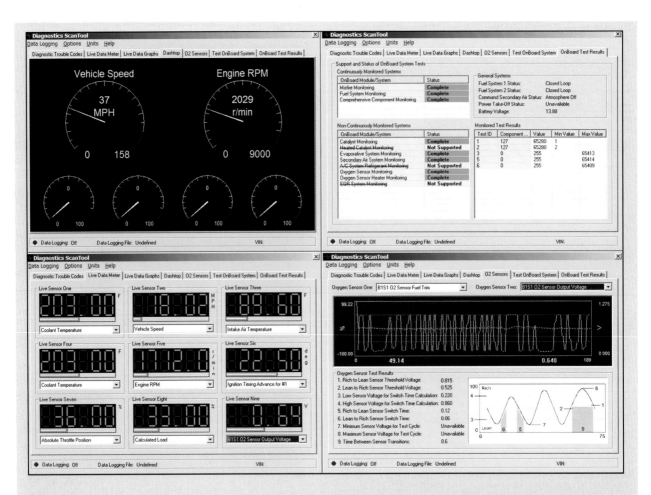

2 The AutoEnginuity software has several screens that allow you to monitor the system in real time. The lower-left screenshot shows the live data screen, which can be customized to show any one of the OBD-II sensors. You can output oxygen sensor voltages, engine rpm, coolant temperature, ignition timing advance, intake air temperature, and several other sensor values. The software allows you to capture and freeze the data, or log it to your local hard drive. On the upper left is the Dashtop screen, which allows you to monitor various sensors in analog format. This is useful when the car is in motion and you want to quickly glance at the "gauges" to get an idea what their values are. This screen functions much like the sensor screen with the digital readouts. There is a separate screen specifically tailored to monitor the oxygen sensors (lower right). The oxygen sensor (O2 sensor) is one of the best indicators of your engine's health and performance. The oxygen sensor changes its value based upon the amount of oxygen present in the exhaust. This percentage directly relates to the air/fuel mixture fed into the engine's intake manifold. If the mixture is too rich or too lean, the engine will not generate an ideal fuel burn, resulting in increased emissions and decreased power. The onboard test results screen (upper right) shows the results from several diagnostic evaluations of various system modules. The system monitors the engine in real time for misfires, fuel compensation, and comprehensive component monitoring. The results of the tests are shown on the right.

results, thereby ensuring accurate and repeatable results. Even if you have modified your BMW, you can change the default values specifically to fit your car.

SpeedTracer is definitely a fun tool to play around with. However, like the big roller dynos (see Project 101), the horsepower figures are somewhat subjective. Driving ability and habits may slightly skew results in the software. As with the traditional dyno, SpeedTracer is best viewed as a comparison and tuning tool. Although not as precise as a real

dyno, you can test your car indefinitely and use the results to determine if you're gaining any horsepower from minor modifications and tweaks. As with the big dyno, the results are often dependent on environmental factors, so you should only compare numbers from same-day runs. Results are also highly dependent on the characteristics of your driving, including the speed at which you shift through the gears. Another downside, of course, is that you need a laptop computer to make the whole system work.

Time: 2 hours

Tab: $20–600

Talent: 👨👨👨

Tools: 8-millimeter or 9-millimeter crescent wrench

Applicable Years: All

Tinware: Injector O-rings, new injectors, white lithium grease

Tip: Be extra careful of the plastic injector tips

PERFORMANCE GAIN: Cleaner, better-running fuel injection system

COMPLEMENTARY MODIFICATION: Replace your fuel filter

There are several myths and misconceptions regarding fuel injectors. The first one is that bigger injectors will give you more power. This statement is completely false. It's the equivalent of saying that adding more lights to your already-bright living room will make you see better.

The fuel injectors in your BMW are more than adequate for stock engines and supply abundant fuel for maximum power and open throttle. For your engine to achieve maximum power, it must have an air/fuel ratio maintained within a certain range. Adding more fuel to the mixture makes it richer but won't necessarily give you any more power. In fact, it is often the opposite—a richer mixture will foul plugs and won't ignite as easily. The goal of any good fuel injection system (whether carburetors or electronic fuel injection) is to maintain the ideal air/fuel ratio (typically about 14.67:1) for ideal combustion and power. Adding higher flow, or larger injectors, disrupts the balance of the engine, makes the engine's fuel management system run richer, and generally decreases power from ideal levels. Just as adding more high-powered lights to your living room won't help you see better if it was adequately lit to begin with, you'll actually see worse, because it will be too bright for your eyes.

So are there exceptions to the rule? Yes, a few. Major changes in the displacement or flow of the engine can cause the engine to run lean. Examples would include increasing the displacement of the engine, changing the camshafts, or adding a turbocharger or supercharger. The supercharger compresses the air/fuel mixture and pushes this denser mixture into the same size combustion chamber. Therefore, the engine should have more fuel injected into the combustion chamber when compressed with a supercharger than is injected in a normally aspirated engine. Owners who add a supercharger or turbo to their car need to be especially concerned about keeping the engine's mixture correct. These cars

FUEL INJECTION

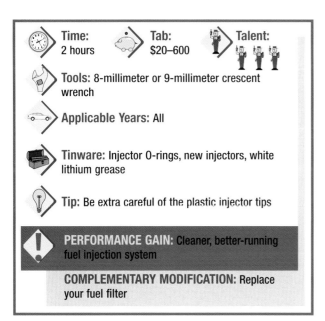

1 Remove all six connector clips (yellow arrow) prior to removing the wire harness box (E36 engine bay shown). Using a pair of needle-nose pliers, reach in and disconnect the small retaining wires that hold the connectors onto the ends of the injectors. Be careful not to drop these, as they can fall into the recesses of the engine and are very difficult to fish out. In most cases, you only need to undo one side of the metal clips, and the side will pop out when you lift up on the wire harness box. Start with the injector closest to the front of the car, and work toward number 6, which is located at the rear.

tend to run too lean, which can lead to destructive problems like detonation or overheating (see Project 22).

In general, you should not upgrade or replace your injectors with larger ones unless you have made a significant engine modification that would cause the engine to run lean. If you replace injectors, use injectors that have stock flow rates for your engine. Don't buy injectors that have higher flow rates thinking that it will give you more power—it won't.

So why would you want to replace your injectors, then? As engines age, their injectors tend to fail and leak. If you pull fault codes out of the computer (see Project 28), it may tell you there is a faulty or leaking fuel injector. You may also find that you can see or smell a particular injector leaking. If this is the case, you may not have to replace the entire injector, but rather only its O-rings.

E30 and E36 cars have a similar fuel injector setup, so the replacement process is much the same for all models. The first step is to prep the car by pulling out the fuse for the fuel pump (see Project 4), and then trying to start the car. The car will turn over and then die. Do this about ten times, as it will help drain excess fuel out of your system. Then let the car has cool down, since you don't want to work with gasoline when the car is hot. **Always** have a fire extinguisher handy, as there will be some fuel spillage—it's nearly impossible to prevent. Also, wear chemical-resistant gloves if you don't want to get gasoline on your hands. Have plenty of paper towels or rags on hand to help clean up. Perform this project in a clear, open, and well-ventilated space; it may not hurt to have a helper around in case any problems arise.

Begin by removing the top two plastic covers from the engine (E36 owners, see Project 8). Pop off the long, thin plastic cover in the center that covers the wire harness for the spark plugs and the injectors, and remove the two small bolts that fasten this wire harness box to the top of the intake manifold (E36). At this point, you will need to remove the connectors from each of the fuel injectors (see Photo 1). With these clips disconnected, remove the wire harness bar from the tops of the injectors and move it out of the way. Now you should have much better access to the injectors, as it's time to remove them from the fuel rail. The fuel rail is the long, thin metal bar that runs along the top of the injectors and it is held onto the manifold with a few bolts (see Photo 2).

You should be able to pull off the fuel rail from the top of the injectors. Use caution, however—although the fuel rail is made out of metal, it easily bends and/or breaks. Carefully work your way from the front to back of the car, slowly lifting the rail. You'll notice the injectors have big, fat O-rings that press into the bores in the fuel rail, and you have to battle these O-rings as you pull the rail up and out.

Once you've lifted out the fuel rail (expect some fuel spillage), you should be able to push it aside enough to reach the injectors. If you don't have access or can't move the fuel rail, you may have to loosen some connections on either side (the rail has rubber fuel lines attached with hose clamps) to help a bit. Fortunately, for my E36 325is, I did not have to remove or loosen these connections.

With the injectors no longer attached to the fuel rail, you can pull them out of the manifold. They are held in place using the same big O-rings at the tips of the injectors. Pull straight up on each injector, and it should come out of the manifold. You may have to tug a little bit to get it out, but don't use excessive force. Sometimes repeated wiggling helps. Be careful of the plastic injector tips—they are not sold separately from the $80 injectors. Do not damage them.

With the injectors out of the manifold, you can take them to a fuel injection specialist shop to be cleaned and calibrated. Over time, injectors become dirty and may not distribute their flow evenly across all cylinders. It costs about $150 for six injectors to be cleaned, tested, and calibrated; new injectors cost anywhere from $80–120 apiece, making their replacement a somewhat pricey endeavor.

There are three types of injector leaks. First, injectors can leak fuel into the manifold from the nozzle. Second, they can leak fuel into the engine compartment from the fuel rail. Third, they can leak air (vacuum leak) from the manifold.

The first leak cannot be fixed at home. You will need to have the injector repaired or replaced. Of these two options, I recommend replacement, as your injector may already be fairly old.

The second fuel rail leak is easy to contend with. Simply replace the old, fat O-ring that seals the injector to the fuel rail. This should be done any time the injectors are out of the car.

The third leakage area is a bit of a "Catch-22." To replace the lower O-ring, the tip of the injector needs to be removed from the injector. While this may seem easy, and indeed it is, it is just as easy to damage the tip in the process. As of this writing, I have not found a replacement source for the tips other than purchasing a new injector ($80–120), so the risk remains somewhat high. The method I used to replace one of the seals in the tip works well, but it can (and did) slightly ding and damage the fragile, green plastic injector tip (see Photo 5).

Because of the danger in damaging the injector tip, I do not recommend replacing the O-ring behind the tip unless you've definitely had a manifold leak. Instead, put some sealant or silicone around the edge of the seal. It's just too easy to damage the fragile green tip.

If you are committed to replacing the injectors or O-rings, place a tiny dab of white lithium grease on the edges that press into the fuel rail and manifold. This will aid in the insertion of the injector and the reassembly of the fuel rail. It will also prevent the O-ring from pinching and will guard against tiny leaks as well.

Installation is simply the reverse of removal. In fact, you may find it easier to insert the injectors into the manifold first, if you have enough room. Double-check to make sure that the O-rings are securely seated when you reattach the fuel rail. Don't attach the two top plastic covers just yet—leave them off until you've checked for fuel leaks. Then, when you are ready to fire up the car, have an assistant on hand to help you spot any leaks in the injectors or fuel lines. If all checks out okay, button up the top two covers (E36) and you're done!

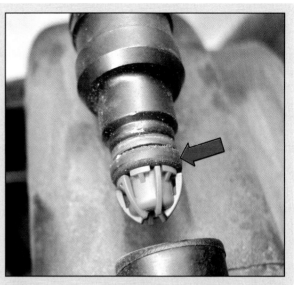

2 Release the fuel rail from the tops of the injectors by removing the small, black, square retaining clips that fasten and secure the injectors to the fuel rail. Use a pair of needle-nose pliers to pull this clip off (blue arrow). It pulls off from the side (it's C-shaped) and should slide off with a reasonable amount of force. Remove all six—this will allow you to remove and detach the fuel rail from the tops of the injectors. When the clips have been removed, remove the two bolts that attach the fuel rail to the manifold. Perform this task with the rail still installed on the engine (it is shown off the engine in this photo for clarity).

3 Depending on the characteristics of your car, it may be easier to remove the injectors from the manifold first. As you pull up on the fuel rail, some may stick in the manifold, or some may come out with the fuel rail—it depends upon a variety of factors. It doesn't really matter on E36 cars, but E30 cars need to have the injectors detached from the fuel rail first. The same O-ring that holds the injector into the fuel rail (red arrow) also holds the injector into the manifold.

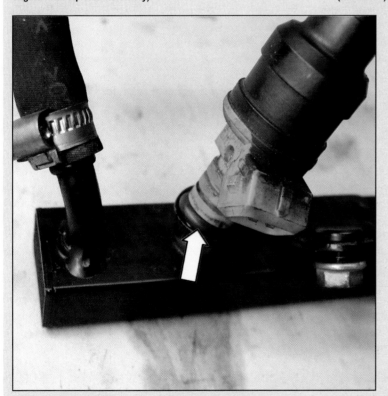

4 With the connector out of the way, pull the injector out of the fuel rail. The big O-ring will offer quite a bit of resistance (yellow arrow). When pulling up on the fuel rail, apply your force locally to the injector—you don't want to accidentally bend or damage the fuel rail by pulling up on the end.

5 To remove the nozzle O-ring, first cut it off with a razor blade. Be careful not to damage the green plastic tip when you cut through the O-ring. Remove the O-ring with a pick, again taking care with the tip. To get the new O-ring on, you will need to remove the tip. The best method I have found to remove the tip is to get a small 8- or 9-millimeter crescent wrench and apply uniform pressure against the tip. However, this will still mar some of the plastic on the tip. Pressing up with the wrench, using a surprising amount of force, will make the tip pop off of the injector. At this point, you can attach the new O-ring and snap the tip back on.

Replacing the Fuel Pump/Fuel Level Sender

FUEL INJECTION

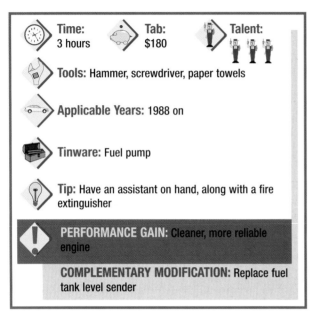

Time: 3 hours

Tab: $180

Talent: 🔧🔧🔧

Tools: Hammer, screwdriver, paper towels

Applicable Years: 1988 on

Tinware: Fuel pump

Tip: Have an assistant on hand, along with a fire extinguisher

PERFORMANCE GAIN: Cleaner, more reliable engine

COMPLEMENTARY MODIFICATION: Replace fuel tank level sender

Some common fuel injection problems can be traced back to a faulty or nonoperational fuel pump. If the pump is noisy and loud, or the fuel pressure in the engine compartment is lower than what is needed for proper fuel injection operation, it's probably time to replace the fuel pump. The fuel pump is not as simple as one might think. The fuel runs through the pump and acts as a coolant and lubricant for the entire assembly. Therefore, if you let the car run out of gas, make sure that you turn off the pump immediately or you might damage the internal components of the pump. There's nothing worse than having a broken or faulty pump leave you stranded on the side of the road.

Typical fuel pump problems can sometimes be headed off in advance. If the pump is noisy or making loud clicking noises, chances are that the bearings inside are worn and the pump should be replaced. If the pump continues to make noise even after the ignition is shut off, internal check valves in the pump may be showing signs of failure. The pump could seize up at some time, or the pressure to the fuel injection system could drop. Either way, the car will not perform at its peak. In another form of failure, the pump motor may get stuck and then finally kick in after turning the ignition on and off a couple of times. This could be a sign that you're living on borrowed time and should replace the pump immediately. Just to be sure, check the electrical connections to the pump before replacement to verify it's the pump and not an electrical problem.

Some early E30 cars have a standard fuel pump underneath the car. For these E30 owners replacement of the fuel pump is quite similar to replacement of the fuel filter (see

Project 4). This text, however, will focus on the fuel pump and tank sender replacement for 1988-and-later models.

First, prep the car by removing as much gasoline from the car as possible. Get a long piece of fuel hose and place it down the fuel filler hole. Then hook up a small battery-operated carburetor fuel pump, and pump the gasoline from one car to another. Or, you could buy a gasoline hand pump from most auto parts stores. Either way you go about it, try to remove every drop of gas from the tank.

Another essential step: Always disconnect the battery before you begin working near the tank. You don't want any accidental sparks from electrical connections. Some additional warnings:

- Always have a fire extinguisher handy in case an emergency arises.
- Gasoline is highly flammable. When working around fuel and fuel line connections, don't disconnect any wires or electrical connections that may cause electrical sparks.
- Always remove the gas cap to relieve any pressure in the tank prior to working on the fuel system.
- Do not use a home office or work lamp near fuel or fuel tanks. If you need more light, use a cool fluorescent lamp, and keep it far away from the pump.
- Gasoline vapors are strong, harmful, and toxic. They can make you drowsy and cloud your judgment. Therefore, always work in a well-ventilated area with plenty of fresh air blowing through.
- Always disconnect the battery prior to working on the fuel system. Leave it disconnected for at least 30 minutes before you begin in order to allow any residual electrical charge in components to dissipate.
- Keep plenty of paper towels on hand, and wear rubber gloves to prevent any spilled gasoline from coming in contact with your hands or eyes.
- Be well grounded. Don't do anything that will create static electricity. Keep all cell phones and pagers a safe distance away.

Next, remove the back seat from your car. It's simply clipped in place. Move both the driver and passenger seat all the way forward, crawl in the back of the car, and tug up on the rear seat from the bottom edge. It should pop up with minimal force. BMW designed the car intelligently, so the fuel tank senders and the fuel pump are very easy to get to. (On other makes, you may need to drop the fuel tank to do the replacement.)

With the back seat removed, you will see sound-deadening material with two flaps, one on the right side and one on the left. The fuel pump is located on the right side of the car, so lift up the right-side flap. You will see a circular cover with some wires emerging from it. Remove this cover and the thin

104

1 In this photo, the back seat has been removed to get down to the fuel pump. On the left, you see the sound-deadening material with the access flap (yellow arrow). In the middle frame, you see the access cover with the fuel pump wires exiting out the top. On the right is the pump with the hoses and electrical connections removed. Tie the old hoses out of the way while you are working on the pump.

2 This is what the pump looks like when you remove it from the tank. Try to wear gloves when handling the pump. The yellow arrow points to the large O-ring that seals the fuel pump with the top of the tank. The red arrow shows the screen on the bottom of the tank; it was originally white.

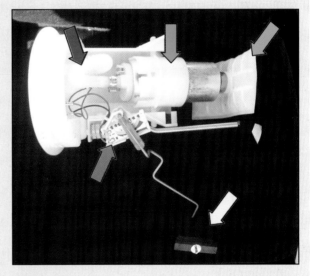

3 This photo shows the brand-new fuel pump assembly. The yellow arrow points to the fuel tank level sender float. The purple arrow shows the electrical pickup for the sending unit. The blue arrow indicates the fuel pickup screen. The red arrow shows a flexible hose that fuel pumps through to get to the top of the pump, and the green arrow points to the fuel pump motor itself.

4 Mate the new large O-ring to the outside of the pump prior to installation. You will have to negotiate the pump into the hole in the tank, and the fuel level sending float tends to get in the way. When you mate the pump with the tank, make sure the O-ring firmly and securely seals the pump to the tank. Otherwise, you may end up with a fuel smell in your car in the future.

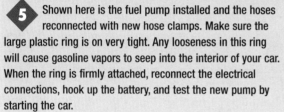

5 Shown here is the fuel pump installed and the hoses reconnected with new hose clamps. Make sure the large plastic ring is on very tight. Any looseness in this ring will cause gasoline vapors to seep into the interior of your car. When the ring is firmly attached, reconnect the electrical connections, hook up the battery, and test the new pump by starting the car.

6 This photo shows an undercarriage fuel pump on a 1984 E30 318i. When replacing these types of pumps, be sure to get the fuel level in the tank as low as possible. This will reduce the pressure in the fuel line leading to the pump. Be prepared to clamp the line, and also have paper towels and a bucket handy to catch any fuel that may spill out of the pump or fuel line.

foam seal underneath it. Beneath that, you'll see the top of the fuel pump.

Carefully disconnect the two electrical connectors that mate with the pump. Then, while wearing protective gloves, disconnect the fuel lines that feed into the top of the pump. There will be some gas spillage here, so have paper towels on hand. Plug the lines quickly with a bolt or a pen, and use a hose clamp to prevent further leaks.

The pump is held in place by a big circular disc with risers on it. BMW makes a special tool to remove and tighten this black plastic ring. However, using a large flathead screwdriver and a small hammer, you can easily tap the plastic ring loose. Carefully remove the ring from the top of the pump.

Now comes the fun part. Make sure you are fully prepared with a well-ventilated garage, plenty of paper towels, and those trusty rubber gloves. Ready? Pull up on the pump, and the entire assembly should come right out of the tank. There is a big, thick O-ring that seals the pump to the tank. Be careful—it will probably fall to the bottom of the pump. Don't let it fall into the tank, or you'll have to somehow fish it out later on. Notice in Photo 2 how brown the bottom filter of the pump looks? Well, the new pump's screen is completely white.

You now have an open tank of gas in your back seat. Needless to say, you don't want to leave the car like this for too long. However, you also don't want to work too quickly, as you don't want to make any big mistakes.

You can reuse the old sealing O-ring, but I usually opt for a new one. If you do use the old one and it doesn't seal well, you will be plagued with a fuel smell in the interior of your car from this point on.

Insertion of the pump into the tank is the reverse of removal. Make sure the big O-ring is properly sealed around the outside of the pump and that it will seal with the opening of the tank. The new pump needs to sit snuggly on the top of the tank. To safely seal it, spin on the large circular ring, and tap it with a hammer or screwdriver to tighten it. For this project I tightened mine about as far as I could go without feeling that I'd break the ring. Next, reconnect the fuel hoses using new hose clamps.

Once all fumes have subsided, plug in the new fuel pump and reconnect the battery. Then crank the car over and see if it starts. If the car starts and runs for any length of time, the pump is working fine. Replace the top cover and foam seal. Finally, reinstall the back seat by pushing it down into its home position.

Replacing the fuel tank level sending unit follows a very similar process. On late-model E30 and E36 BMWs, there are two level sending units—one on the left side, and one on the right side that is integrated into the fuel pump. The procedure for the replacement of the fuel sender on the left side is identical to the procedure for replacement of the fuel pump on the right side.

Installing a Performance Chip

Time:
2 hours

Tab:
$300

Talent: ♦♦

Tools: Torx T-20 driver

Applicable Years: All

Tinware: Performance chip

Tip: Properly ground yourself before opening the DME unit

PERFORMANCE GAIN: More horsepower, better throttle response

COMPLEMENTARY MODIFICATION: DME compartment rain gutter upgrade (Project 87)

1 The DME computer is located on the left side of the car, inside the engine compartment. Disconnect the harness, and it should pull out of the compartment (inset). Check the compartment while you're in here—it's common for the windshield water channels to clog up and for water to overflow and leak into this compartment and fry the DME computer (see Project 87).

In terms of price and performance, the Motronic system (also called the "digital motor electronics," or DME) is hands down the best overall fuel injection system you can use. A digital map—recorded in a removable chip within the main fuel injection (DME) computer—controls ignition timing and fuel delivery. The computer takes input from a variety of sensors to monitor cylinder head temperature, altitude (ambient air pressure), crank angle, throttle position, exhaust gas oxygen (mixture), ambient air temperature, and mass airflow. The factory programs the DME chip with certain performance characteristics (mostly conservative) so the engine will react well under varying conditions. Major changes to the engine (including new camshafts) require an updated chip map to take full advantage of the modifications.

Each system is matched directly to a specific engine configuration. Because of the proprietary nature of the Motronic system, there aren't a whole lot of changes you can effectively perform without updating the DME chip. In fact, major changes to the engine (different camshafts, increased displacement) will not work well with the stock Motronic system, because the computer chip is designed to deliver the proper amount of fuel and spark only for a particular stock engine. Therefore, in order to gain the maximum benefit from engine modifications, you will need to either upgrade your DME chip or install a programmable aftermarket engine management system.

The Motronic system is generally very reliable, with the occasional exception of its sensors, which may transmit faulty data back to the DME computer. Another odd failure point appears to be the DME relay. Corroded contacts cause this

mission-critical part to fail somewhat intermittently. Many people claim their cars run much better right after they have replaced the DME relay. While I don't have empirical data to back this up, I know scores of people who replace their DME relays once every two years. I do recommend that you carry a spare one (see Project 87), because a failure could leave you stranded on the side of the road.

If you run a stock engine with Motronic injection, the best upgrade you can perform is the installation of an aftermarket DME chip (for models through 1995). As noted, the factory programmed the original chip to compensate for a wide variety of driving characteristics. These days, you can find chips that will elevate the rev limiter, advance your timing, and generally run the engine less conservatively than the factory chip. However, the timing curves of a more aggressive chip may be a bit too advanced and may cause detonation on low-octane pump gas (as we have here in California). However, the E36 BMWs have a knock sensor that reduces detonation if the timing is too far advanced.

Another downside to installing a performance chip is that you need to run premium fuel with the chip installed. Whereas the stock chip is designed and mapped to provide good performance across a wide variety of operating conditions, performance chips are specifically mapped to assume you are running high-octane gasoline. If your car doesn't have a knock sensor, and you run low-octane gasoline with

FUEL INJECTION

107

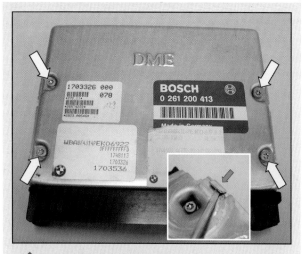

2 Remove the Torx screws (yellow arrows) and pop off the six small tabs (green arrows). Removing the cover exposes the circuit board. Remove and replace the chip with the new one, making sure that the small mark on the new chip goes in the same place as the mark on the old one (blue arrow).

maps, alters cam and ignition timing, raises the factory-set rpm limiter, changes accelerator enrichment, alters VANOS control, and optimizes other engine characteristics for increased performance.

For pre-1996 cars, installing a new chip is easier than you might imagine. First, disconnect the battery. The DME computer is located on the right side of the engine compartment. Pull back the rubber foam, and you will see the cover that protects the compartment. Remove the cover (attached by four screws) from the compartment, and you should see the DME and its harness. Pull back on the small lever on the harness, and you should be able to disconnect it.

The DME is held in place by two clips, so it should simply slide out. Place the unit on your workbench, and remove the four Torx screws (see Photo 2) that hold the cover on. Then, flip the unit over and pry off the six tabs on the bottom. Don't be too concerned with damaging these tabs, as they aren't too important in holding the case together. With the tabs detached, pull the metal cover off and you should see the circuit board. The chip is covered by a small piece of white plastic.

You may want to put on a static wrist strap or touch something that's grounded (like a metal lamp housing or a radiator). Then, carefully pop the chip out of the DME unit, and put the new one in. Make sure the small divot in the new chip faces the same direction as the old one (it is possible to put it in backward).

Seal up the unit, reinstall it, hook up the battery, and you're done!

Here's my rule of thumb: Find a chip manufacturer that not only offers different levels of performance but will also guarantee you're happy with the system.

a performance chip, harmful detonation may occur. If you run low-octane fuel in a car that does have a knock sensor, you can prevent detonation, but most likely you will not fully utilize the performance improvements of the chip.

If you have an OBD-II car (1996 and later), the computer inside the car requires flash programming instead of a chip. The Shark Injector Engine Software by Jim Conforti is a good choice for anyone seeking more performance from their engine. The software upgrade alters the fuel enrichment

3 **A:** With the cover of the DME computer popped off, you can see the electronics and the chip socket (red arrow). **B:** The chip is protected by a small plastic cover; simply pop it off. **C:** Use a small screwdriver on each end of the chip to gently pry it from its socket. **D:** Insert the new chip into the empty socket, making sure the small mark on the new chip goes in the same place as the mark on the old one (blue arrow).

SECTION FOUR

Water Cooling

BMW has certainly built some great engines for its 3 Series cars. However, history has proven that the cooling system is a weak point in these engines. Failures in the cooling system account for a large portion of overall engine failures and breakdowns. Fortunately, upgrades and careful maintenance of the cooling system can significantly increase the engine's reliability.

WATER COOLING

Cooling system maintenance is often neglected on many cars. BMW recommends you flush and clean the cooling system every three years. I perform this task on my own cars about once a year or, if I let it slip, every two years. Old, exhausted coolant can actually cause irreversible damage to engine components, which I learned firsthand when I replaced the head gasket on my '93 325is. The previous owner apparently hadn't changed the fluid once in the past 10 years. As a result, many parts of the engine were corroded and showed severe signs of wear.

A properly maintained cooling system must have several components in proper working order: an adequate supply of coolant, a radiator that acts as a heat exchanger with outside air, a fan or airflow source, a water pump to circulate the coolant, and a thermostat to keep the engine at its optimum operating temperature. The coolant must have the correct mixture and chemical compound to promote heat transfer, protect against freezing, and inhibit corrosion. To keep your BMW operating correctly, check the level, strength, and condition of the coolant regularly. Change the coolant before it degrades to the point that it doesn't perform its job adequately.

The U.S. Department of Transportation reported that cooling system failures are the leading cause of mechanical breakdowns on the highway—not exactly surprising, since proper cooling maintenance is one of the most neglected areas of cars.

Electrolysis

One failure mode associated with dirty coolant is known as electrolysis. Electrolysis occurs when a stray electrical current routes itself through the engine coolant. The electricity attempts to find the shortest path, and impurities in the coolant often generate a path of least resistance across which electricity travels. The source of this stray electricity is often electrical engine accessories that have not been properly grounded. A missing engine or transmission ground strap can also cause the coolant to become electrified. Sometimes, the path of least resistance becomes the radiator, the heater hose, or even the heater core. These components are typically well grounded and offer a ground path from the engine to the chassis by means of the semi-conductive coolant.

Electrolysis can destroy your engine quickly. Although it's somewhat normal to have very small amounts of voltage potential in the coolant system, values greater than 0.10 volt can start reactions between the coolant and the metal in the engine. Electrolysis primarily affects aluminum engine components, resulting in pitting and scarring of the aluminum surface. This corrosion can cause coolant system leaks, particularly radiator leaks around aluminum welds. Cast-iron components are also vulnerable, but the aluminum metal

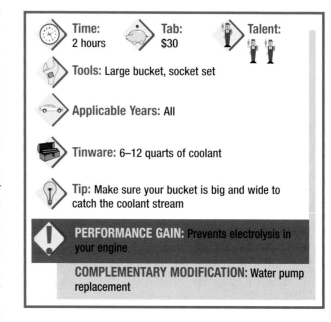

Time: 2 hours

Tab: $30

Talent:

Tools: Large bucket, socket set

Applicable Years: All

Tinware: 6–12 quarts of coolant

Tip: Make sure your bucket is big and wide to catch the coolant stream

PERFORMANCE GAIN: Prevents electrolysis in your engine

COMPLEMENTARY MODIFICATION: Water pump replacement

parts typically fail first. On BMWs, electrolysis often attacks aluminum cylinder heads (see Photo 1).

How can you test for electrolysis? Other than actually spotting signs of corrosion, you can perform a current flow test. Connect the negative terminal of a voltmeter to the chassis ground. Test for adequate continuity by touching another point on the chassis—the resistance should be near to zero. With the engine cold and running, submerge the positive probe into the coolant tank; make sure that the probe does not touch any metal parts. The voltage should be less than 0.10 volt. If not, methodically turn off or unplug each electrical accessory until the meter reads below 0.10 volt. Have an assistant switch accessories (A/C compressor, heater blower, etc.) while you measure the voltage.

If an accessory doesn't have an on/off switch, test it by temporarily running a ground from the accessory's housing to the chassis. Ground each component, and then check the voltmeter. If the wire restores a missing ground connection to the accessory, then you've found a component with a faulty ground.

During this test, be sure to check the starter. A poorly grounded starter will struggle to turn over the engine, and it will zap away tremendous amounts of metal in the cooling system components. Watch the meter carefully when starting the engine. Any voltage spike will indicate a faulty ground connection.

Coolant system additives

Many people are wary of coolant system additives. There are a lot of myths in the automotive industry, and a little skepticism can be a good thing. Luckily, the coolant system additives fall into the category of good practice, for reasons I'll explain here. Like today's modern oils, many of today's modern coolants incorporate chemicals that help cooling and increase heat flow around the cooling system components. As more and more automotive components are made out of aluminum and radiators become smaller, using these additives becomes more advantageous.

Aftermarket coolant system additives are known as surfactants. A surfactant, or surface-active agent, is a molecule that has a water-loving end (hydrophilic) and a water-fearing end (hydrophobic). Localized boiling of coolant in a cylinder head can create large shock waves that can wreak havoc on the engine, particularly on aluminum components. These surfactants reduce the amount of air in the cooling system and control the amount of foam within the system.

There are three main reasons why these additives are beneficial to the cooling system. First, they reduce harmful cavitations and foaming that may occur when the water pump kicks out fluid rapidly. This reduced foaming helps prevent damage to aluminum surfaces. Second, these additives aid in transmitting heat from the coolant to the radiating surfaces within the radiator. Even if your car runs very cool, these additives add an extra level of protection in case a thermostat or similar component fails. Third, the additives contain corrosion inhibitors. Most cars on the road have cooling systems that do not contain the ideal 50/50 water/antifreeze ratio that antifreeze is designed for. The

additives minimize potential corrosion by maintaining adequate pH levels. Even if the antifreeze already contains surfactant additives, these additional additives are typically beneficial because most cars are shortchanged on the 50/50 water/coolant mix.

Additives like Water Wetter help to reduce corrosion due to rust and electrolysis; increase the wetting ability of water while improving heat transfer, thus reducing cylinder head temperatures; clean and lubricate coolant system seals like those in the water pump; reduce foam and cavitations that can cause corrosion; and reduce the effects of hard water in the cooling system.

In general, these additives are inexpensive and provide proven benefits. Using the additives on a perfectly maintained car also provides a significant margin of error in case something goes wrong. BMWs are infamous for cooling system failures. Keeping the odds on your side can prevent a costly head gasket replacement.

It's important to keep the cooling system at the correct pH level. Pure water has a pH of seven and is considered neutral. Battery acid is highly corrosive and has a pH of about zero to one, whereas liquid drain cleaner is very alkaline, and has a pH of 13 to14. Make sure your coolant has a pH greater than 7.0. Any pH less than 7.0 indicates an acidic mixture, which will corrode the engine. The corrosion inhibitors in additives and antifreeze are added specifically to keep the pH above seven. A properly mixed 50/50 split between water and antifreeze will yield a pH of eight or nine. Over time, the

1 This photo shows a picture of the thermostat area of a cylinder head that has been partially damaged by electrolysis. Notice how the aluminum has been eaten away and eroded by the chemical/electrical reactions. The process works somewhat like electrical discharge machines (EDM). These machines pass a large electrical current through metal, literally zapping away bits of material until nothing remains. Unfortunately, the electrolysis process works in a similar way, zapping bits of metal in proportion to the amount of electrical current passing through the coolant. A poorly grounded starter can literally destroy a radiator or head within a matter of weeks, depending upon how often the car is started. A smaller current drain, like an electric cooling fan, may slowly erode components over many months.

2 Having the proper radiator cap on your car is very important. This is the proper cap for an E36. Make sure the cap is not cocked, as this will let coolant flow out and cause the car to overheat. This type of failure caused the head gasket to fail on the engine featured in Project 17. Inset: Bleed the system until no more bubbles come out the top of the radiator.

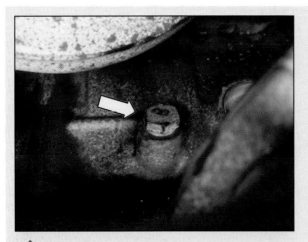

3 The coolant drain plug on the left side of the engine blends in with everything else and is difficult to see. Even more difficult is the task of staying dry and not spilling coolant everywhere when emptying it out from underneath the car. When you remove the plug, coolant will not flow gently out of the hole but will exit like it's being forced out of a garden hose. Have a large catch pan, and keep paper towels handy. Also, wear eye protection when removing this plug.

4 The bottom radiator plug is a bit tamer than the engine plug. The fluid will pour out fast, but you will have a better chance of controlling the stream and minimizing cleanup.

glycol (a main component of antifreeze) will break down and degrade, creating acidic compounds. The alkaline corrosion inhibitors must be adequate enough to neutralize these acidic by-products over the life of the coolant. Minerals in the water, heat, dissolved oxygen, and other pollutants gradually deplete the coolant of its corrosion inhibitors. Once gone, the mixture will become acidic and begin to eat away at the engine.

Cooling system maintenance: checking the level

Check the coolant level regularly to detect leaks that can siphon off coolant and cause the engine to overheat. Regularly check the coolant level in the coolant reservoir, making sure it is within the prescribed high/low marks printed on the side of the coolant container. The container is nearly transparent, so you can also eyeball the current level.

Over time, coolant will evaporate gradually from your BMW's coolant reservoir. However, a significant coolant loss in a very short period of time almost always signals a leak in the system. Sometimes this leak can be seen when you park your car overnight. However, coolant can also leak out and evaporate while you're driving, leaving no telltale marks on the pavement.

If you suspect a coolant leak, immediately inspect the hoses, water pump, reservoir, and radiator for coolant seepage or weeping from seams and gaskets. Check the seal on the radiator cap, and be sure the cap is fastened securely. The way BMW radiator caps are designed, it's easy to make the simple-yet-deadly mistake of leaving the cap cocked—allowing coolant to leak out when the engine is running. If you suspect a leak you cannot see, a professional mechanic can conduct a pressure test to verify the integrity of the system. If you can't

find any visible leaks and the system appears to hold pressure, make sure the radiator cap is the right one for your engine and rated for the proper pressure (see Photo 2).

If the system does not hold pressure and you're still at a loss as to why coolant might be disappearing, look in the engine oil. A faulty head gasket can cause coolant to leak into the oil. If you remove the oil cap and find a yellow murky substance, you probably have a leaky head gasket (see Project 17). The oil level may be elevated, and you will see droplets of coolant inside the oil filler hole. If coolant leaks past the gasket into a combustion chamber, you will see steam exiting the tailpipe, and the spark plugs will foul easily. In addition, the exhaust will be contaminated with silicate corrosion inhibitors from the coolant, and the oxygen sensor will be destroyed. Plan to replace the oxygen sensor (see Project 17) if you have experienced this problem.

If you can't discover what happened to the coolant, the engine may have temporarily overheated, causing some of the coolant to boil over. In this case, top off the coolant and keep a very close eye on it. BMW overheating issues can flare up and unexpectedly destroy a head gasket.

Checking coolant strength and condition

Periodically test the strength and condition of the car's coolant to ensure the optimum balance is achieved for your BMW. This is equally important for protection against both hot and cold temperatures. An imbalance between water and antifreeze levels will change the boiling and/or freezing point of the mixture. A 50/50 mixture of water and ethylene glycol (EG) antifreeze protects against boiling up to approximately 255 degrees Fahrenheit (with a 15-psi radiator cap). This mixture also protects against freezing to a chilly –34 degrees Fahrenheit. A similar 50/50 mixture of propylene glycol (PG) antifreeze and water protects from –26 degrees Fahrenheit to about 257 degrees Fahrenheit.

Increasing the concentration of antifreeze in the coolant raises the effective boiling point and lowers the freezing point. While this may seem beneficial, having antifreeze content of greater than 65 or 70 percent significantly reduces the ability of the coolant to transmit and transfer heat, thus increasing the chances of overheating. As with most things in life, it's good to maintain a healthy balance.

But a word of caution: You can't accurately determine the condition of the coolant simply by looking at it. The chemical composition and concentration of the coolant is very important. If the chemistry is off, the coolant may be harming your engine rather than protecting it.

As mentioned previously, keep the coolant fresh. Ethylene glycol typically accounts for 95 percent of antifreeze by weight. While it does not generally wear out, the corrosion inhibitors that comprise the remaining 5 percent do degrade over time. Keeping the coolant fresh is especially important in engines with aluminum heads and cast-iron blocks.

At a minimum, change the coolant every two years or every 25,000 miles. I'm not a huge fan of long-life antifreeze. If these so-called long-life fluids mix with conventional antifreeze (a very easy mistake to make), the corrosion inhibitors react with each other and reduce the effective protection of the long-life fluid. If you use long-life antifreeze in your car, be sure to add only the same type of antifreeze in the future. Don't mix and match regular and long-life fluids.

Unfortunately, it's tough to determine if long-life coolant has been mixed or topped off with ordinary antifreeze. Although some coolants are dyed a separate color (like Dex-Cool in GM vehicles), most aren't usually potent enough when mixed with standard antifreeze to overpower the bright green color. Unless you know the entire service history of your BMW, err on the side of caution, and use a shorter service interval for changing the coolant.

How do you check the coolant in your system? Use chemical strip tests to measure how much reserve alkalinity is left within the coolant. The test strip changes color when immersed in the coolant. Compare the final color to a reference chart to determine the condition of the coolant. If the coolant tests poorly, or is borderline, plan to replace it very soon.

Note: EG and PG antifreeze have differing specific gravities and require different test strips. Be sure to use the correct test strip, or you may end up with false readings.

Changing the coolant in your BMW

Now that I've convinced you to change the coolant regularly, I have some good news: It's relatively easy on BMW 3 Series cars. Place a large drip pan underneath your car. I use a kitty litter box because it is plastic, big, and holds a lot of coolant. The BMW 3 Series six-cylinder engine cooling systems hold just shy of 3 gallons (10.5 liters), so whatever container you use needs to hold all that liquid.

With your BMW cold, elevate it on jack stands (see Project 1). Place the heater control knobs all the way on hot, turn the ignition to the on position, and turn on the passenger compartment fans to their lowest setting. Do not start the car. By turning the heater knobs on, you open the valves to the heater core, which will allow you to drain the coolant located in the core. For cars with electronic climate control, make sure the ignition is on and the heater is set to maximum heat.

On the right side of the engine (passenger side for U.S. cars), just under the manifold, you will see the drain plug for the coolant (see Photo 3). Place your collection container underneath the plug. Remove the plug and let the coolant empty into the catch pan. **Beware:** I have found it nearly impossible to empty the coolant without spilling it on myself. Don't undertake this project while wearing your Sunday best, and do be sure to wear safety glasses and protective gloves when you're working underneath the car. The coolant will empty out much like water out of a shower—it will spray all over and much will miss your drain pan. Have plenty of paper towels on hand to clean up these spills.

When the coolant has been released from the engine block, replace the plug using a new aluminum sealing ring, and tighten it to 25 N-m (18 ft-lbs).

Next, move on to the radiator. There should be a plastic drain plug at the bottom of the radiator (see Photo 4). Position your drain pan, and slowly remove this drain plug. Fortunately, the flow of coolant from the radiator is a bit more predictable and should empty in a steady stream. When the coolant has drained from the radiator, replace the plug. Tighten to 2–3 N-m (18–27 in-lbs). This torque is very, very small. Don't overtighten the plug, or you may damage either the plug or the radiator.

With a funnel, pour the old coolant from the drain pan into some plastic containers. One-gallon spring water or milk containers make excellent storage vessels for used coolant. Do not pour the coolant down the drain; this toxic liquid can easily wind up as waste or runoff in one of our rivers or oceans. Instead, take your containers to a hazardous waste recycling station. Note: Coolant is highly toxic and therefore dangerous to both family pets and children. Close up used coolant containers right away. Less intelligent animals are attracted to the smell and taste of coolant. Package it up and seal it off. And when you're done, be sure to rinse and dilute any contaminated areas with water.

Now, remove the small plastic bleed screw to the right of the radiator cap. On M3 engines, this screw is located on the thermostat housing. Using a large funnel, slowly fill the radiator's expansion tank with new coolant. Be sure to use a 50/50 mixture of antifreeze and distilled water. Do not use tap water or spring water, as these have impurities that will contaminate your system. Distilled or ionized water is 100 percent H_2O and does not contain any minerals, additives, or impurities. Fill the system very slowly, as it will take a bit of time for the coolant to get to all points in the system. On four-cylinder cars, you will need about 7 quarts (6.5 liters).

For six-cylinder cars, you will need 10.6 quarts (10 liters). M3 motors require 11.1 quarts (10.5 liters).

When the system is full of coolant, you will need to bleed air out of it. This applies only to the cars that have the expansion tank attached to the side of the radiator. (Other BMWs with a separate, external expansion tank are self-bleeding.) The procedure for bleeding BMWs is somewhat sloppy and not too slick. With the bleed screw removed, fill the expansion tank until fluid comes out of the bleed screw. Continue filling until there are no more bubbles visible out the top (see inset of Photo 2). Plenty of coolant will spill all over your radiator and down onto the ground; have a catch pan ready to capture this excess. When no more bubbles come out of the bleed screw, tighten it to 8 N-m (71 in-lbs).

Now, with the garage door wide open (or, better yet, with the car in the driveway), run the engine until it reaches its operating temperature. Then turn off the engine and let it cool down. Top off the coolant in the expansion tank to the appropriate level as needed.

You may be wondering, "What type of coolant should I use?" In 1991, BMW issued technical bulletin 17 01 88(1743), detailing problems with what is known as "silicate gel precipitation" in engines. This green goo (yes, it actually says "green goo" in the BMW tech bulletin) is a consequence of antifreeze overconcentration combined with hard water and the phosphates commonly used in antifreeze. BMW factory antifreeze has been formulated to prevent the problem of silicate drop-out without any coolant performance loss. This antifreeze contains no nitrites and no phosphates. The part number for a 1-gallon container is 88-88-6-900-316, and it costs $15–20 per gallon from a number of sources, including PelicanParts.com. Although I am always eager to find alternatives to expensive BMW factory products, I recommend sticking with the factory coolant for now.

PROJECT 34

http://www.101projects.com/BMW/34.htm

Radiator and Hose Replacement

Proper maintenance of your coolant will go a long way toward extending the life of your radiator. The cooling systems on most cars are neglected, as few owners know much about them (see Project 33). The most vulnerable components in the entire system are the radiator and heater core, as they tend to be damaged by corrosion and electrolysis. Poor maintenance of your car's system can result in a buildup of corrosive elements in the radiator and heater core, creating clogs and leaks that decrease cooling performance. If the engine overheats, the added heat from the coolant can also damage sensitive plastic attachments and components.

When replacing the radiator, replace it with one that meets or exceeds the OEM cooling standards. BMW cooling systems are infamous for overheating problems, and an aftermarket radiator may offer enhanced performance. See the 101Projects.com website for recommendations on aftermarket radiators. If you replace the radiator, also replace the water pump, radiator hoses, thermostat, and hose clamps, too. (A number of sources, including PelicanParts.com, sell complete kits for this replacement.) All of these components can be damaged by a cooling system that has overheated. It may also be a good time to swap out your old or worn belts.

To replace the radiator, first remove all the coolant from the system (see Project 33). Next, you will need to gain access to the radiator. Remove the front plastic panel that covers the front inside section of the engine compartment. (Four screws hold this panel to the car.) Though it's not 100 percent necessary, I recommend that you also remove the cooling fan for better access. For this step, you will need a 32-millimeter wrench and a special fan removal tool. Unfortunately, I have not found an easy removal method that does not require this tool. The tool holds the two pulley

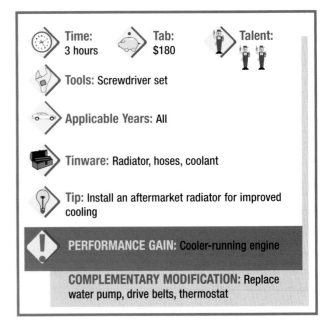

Time: 3 hours

Tab: $180

Talent: ▮▮

Tools: Screwdriver set

Applicable Years: All

Tinware: Radiator, hoses, coolant

Tip: Install an aftermarket radiator for improved cooling

PERFORMANCE GAIN: Cooler-running engine

COMPLEMENTARY MODIFICATION: Replace water pump, drive belts, thermostat

nuts in place, enabling you to remove the fan pulley nut. Holding the fan pulley steady with the tool, twist and remove the fan nut. This nut has reverse threads and needs to be turned clockwise to loosen it.

Next, remove the cooling fan housing frame from the integrated reservoir. It is held in place with small plastic rivets. Pop these out to loosen the frame from the radiator. Disconnect the overflow hose prior to removing this frame. This hose is also attached to the frame. The hose winds around to the left side of the car and needs to be disconnected near the power steering pump. Now, disconnect the coolant level sensor. With all these hoses and connectors

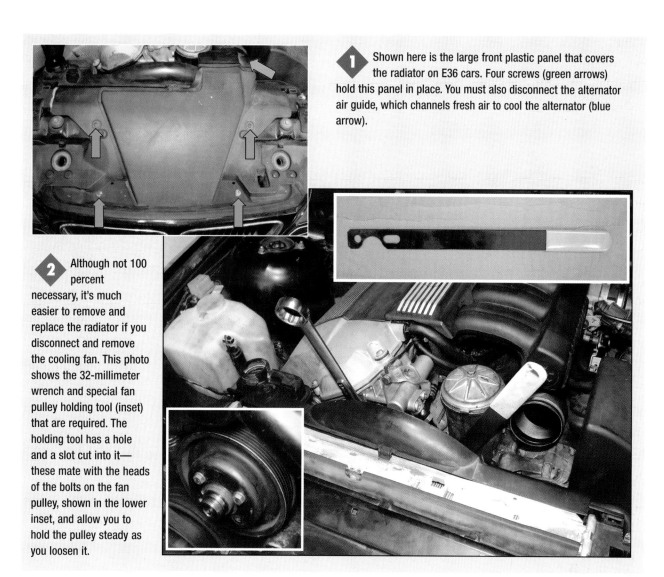

1 Shown here is the large front plastic panel that covers the radiator on E36 cars. Four screws (green arrows) hold this panel in place. You must also disconnect the alternator air guide, which channels fresh air to cool the alternator (blue arrow).

2 Although not 100 percent necessary, it's much easier to remove and replace the radiator if you disconnect and remove the cooling fan. This photo shows the 32-millimeter wrench and special fan pulley holding tool (inset) that are required. The holding tool has a hole and a slot cut into it—these mate with the heads of the bolts on the fan pulley, shown in the lower inset, and allow you to hold the pulley steady as you loosen it.

disconnected, you should be able to remove the fan frame/reservoir from the car.

With the frame out of the way, disconnect the hoses linked to the radiator. There are two large hoses—one on the top left side of the car, and one on the lower right. Loosen the hose clamp on the top left hose, and pull it away from the thermostat housing. Now, disconnect the lower radiator hose on the right. Then remove the electrical connector for the radiator temperature sensor. After the hoses are disconnected, disconnect the automatic transmission lines, if your car has them (see Project 37).

In most (if not all) BMWs, the radiator is held onto the chassis with odd, complicated plastic clips that are somewhat difficult to remove. Because you may end up breaking them while getting the old radiator out, have new ones ready and waiting. Using a screwdriver in the center of the clip, pry it out from the chassis and the radiator. You may have to play with these clips a bit to remove them. With the clips removed, the radiator will no longer be attached to the car and can be easily lifted up and out of the engine compartment. In some models, though, there's a small radiator—the

automatic transmission cooler—attached to the front of the main radiator. Have a catch bucket (kitty litter boxes work well) to capture the excess coolant and automatic transmission fluid that will spill out when you lift the radiator.

When you install a new radiator, or reinstall the old one, make sure it sits firmly on the rubber mounts attached to the chassis. It is possible to install it slightly cocked if you're not paying close attention to these mounts. If you damaged the plastic clips while removing the radiator, this is the time to replace them with new ones.

Reattach all the hoses and connectors. Replace the large upper and lower radiator hoses. If your clamps look worn, replace them too, but only with clamps specifically designed for large rubber hoses (some generic hose clamps can cause chaffing on the rubber when tightened).

Finally, button up the front cover, replace all the coolant, and bleed the system (see Project 33).

While this project only outlines radiator replacement for E36 engines, the procedure for E30 engines is very similar. See the 101Projects.com website for more information and specific details on E30 cars.

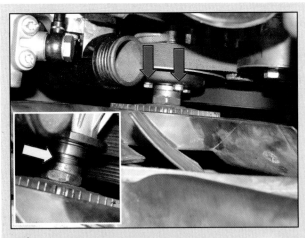

3 Removing the fan requires the pulley holding tool shown in Photo 2. The holding tool mates with the heads of the bolts used to fasten the pulley to the water pump (blue arrows). A large reverse-thread nut (yellow arrow) attaches the fan to the water pump. The reverse thread is used so that the spinning action of the fan won't accidentally loosen the nut (turn the nut clockwise to loosen it for removal).

4 Shown here are some radiator connections that need to be disconnected. The red arrow shows one of the plastic mounting clips that hold the radiator in place. The purple arrow points to where the small plastic rivets hold the reservoir-retaining frame to the radiator. The yellow arrow points to a coolant temperature sensor. The green arrow shows the coolant level sensor, and the blue arrow shows the point where the lower radiator hose needs to be disconnected.

5 On the opposite side, the red arrow points to the place where the upper radiator hose meets the thermostat housing. The green arrow shows where this hose connects to the radiator. The reservoir overflow hose (yellow arrow) wraps around the reservoir-retaining frame. The plastic mounting clips (blue arrow) hold the radiator in place. The inset photo shows the lower overflow hose that must be disconnected from the lower recesses of the engine.

6 The upper left shows the radiator (green arrow) held in place with the plastic mounting clips. In the upper right, the transmission cooler is mounted in front of the radiator. The lower left shows the indentation where the bottom of the radiator sits when it is properly mounted. The lower right shows the attachment points for the automatic transmission coolant lines (see also Project 37).

Water Pump and Thermostat Replacement

Time: 2 hours

Tab: $250

Talent: 👤👤👤

Tools: 32-millimeter wrench, fan-holding tool, socket set

Applicable Years: All

Tinware: Water pump and gasket

Tip: Apply silicone to the thermostat housing O-ring to help seal against the head

PERFORMANCE GAIN: Protects your engine against overheating

COMPLEMENTARY MODIFICATION: Replace radiator, radiator hoses

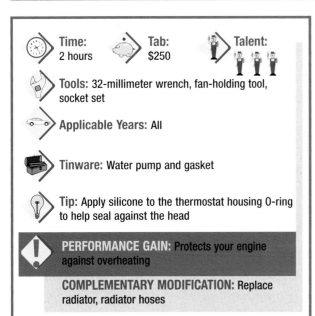

1 Shown here is the front of an E36 six-cylinder engine with the fan removed. The fan pulley is held on with four small bolts. When you remove the pulley, you will expose the water pump and its shaft (inset). The thermostat housing (yellow arrows) is made of black plastic and covers the thermostat assembly.

2 Tap on the water pump with a rubber mallet to free it from the engine block. The pump should pull off of the block after the seal is broken.

BMW cooling systems are known for being troublesome. The thermostat and water pump are two of the principle areas of failure. Some of the old-style water pumps have a plastic impeller that becomes brittle and breaks off after many years of service. BMW has replaced the plastic impeller in recent years with a metal one. If you know you have a plastic impeller in your car, replace it as soon as possible. Overheating problems are common on these cars, and if your engine overheats, you may find yourself replacing the head gasket, which is not cheap (see Project 17).

Begin by gaining access to the water pump. Remove the fan and belts (Projects 5 and 34), and remove all coolant from the system (Project 33).

With your equipment removed, the front part of the engine should be very accessible. Remove the fan pulley from the water pump; it is held on with four small nuts (see Project 34). Loosen the four nuts that hold the water pump to the engine block. Then, using a rubber mallet, softly tap the side of the water pump. It should separate from the block after a few taps. Once the water pump is loose, pull it out of the engine block.

With the pump removed, check the inside bore (where the water pump fits) for debris or corrosion. Use a wire brush to remove any corrosion or debris that may have built up there. Install the new water pump using a new O-ring. Place a bit of white lithium grease around the O-ring to ensure a good seal and to ease installation of the pump into the engine block. Insert the new pump, and tighten the four bolts that attach it to the block. Torque them to 11 N-m (8 ft-lbs) but no tighter.

At this time, I recommend that you remove the thermostat housing (located above the water pump) and replace the thermostat as well. The thermostat is a relatively cheap part that fails easily and can cause your engine to overheat.

This project details water pump and thermostat replacement on E36 engines. For information on E30 water pump replacement, please see the 101Projects.com website.

WATER COOLING

117

3 The old-style pump (right) has a plastic impeller and the new water pump (left) has an upgraded metal impeller. Although this plastic impeller does not have any broken pieces, the plastic has become very brittle and likely to break in the near future. There is no functional difference between these two—they will both pump the same amount of coolant through the system.

4 The interior of the water pump housing will most likely be coated with dirt and debris. Clean the inside bore of the water pump housing with a wire brush attachment and a hand drill prior to installing the new pump. Also consider replacing the thermostat housing. It is manufactured out of plastic and can often crack with age—metal replacements are available.

5 The new thermostat has been installed. Be sure to use a new O-ring to seal the thermostat to the cylinder head. Electrolysis caused by dirty coolant (see Project 33) has done some damage to this head. As a result, I applied a liberal coat of black silicone to the orange O-ring that is embedded in the thermostat housing (O-ring without silicone is shown in the inset photo). The silicone will help to seal the areas that have become somewhat porous on the cylinder head (green arrow).

SECTION FIVE

Transmission/ Drive Axles/ Shifter

These three areas have been combined into one section because they are all interrelated and linked together. The transmission and clutch can be a mysterious setup—leading many owners to ignore and neglect maintenance until it's too late. This section aims to demystify the transmission, clutch, and rear axle assemblies, and also provides some upgrades and improvements for performance.

Replacing your engine oil is easy. BMW knows this needs to be performed about once every 3,000 to 5,000 miles and has designed its cars with ease in mind. On the other hand, E36 transmissions are supposedly designed with a lifetime fluid that does not need to be changed. Despite the dealer's recommendations not to change the transmission fluid, I prefer to change mine every three years or 30,000 miles. Changing the tranny fluid is not an easy task, however, and probably hasn't been recently performed on your car.

Despite some cars having a lifetime fluid in the transmission, BMW did indeed give easy access to the bottom of the automatic transmission. Replacing the transmission fluid was the very first project I performed on my wife's 1993 325is when we bought it. I purchased the car with a known transmission problem: When the car was stopped, if the accelerator was then pressed, the transmission would slip, and then slam into gear, lurching the car forward. I had a strong suspicion that the transmission fluid was low.

 Time: 3 hours
 Tab: $75
 Talent: ⚒⚒

 Tools: Transmission fluid pump

 Applicable Years: All

 Tinware: Automatic transmission filter and gasket kit

 Tip: Don't neglect this maintenance—transmissions are expensive to replace

 PERFORMANCE GAIN: Longer transmission life

COMPLEMENTARY MODIFICATION: Oil change

TRANSMISSION/DRIVE AXLES/SHIFTER

1 The main chamber is about 1 square foot, and the chamber in front of it is about 1 foot by 3 inches. Start the draining process only when the car is cold. When the car is warm, a lot of transmission fluid will still be trapped within the transmission itself. When the car is cold, almost all of the transmission fluid has seeped out and is trapped in the lower sumps. Note: This is the opposite of the procedure for changing the oil, in which you would drain when the engine is hot. Engine oil is thinnest and flows best when it's hot. The transmission fluid has a totally different viscosity. Working on the car when it's cold also ensures that hot exhaust, transmission, or engine parts will not burn you.

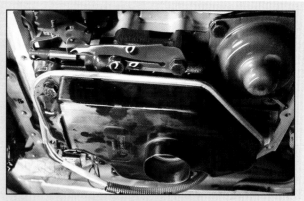

2 This photo shows the bottom of the transmission with both sumps removed. Automatic transmissions have many tiny passages that supply fluid and cooling. Keep this exposed area completely clean and free of dirt and debris.

3 The transmission fluid filter is a large black canister attached to the bottom of the transmission, and it needs to be removed and replaced. Remove the three bolts that attach it to the transmission, carefully pull off the filter, and discard it in the trash. Check the mounting surfaces where the sumps attach to the transmission, and remove any excess gasket material that may have been left there. When you reinstall the filter into the transmission, use the same bolts you previously removed. Torque these bolts to 20 N-m (15 ft-lbs) for the A4S 270R and A4S 310R transmissions. Torque the bolts to 6 N-m (53 in-lbs) for the A5S 310Z transmission.

Why did I suspect this? A thorough inspection had shown that the previous owner smacked the front of this car into one too many parking blocks and had scraped the underside of the car—right behind the radiator. One of the transmission lines had been damaged and was leaking a slow but steady drip of transmission oil. The underside of the engine was coated with transmission fluid, indicating this problem had been occurring for quite some time.

What causes the transmission to slip and then engage suddenly? When you slam on the brakes, the transmission fluid flows to the front of the car and away from the fluid pickup, which is located toward the rear of the transmission. With the fluid at the front of the car, the transmission loses fluid briefly. Automatic transmissions use the fluid as both a hydraulic fluid and a coolant, and they won't work if there isn't any fluid running through them. After my car was fully stopped, the fluid moved back toward the pickup, and the transmission began to work normally. If the transmission has the proper level of fluid, this condition will not occur.

After I replaced the transmission fluid and checked the levels, the problem disappeared. The previous owner had let it run down about 2 quarts low (the whole transmission takes about 5 quarts). Driving for any more time with the transmission in this state would have led to substantial damage and could have wrecked the tranny (replacement cost: $2,500). This is such a common problem, that I've actually owned 3 BMWs that have had this same problem.

Now let's get to work. First, jack up your car so you can reach the underside of the transmission (see Project 1). It is very important that the car be level—don't jack up just the front or rear of the car, make sure that it is as level in the air as it is on the ground. The reason for this is that you will be checking the transmission fluid level by removing a drain plug and looking at the fluid. If the car is not level, you will not obtain an accurate reading.

Additionally, elevate the car with the rear tailpipe sticking way outside your open garage door. You will need to run the car while it's on the jack stands in order to top off the fluid, and adequate ventilation is vital.

With the car elevated, locate the two lower sump chambers that hold the transmission fluid (Photo 1). Next, remove all of the existing fluid from the main transmission sump. As always, wear safety glasses when you're under the car. Between the dirt and the rust, you never know what might fall into your eyes.

The drain plug on the rear right corner of the sump can be used to empty most of the fluid inside. Remove this plug, and let the fluid drain out into a sturdy container that can hold at least 1 gallon (about 4 liters). Once the fluid has fully drained, replace the drain plug using a new sealing ring. Torque the plug to 25 N-m (18 ft-lbs) for the A4S 270R and A4S 310R transmissions. Torque the M10 plug to 16 N-m (12 ft-lbs) for the A5S 310Z transmission.

Now, remove the larger of the two sumps from the bottom of the transmission so you can replace the transmission filter, clean the sump magnet, and remove any extra fluid that may be trapped inside. To remove the sump, loosen the small bolts that attach it to the bottom of the transmission. Once they are out, you should be able to pull the sump cover off. Warning: There may be transmission fluid in the sump that can spill out if you're not careful.

121

4 Using a lint-free cloth, carefully wipe down the inside of the sump (I like Kimwipes, see Photo 23 in Project 17). Any tiny cloth fibers left in your transmission sump can clog the transmission and filter. Pay close attention to the magnet (left) in the bottom of the sump. You should be able to pluck this magnet from the bottom of the sump and clean it. The sump needs to be clean, spotless, and look brand-new, as shown on the right. Remove any remaining gasket material from the edge of the sump cover. In a similar manner, take the small sump and clean the inside completely.

Next, turn your attention to the smaller sump at the front of the transmission. This sump doesn't have a drain plug, so you will have to be extra careful when emptying it. Empty the sump by removing all but one of the small bolts that attach it to the transmission. Leave one bolt on one of the short sides of the sump. With a large and wide container positioned below the small sump, slowly loosen the last bolt. At this point, the small sump should be sticking to the transmission because of the gasket that seals it. Pull down slightly on the small sump, and one end should drop down, emptying some of the fluid into the container below. Plastic cat litter boxes make excellent containers for catching fluid. They are wide and large enough to prevent you from making a huge mess on your garage floor.

With much of the fluid already emptied from the small sump, remove the remaining bolt completely, and carefully detach the sump from the car. Keep it level, or simply lower it into your catch pan.

Turn your attention back to the sumps and clean them out. Then, remove the transmission filter from the bottom of the transmission.

What type of fluid do you use in your automatic transmission? Most BMW transmissions are filled with standard Dexron III fluid. Dexron is a registered trademark of General Motors Corporation and is a transmission fluid specification that is required for use in the majority of 3 Series E36 BMW automatic transmissions. GM manufactured many transmissions for BMW (the 325is tranny featured in this project has a big "GM" stamp on the side). The side plate on your transmission should say which type of fluid to install. There may

also be a sticker on the side of one of the bottom sumps. On my car, I found neither, but since it was a GM transmission, I used the Dexron fluid. Be aware that mixing and matching different types of transmission fluid can cause the transmission to fail, so be sure to drain the old fluid completely.

With the new filter in place, reinstall the lower sumps. The front, smaller sump is the trickiest because it needs to be full of fluid when you install it. With the small sump in place, you can then install the larger one. Bolt it up into place and then fill it with fluid (see Photo 6).

At this point, you can start the car. The transmission fluid level can only be checked when the transmission temperature is within 86–131 degrees Fahrenheit (30–55 degrees Celsius). After you start the car, let it warm up before checking the levels. For my 325is, it took approximately 45 minutes on a chilly day to reach this temperature.

Warning: You will be running the car while it is up and on jack stands. This can be dangerous if the car is not secure on the jack stands, so check them again before you continue. You will also be running the car for an extended length of time while it warms up. For this reason, it is best to perform the test outside (on level ground). Otherwise, you will need to funnel the exhaust gases out of the tail pipe and out of your garage. For this method, I recommend a long, flexible aluminum tube—the kind used for venting gas clothes dryers—from the hardware store. Clamp one end of the aluminum tube tightly to the end of the tailpipe, and run the other end out of the garage. With the garage door open, you should be able to safely idle your car inside the garage for the test run. For added safety, use an electronic

TRANSMISSION/DRIVE AXLES/SHIFTER

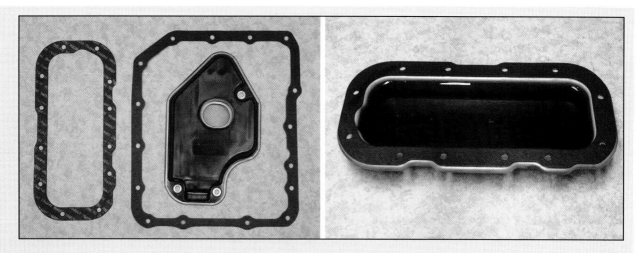

5 On the left is a complete filter and gasket kit for the automatic transmission. The kit contains a single transmission filter, and a gasket for each of the sumps. The small sump is tricky to reinstall without spilling fluid. Fill the sump almost to the top with new, clean transmission fluid, and place the new transmission gasket on the top edge of the sump. No gasket sealant is necessary here—if any sealant got into the sump, it could clog the passages of the transmission. Use red Loctite 271 on the bolts that mount the sump to the transmission to ensure they do not come loose. Keeping the sump perfectly level, carefully raise it up and install it onto the bottom of the car. Expect to spill at least a small bit of fluid unless you are an expert juggler. Just don't spill too much, as you don't want to significantly reduce the level in the lower sump. Reuse the old bolts and torque them to 12 N-m (9 ft-lbs) for the A4S 270R and A4S 310R transmissions. Torque the bolts to 6 N-m (53 in-lbs) for the A5S 310Z transmission.

carbon monoxide monitor inside your garage (also available from most hardware stores).

When you're ready, climb into the car, place your foot on the brake, and then start it. If you hear anything amiss, or encounter any unusual problems, shut off the car immediately. If everything is in working order, it should start and idle normally. Allow the transmission to warm up until it reaches the correct operating temperature, as indicated above. (The bottom of the sump will feel warm to the touch but not hot.) Use a standard body-temperature thermometer to check the temperature of the bottom sump—it should have enough range to give an accurate reading. Again, it should take about 45 minutes to heat the transmission to the necessary level with the car simply idling.

Once your car is at the proper temperature, sit inside it, apply the brake pedal, and slowly shift the transmission through all of its gears. Repeat this about 10 times. Then turn the engine off.

Move underneath the car again to remove the fill plug from the side of the transmission. Then restart the car with the transmission in neutral. With the engine running, refill the transmission until fluid comes out of the fill hole (see Photo 6). When you remove the plug, the fluid will not be pressurized and will not fly out of the hole. Be careful, though, as the fluid may be hot now and could burn you.

Replace the fill plug, using a new sealing washer. Torque the plug to 33 N-m (24 ft-lbs) for the A4S 270R and A4S 310R transmissions. Torque the M30 plug to 100 N-m (74 ft-lbs) for the A5S 310Z transmission.

That's about all there is to it. After you've topped off the fluid, lower the car off the jack stands, and take it for a

6 You will need a transmission fluid pump, which you can find at most auto parts stores, in order to fill the larger sump. The pump works just like a liquid soap dispenser. Pump the transmission fluid into the side of the main sump through the transmission fill hole. Remove the plug, place one end of the pump into a bottle of transmission fluid, and start pumping. Continue pumping into the filler hole on the side of the large sump until fluid begins to run out of the filler hole. Clean up the small spill and replace the fill plug only slightly tighter than hand tight (you will remove it again shortly when you recheck the levels).

short drive. If all is well, you won't notice any difference in performance or operation. Of course, if you were having problems with the transmission slamming into gear, they should be gone now.

TRANSMISSION/DRIVE AXLES/SHIFTER

Replacing Automatic Transmission Lines

BMW claims its transmissions are "sealed" units. I find this an ironic statement, as BMW cars have very significant (and very vulnerable) transmission cooling lines that run to the front of the car. It's not uncommon for these lines to become damaged and start leaking. On my 1992 325is, which I purchased from a private party, the transmission fluid was about 2 quarts low and had been slowly leaking for quite some time. If I hadn't caught the problem, the transmission would have run dry and may have been damaged beyond repair. I recommend that you check the fluid in your BMW automatic transmission often, as the alternative can be very expensive.

From underneath the car while raised on jack stands, you can clearly see the two transmission lines. Each has a unique bend designed to fit around the engine and front suspension components. The lines are part hard line and part rubber line. Most leaks occur at the rubber-to-metal interface point.

Start by disconnecting the lines from the transmission. Use the proper wrench, as there will be some resistance to loosening couplers. Pull the lines away from the transmission when the couplers are loose. Also, have a bucket or drip pan underneath the connection, as fluid will immediately drip out.

With the rear part of the lines disconnected, move to the front of the car. Photo 2 shows how the lines attach to the front transmission cooler in front of the engine radiator. Remove the clamp bolt, and pull the lines out of the connector. Again, have a pan or bucket underneath to catch the transmission fluid that spills out.

Then snake the line out and around the suspension for removal. It took me quite a while to figure out how to do this.

Time:	Tab:	Talent:
4 hours	$150	👤👤👤👤

Tools: Set of crowfoot wrenches, drain pan

Applicable Years: All

Tinware: Transmission lines

Tip: Top off the transmission fluid when you're finished

PERFORMANCE GAIN: Smoother-running transmission with no loss of fluid

COMPLEMENTARY MODIFICATION: Change transmission fluid

One of the lines was far easier than the other one. Depending upon which engine you have, you may need to remove some suspension components (like the front A-arms) in order to gain enough clearance to maneuver the lines so they can be removed (see Project 59).

Installation is basically the reverse of removal. When you're done, check the fluid level in the transmission, as you will have lost some in the process of changing out the lines. Top off the fluid if necessary (see Project 36).

1 These two new E36 automatic transmission lines are waiting to be installed. The convoluted shape of the lines means you may have to temporarily remove some suspension components in order to make them fit during the installation. I was able to install the shorter of the two lines without removing anything else.

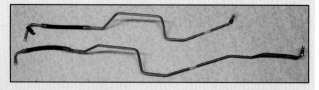

2 On the left is shown the threaded connector that attaches to the transmission. In order to remove this line, I had to use a crowfoot socket attached to a short extension. The connector on the right attaches to the transmission cooler located in front of the radiator. Remove the fastening bolt, lift up the retainer, and pull out the lines.

TRANSMISSION/DRIVE AXLES/SHIFTER

124

Replacing Transmission Mounts

The engine and transmission mounts often deteriorate with age on BMW cars. After many years, the rubber within the mounts becomes old and brittle, and fails to isolate the drivetrain from the rest of the chassis. Old, worn-out motor and transmission mounts can cause shifting problems because the drivetrain is no longer firmly held in its position.

One sign of this failure mode is the gearshift knob jerking backward under hard acceleration, or difficulty selecting gears during cornering. Cracks in the rubber indicate the mounts should be replaced. The rubber deteriorates over the years and needs to be replaced, even if the car has relatively few miles on it. Transmission mounts are easier to replace than the engine mounts and are very similar on both the E30 and E36 BMWs. A transmission mount bar is bolted to the rear of the car and supports the transmission.

Begin by jacking up the car, and place it on jack stands (see Project 1). Place a jack under the transmission to support the weight. Then, carefully remove the transmission mount bar from the car. You may have to bend the heat shield

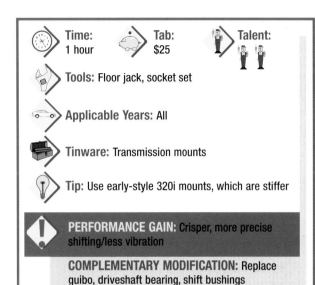

Time: 1 hour

Tab: $25

Talent: ♦♦

Tools: Floor jack, socket set

Applicable Years: All

Tinware: Transmission mounts

Tip: Use early-style 320i mounts, which are stiffer

PERFORMANCE GAIN: Crisper, more precise shifting/less vibration

COMPLEMENTARY MODIFICATION: Replace guibo, driveshaft bearing, shift bushings

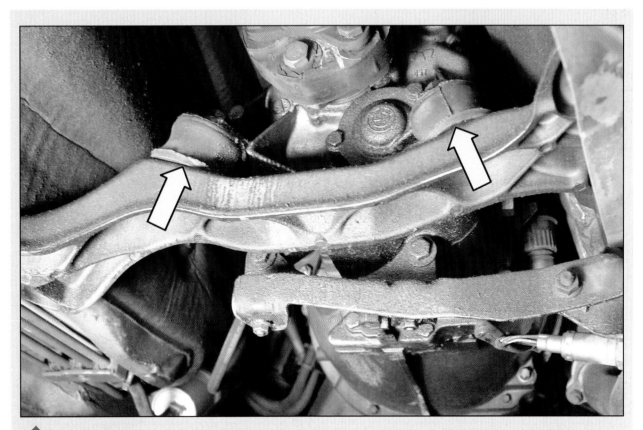

1 From underneath the car, you can see the transmission mount bar that runs across the center of the chassis, attaches to the sides of the driveshaft tunnel, and supports the transmission with the mounts sandwiched in between. The yellow arrows indicate the original stock mounts.

TRANSMISSION/DRIVE AXLES/SHIFTER

2 The upgraded E36 UUC transmission mounts are available in black or red. The black versions are tailored to street driving, while the red mounts are designed for track or autocross use. Be sure to line up the notch in the motor mount with the appropriate boss on the transmission mount bar (green arrow).

3 The tranny mount enforcers (TMEs) are installed on the top of the transmission mounts, beneath the transmission mounting flange. The TMEs prevent the mounts from expanding significantly under compression. Grease up the inside of the TME prior to installation in order to minimize chaffing of the mount. The flange from the transmission mount should fully protrude through the TME.

slightly out of the way to access the bolts that mount the transmission bar to the chassis.

Remove the old mount by removing the nut on the underside of the mount bar. New mounts simply bolt in place of the old ones. The boss on the bottom of the mount lines up with a notch on the transmission mount bar. This boss/notch combination prevents the transmission mount from rotating.

Stock BMW transmission mounts are not known for their performance or reliability. The transmission mount is intended to isolate the chassis of the car from vibration that the transmission emits during normal driving. Since the transmission is connected to the engine, it has a tendency to twist and turn as the car accelerates or decelerates under heavy braking. If the transmission mounts are flexible and sloppy, there may be a misalignment of the transmission with respect to the chassis of the car. This misalignment may cause what is commonly known as a "mis-shift," or in laymen's terms, a "moneyshift." A mis-shift may cause the driver to accidentally shift from a high gear to a much lower gear and overrev the engine. An overrev is very damaging to an engine and typically results in valves hitting the tops of pistons and bending. This, in turn, may result in the need for a very expensive engine rebuild.

One solution is to use early-style BMW 320i transmission mounts. They are thicker, tend to flex less than stock mounts, and, for the most part, are a bolt-in application. Another solution is to use better-designed transmission mounts and brackets, such as those produced by UUC Motorwerks. These new-and-improved mounts not only isolate vibration, but also do a better job of keeping the transmission correctly aligned with the chassis.

I also recommend the UUC tranny mount enforcers (TME). The TMEs hug and constrain the transmission mount and reduce the amount of deflection under vigorous driving. Adding UUC mounts and TMEs provides the best insurance against expensive mis-shifts.

When installing the mounts back into the car, fasten the bracket to the chassis first. Then lower the transmission onto the bushings and tighten the top nuts, securing the transmission to the bar. When you are finished, you should feel an improvement in the shifting of your car, and the drivetrain vibration should feel a little tighter and less sloppy. If you still have shifting problems, you might want to replace the shift bushings (Project 41). You may also want to inspect and replace the driveshaft flex disc (Project 39) or the driveshaft center bearing (Project 40) while working in this area.

Replacing the Driveshaft Flex Disc/Guibo

🕐 **Time:** 4 hours

🐭 **Tab:** $50–75

Talent: 🔧🔧🔧

🧤 **Tools:** Socket set and wrenches

🚗 **Applicable Years:** All E30/E36

🧰 **Tinware:** Flex disc, mounting hardware

💡 **Tip:** Install the bolts according to the arrows on the disc

❗ **PERFORMANCE GAIN:** Less vibration from the drivetrain, no breakdowns

COMPLEMENTARY MODIFICATION: Replace driveshaft center bearing

A flexible coupler joins the transmission output shaft and the driveshaft together. This rubber-reinforced coupler isolates vibration from the rest of the drivetrain while transferring power from the engine and transmission to the rear differential and wheels. As the car ages and is exposed to the elements, these discs (or "guibos," as they are sometimes called) develop cracks and begin to disintegrate. Although the rubber shell is reinforced with rope cords on the inside, it is not uncommon to see one completely fall apart with the cords flying everywhere. Inspect this rubber joint every 10,000 miles or so (about once a year). If this part fails, it does have the potential to leave you stranded. If it fails, bits and pieces can fly off and damage your shift linkage, preventing you from shifting.

Replacement is not too difficult, but you need to take a few things apart to reach the flex disc. Raise the car off the ground and support it on jack stands (see Project 1). Next, remove the muffler and catalytic converter. It is best to disconnect the entire rear exhaust system from the forward flange and drop it as a single unit. This sounds a lot harder than it really is; disconnecting the exhaust is quite easy (see Project 48). Undo the rear muffler clamps and front exhaust flange, and drop the muffler/catalytic converter as a complete assembly. Be aware, though, that this assembly weighs about 50 pounds. Exercise caution as you loosen clamps and bolts, and drop the entire system down.

With the exhaust removed and out of the way, remove the light heat shield that covers and protects the underside of the car. This heat shield is made of an aluminum-foil type of material and easily unfastens from the underside of the

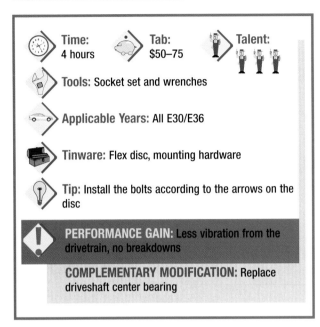

1 Using some paint or white corrective fluid, mark the transmission output flange and the driveshaft to clearly indicate how the flanges connect to each other for reference when you reassemble the unit. Place a mark at the point indicated by the yellow arrow and a mark in the same place on the transmission flange on the opposite side of the flex disc. This will help you align the driveshaft with the transmission output flange later on. You can see how the flex disc has begun to fail—small surface cracks in the rubber. The inset photo shows a nearly destroyed flex disc from a 1994 E36 that only had traveled 63,000 miles.

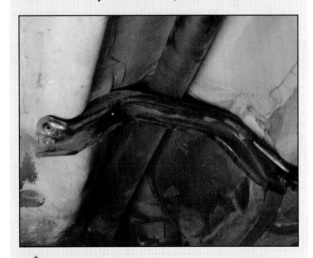

2 This photo shows the support beam that spans the driveshaft tunnel. Remove this crossmember so you can drop the driveshaft and gain enough clearance to separate the driveshaft from the transmission output flange.

TRANSMISSION/DRIVE AXLES/SHIFTER

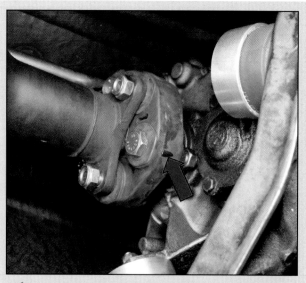

4 If you look closely at the photo, you will see that the flex disc has an arrow cast into the side of the rubber disc (red arrow). This arrow indicates where the flanges are to be mounted. The transmission or driveshaft flange will mate against the opposite surface. The flex disc arrow indicates which way the mounting bolts are pushed through the flex disc. These nuts are hand tightened at this time. The gold-colored bar in the background is part of the shift linkage, which is often damaged when the flex disc disintegrates while the car is in motion.

3 This is the rear driveshaft bearing. On some cars, you may need to completely disconnect the center driveshaft in order to remove the flex disc. If you can't get enough clearance to remove the flex disc, remove this bearing (see Proejct 40).

chassis. Although not 100 percent necessary, I recommend removing the lower transmission support bar to improve access to the flex disc (see Project 38). This is a great time to replace the transmission mounts while you have better access to this area.

Clearly mark the driveshaft (see Photo 1), and remove the bolts from the flex disc. There should be six in total, and some might not be very easy to reach. You will need a deep socket and open-ended wrench to get to them.

Release the parking brake and take the transmission out of gear. Use your hand to rotate the driveshaft so you can reach the bolts and their corresponding nuts. Re-engage the parking brake, and remove the now-accessible bolts and nuts. You will have to rotate the driveshaft three or four times in order to remove all of the bolts.

Now, turn your attention to the rear end of the tunnel. Remove the small crossbrace that spans the driveshaft tunnel (see Photo 2) in order to drop down the driveshaft and remove it from the transmission flange. Focusing on the rear driveshaft bearing (Photo 3), use one hand to remove the two nuts that secure the bearing to the chassis, while holding up the driveshaft with the other. When the nuts are removed, drop down the driveshaft and remove the shaft from the transmission output flange. During this step, be sure to support the driveshaft with a jack stand.

When you can get to the flex disc, completely remove it from the driveshaft. Since you have access to this area, this would be an excellent time to replace and replenish the shift bushings (Project 41) or to install a short shift kit (Project 42).

I generally install a brand-new flex disc along with new mounting hardware (available as a kit from PelicanParts.com). BMW recommends replacing the self-locking nuts, but I also replace the bolts if they look even slightly corroded. These six bolts transmit 100 percent of the engine's power to the rear wheels. Attach the new flex disc to the driveshaft, taking care to properly align the arrows on the side of the disc (Photo 4).

You can torque the flex disc bolts onto the driveshaft first, while you have easy access, but only if you have enough clearance to get the entire assembly back into the transmission output flange with the flex disc attached. Then, move the rubber disc back up to the transmission flange, and insert the remaining three bolts.

Be sure to align the white mark on the driveshaft with the matching mark on the transmission output flange. Also verify that the arrows on the rubber flex disc point toward the transmission output flange. With the flex disc bolts loosely connected, reattach the rear driveshaft bearing. Push it toward the front of the car as you tighten it. The bearing should not have any slack on the rearward side (see Project 40).

When the bearing is reattached, tighten the bolts on the flex disc. Reattach the heat shield, the exhaust system, and any oxygen sensor connectors you may have disconnected.

Center Driveshaft Bearing Replacement

Time:	3 hours	Tab:	$50–75	Talent:	

Tools: Plumber's wrench, socket set, circlip pliers

Applicable Years: All E30/E36

Tinware: Bearing assembly, backing plates, circlip

Tip: Use a plumber's wrench to loosen the driveshaft clamp

PERFORMANCE GAIN: Smoother-running drivetrain

COMPLEMENTARY MODIFICATION: Replace driveshaft flex disc (guibo)

1 The driveshaft spline clamp is difficult to remove with a standard crescent wrench, which keeps slipping off and doesn't grip well. Instead, I used a plumber's wrench that gripped the clamp much more securely.

2 The bearing cup is held in place by a large circlip (green arrow). Remove the clip with a pair of circlip pliers, and the cup should easily pry away from the bearing. With the cup removed, the bearing and support assembly should slide off the driveshaft. If your bearing is frozen on the shaft, you may need to use a bearing puller.

While replacing your driveshaft flex disc, you have to disassemble the rear part of the driveshaft. If so, take the time to inspect and/or replace the center driveshaft bearing. The bearing supports the rear part of the driveshaft, just before it connects to the rear differential. A worn bearing will generate strange vibrations you can feel in the cockpit and may also increase the amount of gear noise you hear while driving.

To replace the center driveshaft bearing, remove the driveshaft flex disc. (See Project 39 for instructions on how to disconnect and drop down the driveshaft.) With the flex disc removed, also remove the driveshaft tunnel support brace and loosen up the bracket that holds the rear driveshaft bearing. Mark the center driveshaft and the rear driveshaft with some paint or white correction fluid (see Project 39). They are a balanced assembly and need to be put back together in the same location in order to avoid vibration later on. The large clamp that secures the middle driveshaft to the rear driveshaft needs to be loosened. I have found it difficult to fit a normal wrench on this clamp, so I use a plumber's wrench for a better grip. (It's a little unprofessional, but it seems to work the best of any tool I've tried.) Loosen up the clamp so the center driveshaft can be removed. With the clamp loosened, you should be able to pull on the center driveshaft and remove it from the rear driveshaft. If the driveshaft will be hanging like this for an extended period of time, I suggest that you support it with some wire or a jack stand.

Remove the driveshaft clamp from the splined end. Then remove the large circlip, using a pair of circlip-removal pliers. Wear eye protection, as circlips can fly off if you're not careful. Pull the large support cup away from the bearing and

remove the entire bearing and support bracket assembly. If the bearing is stuck, you may need to use a bearing puller or tap it with a small hammer.

On the flip side, use a pair of pliers to remove the back support plate. Then tap in the new one, aligning it in the same orientation (flat side goes to the bearing). Tap it all

3 The rear support plate is pressed onto the driveshaft (green arrow). Pry it loose or tap it off with a hammer. Press the new one on in the same orientation—flat side goes up against the bearing when mounted on the shaft.

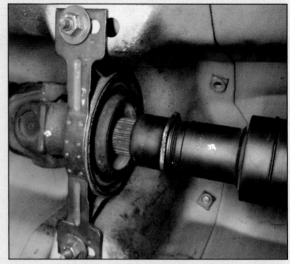

5 Shown here is the new center driveshaft bearing is installed back into the chassis. When tightening the bolts, push the bearing toward the front of the car to remove any slack in the rear driveshaft.

4 The new bearing is shown here. I also like to replace support components when performing a job. You would hate to have a part fail because you were too cheap to replace the one-dollar circlip that holds it in. The picture shows the bearing/support (sold as an assembly), the front and rear support plates, and a new circlip. See the 101Projects.com website for a list of the part numbers you may need for your car.

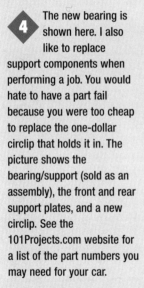

the way onto the driveshaft so that it mates flush with the end. This piece is fixed to the driveshaft and rotates around with the driveshaft when the car is moving.

Now, place the new bearing assembly on the shaft. If it doesn't slide on easily, tap it onto the shaft carefully, using a piece of pipe to fit around the splined shaft. The bearing should be a snug fit, and it should spin freely. Do not grease this bearing as you insert it—you don't want it to spin on the shaft itself. Attach the new support cup, and insert the new

large circlip into its groove on the driveshaft. Reinsert the driveshaft clamp onto the splines and reattach the center driveshaft, lining up the marks that you made previously. Clamp down and tighten the driveshaft clamp.

Photo 5 shows the new driveshaft bearing reinstalled. Refer to Project 39 for instructions on how to reconnect the flex disc. When tightening the rear driveshaft bearing to the chassis, push the bearing all the way toward the front of the car to preload it.

PROJECT 41

http://www.101projects.com/BMW/41.htm

Replacing Your Shift Bushings

On older BMWs, the shifting ability often deteriorates as the years go by. While many people blame their transmissions and prepare for a full rebuild, those worries may be unfounded. In many cases, the shift bushings have worn out and need to be replaced. Worn bushings can result in sloppy shifting, misplaced shifts, and grinding when engaging gears. Most people are amazed at the improvement that occurs when they replace their bushings. A mere $45 for a new bushing kit is a heck of a lot cheaper than a $1,500 transmission rebuild.

First, jack up the car to gain access to the undercarriage (see Project 1). The main shift linkage components are located above the driveshaft. The photos for this project were taken with the driveshaft removed, as I was replacing the clutch at the same time. During the normal process of replacing these bushings, your access and viewpoint will be restricted by the driveshaft. The driveshaft makes things a bit more difficult, but you can certainly accomplish all the tasks without removing it.

Before working underneath the car, move to the cockpit and remove the gearshift knob (see Project 68). With the gearshift knob removed, remove the foam padding beneath the shift boot. Then pull up the rubber shift boot so that it is only connected to the shifter lever.

Now, move underneath the car. The shifter assembly is shown in Photo 1. The inset photo was taken without the driveshaft installed, but you will have to maneuver around the driveshaft while working on the shifter mechanism. Begin by removing the lower shift selector rod (see Photo 2). Next, pry out the shifter arm bushing, which is attached to the chassis and supports the shifter arm (see Photo 3).

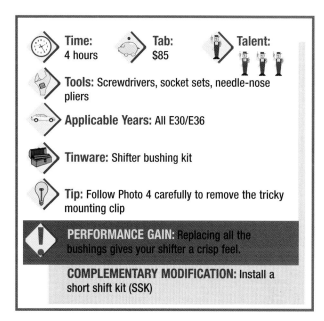

Time: 4 hours **Tab:** $85 **Talent:**

Tools: Screwdrivers, socket sets, needle-nose pliers

Applicable Years: All E30/E36

Tinware: Shifter bushing kit

Tip: Follow Photo 4 carefully to remove the tricky mounting clip

PERFORMANCE GAIN: Replacing all the bushings gives your shifter a crisp feel.

COMPLEMENTARY MODIFICATION: Install a short shift kit (SSK)

This will leave the shifter arm attached only to the transmission hinge point. This part is very tricky if you have never done it before or don't know what to expect (see Photo 4). Examine the angles in this photo to orient yourself. There's a clip attached to the transmission that secures the shifter arm. You need to remove this clip from the transmission in order to remove the arm. However, you cannot see the clip, what you're doing, or how to release the clip. If you have enough photos and understand how it's mounted, removing the clip should be a snap. With the clip removed, tug on the shifter arm and the entire assembly should drop from the car.

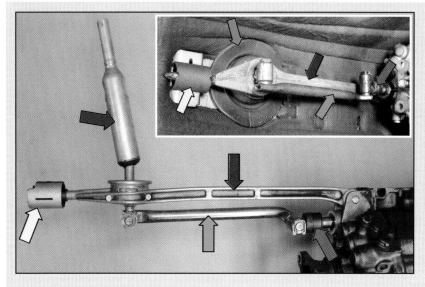

1 If you have any doubts about how the whole assembly fits back together, this photo shows the gearshift mechanism fully assembled and attached to the transmission, but removed from the car. The inset shows the assembly as it looks from underneath the car, with the driveshaft out of the way. The components are shifter arm bushing (yellow arrow), shifter arm (red arrow), selector rod (light blue arrow), shift coupler (purple arrow), shift lever (dark blue arrow), and shift lever boot (green arrow).

TRANSMISSION/DRIVE AXLES/SHIFTER

131

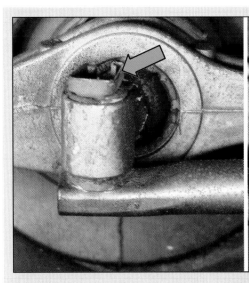

2 The shift selector rod is held onto the shifter handle and transmission coupler by two small circlips (arrows). Using a small screwdriver, remove both circlips and the rod should slide off. Catch the yellow plastic washers as they fall out of the assembly when you remove it. The shift coupler on the right is covered with oil, which is a sign that the shift rod selector seal has been leaking.

3 Use a small flathead screwdriver to remove the shifter arm bushing. This bushing holds the back end of the shift rod to the chassis and may require some force to insert or remove it from its bracket.

4 The side of the clip that attaches the shifter arm is shown in the upper left. The other three photos show the clip from various angles. You can't see this clip from under the car, and it will drive you crazy trying to get this off if you don't know how it's attached. The best way to remove the clip is to get under its back side with a small screwdriver. It's not easy doing this underneath the car, but it is possible. These photos also show aftermarket Delrin carrier bushings from UUC Motorwerks. They are direct replacements for the factory rubber bushings and offer a more precise fit than the originals.

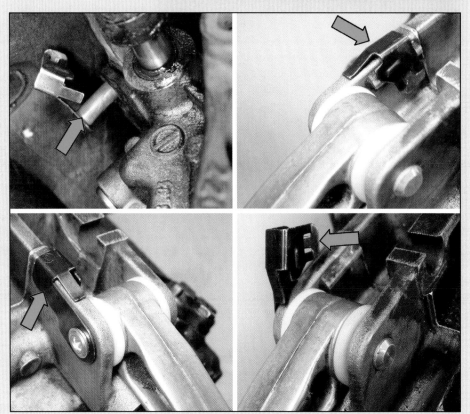

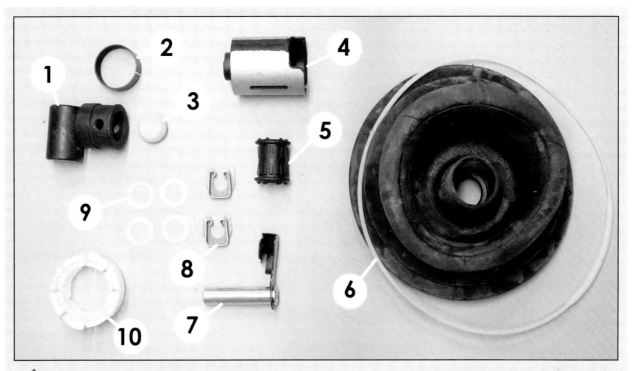

5 Renewing the shifter bushings is as simple as replacing all of the parts that have tend to wear out. Replace all of the pieces and bushings in this photo to give your shifter a pristine, precise feel. The only place that currently sells this complete kit is PelicanParts.com. Of course, some of your existing components may be reusable, so inspect them carefully. But if you want everything to be 100 percent crisp, then replace them all: **1:** Shift coupler with internal bushing. **2:** Pin retaining clip (often destroyed or weakened when removed). **3:** Ball cup sponge (typically disintegrated). **4:** Shifter arm bushing (attaches to chassis). **5:** Shifter arm bushing (attaches to transmission). **6:** Lower shift boot (often cracked). **7:** Shifter arm pin (often damaged when removed). **8:** Shift selector rod circlips. **9:** Yellow plastic washers/bushings for shift selector rod. **10:** Shift handle ball cup bushing (almost always heavily worn).

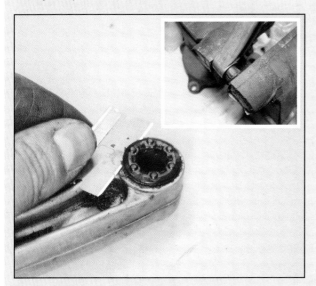

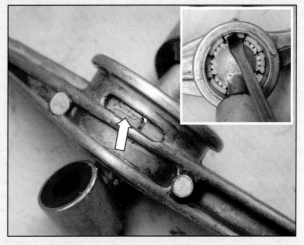

6 Cut away the outside of the carrier bushing. The inside of the bushing may have some metal parts reinforcing it, so be aware of this while you are cutting. The new bushing is simply inserted into the arm, although you may have to use a press or a vice to get the bushing seated completely in the arm (inset).

7 There is a small, special tool used to remove the ball cup bushing from the shifter arm. However, you can use two screwdrivers instead to rotate the bushing counterclockwise, and it should snap out of its housing. If the bushing offers resistance, chip at it with a screwdriver or pick. Don't worry about destroying the bushing, as you will replace it anyway. To get the bushing off the shift lever, pull on it with your fingers and it will slide out over the ball attached to the lever.

133

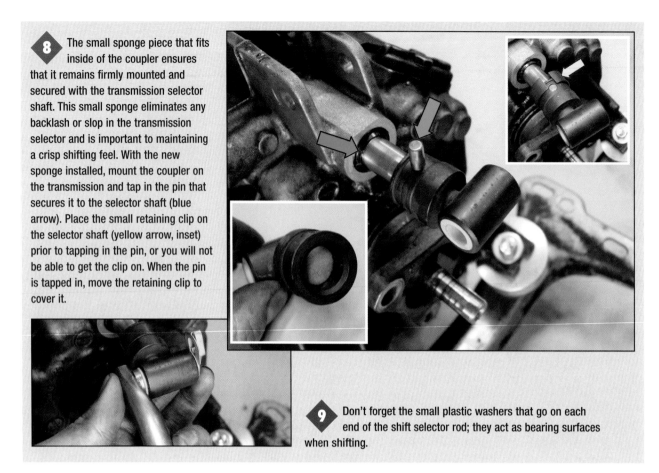

8 The small sponge piece that fits inside of the coupler ensures that it remains firmly mounted and secured with the transmission selector shaft. This small sponge eliminates any backlash or slop in the transmission selector and is important to maintaining a crisp shifting feel. With the new sponge installed, mount the coupler on the transmission and tap in the pin that secures it to the selector shaft (blue arrow). Place the small retaining clip on the selector shaft (yellow arrow, inset) prior to tapping in the pin, or you will not be able to get the clip on. When the pin is tapped in, move the retaining clip to cover it.

9 Don't forget the small plastic washers that go on each end of the shift selector rod; they act as bearing surfaces when shifting.

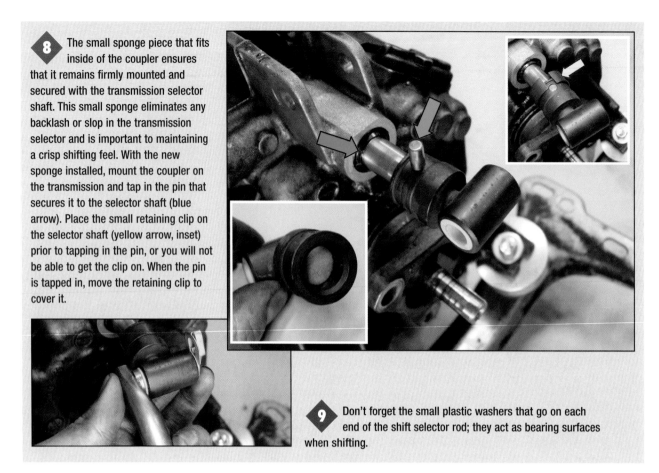

Now, replace each bushing, starting with the shifter arm bushing (sometimes called a "carrier bushing") that attaches to the transmission. Remove the old bushing by cutting it off with a razor blade or knife (see Photo 6), and simply press in the new one.

The shifter arm bushing is located on the bottom of the shift lever. Unfortunately, if this bushing is worn, you will have to replace the entire arm. If you happen to be installing a short shift kit (see Project 42), then you'll be replacing this arm anyway.

The main bushing that wears out is the ball cup bushing, which the shift handle sits in. Pull back on the shift boot that holds this bushing, and remove it by twisting it counterclockwise (see Photo 7).

Clean the shifter arm thoroughly before installing the new ball cup bushing. Now is also a good time to install a new shift lever boot. Clean the inside of the shifter arm where the ball cup bushing fits; get all the dirt and old grease out of the inside. Apply white lithium grease to the ball of the shifter arm prior to installation. Push the new ball cup bushing onto the shift lever and insert it into the shifter arm. Push the bushing in and rotate it clockwise with a screwdriver until the tab on the bushing clicks in place with the slot in the shifter arm.

Now, turn your attention to the shift selector coupler (see Photo 8). The coupler attaches to the transmission with a small press pin. Remove the covering clip and tap out this pin to remove the coupler from the transmission. With the

coupler removed, take a close look at the shift selector seal (Photo 8, green arrow). If it appears worn, this is an ideal time to replace it. To remove the seal, pry it out of its bore with a pick or screwdriver. Push the new shift selector seal onto the shaft and press it into its bore. It's easy to tap the seal in with a deep socket placed over the shaft. Tap the seal in until it is flush with the transmission housing. Then, using a wire brush, ensure that the ball on the transmission selector shaft is clean and clear of debris. Replace the coupler if the internal plastic bushing on the inside of the coupler is severely worn.

With all the bushings and couplers installed, reinstall the shifter arm. Installation of the retaining clip is the opposite of removal. Fit the shifter arm back onto the transmission with a new clip (see Photo 4). Next, install the new shifter arm bushing onto the shifter arm and chassis of the car. Place the bushing on the end of the shifter arm and snap it into place in its bracket on the bottom of the chassis (Photo 3). It may require some significant force pushing upward to get this bushing to snap properly into place.

With the arm securely in place, reinstall the shift selector rod. Photo 9 shows how the yellow washers, circlips, and selector rod are installed with respect to each other. Mount the rod to the shift lever in a similar manner.

When the assembly is put back into the car, re-fit the foam padding and gearshift boot properly in the cockpit, and reinstall the gearshift knob.

TRANSMISSION/DRIVE AXLES/SHIFTER

134

PROJECT 42

http://www.101projects.com/BMW/42.htm

Installing a Short Shift Kit

One of the most popular performance upgrades available for the BMW 3 Series is the addition of a short shift kit. The kit shortens the throw length of the shift lever, theoretically giving you the ability to shift faster. Installation is a moderate task and will probably take the better part of an afternoon.

There are currently many popular short shift kits on the market that are basically all the same—they each replace the shift lever with one that has a shorter throw. A little-known secret, however, is that you can swap out a shift lever from another BMW model into your car for a lot less money than a short shift kit will normally cost you.

If you have an E30 or E36 (models 318, 325, or 323), you can swap in the BMW E46 325Xi lever (part number 25-11-1-434-148, about $55) to obtain a 29 percent reduction in the shift throw. Or, you can swap in the E36 M3/328 lever (PN 25-11-1-221-977), which is basically a pre-built-in short shift kit for these cars and offers nearly a one-third reduction in lever travel. If you own an E36 M3 or a 328 and you want

Time:
6 hours

Tab:
$150–350

Talent:

Tools: Screwdrivers, socket sets, needle-nose pliers

Applicable Years: All E36

Tinware: Short shifter kit (SSK)

Tip: Replacing your shift arm with a stock one from another BMW is an inexpensive upgrade

! PERFORMANCE GAIN: Shorter shift throws

COMPLEMENTARY MODIFICATION: Replace your shifter bushings

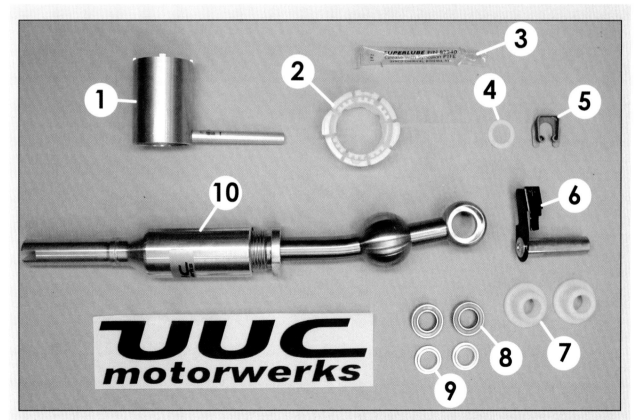

The UUC short shift kit (SSK) contains: **1:** Ball cup removal tool. **2:** New ball cup bushing. **3:** Grease. **4:** Yellow plastic bushing. **5:** New circlip. **6:** New pin clip. **7:** Delrin shifter arm bushings. **8:** Ball bearing cartridges. **9:** Bearing spacers. **10:** Height-adjustable short shift lever.

TRANSMISSION/DRIVE AXLES/SHIFTER

135

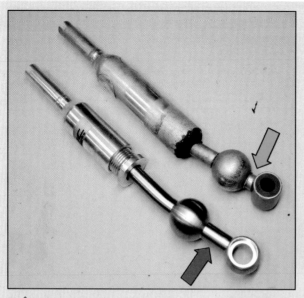

2 The lever itself is the heart of the short shift kit. The throw is made shorter by extending the distance from the ball to the lever arm bushing. The stock shifter distance (green arrow) is significantly shorter than the short shifter (red arrow).

3 The UUC kit includes ball bearing cartridges that insert in the end of the short shift lever. These precision bearings will last the life of your car and will never wear out like the factory plastic bearings.

an even shorter throw, you can swap in the shift lever from an M roadster (PN 25-11-2-228-384, about $55). However, if you want to use the M roadster lever, you may have to bend it slightly to make it fit properly. Use a bench vise and bend it to match your stock lever. All of these levers, as well as short shift kits, are readily available from PelicanParts.com.

For the purpose of this project, I chose the short shift kit (SSK) from UUC. This kit allows you to adjust the height of the shift lever to suit your driving style. I also like AutoSolutions short shift kits. AutoSolutions offers an amazingly detailed kit that replaces many shift bushings and eliminates many points of failure for the shifter.

The UUC kit, shown in Photo 1, comes complete with everything you need to replace your shift lever, and replaces many of the shift bushings that tend to wear out. Specifically, this kit contains Delrin bushings for the shifter arm and ball bearing bushings for the shift lever. The kit is very well constructed, and all the parts fit together with very tight tolerances.

Installing a short shift kit generally involves swapping out the old shift lever for the new one. Look to Project 41 for precise, detailed instructions for removing and replacing the shift lever.

The short shift kit replaces the old shift lever with one that has a longer throw on the bottom half. Photo 2 shows the original lever along side the UUC short shift lever. Note the difference in the length of the rod between the ball and the bottom bushing.

This particular shift kit comes with ball bearings that fit into the bottom of the shift lever. These bearings will virtually last forever. A set of small aluminum spacers is required, however, to make the bushings fit with the stock shift selec-

tor rod. During the installation process, I found my shift selector rod was a tad too big for the new bearings and required a bit of sanding to insert the rod into the bearing cartridge. Once in there, the fit was very tight.

After you install the kit, double-check the shift selector rod and its location with respect to the driveshaft and driveshaft flex disc. Because the throw on the short shift kit is longer underneath the car, the selector rod may tend to interfere with the driveshaft. If this is the case, slightly bend and bow the shift selector rod to clear any drivetrain components. Once you bow the shift selector rod, the shifter will lean backward slightly when fully installed.

At first, I didn't really care for the short shift kit. But after driving the car with the kit installed, I didn't want to go back to the standard shifter. If you're not sure whether you'll like the short feel, drive someone else's car that has a short shifter installed. The procedure to remove the kit takes as long as the installation, so try it out beforehand if you're not sure.

On a side note, many people install short shift kits in their cars thinking it will fix transmission problems. A short shift kit will not solve any problems and may make a poorly shifting car shift even worse. The reason for this is that with the short shift kit, the torque arm on the shift lever is much shorter, giving you much less resolution on the shifter. It's similar to having a gas pedal that only travels 1 inch over its range instead of 2 to 3 inches. You have less precision as to how much throttle you give the car. Similarly, the short shift kit has less precision with respect to gear position placement. Tackle the core problems with your transmission (synchros, shift bushings, etc.) prior to installing a short shift kit (see the other transmission projects in this book).

Time: 2 hours

Tab: None

Talent: 👤👤👤👤

Tools: Torx socket set, floor jack, jack stands, socket extension set

Applicable Years: All

Tinware: None

Tip: Have an assistant help you remove the topmost Torx bolts

PERFORMANCE GAIN: Enables you to perform a variety of other projects

COMPLEMENTARY MODIFICATION: Clutch replacement

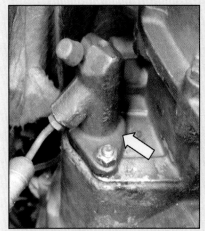

1 The slave cylinder is located on the left side of the transmission (yellow arrow). Simply unbolt it and tie it out of the way. Don't let it hang by its rubber hose.

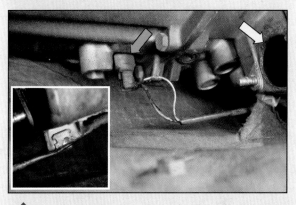

2 Here is the backup lamp switch (blue arrow). Remove the connectors and also unclip the harness from the side of the transmission (inset). The yellow arrow indicates where the slave cylinder mounts.

There are quite a few projects that require removing the transmission. An important one is clutch replacement, which is detailed in Project 44. There are several steps you will need to perform prior to dropping your transmission: disconnect the battery (Project 84), jack up the car (Project 1), remove the exhaust (Project 48), remove the driveshaft (Projects 39 and 40), and remove/disconnect the shifter (Project 41).

With these tasks completed, move to the side of the transmission and unbolt the slave cylinder. Also disconnect the backup lamp switch and detach its corresponding harness. If you are removing an automatic transmission, disconnect the transmission fluid lines on the left side (see Project 37) and the transmission control wire harness.

Support the transmission with your floor jack, and remove the lower transmission support bar (see Project 38). Then, move the floor jack under the transmission and support it. Now undo the bolts that hold the transmission to the engine.

This is where the going gets tough. First, these bolts are special Torx head bolts that require special sockets to remove them. You need to apply a phenomenal amount of force to remove these bolts from the transmission. If you don't have the right tools, you will not succeed. Buy yourself an external Torx socket set with sizes E6 through E16 (available from PelicanParts.com), and you will be covered for all of the bolts on the car. These Torx bolts are designed for applications where a good grip is required, and a lot of torque needs to be applied.

The inset in Photo 3 shows two of the Torx bolts you will need to remove. These bolts will be very difficult to remove

(see Photo 3 for bolt locations). Conversely, the bolts on the sides and bottom of the transmission will be relatively easy to remove. The two bolts at the top of the engine near the cylinder head are very difficult to remove, especially the one at the very top because there is no room to reach in to apply any significant amount of force. In order to remove the top bolt, I used the following tool combination: ⅜ Torx socket, ⅜ 1-foot extension, ⅜ extension U-joint, ⅜ 3-foot extension, ⅜ to ½ adapter, 3-foot ½ breaker bar. This combination of tools was the only way to reach the topmost bolt and remove it. I could place a smaller tool on the bolt, but then I had no leverage to remove it. With this combination of tools, hold the socket in place with your fingers and have an assistant rotate a breaker bar located about 3 feet from the rear of the engine.

As if the top bolts weren't enough of a pain, the starter bolts are even more difficult. Depending upon the year of

TRANSMISSION/DRIVE AXLES/SHIFTER

137

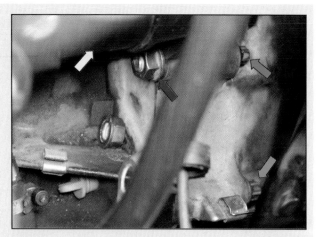

4 Perhaps the most difficult are the starter bolts (E36 318 shown here). These are made even more difficult to remove if your starter (yellow arrow) does not have threaded holes on its flange and requires a nut, as shown in the photo (red arrow). The green arrow indicates the head of the Torx bolt that attaches to this nut. The light blue arrow shows one of the M-10 Torx bolts that screws into the engine case. In general, the nut on this side of the starter is much easier to get to than the one on the opposite side. You'll likely drop one or two nuts while you're working in this area, so have a magnetic pickup tool handy.

3 This photo shows the flywheel end of the engine with the transmission and flywheel removed. The arrows indicate all of the headache bolts that need to be removed. They are mostly Torx bolts, similar to those in the photo inset. The red arrows indicate M-10 Torx bolts, the yellow arrows show the two M-10 Torx bolts that secure the starter, and the green arrows show M-8 Torx or regular bolts. Depending on which engine you have, the location and type of bolts may vary slightly.

The engine (red arrow) and the transmission (green arrow) are ready to be separated. The transmission is supported by a floor jack and a 4x4 piece of wood. Place a jack stand underneath the engine sump to support it after the transmission has been removed. **5**

your car, you may or may not have what is known as a "threaded starter." If the starter housing is threaded, simply remove the bolts from underneath the car. If your starter has nonthreaded holes, place a wrench on the nuts that are on the opposite side of the bolts. This can be nearly impossible on the six-cylinder cars. In order to reach these nuts, you may need to remove the six-cylinder intake manifold, which is a huge project in itself (see Project 12). If you have a 318 (like the E36 318 used for the photos in this project), it is possible to squeeze your hand down into the engine compartment and reach them. The nuts in question are shown in Photo 4.

Once these hard-to-reach nuts are removed, pull the transmission away from the rest of the engine. (Make sure

you haven't overlooked any bolts on the back side of the transmission; there's at least one that holds on a metal shield.) Now, with the transmission supported on your jack, pull it away from the engine. If all of the bolts, hardware, and accessories are properly disconnected, the unit should simply pull apart. If it doesn't, go back and double-check everything. It should pull away quite easily, so don't use the iron grip of death to pull it out or you could damage something.

Work slowly and carefully at this point. Make sure the transmission is well balanced on the jack—you don't want it to accidentally fall on you. Also, be sure the transmission is well supported as you pull it out. Don't let it hang on the center input shaft, as it could bend. Pull the transmission away from the car and lower it to the ground.

6 Here's the view from underneath as you pull the transmission away from the engine (manual transmission). The yellow arrow shows the engine; the green arrow indicates the metal shield wedged between the transmission and the engine block. The red arrow points to the flywheel, the purple arrow shows the pressure plate, and the blue arrow indicates the transmission.

PROJECT 44
http://www.101projects.com/BMW/44.htm
Clutch Replacement

Clutch assembly replacement is a common repair procedure for the BMW 3 Series. Unfortunately, it is a rather big process involving transmission removal. The good news: It's really not a difficult job if you have some information, hints, and tips.

The first step is to follow Project 43 to remove your transmission from the car. Once the transmission has been removed, remove the pressure plate. While working on my E36 318is, some of the pressure plate bolts began rounding out when tried to remove them. If this happens, dig out your trusty Dremel tool and cut them off. Don't worry about damaging the pressure plate, because you're going to be replacing it anyway. When you're ready to remove the last bolt, hold the pressure plate with one hand because it can fall off when the last bolt is removed. The disc should also pop out when you remove the pressure plate.

With the pressure plate removed, you should be able to see the flywheel. This particular flywheel was used on an E36 318is with air conditioning. The 318 with air conditioning uses a dual-mass flywheel (to reduce vibrations from the high-compression four-cylinder engine). Unfortunately, this flywheel can be expensive to replace, so consider replacing it

Time: 12 hours

Tab: $450

Talent: 👤👤👤👤

Tools: Allen-head socket set, clutch alignment tool, pilot-bearing puller

Applicable Years: All

Tinware: Complete clutch kit

Tip: Purchase a kit with everything in it, not a simple version

! PERFORMANCE GAIN: Smoother shifting, no power loss

COMPLEMENTARY MODIFICATION: Replace starter, overhaul shift bushings, replace flex disc and driveshaft bearing

1 Here's what your engine will look like after you have removed the transmission. The blue arrow shows the pressure plate. Notice the jack stand underneath the engine (yellow arrow), supporting the weight normally supported by the transmission.

2 An impact wrench can be your best friend in cases like these. Zapping off flywheel bolts can take a matter of seconds, versus several minutes with a long breaker bar. If you don't have an impact wrench, use a flywheel lock to hold the flywheel (see Photo 10).

3 Here's a revealing view of the engine after the flywheel has been removed. Some points of interest: starter (yellow arrow), cylinder head (red arrow), exhaust manifold (green arrow), flywheel seal (blue arrow), and pilot bearing (purple arrow).

with a non-dual-mass flywheel if yours is worn out (the engine's idle may be a bit rougher).

Next, remove the flywheel bolts. You can use a socket and breaker bar, or zap them off with an impact wrench. (I use an electric impact wrench for this task.) With the bolts removed, tug the flywheel off the crankshaft. The dual-mass flywheel is a two-piece component that is bonded together, which changes the natural frequency of the flywheel and reduces vibrations in the engine when the A/C system is running. For this car, I could have substituted a non-dual-mass flywheel, as I don't use the air conditioning system very often.

At this point, turn your attention to the transmission to refurbish the throwout bearing and arm. Start with the throwout bearing guide tube. The throwout bearing rides on this small tube when the clutch is disengaged. As the throwout bearing slides back and forth on the tube, it tends to wear out. Remove the bolts that hold the guide tube to the transmission. Remove the guide tube, and underneath you will find the mainshaft seal. Using a small screwdriver, punch a small hole in one of the indents in the surface of the seal, pick out the old seal, and remove it (Photo 6).

Clean the inside of the bore where the seal fits, and then install the new seal. Tap it in lightly with the end of a socket extension, taking care that it doesn't go in half-cocked. Install the seal so it is flush with the flange. Then install the new throwout bearing guide tube, applying a liberal coat of white lithium grease. Place the new throwout bearing on the throwout arm, and attach the arm to the transmission. The throwout arm is now ready for reinstallation.

This would be an excellent time to replace your starter if you've been having problems with it. Access is very easy when the transmission is out of the car; otherwise, getting at the starter is quite difficult (see Project 84).

4 Gather all the required parts for the job before you begin. It is very frustrating to get halfway through a replacement job, only to find out you need a part or a tool that you don't have. Here is a list of typical clutch replacement parts for a BMW 3 Series: **1:** Flywheel (optional). **2:** Pilot bearing. **3:** Throwout arm pivot. **4:** Clutch alignment tool. **5:** Throwout arm clip. **6:** Pressure plate. **7:** Clutch disc. **8:** Throwout bearing. **9:** Flywheel bolts. **10:** Flywheel seal. Not shown: pressure plate bolts, exhaust gaskets, selector rod seal, slave cylinder, and hose.

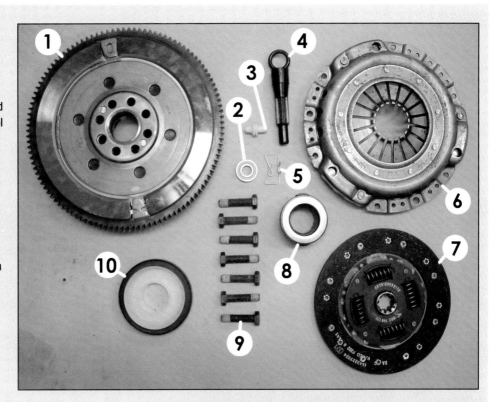

Turn your attention back to the flywheel end of the engine. First, replace the flywheel pilot bearing and the flywheel seal (see Photos 8 and 9). Next, reinstall the flywheel onto the engine. Always use new flywheel bolts, and have the flywheel resurfaced at a machine shop if you plan to reuse it. Install the new or resurfaced flywheel onto the engine, install the new flywheel bolts, and torque them down. Use a torque wrench and a flywheel lock to tighten the flywheel (see Photo 10).

After the flywheel is mounted, place the clutch alignment tool in the center of the pilot bearing. Install the clutch disc onto the flywheel (see Photo 11). Then install the pressure plate onto the flywheel, compressing the clutch disc. Use new pressure plate bolts if you damaged them when you removed the old pressure plate. When the pressure plate is tightened to its proper torque, remove the alignment tool. The disc, pilot bearing, and pressure plate should all be aligned.

Balancing the transmission on your jack, mate it with the engine. Be careful not to let the transmission mainshaft support any of the weight of the transmission—keep it well balanced on the floor jack. You may have to play around with the height and rotation of the transmission to line it up well with the engine. Once you have everything aligned, reattach all the Torx bolts you removed earlier. Remember to use a wrench on the nuts in the engine compartment if your starter isn't threaded through.

Next, reattach the slave cylinder, backup lamp switch, driveshaft, and exhaust. At this time, I also recommend you bleed the clutch system (see Project 49).

5 The throwout fork is attached at one end with a small metal clip (yellow arrow). Remove the fork from the transmission by pulling out the small plastic pivot from the hole in the transmission. Assemble the clip onto the pivot as shown in the photo inset (lower left). Lubricate the whole pivot piece well with white lithium grease. Grease the bearing and plastic pivot prior to installing them (inset, upper right).

I wish I could say this was an easy job, but it's not. It's not impossible, but there's a lot of stuff to remove and a lot of tricky spots. Purchase a kit that contains everything that you need for the job—all of the nuts, bolts, and bushings—as this will be a huge timesaver. The only place that currently sells such a kit is PelicanParts.com.

6 These steps are associated with replacing the seal: removal of the seal (**A** and **B**), tapping in the new seal (**C**), and replacement of the throwout bearing guide tube (**D**).

7 If the backup lamp switch is giving you trouble, now is the perfect time to replace it. The switch is located on the left of the transmission. Simply unscrew it from the side of the transmission case and replace with a new one.

8 The pilot bearing holds the transmission input shaft in place and aligns the transmission with the crankshaft. To remove the flywheel pilot bearing, you may need a bearing puller. Place the puller inside the bearing and use a socket on the puller tool to slowly remove the bearing from the crankshaft. In some cases, you may be able to reach in with your finger and pull the bearing out. Try pulling it out by hand before you resort to using the puller. The new bearing should fit easily inside the hole in the crankshaft. Use a deep socket to evenly tap in the bearing (inset).

9 Using a screwdriver, puncture and remove the flywheel seal. Be careful not to damage any of the side surfaces where the seal mates to the engine case. Coat the new seal lightly with Curil-T. Then install it onto the engine, taping lightly around the edge with the end of a ⅜ extension. Tap lightly and carefully—make sure the seal doesn't become cocked in its bore. Clean up any excess sealant that squeezes out.

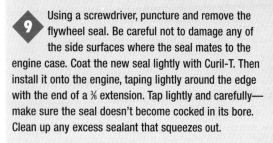

10 I use a simple flywheel lock that is basically a strip of metal with two large slots in it (arrow, right). This allows me to attach the lock to a bolt affixed to the engine case and one affixed to the flywheel, where the pressure plate bolts normally mount. This inexpensive lock works great on almost any car. With the lock in place, torque the bolts, working in a crisscross pattern. Start by tightening all the bolts to 50 percent of their final value, and then go around again and tighten them to the final value.

12 Without the alignment tool (blue arrow), it would be nearly impossible to insert the transmission input shaft into the pilot bearing when mating the engine and the transmission back together. When the pressure plate bolts are all tightened, you should be able to pull out the alignment tool, and the pressure plate and clutch disc should be centered with respect to the pilot bearing (photo inset). Use new pressure plate bolts when performing a clutch replacement project.

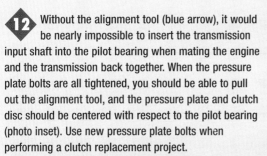

11 The clutch alignment tool (yellow arrow) aligns the clutch disc (red arrow) with the pilot bearing, pressure plate, and flywheel (blue arrow).

Replacing the Clutch Slave Cylinder

TRANSMISSION/DRIVE AXLES/SHIFTER

Time: 2 hours

Tab: $65

Talent: ▮▮

Tools: Socket set

Applicable Years: All

Tinware: Clutch slave cylinder

Tip: Use flare-nut wrench on supply fitting

PERFORMANCE GAIN: Reliable shifting and clutch operation

COMPLEMENTARY MODIFICATION: Bleed brake system

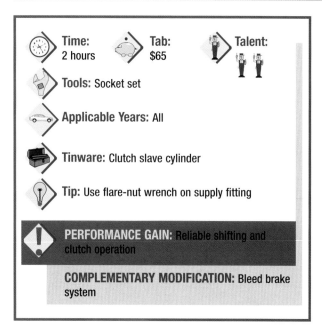

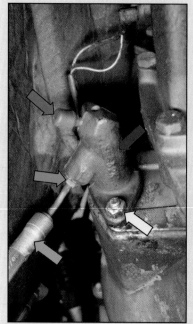

1 Shown here are the various components associated with the slave cylinder: red arrow—the slave cylinder; yellow arrow—one of two attachment nuts; blue arrow—hydraulic feed line; green arrow—fitting for attaching the line (use flare-nut wrench); purple—bleed nipple cover.

The BMW 3 Series cars have a hydraulic clutch engagement system; there are no cables involved with clutch actuation. Although this creates a more reliable clutch system, there can be a failure or breakdown of the system if the slave or master cylinder gets old and begins to leak or fail. A spongy feel to the clutch pedal, gears grinding when shifting, long pedal travel, and hydraulic leaks under the car are signs that one or more components of the system have failed. Start with the clutch slave cylinder, as it is one of the easiest and least expensive parts to replace.

Replacement of the slave cylinder is a snap. It is easy to get to from underneath the car. Start by jacking up the car (Project 1). The slave cylinder is located on the left side of the transmission. Two nuts fasten it to the transmission. Disconnect the hydraulic line from the cylinder. Use a flare-nut wrench to remove the hose—these hydraulic fittings have a tendency to strip if you use a regular wrench. Also, inspect the clutch slave line. Replace it if it's bulging or if it shows signs of cracking in the rubber. Before you disconnect the hydraulic line, have a small drip pan or plate to catch the few drops of fluid that will leak out. Now, remove the two nuts that hold the cylinder to the transmission. The slave cylinder should remove easily. Install the new one and reattach the clutch fluid line. Place a bit of white lithium grease on the tip of the slave cylinder prior to installation.

Now bleed the system. I like to use the Motive Products power bleeder (see Project 50), available from PelicanParts.com, for this task. Attach the power bleeder to the top of the master cylinder reservoir and pump up the pressure in the bleeder. Move underneath the car and attach the bleeder hose

2 Bleed the slave cylinder using a similar procedure to how you bleed each of the brake calipers (see Project 49). When you disconnect the fluid supply line to replace the slave cylinder (green arrow), use a flare-nut wrench (inset). These fittings easily strip, and the flare-nut nut wrench is the best way to prevent this.

to the bleed nipple on the slave cylinder. Let the system bleed out until no more bubbles appear.

When finished, remove the bleeder system, lower the car, and try the clutch again. The pedal should have a good feel to it, and the clutch should engage normally. If you still have problems, try replacing the clutch master cylinder.

http://www.101projects.com/BMW/46.htm

Replacing Manual Transmission Fluid

Time: 30 minutes

Tab: $15–50

Talent:

Tools: 14-millimeter Allen wrench socket

Applicable Years: All

Tinware: Transmission fluid, 5-quart drain pan

Tip: Make sure you have a drip pan and plenty of paper towels

PERFORMANCE GAIN: Longer-life transmission and differential

COMPLEMENTARY MODIFICATION: Use Swepco transmission fluid for better shifting

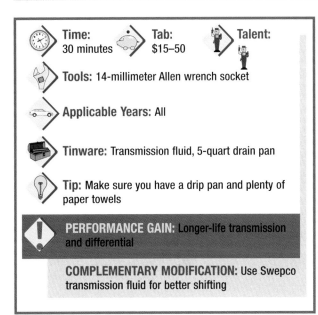

1 Shown here are the filler (green arrow) and drain plug (yellow arrow) for a typical 3 Series E36 manual transmission. The drain plugs on the other transmission models are similar.

2 Shown here are the filler (green arrow) and drain plug (yellow arrow) for the average 3 Series E36 differential. You will need a 14-millimeter Allen wrench to remove these nuts. The drain plugs on the other differential models are similar.

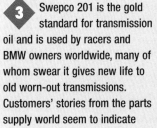

3 Swepco 201 is the gold standard for transmission oil and is used by racers and BMW owners worldwide, many of whom swear it gives new life to old worn-out transmissions. Customers' stories from the parts supply world seem to indicate that using Swepco on a transmission with worn synchro rings can prolong its life and fend off that costly transmission rebuild.

One of the easiest tasks to perform on your BMW is to change the manual transmission and differential fluid. The differential and manual transmission both use the same lubricating fluid. It's very important that the fluid in your transmission is at the proper level, or your transmission will experience significant wear. The synchro rings and sliders depend on a slick surface to match speeds when shifting. If your transmission is low on oil, the wear on these components will accelerate significantly and shifting the car will be more difficult. If your BMW is having problems shifting, check the level of the transmission oil. In addition, keeping the differential and its associated gears well lubricated should help increase your fuel mileage.

The transmission oil also keeps temperatures down inside the transmission. The engine is a primary source of heat for the transmission, as the heat conducts and radiates through and around the points where the engine and transmission are mounted. The transmission creates heat itself as the gears and synchros turn within its case. Keeping the transmission fluid at its proper level helps to mitigate heat problems. Note that on some higher-performance BMW transmissions, there is an external transmission cooler that operates similarly to the engine cooler.

Change the transmission fluid every 30,000 miles or about once every two years. Check your owner's manual for more details on the scheduled requirements for your BMW. This number is a rough estimate, and may vary depending upon the use of your 3 Series (track vs. street). There are many moving parts in the transmission, and they tend to drop microscopic metal particles into the tranny oil. Specifically, the synchro rings wear down each time you shift. While transmission bearings are not as sensitive as engine bearings, they can exhibit wear from these particles in the oil.

The 3 Series manual transmission has two plugs for filling and emptying the transmission oil, located on the side and bottom of the transmission case. To check the level of the transmission oil, remove the top filler plug on the side of the transmission (where you usually add fluid). When you have the plug removed, stick your finger inside the hole, angle it toward the ground, and see if you can feel any fluid. Do this when the car is cold and parked on level ground. If you can feel the fluid level with your finger, your fluid level is about right, or perhaps will need only a little topping off.

If you cannot feel the fluid level, add transmission oil to the case. If you plan to change the oil, remove the small plug on the bottom of the transmission case. Empty the transmission oil when the car is still warm, as it will drain easier. For

TRANSMISSION/DRIVE AXLES/SHIFTER

this task, have a drain pan capable of handling at least 5 quarts of transmission oil. Check the fluid in the pan for any unusual metal pieces or grit in the oil.

While the fluid is emptying, clean out the drain plugs. Using a cotton swab or a paper towel, carefully clean out any black debris and particles present.

Replace the bottom plug on the transmission, but don't tighten it too much (50 N-m or 37 ft-lbs maximum). Fortunately, this plug does not tend to leak (transmission oil is thicker than engine oil). If the plug does leak later on, however, you can always tighten it a little more. Now, add transmission oil to the case with a hand-operated oil pump. These pumps are available from most auto parts stores, and attach to the top of the plastic transmission-oil bottle. They work similarly to liquid soap dispensers. Pump the transmission case full of fluid until it just starts to run out the filler hole. It should take a little more than 1 quart to fill. Replace the filler plug and

clean up the few drips that might have come out of the hole. Tighten the filler plug in a similar manner to the drain plug.

Replacement of the differential fluid is nearly identical, except you will need a 14-millimeter Allen wrench for the plugs. If you have one of those semi-rare, four-wheel-drive 3 Series cars (like the 325ix), don't forget to change the fluid in the forward differential and center transfer case as well.

In many cases, generic transmission gear oil will suffice. However, for those BMW 3 Series owners wishing to have the best of everything for their cars, there is Swepco 201 multi-purpose gear lube. This gear oil is excellent for transmissions, and many of our loyal Pelican Parts BMW and Porsche customers swear by it. Rumor has it that adding Swepco 201 will prolong transmission life and help to postpone a costly rebuild. While this can hardly be proven, a lot of our customers agree that Swepco 201 creates a difference they can feel while shifting.

PROJECT 47
http://www.101projects.com/BMW/47.htm
Replacing CV Joints, Boots, and Axles

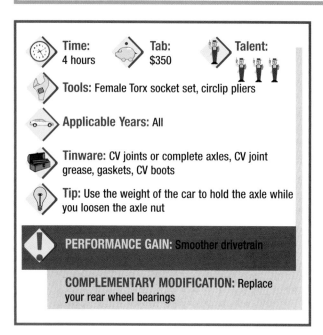

Time: 4 hours

Tab: $350

Talent:

Tools: Female Torx socket set, circlip pliers

Applicable Years: All

Tinware: CV joints or complete axles, CV joint grease, gaskets, CV boots

Tip: Use the weight of the car to hold the axle while you loosen the axle nut

PERFORMANCE GAIN: Smoother drivetrain

COMPLEMENTARY MODIFICATION: Replace your rear wheel bearings

One of the most common sets of suspension items to replace or service on the 3 Series are the "constant velocity," or CV, joints that connect the wheels to the transmission. These bearings, packed in grease, get a tremendous amount of wear through the years and tend to wear out after about 100,000 miles. One of the clear signs the joints need replacing is a distinct "clunk, clunk, clunk" sound coming from the rear axle when the car is in motion.

In some cases, the boots that cover and protect the CV joints will be torn and need replacing. The procedure for replacing the boots is very similar to the procedure for replacing the entire joint. Install new boots each time you install a new CV joint.

For both the E30 and E36 cars, BMW sells only a complete, replaceable axle. The new axle contains both the inner and outer CV joints, as well as the boots that cover and protect them. Although the inner E30 CV joints are available separately, I recommend installing the complete axle. It simply bolts up to the car, and you don't have to mess with disassembly or CV joint grease.

First, jack up the car (see Project 1) and remove the road wheels. Then, pry off the dust cover cap on the wheel hub if your car has one in place (Photo 1). Now, knock out the back of the center hubcap of the wheel, remount the wheel to the car, and then lower the car. With the car in gear and the emergency brake on, use a long breaker bar to loosen up the drive shaft flange collar nut. This nut is tightened to more than 250 N-m (184 ft-lbs), so it will take quite a bit of force to loosen it up. Lift the car up again and remove the wheel once more.

Next, start removing the bolts from the inner CV joint (see Photo 2). You'll need a properly sized Torx socket set for this task. Warning: You must have the correct tool for this task, or you might strip the CV bolts. If you do strip the bolts, the only way to remove them is to grind them off, which is not a fun task.

To access the CV bolts, rotate the wheel until you can clearly get your Torx socket wrench on the bolts. Then, pull the emergency brake and place the transmission into first gear. This will allow you to loosen the bolts without having the axle spin. When you have removed all the bolts you can access from this angle, release the brake, take the car out of gear, and rotate the wheel until you can reach the next set of bolts. When all of the bolts are removed, suspend the end of the drive axle with some rope or wire.

1 The driveshaft flange collar nut is hidden by a metal cap (green arrow). Pry this cap off after you remove the wheel to gain access to the nut (red arrow). Pop out the center hubcap to your road wheel, remount the wheel to the car, and lower the car so the wheel will be held steady as you loosen the driveshaft flange collar nut. When reinstalling the axle, deform the retaining nut around the stub axle splines (purple arrows).

Once you have the CV bolts disconnected, it's time to remove the axle. Disconnect the brake caliper and brake rotor assembly, and hang the caliper out of the way (see Project 57). Place your floor jack under the rear trailing arm to support it. Remove the lower shock mount bolt (see Project 61). Now, lower the rear trailing arm so you have enough clearance to remove the stub axle from the hub. If you cannot pull the axle out of the hub, you may need an axle-pulling tool to push the center of the axle out of the hub.

Remove the axle and take it to your workbench. The inner CV joint is held onto the axle by a large circlip, which is located under the large rear dust cap. The outer CV joint is not removable. If you wish to replace the CV joint boot on the outer joint, you must remove the inner joint first. Remove the inner circlip, release the boot clip, and the joint should come right off. It's generally a really bad sign if large balls from the bearing start falling out. That's a clear indicator you need to replace the joint. If you reuse the joint, carefully place it in a plastic bag to avoid getting any dirt or grime in it. Even a grain of sand in the CV joint can cause it to wear out prematurely. Carefully inspect both CV joints for any wear prior to installing them back into the car.

Once you remove the joint, replacing the boots should be easy. Simply disconnect the small clips that hold the boot to the shaft and slide it off. The new boots are installed in a reverse manner. Rotate the joint through its entire motion before tightening the small, inner boot clamp—you don't want it to be too tight.

When installing new CV joints, pack them with plenty of CV-joint grease before you install them. Also place plenty of

2 The four CV joints are located in the rear of the car, attached to the transmission flanges and the stub axles on the trailing arms. Replace the joints in pairs—either both of the inside ones or both of the axles. Chances are, if one of the joints is showing signs of wear and deterioration, the other three will not be far behind. The inset photo shows the inner CV joint dust cover that must be pried off in order to access the retaining circlip underneath. The yellow arrows show four of the six Torx bolts that attach the axle to the rear differential.

3 This complete axle has a new nut and retainer plate, an inner CV joint, and a CV boot kit for an E30 3 Series. On the 3 Series cars, the outer CV joint is not available separately but must be purchased as a complete axle, because the joint is integrated into the stub axle and cannot be separated. If the boots are damaged and leaking, you should replace them, because dirt and debris can find their way inside. Apply the Loctite 2701 that comes with the CV boot kit to the CV bolts just prior to installation.

grease in and around the boot. Move the joint in and out as you insert the grease to ensure it's well lubricated, as new CV joints do not come pre-greased. When ready, place the new boot on the axle, and then place the CV joint on the axle. Reattach the circlip so the joint is attached to the axle. Reinstalling the axle is essentially the reverse of the removal process. Use a new driveshaft flange collar nut and retainer plate when you mate the axle back with the hub. Deform the nut and/or retaining plate after the nut is tightened.

Once you have the entire assembly back together, take the car out for a drive and check the rear for noises. All should be smooth and quiet, and the boots should no longer leak.

Exhaust

These projects are designed to help you get the most out of your exhaust system. Fortunately, BMW exhaust systems are relatively simple, and the processes of replacing/upgrading the components are fairly easy. This section will show you how to swap out mufflers and also how to replace a cracked exhaust manifold.

Muffler and Hanger Replacement

Time: 2 hours

Tab: $250

Talent: 🔧🔧🔧

Tools: Socket set

Applicable Years: All

Tinware: Muffler, new rubber hangers, new exhaust gaskets

Tip: Have a helper assist you with lowering the heavy exhaust system

PERFORMANCE GAIN: Sporty-sounding exhaust

COMPLEMENTARY MODIFICATION: Short shift kit, driveshaft bearing replacement, flex disc replacement

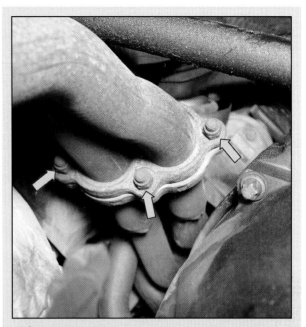

When I first bought my darling wife her own E36 BMW 3 Series, one of the first comments she made about the car was, "It's too loud." The car had been originally ordered with a factory sport muffler option that was a bit too macho for her sensibilities. I promptly ordered the standard factory muffler and installed it on her car.

1 This photo shows where the exhaust system meets up with the manifold. Remove the six bolts (orange arrows) from the exhaust flanges near the front of the transmission, and then unfasten the small exhaust retainer clamp from the bottom of the transmission. You may want to use WD-40 or another penetrant on the bolts before you attempt to remove them. If you have a late-model BMW, disconnect any oxygen sensor wires that may be attached to the exhaust pipes.

2 Old, worn-out exhaust gaskets are a prime source of loud and annoying exhaust leaks (upper left). It's very common for the exhaust gasket to break when you try to remove it from the exhaust pipe. In fact, breaking it in two is sometimes the only way to remove it from the exhaust pipe. New gaskets (lower left) press onto the exhaust pipe. Use a small plastic hammer if the gasket offers any resistance. The exhaust flanges should compress and crush the new exhaust gasket as they are bolted together (right).

EXHAUST

149

The E36 cars use a very long muffler and tailpipe assembly that connects to the catalytic converter in the center of the car. Replacement is a very easy process, primarily because the exhaust components and bolts are so accessible. One thing to remember, though: The muffler assembly is quite heavy and very unwieldy to manipulate under the car, so this is a project best performed with a helper. The muffler is suspended from the bottom of the car with rubber mounting brackets. These brackets and two muffler gaskets, or "donuts" as they are sometimes called, should be replaced when you remove the muffler, as they tend to get old and break.

First, raise the rear of the car off the ground and support it on jack stands (see Project 1). Then, using two wrenches, disconnect the bolts on either side of the muffler flanges. With a few taps of a hammer, the flanges should separate from the muffler. Always replace the donut gaskets that seal the muffler to the rest of the exhaust system whenever you disturb them. In most cases, they will already be cracked when you go to remove them. Press on a new gasket before you mate the new muffler.

The main body of the muffler is held in place with the rubber muffler hangers and a few brackets that clamp the side of the muffler. Carefully unbolt and release the clamps from the side of the muffler. The muffler will fall once you release the clamps, so have your helper hold the muffler while you release them. Also, wear eye protection when working underneath the car. It's very easy to drop the muffler on your face if you're not paying attention. Even if you don't drop the muffler, it's rusty and dirty under the car.

The rubber hangers bolt to the frame of the car. Remove them, transfer over the muffler hanger bracket, and remount

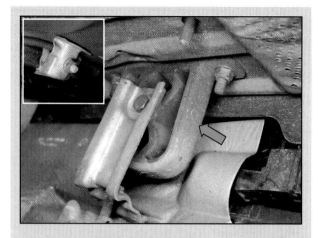

3 The inset photo shows one of the two muffler clamps. These clamps squeeze the edge of the muffler and hold it in place. The entire assembly hangs from the body of the car by flexible rubber muffler hangers (green arrow). These hangers allow the muffler some flexibility in movement as the car is being driven.

the hangers to the car. When mounting the new muffler, loosely attach the pipes to the rest of the exhaust system, and then loosely hang the muffler in place. Again, ask for the help of a friend to hold the muffler while you fasten the exhaust flanges and muffler clamps. With the muffler loosely attached to the clamps and loosely connected at the flanges, tighten the flange, compressing the exhaust gasket. Then tighten up the clamps on the muffler, and you're good to go.

PROJECT 49
http://www.101projects.com/BMW/49.htm
Exhaust Manifold Replacement

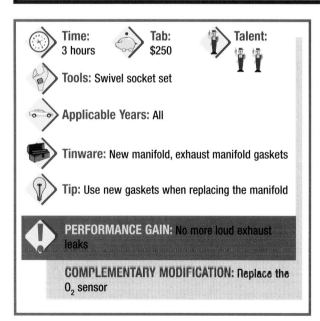

Time: 3 hours

Tab: $250

Talent: 🔧🔧

Tools: Swivel socket set

Applicable Years: All

Tinware: New manifold, exhaust manifold gaskets

Tip: Use new gaskets when replacing the manifold

PERFORMANCE GAIN: No more loud exhaust leaks

COMPLEMENTARY MODIFICATION: Replace the O₂ sensor

Cracked exhaust manifolds have plagued the E30 and E36 models through the years. The manifolds installed on these cars are made of cast alloy steel. This alloy is heavy and durable, but over the years, it can become increasingly susceptible to cracks. It's not uncommon to discover a loud exhaust leak coming from the engine compartment. If it's not a worn-out exhaust gasket, it's most likely a cracked manifold. A cracked manifold will introduce an exhaust leak into the system. Besides making the engine noisy, it can cause the engine to run roughly and erratically.

The exhaust manifold connects each cylinder's exhaust ports to the exhaust system. Before you go near the manifold, make sure the car is completely cold. To remove the manifold, you will need to remove the nuts from the exhaust studs on the head. A set of swivel sockets comes in handy, as they are great for reaching nuts in hard-to-reach places. It is highly likely that the exhaust studs will come out of the manifold when you try to remove the nuts. If this happens, replace the studs with new ones, as you cannot properly

1 Here's a shot of the old exhaust nuts and the rusty studs. I recommend spraying the area with a penetrant prior to removing the studs. With this E36 manifold, a lot of force was required, and the nuts froze to the studs. However, with the right amount of leverage, the studs came loose. In the lower left, you can see new exhaust gaskets, new studs, and new copper nuts. Use anti-seize compound on the nuts when you reinstall them (lower right).

2 When I removed the cylinder head to replace the head gasket on this E36 (see Project 17), 100 percent of the exhaust studs came out of their holes in the head. The exhaust nuts had frozen solid on the studs. When attempting to remove just the nut, the stud loosened up in the head. I ordered 24 new studs (yellow arrow) to replace the ones that had been removed—it would have been impossible to remove the nuts without damaging the threads. The inset photo on the left shows the old exhaust studs with the nuts still firmly attached to them. The inset photo on the right shows the swivel sockets that are perfect for getting into these tight spaces.

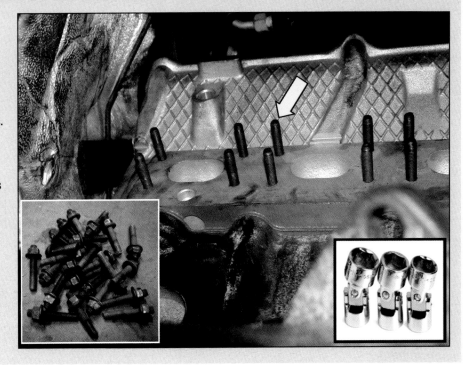

install the manifold again using the studs if the nuts are frozen on them. You won't know if the stud bottoms out in the head or if it's actually holding on the exhaust manifold, and that's why it's best to just use new studs and nuts.

On 1996-and-later cars, you have to remove the secondary air check valve and pipe from the exhaust manifold.

Also, on some models, you may need to remove the oxygen sensor prior to removing the manifold (see Project 27).

A word of caution: Always use new exhaust gaskets when reinstalling the manifold. If you reuse gaskets, you may introduce an exhaust leak into the system, which can result in a noisy engine and erratic engine performance.

Brakes

The brakes are probably the most important system on your BMW. No matter how fast you go, you will always need to stop—and sometimes rather quickly. It's of paramount importance to keep your brakes in top condition. The stock 3 Series braking system is a very capable setup if properly maintained. The projects in this section detail the troubleshooting, restoration, upgrades, and maintenance of this all-important brake system.

Time: 2 hours

Tab: $20

Talent: ♟♟

Tools: Power bleeder, 7- or 9-millimeter wrench, floor jack, jack stands

Applicable Years: All

Tinware: 3 or more quarts of brake fluid

Tip: Use different-colored brake fluid so you know when your system is flushed

PERFORMANCE GAIN: Quicker, firmer stopping

COMPLEMENTARY MODIFICATION: Rebuild brake calipers

1 There are a few little tricks for changing the brake fluid. ATE makes a brake fluid called SuperBlue that comes in two different colors. Fill your reservoir (green arrow) with a different-colored fluid when you bleed the brakes. When the new colored fluid exits out of the caliper, you will know there is fresh fluid in the system. Use DOT 3 or DOT 4 brake fluid in your car. Some of the later-model BMWs with anti-lock braking systems require DOT 4 fluid. Do not use silicone DOT 5 fluid for street use. Shown here is the Motive Products Power Bleeder is attached to the brake fluid reservoir (blue arrow). Available for about $50 from PelicanParts.com, it is a huge time saver when it comes to bleeding the brakes.

Bleeding brakes is not one of my favorite jobs. There always seems to be a bit of black magic involved with the bleeding process. Sometimes it works perfectly, and other times it seems like you end up with a lot of air in the system. When bleeding the brakes, repeat the procedure several times to make sure you have removed all the trapped air from the system.

There are two popular methods of bleeding the brake system—pressure bleeding and vacuum bleeding. Pressure bleeding uses a reservoir of brake fluid with a positive air pressure force placed on the opposite side of the fluid, forcing it into the brake system. In vacuum bleeding, you fill the reservoir and then apply a vacuum at the bleeder nipple to pull fluid through the system.

Of these two methods, I advocate pressure bleeding, and then having a family member stomp on the pedal to free up any trapped air in the system. If the family member really owes you big time, you will be the one stomping on the pedal, and they can spill brake fluid all over themselves.

To begin, fill the system with brake fluid. I recommend using colored brake fluid, such as ATE SuperBlue, in order to determine when fresh fluid has been flushed through the entire system. One of my favorite pressure bleeding tools is the Motive Products Power Bleeder. This system has a hand pump you can use to pressurize the brake fluid to just about any pressure. A small gauge on the front of the brake fluid reservoir indicates the pressure of the brake fluid inside. The large reservoir can hold about 2 quarts of brake fluid—more than enough for most brake flushing and bleeding jobs. Retailing for about $50, the bleeder kit is a highly useful and cost-effective tool to have in your collection.

The system bleeds by pressurizing a bottle filled with brake fluid from air from an internal hand pump. The procedure is to add fluid, attach the bleeder to the top of the reservoir cap, and pump up the bleeder bottle using the hand pump. This will pressurize the system. Check to make sure that there are no leaks around the bleeder or where it attaches to the top of the master cylinder reservoir.

Now start bleeding the system. Start with the right rear caliper, located furthest away from the master cylinder (for left-hand drive cars). The whole process is a lot easier if the car is off of the ground (Project 1) and the rear wheels have been removed. Turn the front wheels for access to the calipers if you don't want to lift the front end. To bleed the right rear caliper, attach a hose to the bleed nipple, place it in a jar, and open the valve by turning the bleeder nipple counterclockwise with a 7-millimeter wrench. Let the fluid drain until there are no more bubbles. If you don't have a pressure bleeder system, you need someone to press on the pedal repeatedly to force fluid through the system.

153

2 Open the bleed nipple by loosening it in the caliper about one-quarter of a turn. Let the brake fluid run out of the caliper until no more bubbles appear (inset). Routinely flush and replace the brake fluid every two years. Deposits and debris can build up in the lines over time and decrease the efficiency of your brakes. Bleeding the system regularly can also help you spot brake problems you wouldn't notice simply by driving the car. Never reuse brake fluid, and don't use brake fluid from an open can that has been sitting on the shelf (or in your Power Bleeder) for a while. Brake fluid tends to absorb moisture when sitting on the shelf. This moisture "boils" out of the brake fluid when you start using the brakes and can result in a spongy pedal.

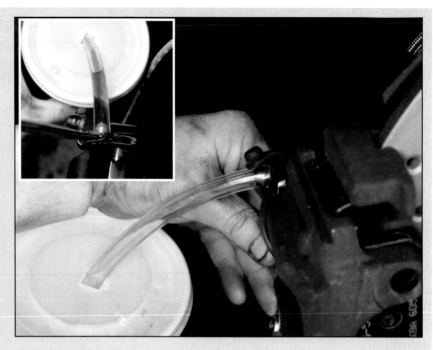

3 There is a relatively new product out called Speed Bleeder. These small caps replace the standard bleeder valves on your calipers. The Speed Bleeders have a built-in check valve that eliminates the need for a second person when pedal-bleeding the brakes. Simply

open the bleeder valve for a particular caliper and step on the brake pedal. The Speed Bleeder allows brake fluid to cleanly bleed out of the system without sucking air back in when you release the pedal. When used in conjunction with a pressure bleeder system, you can achieve a pretty firm pedal bleeding the brakes by yourself. I still recommend the two-person pedal-stomping method as a final procedure, simply because the high pressure from this method can help to dislodge trapped air bubbles.

Another solution is to get a check valve and place it on the nipple while you stomp on the pedal (see Photo 3). This will get fluid into the system, but you will still need a second person for the final step to ensure you have bled the system completely. If your caliper has two bleed nipples (some have one, others have two), bleed the lower one first.

When no more air bubbles come out, move on to the next caliper. Bleed them in this order: right rear caliper, left rear caliper, right front caliper, left front caliper. Bleeding in this order minimizes air getting into the system.

Repeat the process until you no longer see any air bubbles coming out of any of the calipers. Make sure you don't

run out of brake fluid in the reservoir, or you will suck in air and have to start over. Start out with about 1/2 gallon of brake fluid in the pressure bleeder and another 1/2 gallon on the shelf in reserve. Depending on your car, and the mistakes you may make, I recommend having an ample supply. During the bleeding process, don't forget to check the master cylinder reservoir. As you remove fluid from the calipers, it will empty the master cylinder reservoir. If the reservoir goes completely empty, you will most certainly add air bubbles in to the system, and then you will have to start all over. Keep an eye on the fluid level, and don't forget to refill it. Also, always put the cap back on the reservoir. If the cap is off, brake fluid may splash out and damage your paint when the brake pedal is released. If you are installing a new master cylinder, perform what is called a "dry bleed" on the workbench. This is the process of filling the master cylinder with brake fluid. Simply add brake fluid to both chambers of the master cylinder, and pump it a few times. This will save you time when bleeding the brakes.

Now, make sure all the bleeder valves are closed tightly. Disconnect the pressure system from the reservoir. Get your helper to press down repeatedly on the brake pedal at least five times, and then hold it down. Then open the bleeder valve on the right rear caliper. The system should lose pressure, and the pedal should sink to the floor. When fluid stops coming out of the bleeder valve, close the valve and tell your helper to release the pedal. Do not let them take their foot off until you have completely closed the valve. Repeat this motion for each bleeder valve on each caliper at least three times. Then, repeat this entire procedure for all the valves in the same order as described previously.

I recommend that you use the previous procedure as a final step, whether you are vacuum or pressure bleeding. The high force associated with the pressure from the brake pedal can help free air and debris in the lines. If the brake fluid doesn't exit the nipple quickly, you might have a clog in your lines. Brake fluid that slowly oozes out of the lines is a clear indication that the rubber lines might be clogged and constricted. Don't ignore these warning signs—check out the brake lines while you are working in this area (see Project 56).

Now, let the car sit for about 10 minutes. Repeat the bleeding process at each corner. The pedal should feel pretty stiff. If the pedal still feels spongy, make sure you have the proper adjustment on the rear calipers or drum shoes (Project 53). You may need a new master cylinder, have a leaky caliper, or have old, spongy flexible brake lines.

There's one caveat to the whole bleeding process, involving cars with anti-lock braking systems (ABS) and all-season traction (AST) systems. BMW recommends that cars with AST only be bled at the dealer using specific bleeding equipment.

For cars with ABS, however, the bleeding method detailed here works very well. If you find that your ABS-equipped car feels spongy on the brake pedal, take the car to a deserted parking lot and engage the ABS system by stopping short a few times. Then go back and re-bleed the system, and it should take care of the spongy pedal.

Remember that brake fluid kills—paint jobs, that is. Brake fluid spilled on paint will permanently mar the surface, so be very careful not to touch the car if you have it on your hands and clothing. This, of course, is easier said than done. Don't bleed the system in a tight garage. The probability of spilling on yourself and then leaning against your car is too great. Rubber gloves help to protect yourself from getting it on your hands and your car. If you do get a spot on your paint, blot it with a paper towel—don't wipe or smear it. Also, do not try to clean it off with any chemical or cleaning solutions.

PROJECT 51
http://www.101projects.com/BMW/51.htm

Replacing Brake Pads

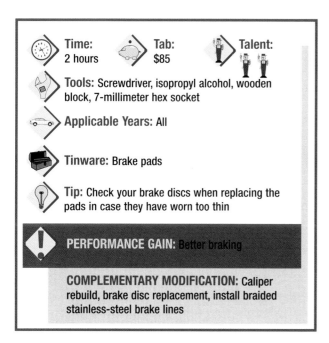

Time: 2 hours

Tab: $85

Talent:

Tools: Screwdriver, isopropyl alcohol, wooden block, 7-millimeter hex socket

Applicable Years: All

Tinware: Brake pads

Tip: Check your brake discs when replacing the pads in case they have worn too thin

PERFORMANCE GAIN: Better braking

COMPLEMENTARY MODIFICATION: Caliper rebuild, brake disc replacement, install braided stainless-steel brake lines

Replacing the brake pads is one of the easiest jobs to perform on your BMW. In theory, you should inspect your brake pads about every 10,000 miles, and replace them if the material lining of the pad is worn down enough to trigger the pad replacement sensor. In practice, most people don't inspect their pads very often and usually wait until they see the brake-warning lamp appear on the dashboard. Replace the pads and inspect your discs as soon as you see that warning lamp go on.

If you ignore the warning lamp, you may get to the point of metal-on-metal contact, where the metal backing of the pads contacts the brake discs. Using the brakes in this condition will not only give you inadequate braking, but will also wear grooves in the brake discs. Once the discs are grooved, they are effectively damaged and there is often no way to repair them. Resurfacing sometimes works, but most often the groove cut will be deeper than is allowed by BMW specifications. Don't run the risk; instead, replace the pads right away.

The procedure for replacing pads on all four wheels is basically the same. There are slight configuration differences between front and rear brakes, but the procedure for replacement is similar. First, jack up the car (see Project 1) and remove the road wheel to expose the brake caliper that presses the pads against the disc. Make sure the parking brake is not engaged when you start to work on the pads.

If you look inside the caliper, you will see the brake pads, which usually look very thin. To replace the brake pads on E36 cars, you first need to remove the caliper. Begin by removing the small plastic cap that covers the caliper guide bolts. Remove both guide bolts from the caliper (see Photo 1). Then remove the brake pad retaining clip, which keeps the pads from rattling (see Photo 2). Wear safety glasses during this step, as the clip can fly off if you're not careful. Then, use a pair of needle-nose pliers to remove the brake pad sensor (see Photo 3). For most E30 cars, you can remove the lower caliper guide bolt and then simply rotate the caliper upward to remove the pads. Some, however, require the complete removal of the caliper (as E36 cars do).

After the guide bolts have been removed, lift the caliper off of its mount. Suspend the caliper using zip ties or rope; don't let the caliper hang from its rubber hose, as it can damage the brake line. At this point, you can remove the outer brake pad from the caliper and use a screwdriver to pry the inner pad out of the caliper piston. Be extra careful not to push the brake pedal while the caliper is removed from the

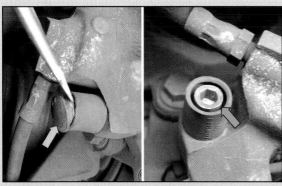

1 The left side of this photo shows the plastic dust caps (orange arrow) that cover the caliper guide bolts. Using a 7-millimeter Allen socket, remove the bolt, and the caliper should simply slide off. When reinstalling the bolt (blue arrow), apply a bit of caliper assembly grease to the long body of the bolt. This special grease allows the caliper to slide back and forth without binding and also withstand the high temperatures that are often experienced by the braking system.

2 With the road wheel removed, you can see the caliper and brake disc assembly. Pry off the retaining clip with a screwdriver (red arrow). Wear safety glasses, as these clips can fly off quite easily.

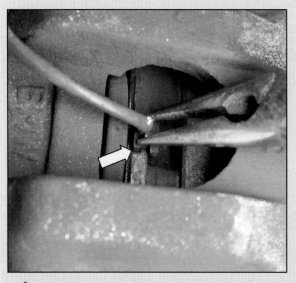

3 Grab the brake pad sensor (yellow arrow) with a pair of needle-nose pliers. If your brake sensors activated the lamp on your dashboard, replace them with new sensors. Disconnect the sensor and plug in the new one. The plug for the sensor is located in the top of the wheelwell.

4 This is what the caliper should look like after you have removed both pads. The BMW 3 Series (and many other BMWs) uses a single-piston caliper design. One piston presses against the side of the brake disc (orange arrow), and the whole caliper slides on the guide bolt to achieve equal pressure on the disc from both pads. When you are ready to install the pads back into the caliper, use a wooden or plastic handle to push back the caliper pistons (inset). Don't use a screwdriver, as you might damage the piston seals. Keep your eye on the fluid level in the master cylinder reservoir—it can overflow when you push back on the pistons.

disc, or you'll have a hard time pushing the pistons back far enough to get around the disc when you are ready to reinstall the caliper.

Once you have the pads removed, inspect the inside of the caliper. Clean this area with compressed air and isopropyl alcohol. Make sure the dust boots and clamping rings inside the caliper are not ripped or damaged. If they are, the caliper may need to be rebuilt (see Project 52).

Now, inspect the brake discs carefully. Using a micrometer, take a measurement of one disc's thickness. If this disc is worn

beyond its specifications, it's time to replace it—along with the one on the other side (see Project 57).

Installing new brake pads is quite easy. Take a small piece of wood or plastic and push the caliper piston back into the caliper. The new pads will be quite a bit thicker than the worn-out pads, and the piston will be set in the old

5 Install the inner pad into the caliper by inserting it with your hand. Brake pads should only be replaced in sets—replace all front pads and/or all rear pads at the same time. The same rule applies to the brake discs, which should be checked each time you replace the brake pads. Note the nylon cable tie I used to suspend the caliper (green arrow). Never let the caliper hang from the brake line, as it can damage the line.

pad's position. Pry back the piston with the wood, being careful not to use too much force. A note of caution: Using a screwdriver here can accidentally damage the dust boot and seals inside the caliper, and is not recommended.

As you push back the pistons in the calipers, you will cause the level of fluid in the brake reservoir to rise (see Photo 1 of Project 50). Make sure you don't have too much fluid in your reservoir. If the level is high, you may have to siphon out a bit from the reservoir to prevent it from over-flowing. Also, make sure the cap is securely fastened to the top of reservoir or brake fluid may accidentally spill onto your paint.

When the piston is pushed all the way back, insert the new pads into the caliper. If you encounter resistance, double-check to make sure the inside of the caliper is clean. Then simply snap the inner brake pad into place using your hand.

Mount the caliper back onto its mounting bracket, surrounding the brake disc. If the caliper won't fit, you may need to push the piston in a bit more until the space in between both pads is wide enough for the brake disc. Using a torque wrench, tighten the guide bolt to 30 N-m (22 ft-lbs), and then reinstall the brake pad sensor into the gap in the pad. Use a new sensor if the old one was activated.

You may want to spray the back of the brake pads with anti-squeal glue. This glue keeps the pads and the pistons glued together and prevents noisy vibration. Anti-squeal pads can also available as sheets that are peeled off and placed on the rear of the pads.

When finished with both sides, press on the brake pedal repeatedly to make sure that the pads and the pistons seat properly. Top off the master cylinder brake fluid reservoir if needed. Brake pads typically take between 100 and 200 miles to completely break in. Braking performance may suffer slightly as the pads begin their wear-in period. Avoid any heavy braking or emergency maneuvers, if you can, during this period.

PROJECT 52
http://www.101projects.com/BMW/52.htm
Rebuilding Brake Calipers

 Time: 6 hours   **Tab:** $60   **Talent:**

 Tools: Flared-end wrench to remove brake lines

 Applicable Years: All

 Tinware: Brake caliper rebuild kits, brake fluid, silicone assembly lube

 Tip: Soak the caliper in parts cleaner overnight if possible

 PERFORMANCE GAIN: Better braking, no more sticking calipers

COMPLEMENTARY MODIFICATION: Replace the flexible brake lines, brake pads, and discs

If your car is pulling to one side when braking, you might have a sticky caliper that needs rebuilding. The rebuilding process is actually a lot simpler than most people think. Rebuilding involves removing the caliper, cleaning it, and then reinstalling all of the components, along with new seals. Removing the caliper is often the most difficult part of the task.

First, jack up the car (see Project 1). Then refer to Project 57 for details on removing the caliper from around the brake disc. Moving on, Project 56 will guide you in disconnecting the brake line from the caliper. Once you have the caliper free and clear from the car, take it over to your workbench, and begin the disassembly process.

Start by removing the piston from the calipers. Using a small screwdriver, remove the dust boot that surrounds the piston. Place a small block of wood in the center of the caliper to prevent the pistons from falling out of the caliper. Then blow compressed air through the caliper bleeder hole to force the piston out of its chamber. Start slowly, and gradually increase pressure until the piston reaches the block of wood.

1 Rebuilding calipers is a lot easier than you might think. The basic principle involves tearing apart the caliper, cleaning it, and then reinstalling the pistons with new seals and clips. Professionally rebuilt calipers, like this one, are usually sandblasted and plated so they return to their original gold color. Rebuilding your calipers may solve a lot of mysterious brake problems you've been experiencing. Because rebuilding seems difficult, it's usually the last project tackled when overhauling the brakes. Another option is to purchase rebuilt calipers and mount them on your car.

2 Replace the inner piston seal, which keeps brake fluid from leaking out past the cylinder. Also, clean the inside of the cylinder of dirt, debris, and corrosion. Don't scratch the inside of the caliper cylinder while you are working on it, or the caliper may leak when you reassemble it.

Make sure the piston doesn't come all the way out of its chamber. After the piston is far enough out, you should be able to grip it with your fingers. Be careful when working with compressed air, as it is more powerful than it appears and can make the pistons fly out of the caliper unexpectedly.

Using a rag to protect the sides of the pistons, carefully remove them both from the caliper with your hands or a large pair of Vise-Grips. Don't touch the sides of the pistons with any metal tools, which may scratch their surfaces.

If the piston is frozen, more radical methods of removal may be necessary. Using a block of wood, pound the caliper on the block of wood until the piston begins to fall out. If the piston starts to come out and then gets stuck, push it back in all the way and try again. Eventually, the piston should come out of the caliper half. Another method is to use the car's brake system to release the pistons. Reconnect the caliper to the car, and have an assistant pump the brakes to force out the piston.

Once the piston has been removed from the caliper, carefully clean both the inside and outside of the caliper with brake cleaner or another appropriate solvent. Blow out all of the passages with compressed air. If possible, let the whole assembly sit in parts cleaner overnight. If the piston or its cylinder is badly rusted or pitted, replace the caliper. A little bit of surface rust is okay but should be polished off with a coarse cloth or Scotch-Brite. Thoroughly scrub out the inside of the cylinder and outside of the piston so they are perfectly clean.

After the caliper and piston have been cleaned and dried, coat the cylinder and piston with silicone assembly lube. If you don't have this silicone assembly lube handy (available from PelicanParts.com), coat the entire assembly with clean brake fluid. Be careful not to get any lube or brake fluid on the dust boot.

Insert the new piston seal inside the caliper piston groove. It should fit smoothly in the groove, yet stick out slightly. Wet the seal with a little brake fluid. Now install the dust boot inside-out onto the piston, so the edge of the boot hangs out toward the area where the piston contacts the brake pad. Then, insert the piston slightly into the caliper. It should slide in easily, but make sure it doesn't go in crooked. Wrap the dust boot around the outer edge of the caliper, and then push the piston into the caliper.

As the piston reaches the internal O-ring, you will encounter some resistance. Make sure the piston is pushed in and doesn't become cocked as you insert it. If you have trouble inserting the piston into the caliper, softly tap it with a plastic hammer, or use a small piece of wood to compress the piston into its home position in the caliper housing.

Now install the brake pads (Project 51) and remount the caliper onto the car. Bleed the brake system (Project 50), and you should be good to go. Of course, carefully test the brakes on the car before you do any significant driving.

Parking Brake Adjustment

Time: 1 hour

Tab: None

Talent:

Tools: Long screwdriver, flashlight

Applicable Years: All

Tinware: None

Tip: Properly adjusting the parking brake can reduce the drag on your road wheels

PERFORMANCE GAIN: No more drag on your rear wheels

COMPLEMENTARY MODIFICATION: Adjust clutch cable, replace brake pads

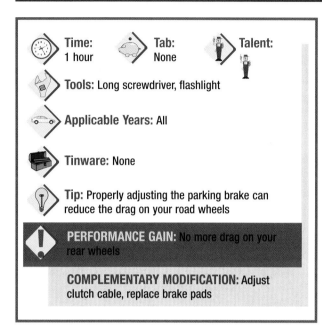

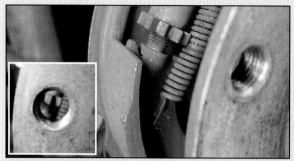

1 Removing the rotor reveals the mechanism for the parking brake adjustment. As the small cog turns, the parking brake shoes are pushed out toward the inside of the disc. The shoes are in proper adjustment when they are just about to touch the inside of the disc. The photo inset identifies the location of the sprocket when you are trying to look through the access hole in the brake disc—removal of the brake disc is not necessary.

2 The ends of the parking brake cables (right side shown by yellow arrow) need to be loosened prior to the adjustment process, and then tightened later on after the shoes are properly adjusted.

Through the years, the parking brake on your BMW may become loose or otherwise fail to perform properly.

First, raise the rear of the car (Project 1) and remove the two road wheels to gain access to the rear calipers. Important: Release the parking brake lever and shift the car into neutral. Using a screwdriver, push back slightly on the brake pads until the brake disc turns freely. Check the fluid level in the master cylinder reservoir, as pushing the pads back will make the fluid level rise and may cause it to overflow.

Once the brake disc moves easily, move to the cockpit of the car, lift up the handbrake boot, and loosen the two nuts that attach the handbrake cable to the inside of the brake mechanism. If there is any pre-tension on these cables, it will be difficult to adjust the handbrake.

Adjust the parking brake shoes by turning a small gear or sprocket with a screwdriver. Unfortunately, this sprocket can only be reached through one of the lug nut holes in the brake disc.

Rotate the brake disc until you can see the small adjusting sprocket through the lug nut hole (see Photo 1). You may need a flashlight for this procedure. Reaching in through the hole, use a screwdriver to rotate the cog until the parking brake shoe is tight and the rotor no longer rotates. If you are working on the right side of the car, turn the cog toward the front of the car to tighten the brake shoes. If you are working on the left side of the car, rotate the cog toward the rear of the car to expand the shoes. If you find that you are turning the sprocket a lot and the brake shoes still aren't tightening up, you're probably turning it in the wrong direction.

Repeat this procedure for the opposite side of the car. After you adjust the sprockets so the brake shoes are just pressed up against the inside of the disc and you can no longer turn the disc, back the brake shoes off until the disc can spin.

Now move back to the cockpit, and pull up on the handbrake several times to seat the cables. Finally, pull up on the handbrake so the ratchet clicks through four notches. Tighten up the cables using the nuts at the bottom of the handbrake lever. Tighten each nut to the point that there is just slight resistance at each wheel.

Now, release the lever and verify that the wheels turn freely. The brake discs should rotate with the handle in the down position but fully lock by the time that the handbrake is pulled up a few notches past four clicks.

When you are finished, recheck the master cylinder reservoir fluid level. Then step on the brake pedal a few times to ensure that the pistons have repositioned themselves properly against the brake pads. Finally, verify that the parking brake lamp on the dashboard illuminates as soon as the handle is pulled up.

BRAKES

159

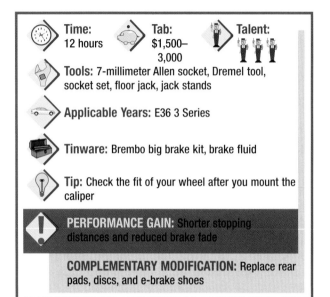

Time: 12 hours

Tab: $1,500–3,000

Talent: 👔👔👔

Tools: 7-millimeter Allen socket, Dremel tool, socket set, floor jack, jack stands

Applicable Years: E36 3 Series

Tinware: Brembo big brake kit, brake fluid

Tip: Check the fit of your wheel after you mount the caliper

PERFORMANCE GAIN: Shorter stopping distances and reduced brake fade

COMPLEMENTARY MODIFICATION: Replace rear pads, discs, and e-brake shoes

BMW braking systems have always been good, but I've often thought that the stock systems could be better. The single-piston design on these cars always seemed inferior to the design used on Porsche 911s. Repeated 80–0-mile-per-hour stop tests by *European Car* magazine found that stock E36 M3 brake fluid boiled and became highly ineffective after about four runs. Needless to say, if you're going to be doing any performance driving, it's time to upgrade your brakes.

Upgrade kits aren't cheap—they range from about $1,500 to $3,000, with the top end of the dollar range dominated by the premium kits from Brembo. Though spendy, these kits include a caliper rebuild, new discs, and new brake lines.

You can expect the following from your upgrade:

Shorter stopping distances. Depending upon the application and road conditions, you can experience 20–30 percent shorter stopping distances. Thus, the faster you are traveling, the greater the improvement.

Repeatability. Even the simplest brake systems can stop a car very well once or twice. However, as the brake fluid and pads heat up, performance decreases, and each stop gets longer and longer. Installing a big brake kit will consistently give you remarkably shorter stops.

Reduced or eliminated brake fade. The larger brake discs on the big brake systems dissipate heat that causes brake fade and failure. Each component in the big brake system is designed for performance braking, which includes the proper cooling of the system. Whether you're coming down a steep mountain, or blasting from turn to turn on a racetrack, big ger brake systems are better equipped to prevent overheating than stock systems.

Better control and modulation. With a performance brake setup, you achieve a better pedal feel. You can brake harder and still maintain control. The big brake systems work flawlessly with the BMW anti-lock braking system (ABS).

Big brake kits typically come with equipment to replace only your front brakes. Front brakes typically perform 80 percent or more of the stopping, and sometimes much more during panic stops. Don't put a high-performance, big brake system on the rear, because it may cause the rear brakes to lock up prematurely and actually increase stopping distances and decrease control—exactly what you're trying to avoid! Cars with performance systems on the rear are often coupled with anti-lock controllers or proportioning valves to prevent rear brake lockup. BMW 3 Series cars only have anti-lock mechanisms on the front brakes.

Brembo manufactured the big brake setup we chose for this project. Brembo is one of the leading brake system manufacturers and an OEM supplier to world-class sports car manufacturers such as Porsche and Ferrari. The Brembo mono-block kit we used for this upgrade is widely considered to be one of the best for the E36 3 Series. It was mounted on a BMW E36 318ti that had a few other performance mods to match.

The kit requires 17-inch or larger wheels on your car. The stock M3 wheels will work and were installed on this 318ti at the time of the upgrade. Not all 17-inch wheels will allow the huge calipers to fit, so plan in advance and verify that your wheel combination will work with the larger brake components.

First, loosen the lug nuts on the wheels and raise the front of the car (see Project 1). You might want to raise the rear as well, as I recommend you inspect and refurbish the rear brakes at the same time, so you have fresh components on all four corners of the car. On this car, I installed rear cross-drilled rotors, new rear brake pads, and new parking brake shoes to match.

For the remainder of this project, I will describe the installation procedure for the right side of the car—the opposite side is exactly the same. With the car on jack stands, remove the two road wheels. When the road wheel has been removed, disconnect the brake pad sensor. Then unbolt and disconnect the brake caliper from the car (see Project 57). Tie the caliper up and out of the way, but **do not disconnect the brake line**. Make sure there is no tension on the brake line. Even though you will replace it, you don't want to make a habit of hanging the caliper by the brake hose. Remove the bracket that normally holds the caliper to the strut.

Next, remove the small screw that holds the brake disc to the hub. The brake disc should lift off. If it does not, tap it with a rubber mallet. Depending on your car, you may

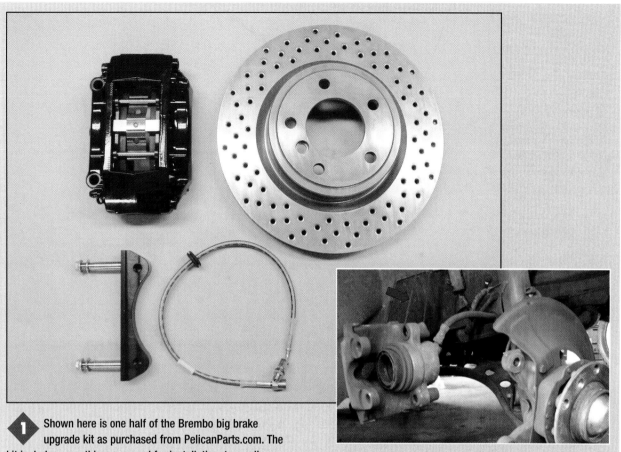

1 Shown here is one half of the Brembo big brake upgrade kit as purchased from PelicanParts.com. The kit includes everything you need for installation: two calipers, two rotors, two brake lines, two brackets, and two sets of pads and retaining clips. Truly a sight to be seen, it's unfortunate this braking beauty has to be hidden behind the wheels. This caliper is painted black, but the kit is available in many different colors, including red.

2 This is what the strut should look like with the caliper, caliper bracket, and brake disc removed. Suspend the caliper from a wire hanger or piece of rope while you perform the assembly (red arrow). See Project 57 for more information on removing the caliper and brake disc.

3 On most strut assemblies, you will have to remove the dust shield. In general, this will not affect the operation of the anti-lock braking system (ABS). However, if you drive through a lot of mud and dirt, periodically clean out the sensor degree wheel. Use a Dremel cut-off tool to slice the metal of the dust shield (left). Be careful not to damage or cut into the sensor (blue arrow) or degree wheel (green arrow) underneath the shield (middle and right).

4 The caliper bracket mounts in the same position as the factory one, using the original bolts and mounting hardware.

5 Mount the disc to the hub and temporarily fasten it with the brake disc locating screw (green arrow). Verify that the disc turns freely and doesn't hang up on any part of the strut or hub assembly. The discs are specific to each side of the car—verify from the diagram that the proper one is mounted according to how the wheel turns when the car moves forward.

need to remove the anti-lock brake sensor dust shield (see Photo 3). The new rotor will not fit on the hub assembly with the dust shield in place. Some dust shields are mounted using bolts, but many are riveted or press-fit onto to the larger back plate and may need to be cut off. On this E36, the dust shield was bolted to the strut assembly. However, it still needed to be cut off using a Dremel cut-off tool. There was no other way to remove the dust shield without disassembling the entire hub and bearing assembly. When cutting, make a large cut through the shield, being careful not to damage the sensor or degree wheel underneath. Make a similar slice on the other side, and the two half-moons should simply fall off. Underneath you will find the ABS sensor and the sensor degree wheel. If there is any dust or debris in this area, clean it out thoroughly.

Now, attach the new Brembo caliper mounting bracket to the strut assembly. Torque the bolts to the value indicated in the kit instructions and apply red Loctite 271 to the threads to ensure they don't come loose.

With the bracket mounted, place the rotor on the spindle. There is a left and a right rotor. They usually have stickers on them, but you can also tell the difference by the way the internal fins are cast into the disc (see inset of Photo 5). Use the brake disc locating and mounting bolt to secure and correctly register the brake disc with respect to the hub. The holes for the wheel studs should be correctly lined up with both the brake disc and the spindle. Use a spare wheel lug nut to help secure the disc to the spindle if needed.

The pads should be pre-assembled in the caliper, but if they're not, now is the time to install them. Remove the two retaining pins by tapping them out with a small hammer and the end of a punch or small screwdriver. Insert the pads and replace the pins. Now, mount the new, huge, caliper to the newly installed mounting bracket. Torque the bolts to 50 N-m (37 ft-lbs). There should be an embossed arrow on the front of the caliper that indicates the direction of the disc rotation. When mounting the calipers on the spindle, the arrow should always point up.

At this point (before you disconnect the brake line to your old caliper), perform a test fit of the wheel to the spindle. Make sure there are no interference problems when the wheel is fully mounted. Cover the caliper with a piece of tape to protect the paint in case the wheel happens to scrape the caliper. Put the wheel on the spindle, and tighten it down with two lug nuts. Then give the wheel a spin—it should turn freely, without rubbing or scraping on the caliper or anything else.

When you have verified the wheel turns freely, remove it again and set it aside. Now, attach the new braided-steel brake hose to the brake caliper. There should be a small copper washer that seals the line fitting to the caliper. Route the brake line through the rubber grommet that secures it to the strut.

Using a flare-nut wrench, quickly disconnect the old rubber hose from the steel hard line that connects the hose to the main brake system (at the top of the inner wheelwell). Don't use a regular wrench on the hard line. Only use a flare nut wrench, as explained in Project 56. Reconnect the new

6 Shown here is the caliper mounted to the strut assembly. The embossed arrow on the caliper should always point upward. The brake pads should be installed in the caliper from the factory.

7 Perform a test fit of the road wheel to the hub to make sure that there are no interference problems. Place some tape on the painted surface of the caliper, just to make sure the inside of the wheel doesn't accidentally scratch the surface of the caliper. The BMW M3 wheels shown in the photo work very well with the Brembo kit. Clearance is still tight, but it fits as if the kit were tailor-made for this particular wheel.

line quickly to minimize the amount of brake fluid that leaks out of the system.

With the brake line attached, clean up any spilled brake fluid (it is very harmful to paint). Repeat the process for the opposite side. When you have completed the install, bleed the brake system (see Project 50). After the brakes have been bled, reattach the road wheels, lower the car, and tighten the lug nuts to 100 N-m (74 ft-lbs).

The brake system needs to be broken in before you can really test its performance. First, make sure the emergency brake system is working properly, just in case anything goes wrong and you need to pull the lever to stop the car. Before you set out to drive the car, pump the brake pedal and make sure that you have firm pressure. Have an assistant push the car while you hold down the brake pedal to test that the system is working.

Drive the car slowly to a nearby parking lot or deserted area. Perform 15 to 20 stops from 55 miles per hour to 10 miles per hour using light pressure on the pedal. This will increase the temperature of the pads, caliper, and rotors,

8 On the left side of this photo, you will see the point where the brake line enters the brake caliper (orange arrow). This line attaches to the lower part of the caliper, and the bleed nipple should be on top of the caliper. On the right, you can see how the stainless-steel brake line routes around the strut. Take note of the grommet in the strut housing (yellow arrow).

and will help mate the pad and the disc's friction surface together. After these repeated stops, drive the car around town for a few miles and try to avoid using the brakes. This will allow the components to cool back down. Now park the car and look at the brake discs. They should be a grey-blue color consistently across the surface of the disc. If this color is not consistent, repeat the 15- to 20-stop heating and cooling procedure.

http://www.101projects.com/BMW/55.htm

Parking Brake Shoe Replacement

Time: 3 hours

Tab: $40

Talent: ♦♦

Tools: 19-millimeter socket, rubber mallet, Allen wrench set

Applicable Years: All

Tinware: New parking brake shoes, springs

Tip: Wear safety glasses when working around the spring-loaded mechanisms

PERFORMANCE GAIN: Better parking brake performance

COMPLEMENTARY MODIFICATION: Replace the brake pads, brake discs

If your parking brake is not functioning properly, perhaps it's time you replaced the parking brake shoes. First, make sure the parking brake cables and handles are adjusted properly (see Project 53).

The parking brake shoes can only be inspected after removing the rear brake discs (see Project 57). With the brake discs off, you can visually inspect the shoes for wear. They should have some brake lining along the top but should not have any heavy grooves cut into them. Compare your brake shoes to the new shoes in Photo 1 to determine if you need to replace yours.

After the brake disc has been removed from the brake assembly, remove the small parking brake adjuster by prying it out from between the upper and lower parking brake shoes. Make sure that the parking brake handle is set all the way down for this procedure. Be very careful during this removal, as the adjuster is spring loaded and the springs may fly out when you remove it.

When you have removed the adjuster, take a set of needle-nose pliers and remove the long spring that holds the upper and lower shoes together near where the adjuster was mounted. Again, be mindful of the spring, as it may fly off unexpectedly. Wear safety glasses during this entire procedure.

Now, remove the washer and conical spring-retaining mechanism at the top of the assembly. Press in the spring, then rotate the special spring washer so you can slide it out of its retainer. Make sure you don't lose the parts if they happen to fly out.

Move to the front of the brake assembly (toward the front of the car), and remove the long spring from the two brake shoes. Use the needle-nose pliers again, and be careful not to catch your fingers in the process.

1 Remove the small adjusting cog assembly by using a large screwdriver to push it out from between the two parking brake shoes. With some effort, the cog assembly should pop out, leaving a bit of slack between the two parking brake shoes. Be very careful when installing the new shoe, as the retaining springs may snap out of place and fly out. Keep your hands out of the way, and wear safety glasses when installing or removing the springs. The inset photo shows a brand-new parking brake shoe. Compare your old one to this to see if you need to replace it.

2 Using a pair of pliers, grab and unhook the parking brake spring from the brake shoes (green arrow). Be careful of the spring, as it is under a lot of tension at this point. Use a pair of Vise-Grips and a pair of needle-nose pliers to twist the spring and unlatch it from the assembly. Also undo the small spring retainer (inset) that secures the brake shoes to the rear trailing arm. If you don't think the parking brake shoes are worn, take a close look at these (red arrows). The brake lining has completely broken off, probably due to the previous owner driving too many miles with the parking brake on.

BRAKES

After the three springs have been removed from the parking brake assembly, both the top and bottom shoes should lift off the assembly.

Install the new shoes in the opposite manner as the removal process. Reassemble the parking brake by attaching the long spring toward the front of the car first, then the upper conical spring, and finally the spring toward the rear.

When you are finished, test the assembly by operating the emergency brake handle a few times. Carefully check that the springs are properly seated in the restraining holes in the brake shoes.

Reinstall the brake disc, and then recheck and adjust the parking brake mechanism (Project 53) before you reinstall the caliper and brake pads.

PROJECT 56
http://www.101projects.com/BMW/56.htm
Brake Line Replacement

Time: 4 hours

Tab: $65

Talent:

Tools: 11-millimeter crescent flare-nut wrench

Applicable Years: All

Tinware: New brake lines, or stainless-steel brake lines

Tip: Make sure corroded rubber from old lines doesn't end up in your caliper

PERFORMANCE GAIN: Better braking performance

COMPLEMENTARY MODIFICATION: Rebuild calipers, replace brake pads, flush brake system, replace master cylinder

1 Old rubber brake lines are often responsible for poor brake performance. As the car ages, the rubber begins to break down and can clog the lines, restricting the amount of pressure getting to the calipers. Renew the brake lines if they are old or if you are having problems with your brakes. The arrow points to the flexible brake line on the front of the car that needs to be replaced.

One of the most popular projects for the BMW 3 Series cars is replacing the flexible brake lines that run from the main chassis of the car to the A-arms and trailing arms. These lines are made out of rubber and, over time, tend to break down and corrode. Carefully inspect the rubber lines every 10,000 miles or so. They can exhibit strange characteristics, such as bubbling and expanding, prior to actually bursting. Failure of these lines is a very bad thing, as you will instantly lose pressure in one-half of your braking system.

Faulty brake lines in the front of your BMW can also cause steering problems when braking. Bad hoses can cause a car to dart from side to side when braking. Bad hoses may also allow pressure to build up in the caliper, but sometimes do not release this pressure properly when the pedal is released.

To replace the lines, first elevate the car (see Project 1). Then remove the wheels from each side of the vehicle for easier access to the brake lines. To prevent a large amount of brake fluid from leaking out, push the brake pedal down just to the point of engagement and block it there. You will lose less brake fluid, and less air will enter the system.

Now it's time to disconnect the brake lines. Have paper towels handy, as some brake fluid will leak out of the lines. Brake fluid is perhaps the most dangerous fluid to your car, as any amount spilled on the paint will permanently mar it. If you do get some on the paint, make sure you blot it—don't wipe it off. Your hands may also be contaminated with brake fluid, so don't touch the paint on the car.

The brake lines themselves can be very difficult to remove. The goal of this job is to remove the lines without damaging anything else. In this case, the easiest pieces to damage (besides your paint) are the hard steel brake lines that connect to the flexible rubber lines. These lines have relatively soft fittings on each end and often become deformed and stripped when removed. The key to success is to use a flare-nut wrench. This wrench is designed for jobs like this, in which the fittings are soft and might be heavily corroded. The flared end of the wrench hugs the fitting and prevents it from stripping. Use only this type of wrench, as it is very easy to damage the fittings using a regular crescent wrench.

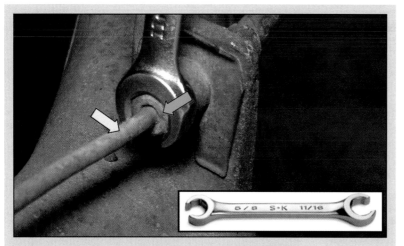

If you do damage the hard line or strip the fitting, the replacement line might be a special-order part that will have to be shipped in from Germany. You can usually find the correct length of line at an auto parts store, but then you would have to bend it into shape—a very difficult process that usually requires a few special tools. The moral of this project, and really this entire book, is that you should use the right tool for the job (in this case, the flare-nut wrench).

2 A required tool is the flare-nut wrench that fully wraps around the brake line. If you use a standard wrench, there is a high chance you'll round off the corners, permanently damaging the hard brake lines. These fittings are not very strong, and will become stripped if you don't use a flare-nut wrench. If the fitting becomes stripped, the line needs to be replaced (usually a special-order part from Germany). Also, make sure the fitting is turning (blue arrow), not the line itself (yellow arrow). It is very easy to twist off the ends of the hard lines when the fitting binds.

After you have disconnected the flexible rubber line from the hard metal line, you can remove it from the car. At the chassis end, the lines are attached using spring clips. Sometimes, depending upon the angle, these clips can be difficult to remove. With a good pair of Vise-Grips, though, they can usually be pulled off the car.

Installation of the new lines is straightforward and easy. Before you attach them, make sure you have the correct ones for your car. There are a few different types, and a few different lengths, so make sure the ones you are putting on match the length and fittings of those you just removed. If the line you install is too short, it may stretch and break when your car goes over a bump.

When it comes to replacing brake lines, many people install braided stainless-steel lines on their cars. Rumor has it the stainless-steel sheath keeps the rubber inner line from expanding under pressure and actually delivers better performance than the standard lines. While this reasoning sounds good at first, it's mostly hype. Stainless-steel braided lines are usually made of the same rubber underneath and are simply protected by the outside sheath. Even if the sheath were tight and strong enough to prevent the lines from expanding, it wouldn't make a difference in braking. If the lines expand a little, the resulting pressure exerted at the caliper will be virtually the same.

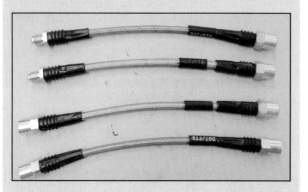

3 New stainless-steel lines are identical in size and length to the original ones that shipped with the car. Stainless-steel lines have a protective coating on the outside that prevents the elements from attacking them as easily. However, the stainless-steel sheath doesn't allow you to inspect the rubber inside for significant deterioration. Some of the aftermarket lines are made out of Teflon (or have Teflon components) to increase their durability.

Still, I recommend braided stainless-steel lines for your car because the outside sheath does protect the lines from dirt, grime, rocks, small animals, and anything you might run over.

Another point to consider is the label of "DOT" (Department of Transportation) certification. The original rubber lines were required to be certified under a certain set of specifications dictated by the DOT for use on U.S. highways. Often, braided stainless-steel lines are aftermarket components that are not DOT-certified and subsequently are listed "for off-road use only." In reality, these lines are typically more than adequate for use on your car, and any concern over their use is not really necessary.

However, for those who want to be absolutely sure and certified, there are manufacturers who make DOT-certified stainless steel lines, but they're usually more expensive than the noncertified ones. (Both types are available at PelicanParts.com.)

The fitting is supposed to turn and rotate on the end of the line, but sometimes it becomes too corroded to break free and can get stuck to the hard line. When this happens, the fitting and the line will usually twist together, breaking the line in half. Thus, be careful when removing this fitting to make sure you do not twist the line.

BRAKES

Time: 3 hours

 Tab: $50–200

 Talent:

 Tools: 5-millimeter hex head tool, rubber mallet, socket set, micrometer

 Applicable Years: All

 Tinware: Brake discs, new pads, new emergency brake shoes (if required)

 Tip: Adjust your emergency brake while you have access

! **PERFORMANCE GAIN:** Better, safer braking

COMPLEMENTARY MODIFICATION: Replace brake pads, emergency brake shoes, install stainless-steel brake lines, install new wheel bearings

Brake discs (or "rotors" as they are often called) are a very important part of the braking system. The brake pads rub against the discs to create the frictional force responsible for slowing the car down. If the rotors become too thin or grooved, their ability to stop the car decreases.

When replacing the brake pads, always measure the thickness of the brake discs. If they fall below the specified value for your car, replace them. Check for grooves in the rotor, and take several measurements of the disc in several different places to guarantee an accurate reading. If the brake disc has a groove in it, it should at least be removed and resurfaced by a machine shop—or, even better, replaced with a new one. Discs with grooves brake less efficiently and also heat up to higher temperatures, further reducing their overall braking ability.

Take the micrometer measurements from the center of the discs. It is common for OEM rotors to have the minimum thickness stamped on the rotor hub. If you can't find this information, use the following chart to determine if your rotors need to be replaced.

Type and Year	Minimum thickness
E36 front solid rotor	10.4 millimeters
E36 front vented rotor	20.4 millimeters
E36 front vented rotor, M3	26.4 millimeters
E30 front solid rotor	10.7 millimeters
E30 front vented rotor	20.0 millimeters
E36 rear rotor, solid	8.4 millimeters
E36 rear rotor, ventilated	17.4 millimeters
E36 rear rotor, M3	18.4 millimeters
E30 rear solid rotor	8.0 millimeters

1 The rear brake discs have a slightly different shape than the front discs, due to the need for an inner "drum" area that acts as the friction surface for the emergency brake. While the BMW 3 Series has disc brakes at all wheels (except for the early 318i), the rear parking brake mechanism is most like a drum brake system.

2 Before you remove your brake discs, measure them with a micrometer to see if they need to be replaced. If you use a dial caliper instead, you might get a false reading, because the disc wears on the area where the pads make contact, not on the edges of the disc. Take several measurements to compensate for potential low or high spots on the disc.

If you need to replace the rotors, the process is relatively simple. The procedure for front and rear rotors is very similar, but for the sake of this project we'll look at replacing the rear rotors, which are slightly more complicated due to the integrated parking/emergency brake assembly.

First, jack up the car (see Project 1) and remove the road wheel. If you haven't already done so, remove the brake pads from the caliper (see Project 51). The flexible rubber brake hose attaches to the trailing arm of the car with a large clip. This clip retains both the flexible line and the hard line that connects to the rear caliper. Remove this clip in order to remove the caliper without bending the hard metal brake line.

BRAKES

167

3 Remove caliper by unbolting the two 7-millimeter bolts that mount it to the arm. The caliper (green arrow) can be pushed out of the away and doesn't need to be physically disconnected from the brake line. Hang the caliper from a string (blue arrow) so you don't put unnecessary tension on the rubber brake line (orange arrow). The caliper mounting bracket (yellow arrow) can be detached from the strut by removing the two bolts on the back side.

4 There is a small locator screw that holds the brake disc in place. Use a 5-millimeter Allen wrench to remove this screw, and the brake disc should slide off of the hub. The lug nuts that hold on the wheel apply the majority of the force that constrains the disc to the hub, not this screw.

5 Tap on the new disc with a rubber mallet. Have your parking brake shoes adjusted away from the inside drum, or they might interfere with the installation of the disc. New discs may not be perfectly flat and may take a few hundred miles of break-in to achieve their maximum braking efficiency.

Installation of the new brake disc is a snap—simply push it onto the hub. Before you install the new disc, though, take a close look at the parking brake shoes to see if they warrant replacing. If you can see metal on the shoes, or if the previous owner had a hard time remembering to remove the emergency brake, then it might be a good time to replace them. After you install the new discs on both sides, test the parking brake and adjust it if necessary (see Projects 53 and 55).

Once the new disc is installed, replace the retaining screw, reattach the caliper, and install the new brake pads. The new rotors should last a long time, and you should see improved braking after the wear-in period for your new brake pads.

On some late E36 models (in particular, the convertibles), the rear brakes came equipped with rear vented rotors and slightly larger calipers. The theoretical reasoning behind the larger caliper in the rear is due to the heavier weight distribution on the rear wheels of the cabriolet. It would appear there is a larger weight bias toward the rear on the convertibles because of increased chassis stiffening.

Are these vented rear rotors a worthwhile upgrade for the nonconvertible cars? If this is a dedicated track car, then the answer is probably yes. Only add the vented rotors if you're approaching the heat dissipation limits of the rear brakes. Simply adding vented rotors over solid ones won't buy you any more braking power under normal conditions where the rotors are adequately cooled. The larger piston diameter of the 328ic caliper might change front/rear brake bias as well, but in general, the stock braking system is designed for the weight distribution of the coupe and sedan. Putting too much braking power on your rear brakes may in fact cause them to lock up sooner, which hurts braking control. Many cars from previous generations are equipped with proportioning valves that limit the braking force applied to the rear just for this reason. Adding the rear vented rotors and calipers would only seem to benefit you if you're on the track all the time, or if you somehow changed the weight bias of your car.

Now, unbolt the caliper from the trailing arm where it is mounted. There should be two bolts that mount the caliper and hold it in place. After you remove these two bolts, you should be able to slightly move the caliper out of the way of the disc. Exercise caution when moving the caliper around, however—do not let the caliper hang from the rubber brake line, as this will most certainly damage the line.

Once you have the caliper out of the way, remove the small screw that holds on the brake disc (once you've made sure the parking brake is off). You will need a 5-millimeter hex head tool for this task. Pull the disc off of the hub. If there is any resistance, use a rubber mallet to rap the brake disc loose.

If you are having a difficult time getting the disc off, the parking brake shoes may be stuck on the back of the disc. Adjust the parking brake so it's not gripping the disc (see Project 53).

SECTION EIGHT

Suspension

As cars age, one thing is almost always certain: suspension components will begin to wear out. This creates a sloppy feel to the car—exactly the opposite of what BMW designers intended. Repairing the effects of age is straightforward. In most cases, suspension components need to be disassembled, evaluated, and possibly replaced. This section details the process of overhauling the 3 Series suspension and offers some projects on suspension upgrades you can perform along the way.

Alignment on Your BMW

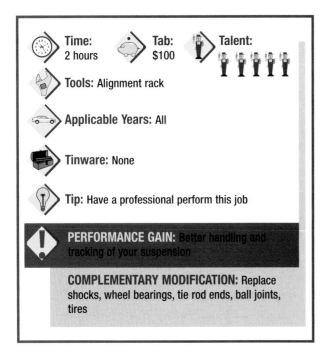

Time: 2 hours

Tab: $100

Talent: 🕴🕴🕴🕴🕴

Tools: Alignment rack

Applicable Years: All

Tinware: None

Tip: Have a professional perform this job

PERFORMANCE GAIN: Better handling and tracking of your suspension

COMPLEMENTARY MODIFICATION: Replace shocks, wheel bearings, tie rod ends, ball joints, tires

The BMW 3 Series cars are known for good handling and an excellent suspension system. Of course, precise handling and cornering are nonexistent if the car is not aligned properly. There are five suspension specifications that must be met to properly align the chassis: front-end caster, camber, and toe; and rear-end camber and toe. Unfortunately, on the stock 3 Series, all but front toe setting are fixed and nonadjustable. Aftermarket racing components can be substituted if you need additional adjustment, but the street cars don't have this ability in their stock form. If the alignment of the suspension is slightly off, you may experience significant tire wear and a loss of power and fuel economy. The most common sign of a misaligned front suspension is the car pulling to one side of the road while you are steering straight.

Although the home mechanic can adjust basic front-end toe-in setting, have a trained professional with an alignment rack make the final adjustments. It's nearly impossible to determine the correct angles and settings for your car without an alignment rack.

"Camber" refers to the tilt of the wheel as measured in degrees of variation between the tire centerline and the vertical plane of the car. If the top of the wheel tilts inward, the camber is negative. If the top of the wheel tilts outward, the camber is positive. On the BMW 3 Series, the camber should be slightly negative and within the standard stock settings. On some older BMWs, chassis deformation due to rust and age can cause the camber adjustments and measurements to be slightly off. If the car has been in an accident, the resulting

chassis damage is often reflected in alignment values not within spec.

With E30 cars, BMW makes an eccentric upper strut mount for the front suspension that allows you to subtract half of a degree from your camber setting (part number 31-33-1-139-484). This upper strut mount can correct the chassis camber when it falls out of factory specifications.

Worn suspension bushings may also add to odd alignment measurements. As the bushings and suspension mounts age, they tend to introduce slop into the suspension system, which can result in poor alignment readings. Lowering your BMW will also change the alignment specifications from the factory defaults. If your alignment specialist says your car's fixed specifications are outside the factory ranges, but your car has not been in an accident, it's likely some of the suspension bushings are worn and need replacement (see Project 59). If you have difficulty achieving proper camber settings, a good-quality camber strut brace can help you tweak the chassis (see Project 64). Tightening or loosening the adjustment nut on the camber bar can move the upper strut towers in or out very slightly.

The rear wheels should be set from the factory for a slight negative camber (about –1 to –2 degrees), as the trailing arms tend to bend slightly outward as the car accelerates under power. Since one-half of the wheel is mounted firmly on the ground, the top of the wheel has a tendency to twist outward. Setting the rear wheels for a slight negative camber means that under power they will be mostly neutral.

"Caster" is the angle that the steering axis is offset from the vertical plane. On the 3 Series, the strut points toward the rear of the car, resulting in a positive caster angle. This angle varies over the model years from 3 to 9 degrees. The amount of caster in the suspension directly influences the control and stability of the wheels when traveling in a straight line. Since the BMW rear suspension utilizes a trailing arm design, which has a tremendous amount of built-in caster, there is no specification for the rear caster. Front suspension caster is very good for high-speed stability because it helps to keep the wheels aligned and straight.

"Toe" refers to the angle of the two wheels with respect to each other. If a car has "toe-in," the front edges of the wheels are closer to each other than the rear edges. Toe-in is adjustable by changing the length of the tie rods (see Project 58). With rear-wheel-drive cars like the BMW 3 Series, the front wheels may try to move toward a toe-out position under power. Setting the wheels to have very slight toe-in can help neutralize this effect. "Toe-out" occurs when the front edges of the wheels are further apart than the inner edges. Some toe-out is necessary when turning, since the angle of inclination of the inner wheel must be tighter than the outer wheel. The rear toe should be set as close to neutral as possible.

SUSPENSION

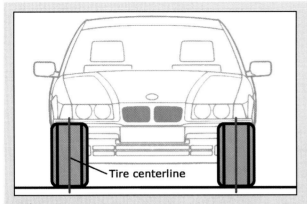

Tire centerline

1 Zero camber. When the car is aligned with zero camber, the wheels are directly perpendicular to the ground. The tires make even contact with the road and exhibit minimal wear and friction when turning. The weight of the car is distributed evenly across the tire tread, but the steering control can be a bit heavy. For ease of illustration in these diagrams, tire sizes are shown smaller than scale and camber angles are exaggerated.

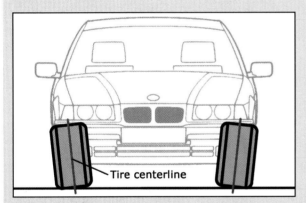

Tire centerline

3 Positive camber. This can cause the outer edges of the tires to wear more quickly than the inside. Positive camber is sometimes designed into the suspension to provide increased stability over bumpy roads or through turns on the typical high-crowned roads.

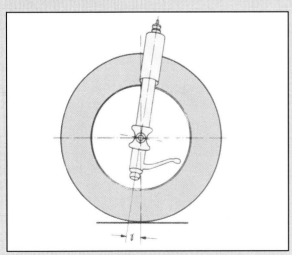

2 Negative camber. The lower parts of the tires are angled outward, causing more wear on the inside edges. The 3 Series cars have an independent front suspension that creates a slightly negative camber when traveling over bumps. As the suspension compresses upward, the top of the wheel tilts in slightly to avoid changing the track (distance between left and right wheels). Although this momentarily changes the camber of the wheel, it prevents the tires from scrubbing and wearing every time that the car travels over a bump. At factory settings, each 3 Series car should have a slight negative camber (between -2 degrees and -½ degree, depending upon the year).

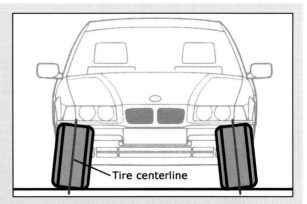

Tire centerline

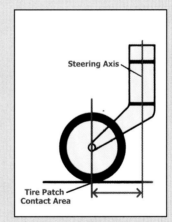

Steering Axis

Tire Patch
Contact Area

4 Positive caster. The wheels of a shopping cart best demonstrate the concept of positive caster. The steering axis of each wheel is located in front of the point where the wheel touches the ground. The load of the cart is in front of the wheels, and, as the cart moves forward, the wheels rotate on their axis to follow the cart's direction. This creates an inherent stability that keeps the wheels straight, unless they are forcibly steered in a different direction.

5 Positive caster. All BMWs have slighty positive caster, which creates an inherent stability when the car is moving in a straight line. With the angle of the strut tilted back, it places the steering axis, and the load, in front of the contact patch where the tire meets the pavement. Like the shopping cart example in the previous illustration, the car tends to move forward in a stable, straight line until the wheels are turned in a different direction. The rear trailing arm of the BMW 3 Series cars, by its design, has extensive positive caster built in.

SUSPENSION

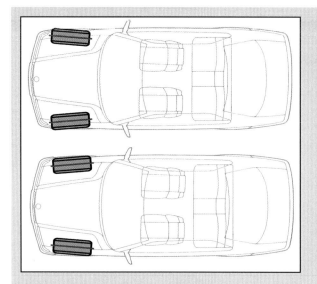

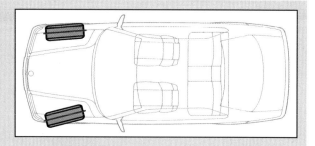

7 Toe-out through turns. When going around a turn, the inner wheels will turn to a tighter radius than the outer ones. This minimizes the amount of tire scrub on the pavement as the car turns.

6 Toe-in (bottom) and toe-out (top). The toe of the front suspension refers to the angle of the two wheels with respect to each other. Significant toe-in or toe-out will cause extreme tire wear, as the wheels constantly try to move toward each other (toe-in) or away from each other (toe-out). The result is severe friction on the tires, and at highway speeds, the tires will wear significantly and power/fuel economy will suffer.

8 To get the proper alignment measurements your car, have a professional perform the work on an alignment rack. Alex Wong of Precision Tech Motorsports owns this alignment rack, which cost in excess of $18,000. The proper BMW alignment is not something the home mechanic can reliably perform. Just don't get snookered into paying for more than you should—the only adjustment on the BMW 3 Series cars is the front toe-in, which should be measured against the fixed rear wheels in a simple four-wheel alignment.

9 If you're racing your BMW, upgrade to an adjustable suspension that allows you to easily change caster and camber. This trick setup for racing includes adjustable camber and caster plates from Ground Control. The outer three bolts are used to adjust camber, and the four center bolts adjust caster. This allows you to dial in your suspension for just about any track condition.

So how should your BMW be set up? If you plan to race your car, you will need aftermarket suspension components and as much negative camber as allowed by the racing rules. The car will tend to straighten out in turns, and you want the maximum tire patch on the road when cornering. When the camber starts to change to slightly positive through turns, a negative camber setting will help neutralize the effect.

There's a common misconception that a lot of caster is good for racing. While adding more caster to the suspension can indeed make it handle better, introducing too much caster into the suspension can negatively impact your track

times. On a perfectly balanced rear-wheel-drive car, adding too much caster can transfer load from the outside front and inside rear tires to the opposite corners. This can upset the balance and cause a corner entry push.

Seek professional help for alignment specifications and answers to questions you might have, and don't accept blanket statements about suspension upgrades—they've led to many common misconceptions. Do your own research. Two books I refer to on these topics are *Race Car Engineering* by Paul Van Valkenburg and *How to Make Your Car Handle* by Fred Puhn.

Front Suspension Overhaul

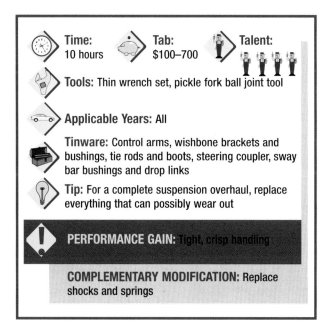

Time: 10 hours

Tab: $100–700

Talent:

Tools: Thin wrench set, pickle fork ball joint tool

Applicable Years: All

Tinware: Control arms, wishbone brackets and bushings, tie rods and boots, steering coupler, sway bar bushings and drop links

Tip: For a complete suspension overhaul, replace everything that can possibly wear out

PERFORMANCE GAIN: Tight, crisp handling

COMPLEMENTARY MODIFICATION: Replace shocks and springs

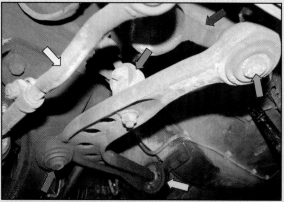

1 This photo shows a typical front left control arm for the E30/E36 suspension. The control arm is attached to the car at three points. The rear fits into a wishbone bracket and bushing that attaches to the chassis (orange arrow). The midpoint pivot attaches to the front axle support bar with an inner ball joint (purple arrow). The outside of the control arm connects to the bottom of the strut (red arrow) with an outer ball joint (blue arrow). A small drop link (green arrow) affixes the front sway bar to the control arm. Finally, the tie rods (yellow arrows) are attached to the front of the strut.

There are lots of bushings and joints on the front end of the 3 Series suspension that can wear and become loose after many miles of driving. If your car's steering wheel vibrates at highway speeds, there are most likely components in the front suspension that need replacement. For a crisp, firm handling ride, replace every wearable part in the suspension every 80,000 to 100,000 miles.

There are four main components that need attention when you overhaul the front suspension: control arms, ball joints, sway bar bushings, and tie rods. The PelicanParts.com online catalog has complete replacement kits with everything you need for your overhaul, making the job of acquiring these parts substantially easier.

Control arms

Both the E30 and E36 use control arms that integrate three joints: two ball joints and a rear rubber bushing contained in what BMW calls a "wishbone bracket." Worn-out control arm ball joints or bushings are often the cause of suspension problems. If the steering wheel shakes at high speeds, the control arm wishbone bushings are worn, the ball joints are worn, or the control arm itself has bent. If you plan to replace the wishbone bushings, upgrade to the 1996-and-later M3 bushings. This bolt-in replacement for the weaker, stock E36 bushings should give you longer life and a better ride.

The inner ball joint is integrated into the control arm and is not individually replaceable (you must replace the entire control arm). The outer ball joint is integrated into the control arm on E30 cars, but is individually replaceable on non-M3 E36 cars. The bushing in the wishbone bracket is a common replacement item in a suspension overhaul. It's typically replaced when the control arm is replaced.

Removing the control arm involves several steps. First, jack up the car and disconnect the two ball joints and the sway bar drop links, and pull the control arm out. (See the next subsection in this project for instructions on ball joint removal and sway bar drop link replacement.)

With the ball joints and sway bar drop link disconnected, unbolt the wishbone bracket from the chassis. The control arm should fall right off.

Use a gear puller to remove the old bushing from the old control arm. Mark the position of the old bushing on the shaft first, since you will need to install the new one in approximately the same spot. I recommend you replace the entire control arm, as you will not be able to tell if it's been bent by a rogue pothole at any time through the years. With the wishbone bracket and bushing assembly removed from the control arm, you'll need to purchase new brackets or cut the old bushing out of the old bracket.

Using a saw, you can cut out the inner rubber part quite easily. Then use a Dremel tool to slice away the outer ring of the original bushing. Avoid cutting through the old bushing and into the wishbone bracket. The brackets are not too expensive, and I typically tell people to replace them with new ones if they can afford it.

SUSPENSION

173

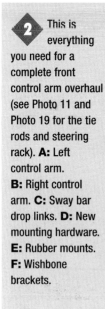

2 This is everything you need for a complete front control arm overhaul (see Photo 11 and Photo 19 for the tie rods and steering rack). **A:** Left control arm. **B:** Right control arm. **C:** Sway bar drop links. **D:** New mounting hardware. **E:** Rubber mounts. **F:** Wishbone brackets.

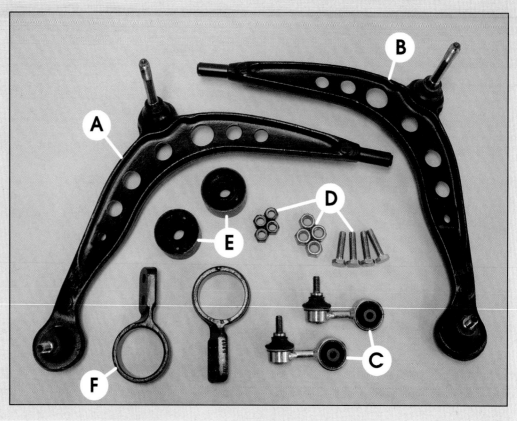

With the old bushing cut out of the wishbone bracket, use a vise to press in the new one (see Photo 7). While I advocate doing most everything yourself, I strongly suggest you have a machine shop press the new bushings onto the end of the control arm. No amount of hammering, pressing, pushing, or swearing will get those bushings onto the end of the control arm without a special tool. Most machine shops can perform this press procedure quite easily with the right equipment.

BMW recommends a special-formula lubricant (part number 81-22-9-407-284) to aid in pressing on the bushing. If you use the lubricant, however, the bushing becomes "glued" to the control arm shaft after about 30 minutes. The BMW factory manuals state that you should set the car back down on its suspension immediately after you press on the bushing. This time constraint makes it very difficult for the do-it-yourselfer to perform the install, particularly if you need to drop the car onto the control arm immediately following the pressing operation. To learn about other solutions, see 101Projects.com for details on homemade tools that may also work in a pinch.

Ball joints

The ball joints are key components in the BMW 3 Series front suspension. These joints, located at the bottom of the strut and attached to the front axle support bar, help the entire assembly pivot and rotate as the control arm turns and pivots and the suspension rides up and down. Needless to say, these critical components can wear out over time and should be replaced

every 100,000 miles, or when the front suspension begins to feel wobbly. Because the inner ball joint is integrated into the control arm, you must purchase a new control arm if you wish to replace the ball joint. On non-M3 E36 cars, the outer ball joint is replaceable.

First, remove the nut that holds on the ball joints. For the inner ball joint, this nut is accessible from the top of the front axle support bar. For the outer ball joint, the nut is easily accessible on the lower part of the strut.

Replacement of the ball joints is relatively simple—if you have the proper tools. Each ball joint attaches with a beveled fit, meaning the ball joint end is securely pressed into the spindle arm and cannot be removed without a special tool. The best removal tool is an angled pitchfork-shaped tool called a "pickle fork," designed specifically for this task. Do not hit the top of the rod end with a large hammer to remove the ball joint, as this will only bend or damage the strut. Place the pickle fork tool between the strut and the rod end, and hit the tool repeatedly with a large hammer. The wedge in the pickle fork tool will drive the rod end out of the arm. You may have to hit the pickle fork tool several times before the rod end pops out of its location. Installation of the new ball joint is easy—simply insert it into its hole and tighten the nut on top.

Sway bar bushings

As BMWs age, the sway bar bushings wear. Carefully inspect your bushings for cracking, and ensure that their inner diameter hugs the sway bar tightly. If they do not appear to be

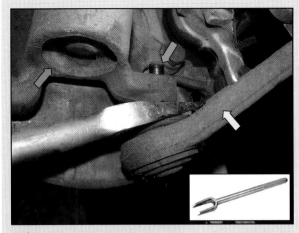

3 Use a pickle fork tool (inset) to remove the ball joints. This pitchfork-shaped tool is wedged between the control arm (yellow arrow) and the strut (green arrow). When the tool is in place, tap the end with a hammer and the wedge will force the ball joint apart from the strut (see also Photo 10). The blue arrow in this photo points to the top of the ball joint thread. For reference, the red arrow points to the brake caliper in the background, which is attached to the strut.

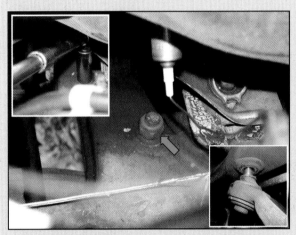

5 The inner ball joint attaches to the front axle support bar, which holds the steering rack. The nut that secures the ball joint is located on the top side of this support bar (green arrow) and must be removed prior to inserting the pickle fork tool. The nut can be difficult to get to—I had to use several socket extensions, a universal joint, and a large breaker bar to remove it (inset photo, upper left). When the nut is removed, use the pickle fork tool to loosen the ball joint from the front axle support bar (inset photo, lower right).

4 On all E36 models except the M3, the outer ball joint is replaceable. This ball joint can be replaced with the control arm still installed in the car. The retaining clip (purple arrow) attaches the ball joint to the arm.

6 Here's a close-up shot of the wishbone bracket on the right side of the car. Although it may appear at first glance that the left and right brackets are the same, they are in fact different for each side of the car. There are small indentations on the inside mounting surface of the bracket that must line up with corresponding bosses on the chassis of the car. Pay attention to which bracket fits on which side of the car.

worn, simply apply a bit of lithium grease inside the bushing. If they are worn, they will need to be replaced.

Replacing the bushings is very easy. With the car elevated (see Project 1) and the front wheels removed, disconnect the bracket that holds on the sway bar bushing. The bar and bushing together will drop down slightly if you release both sides at the same time.

The new replacement bushings are split down the middle so you can easily slide them onto the bar and into the bracket. Remove the old bushings and insert the new ones, coating the bushings with white lithium grease on the inside.

The sway bar drop links are also easy to replace. The upper part of the drop link contains a small ball joint, and the lower part has an integrated rubber bushing. Remove the

7 New bushings usually come separate from the wishbone brackets. Press the bushing into the bracket using a vise or an industrial press. Make sure the bushing is centered width-wise in the bracket when you have finished pressing it into the wishbone. Each bushing has a small arrow cast into the rubber that should line up with the corresponding dot on the outside of the wishbone bracket (inset photo).

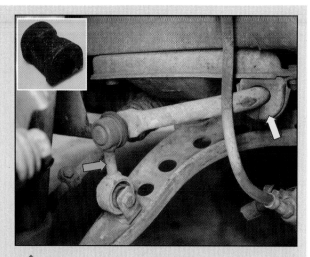

8 This photo shows the front sway bar and drop links (blue arrow). To completely renew the front suspension, replace the sway bar bushings (yellow arrow) and drop links as well. Unbolt the bracket and slide the old one off. The bushings have a slit down the center to easily pry them on and off the sway bar.

9 Drop links can be a challenge to remove, as the ball joint on top of the link may spin when you try to remove the outer nut. If this happens, use a thin wrench (green arrow) to hold the ball joint in place while you loosen the nut. You can purchase a set of these wrenches specifically designed to fit into places where a normal, thick wrench will not. They are typically about ⅛-inch thick, and are a very useful tool to add to your arsenal.

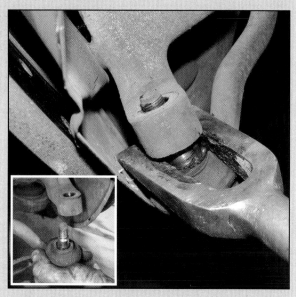

10 Steering tie rods are removed in a similar manner to the ball joints. The pickle fork tool is essential for popping the tie rod ends out of the strut end. The rubber boot will likely be damaged when you remove the tie rod end, but you will replace the tie rod end with its integrated boot anyway.

bolt from the lower drop link to disconnect it. The small upper ball joint may present a challenge. If it does, use a special thin wrench to remove the retaining nut (see Photo 9). Bolt the new drop link into place. Replacing the rear sway bar bushings is nearly identical to the front.

Tie rods

The tie rods commonly need replacement. These rods have two universal joints on each end and control the angular position of each front wheel when the car is steered. If the tie rods' joints are worn, precise steering is impossible and the car will

11 Shown here is a set of new tie rods. The tie rods connect the steering rack to the strut and adjust the critical toe-in alignment specification. If your car's steering wheel shakes on the highway, or if the steering wheel feels like it turns a lot in either direction with no effect on the car, then you may have worn-out tie rods. A complete tie-rod kit comes with the pair of tie rods, a set of rubber boots, and clamps. Beware of cheap kits—the boots in these kits often don't last very long. Purchase only high-quality OEM replacements; otherwise, you may be replacing the boots again in about a year.

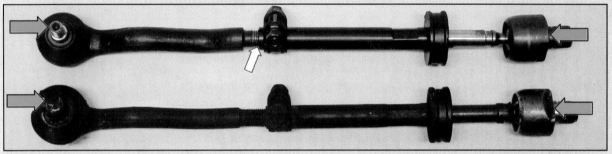

12 Before you install the new tie rods, get each one as close in length to the originals as possible (distance between green arrows should be the same). Place them on your bench and compare the lengths, then mark the position of the tie rod end with white correction fluid (small white arrow). Adjust the new tie rods as necessary to match the lengths of the old ones to get as close as possible to the toe-in alignment adjustment. You'll still need to take the car in for an alignment, but you can minimize tire wear while you're driving to the alignment shop.

13 There are several steps in the tie rod removal process. In Frame **A**, remove the boot clamp using a set of snips. With the two boot clamps removed (inner and outer), cut off the rubber boot, exposing the tie rod. There's a special tie rod wrench for removing the ends of the tie rods, or you can use a plumber's wrench, especially if you secure the entire assembly in a bench vise (Frame **B**). For this overhaul, I removed the entire steering rack, tie rods and all, and placed the entire assembly into the vise. Screw the new

tie rods into the ends of the steering rack, as shown in Frame **C**. Although there is a torque specification for this, it's nearly impossible to measure, as you need the tie rod wrench or plumber's wrench to tighten the assembly. I tighten it as tight as I can with the tool. Insert a new retaining washer—this washer bends over the edge of the tie rod to prevent any accidental loosening of the tie rod. Finally, Frame **D** shows the attachment of the new boots. The OEM clamps are difficult to work with. Place them over the boot and then pinch the inside of the clamp together with a strong pair of needle-nose pliers. Try not to pinch your fingers in the process.

14 Attach the tie rod end to the strut arm. Use a new nut on the threads of the tie rod end. The tie rod end will often turn and rotate as you're trying to tighten it. Place a floor jack underneath the tie rod end and gently apply pressure to wedge the tapered shaft in place. Don't lift the entire car up—just use enough force to raise the strut up slightly. The springs in the strut will be compressed slightly at this point. Tighten the tie rod nut, and it should squeeze itself tightly into the strut arm.

15 Another item you might want to inspect and/or replace is the motor damper shock. Found only on some cars, it absorbs vibrations from the engine and prevents them from being transferred to the chassis. Replacement is easy—simply unbolt each end and replace with a new one. This one is shown installed on a 1984 318i.

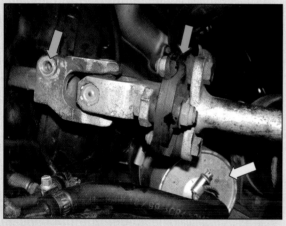

16 Steering rack removal is a somewhat complicated job. Shown here are the lower steering column joint assembly and coupler. Remove the bolt that secures the coupler to the upper steering shaft (blue arrow). Mark the position of the top of this coupler with respect to the shaft that attaches to the steering wheel, as you will need to line these two up later on. Also remove the bolt that attaches this shaft to the steering rack itself (not shown) to loosen the shaft when you remove the rack. Inspect the steering coupler at this time, too. It's made of rubber and can deteriorate over time, leading to a sloppy feel in the steering wheel. For a complete overhaul of the front suspension, replace this rubber joint. For reference, the yellow arrow indicates the fuel filter. Replace the fuel filter as well if it's due (see Project 4).

have wobbly front wheels and a possible alignment problem. Sometimes vibration in the steering wheel can be caused by worn out tie rods too.

As with the ball joints, replacing the tie rods is relatively simple with the proper tools. Each tie rod attaches to the spindle arm with a beveled fit. The tie rod is securely pressed into the spindle arm and cannot be removed without the angled pickle fork tool discussed previously. Do not hit the top of the rod end with a large hammer, as this will only bend the entire spindle arm.

Remove the top self-locking nut with a socket wrench. Place the pickle fork tool between the spindle arm and the rod end, and hit the tool repeatedly with a large hammer. The wedge in the pickle fork tool will drive the rod end out of the arm. You may have to hit the tool several times before the rod end pops out of its location.

Once you have the outer rod ends disconnected, remove the boot clamps that attach and secure each end of the rubber boot (bellows) to the tie rod and steering rack. Using a small clipper, carefully snip the spring retainers from the boot and remove it. You will see the exposed metal shaft of the steering rack. Don't get any dirt or debris on the rack while you are working on it.

Now, unscrew the old tie rod from the rack. This sounds easier than it really is. Bend back the small lock plate that secures the tie rod end. The old tie rod may be snuggly secured to the rack and could require significant force to remove it. There are specialty wrenches designed for this purpose, but I've had good luck with channel locks and/or a plumber's wrench. Bend the small retaining clip backward prior to removing the tie rod.

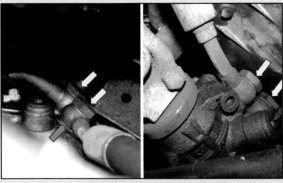

17 Here are two views of the power steering lines, which must be disconnected from the steering rack prior to removal. Remove the two banjo bolts that attach them to the rack (yellow arrow). Warning: The lines are full of power steering fluid and will leak all over the place when you disconnect them. Have an oil drip pan ready, along with plenty of paper towels. When the lines are disconnected, simply bend them up toward the top of the engine, and they should stop leaking. When you reconnect them to the rack, use new aluminum sealing rings (green arrow) to guard against fluid leaks.

Before the final install of the new tie rod, place the new one and old one side by side on a workbench, and adjust the new tie rod so the length from the rod end to the rack-mating surface is the same (see Photo 12). You want to set the two lengths of the tie rods to be equal to minimize the change in alignment of the car. Have the car realigned regardless, but get the alignment close so you can safely drive to the alignment shop. Mark the final position of the tie rod end on the new tie rod (white paper correction fluid comes in handy), and then remove it. Don't install the new rod end just yet. Before you screw the tie rod into the rack, spread a few drops of Loctite onto the threads. Only use a new locking plate, and install it onto the shaft of the rack. Insert the tie rod into the rack, and use a pair of large Vise-Grips or channel locks to tighten it down. There isn't much to grab onto with a regular wrench, and you likely won't have the special thin wrench required to tighten the tie rod. Tap down the retaining clip with a small hammer.

Once the tie rod is tight, place the rubber boot over the tie rod and onto the steering rack. You have to have the tie rod end removed in order to make the boot fit. Getting the boot to cooperate and properly cover the rack and the tie rod may be the most difficult part of this process. Use pliers and screwdrivers to stretch the boot over each end. This may take a few tries, but it is possible. Once the boot is in position, install two new clamps over the two ends of the boot to secure it to the rack housing.

After the boot is installed, reattach the tie rod end. Make sure the length of the tie rod is the same as the measurement of the old one. Adjust the position of the rod end to match up with the mark you made when you compared it to the original tie rod.

18 The steering rack (green arrow) is affixed to the front axle support bar at two attachment points (yellow arrow). Disconnect the rack at these two points. With the tie rod ends disconnected, the power steering lines detached, and the steering column shaft loosened, you can maneuver the steering rack out of the car. On some models, you may have to remove the lower oil pan cover (shown here) to gain enough maneuvering room to remove the steering rack.

19 There's a night-and-day difference between a new and used rack. This photo shows an OEM ZF rebuilt power steering rack-and-pinion assembly. If the rack wears out, the steering will be sloppy. Leaky racks may also deposit power steering fluid on the floor of your garage. However, it may be the power steering lines that are leaking and need to be replaced instead of an expensive rack. Carefully check the rack and lines before spending your money on a rebuilt rack. The most common leakage point for the rack is out the ends. If you cut open your tie rod boot and a lot of power steering fluid comes leaking out, chances are the seals in the ends of your rack are worn, and it needs to be rebuilt or replaced. Unfortunately, there are no individual repair parts available for you to fix the rack yourself—it must be sent back to the manufacturer.

To complete the job, attach the new rod end to the front control arm. Perform the same procedure on the opposite side. Take the car directly to an alignment shop, as it is very easy to mess up the toe-in of the front suspension when you replace the tie rods. If you plan to perform any other front suspension work that might affect the alignment, do it now to save yourself a second trip to the alignment shop.

Replacing Front Shocks and Springs

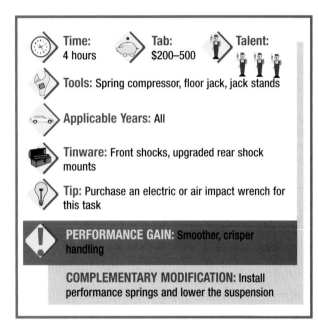

Time:
4 hours

Tab:
$200–500

Talent: ▮▮▮

Tools: Spring compressor, floor jack, jack stands

Applicable Years: All

Tinware: Front shocks, upgraded rear shock mounts

Tip: Purchase an electric or air impact wrench for this task

PERFORMANCE GAIN: Smoother, crisper handling

COMPLEMENTARY MODIFICATION: Install performance springs and lower the suspension

Another popular project among BMW 3 Series owners is replacing the front and rear shocks. Replace both the front and the rear at the same time, as they take roughly similar abuse over their lifetimes, so neither is likely to be more or less worn than the other. The shocks should always be replaced in pairs (left and right together, see Project 61).

I recommend that you replace your shocks every 50,000 miles or so, or if they start to show signs of fading or wearing out. If you push down on a corner of the car, it should spring back with little oscillation up and down. If the car bounces up and down, you probably need new shocks. Different driving patterns may also affect the life of shock absorbers. Cars that are raced or often driven on winding roads may need their shocks replaced more often. It is also important to remember that if you install performance springs that lower the car from its stock level, you will need to have the car realigned. Changing the height of the suspension also changes the alignment of the front suspension.

The replacement process is somewhat similar for E30 and E36 cars with one glaring exception: E30 cars have a replaceable front shock (called a "strut insert"), whereas E36s require you to replace a more complex integrated shock absorber/strut assembly. Although the E36 design requires the replacement of a more complex part, its replacement procedure is actually easier.

Begin the process for both E30 and E36 cars by jacking up the car and removing both front road wheels (see Project 1). E36 owners should read the following E30 section and then the subsequent E36 section, as there are elements of the strut disassembly process that are not specifically mentioned in the E30 section below.

E30 chassis

With the car elevated (see Project 1) and the wheels removed, start with one strut, and remove the brake caliper (see Project 57). Unplug any brake sensors connected to the caliper, and disconnect the caliper from the strut. Use rope or wire to tie the brake caliper aside so it doesn't hang by its rubber hose. With the brake calipers secured out of the way, disconnect the tie rods from the struts (see Project 59). It is difficult to disconnect tie rod ends from struts without damaging the rubber boot that protects the tie rod. Consider replacing the tie rod ends at the same time if you think you might damage the boot.

With the tie rod disconnected, you should be able to rotate the strut quite easily. Now, disconnect the sway bar drop link from the control arm (see Project 59). This allows you to drop the strut downward to its lowest point, so that you can pull it out from the car after you remove the shock insert and spring.

Next, install the spring compressor onto the spring and compress it until it no longer is tight in the strut assembly. While compressing the spring, be sure yo wear safety goggles. These springs are under a lot of pressure, and the spring compressor could suddenly slip off. Place the two halves of the compressor on exactly opposite sides of the spring. Use two ratcheting wrenches (I prefer the ones manufactured by GearWrench) on each side of the compressor to ensure even and equal compression. Failure to maintain even compression when compressing the springs can cause the compressor to slip off.

With the spring compression removed from the strut assembly and the springs loose on their perches, now move to the engine compartment. Pry off the small black cap in the center of the strut mount, and remove the center nut attached to the top of the shock. This, of course, is easier said than done. If you have an impact wrench, simply zap this nut off. The reassembly process requires an impact wrench, so if you don't have one, now is a great time to buy one. I recommend electric impact wrenches that function without an air compressor (see Tools of the Trade in the front of this book).

If you don't have an impact wrench at this time, remove the nut by latching onto the top of the shock rod in the wheelwell with some carefully placed locking pliers, in between the springs. This is not the best method for removal, and if that top nut is on really tight, it may not be possible to remove it this way. If that's the case, remove the entire strut from the car by disconnecting the lower ball joint (see Project 59). Once the strut is out of the car, you have a few more options for removal, including taking the entire strut over to someone who has an impact wrench.

With the top nut removed, place your floor jack underneath the bottom of the strut to relieve some of the pressure

SUSPENSION

1 **E30:** With the car on jack stands and front road wheels removed, remove the brake caliper (see Project 57) and disconnect the brake pad sensor and ABS sensor wires (Project 51). Detach any hoses and sensors that may be clipped to the strut housing (green arrows; E30 shown in main photo, E36 inset photo).

2 **E30:** Now, disconnect the sway bar drop link from the control arm (left) and disconnect the tie rod from the strut (right) to gain enough maneuvering room to remove the front strut.

3 **E30:** Install the spring compressor onto each side of the spring. Be sure to space the compressor equally on both sides. I use a pair of ratcheting wrenches to compress the springs—it turns a 45-minute job into a five-minute task. I recommend the ratchet-style wrenches manufactured by GearWrench.

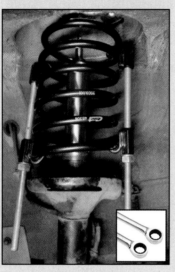

4 **E30:** This photo shows the center nut removed and the three nuts that hold the upper shock mount to the chassis. Use an electric impact wrench for best results.

from the weight of the strut assembly. Next, disconnect the three nuts that hold the top shock mount to the chassis, and lower down the strut. Reach up inside the wheelwell and remove the top strut mount, the upper spring retaining plate, and the old rubber gasket.

Now you're ready to remove the shock insert. Remove the dust cover from the insert and you will see a threaded collar that secures the insert to the strut housing. Lubricate this collar a bit with WD-40 or similar penetrant, as you don't want to damage the threads of the strut. You can use the special BMW tool designed to fit this collar, but I found it just as easy to use a plumber's wrench or a set of channel locks, to loosen it. Once the collar is loose, pull the shock up through the top inside the engine compartment. It's normal for the older-style hydraulic shocks to be submerged in oil, so be prepared that oil will leak and drip everywhere as you pull the shock out. Have paper towels handy.

With the shock removed, lift the old spring off of the bottom spring perch. Swing the strut out and look down

the tube with a flashlight. If the old shock inserts were conventional hydraulic shock absorbers, there should be oil in the bottom of strut. The oil is used as a lubricant and also aids in heat dissipation. If you are going to use new hydraulic shock absorbers, siphon out the old oil and replace it with about 1 quart of new oil. You can use regular motor oil for this. If you are using replacement gas shock inserts (like the Bilstein units), siphon out the old oil in the strut and install the new shock inserts dry.

If you reuse the old springs, simply place them back onto the top of the lower spring perches. If you replace your springs with new ones, move the springs to your workbench and slowly release the spring compressor on your old springs. Compress the new springs in a similar manner. The E30 shown in this project was upgraded to Eibach performance springs, which created a stiffer suspension and lowered the car about 1.8 inches in the front and 1.5 inches in the rear.

Install the compressed spring assembly back onto the lower spring perch. Install the new shock absorber through

181

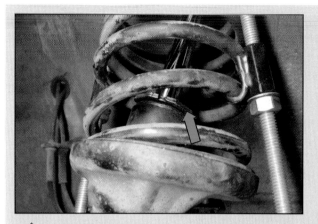

 5 **E30:** Remove the collar (green arrow) in order to remove the shock absorber from the strut.

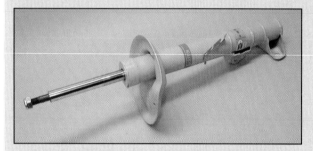

7 **E36:** The E36 shock and strut are integrated. While this makes for a more expensive and more complicated part, it also makes the replacement process quite a bit easier.

8 **E36:** Push the sensor wires (green arrows) and the brake hose (yellow arrow) out from the brackets in the strut. They are attached to the strut by rubber grommets. With the hose and wires detached, remove the upper bolt (blue arrow) that connects the top of the strut to the steering arm assembly.

6 **E30:** The E30 chassis' strut design incorporates a replaceable shock insert. With the springs removed, the insert should pull out from the strut. Support the strut carefully, and don't let it hang on the lower ball joint; the weight of the strut can damage the joint. Use a piece of wire or a few tie wraps to secure the strut, or place a support under the brake disc. The inset photo shows two new E30 front strut inserts (gas shocks) manufactured by Bilstein. Bilstein shocks are the gold standard for German strut inserts, and one pair typically lasts the life of the car. These come complete with new dust boots to protect the top of the insert rod. For E30 cars, simply place the new inserts inside the strut (without any oil), and reassemble the spring and mount assembly on top of the insert.

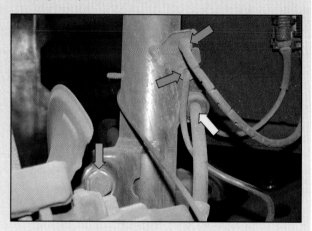

the top of the engine compartment, and tighten the collar to the strut. Reinstall the dust boot/rubber bumper assembly over the shock to protect it from road debris and grime. The Bilstein sport shocks installed on this car have the boot and stopper already integrated into the assembly.

Reinstall the upper spring plate and spring pad, and verify the plate is nestled correctly against the top of the spring. Inspect the upper strut mount carefully. This part is manufactured out of rubber and has an integrated ball bearing inside. It will wear over time, so replace it if it looks old, or if it hasn't been replaced previously. Reinstall the upper strut mount on top of the spring plate, and zap it on with an impact wrench. Unfortunately, the impact wrench is pretty much required here—do not use pliers on the shaft of the new shock inserts.

Once the shock rod nut is affixed, have an assistant raise the strut assembly with the floor jack while you guide the upper strut mount into place. Reattach the three nuts. Now,

carefully release the tension on the spring compressors and the spring should seat between the upper and lower perches. Reattach the sway bar drop links, tie rod ends (Project 59), and brake caliper (Project 57). Plug in any sensor connectors you may have disconnected, and route the wires and hoses back through the tabs in the strut.

E36 chassis

With the car elevated (see Project 1) and the two front road wheels removed, start with one strut and disconnect the brake sensors and brake hose from the strut. They are wedged into a mounting tab in the strut and held in place with rubber grommets. Slide the grommets out of the tabs; this may require some gentle nudging with a screwdriver. Then, remove the upper mounting bolt for the strut. Hold the nut on the other side of this bolt with a crescent wrench. Remove the two lower bolts as well. Place your floor jack underneath the bottom ball joint and lift up on the strut about $1/8$ inch to support the weight of the strut when you disconnect the top from the chassis.

Moving to the engine compartment, remove the three small nuts that hold the upper shock mount to the chassis shock towers. At this point, the strut should be free to be removed from the car. Lower the floor jack and press down slightly on the control arm, and pull the strut out and away from the car. Don't let the steering arm assembly hang. Tie it up with rope and wire, as you don't want to damage the outer ball joint or rubber brake hose.

Take your strut assembly over to your workbench. Compress the spring using the procedure discussed in the above E30 section. Remove the top nut from the shock, also using the procedure discussed in the E30 section. Again, it is very difficult to remove this nut without an impact wrench. Move your spring to the new strut and reassemble, using all of the hardware from the old strut. As with the E30, inspect the top shock mount to see if it needs replacement. Zap in the new top mount with the impact wrench and reinstall the entire assembly into the car.

9 **E36:** The two blue arrows here show the two lower bolts that secure the bottom of the strut to the steering hub assembly.

10 **E36:** With the bottom of the strut disconnected and supported by your floor jack, remove the three nuts at the top of the strut tower in the engine compartment. With these nuts removed, lower the strut with the jack.

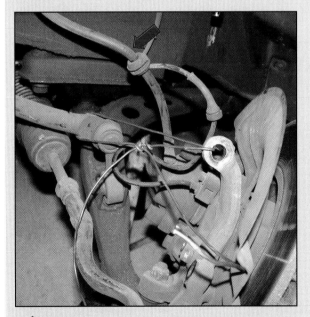

11 **E36:** With the strut removed, the steering arm assembly will hang loose. Tie up the assembly to prevent damage to the ball joint or the rubber brake hose that connects to the brake caliper. If you look closely, you'll see the rubber of the brake hose (red arrow) is cracking and should be replaced as soon as possible.

12 **E36:** Like the E30 strut, the top nut is very difficult to remove without an impact wrench. Bite the bullet and pick up a good electric impact wrench, as you will certainly find it useful on other projects.

SUSPENSION

183

Replacing Rear Shocks and Springs

Time: 4 hours

Tab: $150–250

Talent: 👨👨👨

Tools: Spring compressor, floor jack, jack stands

Applicable Years: All

Tinware: Rear shocks, upgraded rear shock mounts

Tip: Use a long piece of natural gas pipe from a hardware store

PERFORMANCE GAIN: Smoother, crisper handling

COMPLEMENTARY MODIFICATION: Replace rear shock mounts

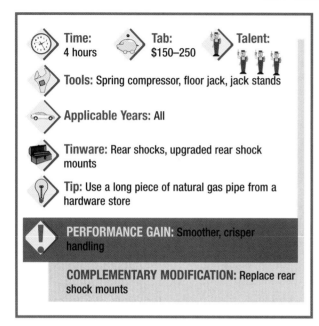

1 Support the rear trailing arm with the edge of a floor jack to take some compression force off of the shock. Remove the bolt (green arrow), and the bottom of the shock will be disconnected from the trailing arm.

Replacing the rear shocks is easier than the front shocks. The rear shocks are basically a bolt-in replacement. Before you begin, jack up the rear of the car (see Project 1). You don't need to remove the rear wheels if you're only replacing the rear shocks.

To remove the rear shock, place a jack under the rear trailing arm and lift it up slightly. The shocks support the weight of the trailing arm when the car is suspended in air, so you need to remove this tension from the shock prior to removal. With the bottom disconnected, remove the top of the shock and the rear shock mount (see Project 62). Replacement simply involves bolting in the new shock.

Replacement of the springs is a bit more difficult, and the procedures for the E30 and E36 vary slightly. First, the E30 procedure: Begin by unbolting the bottom of the shock from the trailing arm. Then undo the straps that attach the muffler to the car, along with the front exhaust mounting bracket. You will need the exhaust to be somewhat loose so you can drop down the trailing arms and they won't get hung up on the muffler pipes.

Disconnect the sway bar drop links. Then place your floor jack underneath the rear differential and support its weight. Remove the mounting bolt from the rubber differential mount. Inspect this rubber mount and replace it if it's worn. Also disconnect the speedometer sender connection. Slowly drop the differential a few inches to lower the pivot point for the CV joints, which will allow you to rotate the trailing arms downward. As you lower the rear suspension, make sure the brake cables and hoses don't catch on the rear sway bar. With the trailing arms lowered, have a helper push

2 Shown here is the rear spring configuration for an E30 (very similar to the E36). The spring sits between the trailing arm and the frame of the chassis.

down on them with their foot so you can remove the springs. Install the new springs and raise the rear suspension back up. Reconnect the sway bar, speed sensor, muffler straps and bracket, and rear shocks.

The E36 spring replacement is a bit easier. With the rear of the car raised, disconnect the rear shock. Be sure the emergency brake is released (handle down). On the 318is in this set of photos, I had to disconnect the rear sway bar from the trailing arm and the chassis. The bar kept getting caught between the exhaust and the trailing arm, and didn't allow the arm to drop down enough. Using a 6-foot-long pry bar, pull down the rear trailing arm by putting your weight on the end of the bar. With the trailing arm depressed downward, reach in and pull out the rear spring. I used a long piece of pipe normally used for gas lines since this type of pipe is cheap and available at most hardware stores. Don't try to muscle your way through it without the pipe—it makes the task a whole lot easier. With the new spring in place, reconnect the rear sway bar and rear shock.

With both the E30 and E36, carefully inspect the rear rubber spring pads. Most of the time they will be perfectly fine, but if they are really old, they may be cracked or worn out. If you encounter tire clearance problems, you can raise up the rear of the car by substituting the upper rear spring pad with a thicker one. Stock E36 thickness is 7.5 millimeters. Replacement spring pads are available in 10 millimeters (part number 33-53-1-136-387) or 5 millimeters (part number 33-53-1-136-385). You can also clip away the center nipple from the pads and combine them for extra height.

Many people purchase spring kits in order to lower the car from its original height. One word of caution: The stock M3 suspension components are designed to already have the car sit low to the ground. So, if you purchase a spring kit designed to lower an M3 and install it on a stock 3 Series, the car will probably sit higher than you want. If you wish to properly lower your stock 3 Series, use the kits that are specifically designed to lower these cars, as they will compensate for the non-M3 components. Also, if you use a spring set to lower your car, you will have to cut down the rubber bumper stop on the shock an amount equal to the amount you're lowering. Otherwise, you'll bottom out the shocks against the stop more often.

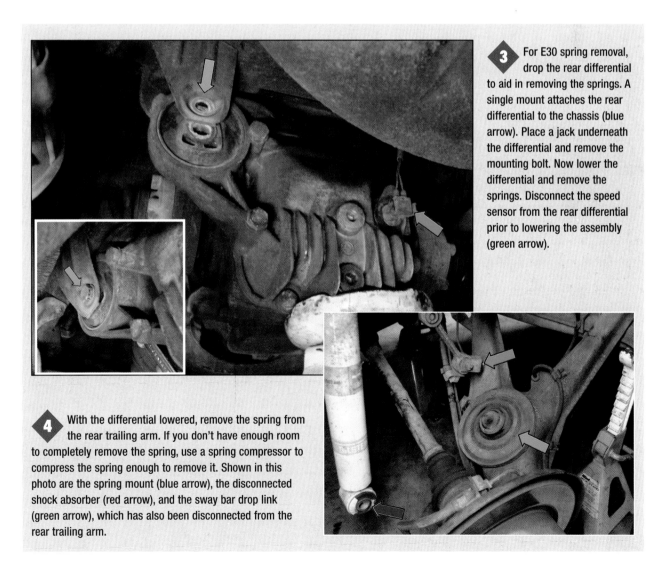

3 For E30 spring removal, drop the rear differential to aid in removing the springs. A single mount attaches the rear differential to the chassis (blue arrow). Place a jack underneath the differential and remove the mounting bolt. Now lower the differential and remove the springs. Disconnect the speed sensor from the rear differential prior to lowering the assembly (green arrow).

4 With the differential lowered, remove the spring from the rear trailing arm. If you don't have enough room to completely remove the spring, use a spring compressor to compress the spring enough to remove it. Shown in this photo are the spring mount (blue arrow), the disconnected shock absorber (red arrow), and the sway bar drop link (green arrow), which has also been disconnected from the rear trailing arm.

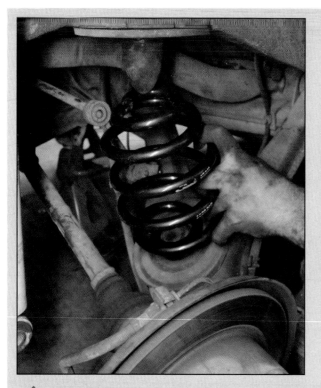

6 Removing the E36's rear springs (yellow arrow) is pretty easy. Simply get a long piece of pipe (blue arrow), and wedge it into the rear trailing arm. Placing your weight on the pipe should enable you to pull the spring out. To gain extra maneuvering room with the trailing arm, you may need to disconnect the rear sway bar drop links (green arrow). Inspect the upper spring pad (red arrow) and the lower one (purple arrow) for cracks due to age.

5 The new springs should simply slide into place. If they don't fit, you may need to compress them slightly with a spring compressor tool.

http://www.101projects.com/BMW/62.htm

PROJECT 62
Replacing Rear Shock Mounts

SUSPENSION

The 3 Series rear shock mounts (RSMs) are weak. These mounts hold the top of the rear shocks to the chassis. Repeated wear and tear on these mounts causes them to crack and break after many years of use. The worn-out shock mounts result in a clunking noise that emanates from the rear suspension while you're driving. Left unchecked and unfixed, the broken mounts can inflict permanent damage on the chassis by tearing the sheet metal in the rear wheelwells.

Begin by opening the trunk and removing everything from it—including the carpeting. If you have an E36, you'll also have to remove the rear speakers to gain access to the rear shock mount (see Photo 1). If you have a convertible, the rear shock mounts are located in the convertible top compartment behind the rear seat. Carefully pull back the molded carpeting in the trunk and remove whatever carpet fasteners hold the carpet down. Then remove the two retaining nuts that hold the rear shock mount to the chassis.

At this time, also disconnect the rear shock where it attaches to the rear trailing arm (see Project 61). Remove the

Time: 2 hours

Tab: $50–150

Talent:

Tools: Floor jack and jack stands, socket set

Applicable Years: All

Tinware: Rear shock mounts, gaskets, mounting hardware, reinforcement plates, or aftermarket kit

Tip: Use the upgrade kit, or the Z3 reinforcement plates

PERFORMANCE GAIN: No more clunking sounds from your rear suspension

COMPLEMENTARY MODIFICATION: Replace rear shocks

entire assembly from the car disassemble it on your workbench (see Photo 3).

Around the time that the Z3 was designed, BMW realized that this rear shock mount design placed a lot of stress on the sheet metal surrounding the rear shock towers. As a result, BMW engineers included a top-mounted support bracket that sandwiches the rear shock mount and distributes the load better (part number 51-71-8-413-359, about $15). BMW also redesigned the mount for the E46 3 Series cars, making sure the mount was backward compatible with the earlier 3 Series cars. This upgraded mount is used on the E46 M3 and E46 convertible cars, and is the mount to use if you swap out your rear shock mounts for replacement stock units (part number 33-52-6-754-096).

If you wish to go a step further in performance, install an aftermarket rear shock mount kit. I prefer the aluminum billet kit manufactured by Ground Control and available from PelicanParts.com for about $150. This kit replaces the rubber inner bushing with a polyurethane bushing that is much stiffer and far more secure than the stock mount. In addition, the aftermarket kit contains a beefy support plate that reinforces the sheet metal at its weak point. Installing the aftermarket kit is very similar to installing the stock mounts.

Reuse the plastic dust cover and the two concave washers from your old shock. Don't reuse the rubber bumper, as these are typically near disintegration by the time most people replace the mounts. Use new self-locking nuts on top of the shock, and affix the rear shock mount to the chassis. Finally, use a new gasket to seal the base of the shock mount to the chassis. Reinstall the shock mount and replace the rubber boot on top if it was there when you removed the old mount. Reattach the shock at the bottom, reinstall any speakers or carpet removed, and you're finished.

If you find your chassis sheet metal torn around the mounts, there is a BMW factory retrofit part that can be welded into place to repair the metal (part number 41-14-8-169-027 for the left side and 41-14-8-169-028 for the right side). Count on spending about $100 or so for a good welder to fit and weld these plates into the rear of your trunk.

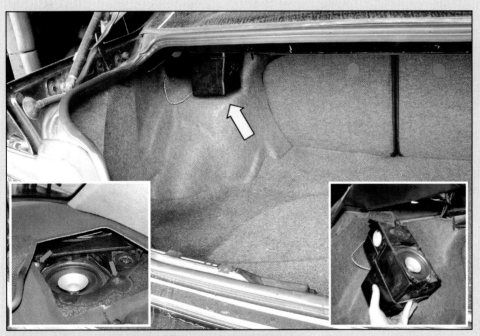

1 To access the rear shock mounts, remove everything in your trunk. On E30 cars, you only need to pull back the carpet, and the mounts should be easily accessible underneath. On E36 cars, the rear speakers interfere with access to the mounts (yellow arrow). From the back seat, pry off the speaker grille and remove the two screws that attach the speakers to the chassis (green arrows, lower left). The speakers should drop into the recesses of the trunk (lower right). No need to unplug them—the wires should be long enough to simply place them aside.

2 Here's a photo of what the rear shock mounts in the rear of an E30. On some cars, there may also be a factory rubber boot installed (inset photo). The red arrow points to the rear shock mount (RSM), and the blue arrow points to the very tip of the rod that runs the length of the rear shock.

3 With the rear shock assembly removed from the car, disassemble it by removing the top retaining nut from the top of the shock. Hold the shock tip with a pair of locking pliers or a similar tool. Closer examination of this rear shock mount upon disassembly reveals a large crack (red arrow).

4 On the left is the aftermarket rear shock mount kit from Ground Control. If you're planning on doing some spirited driving, this kit is just what you need. On the right is a stock mount with the Z3 reinforcement plate, a less-expensive alternative to the aftermarket kit.

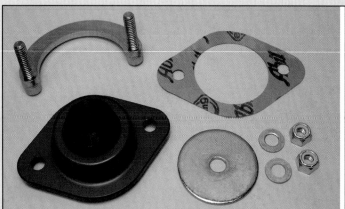 

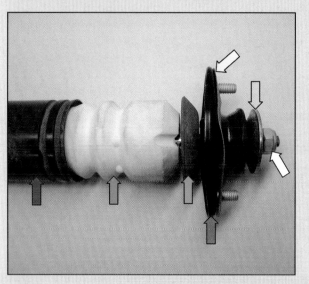 

5 This photo shows the proper assembly order for the rear shock mounts. Red arrow: shock absorber dust cover. Green arrow: rubber/foam bumper stop. Blue arrow: lower cup washer (cup faces the rubber/foam bumper). Purple arrow: rear shock mount (stock unit shown). Yellow arrow: shock mount/body gasket. Orange arrow: upper cup washer (cup faces upward toward the top). White arrow: shock retaining nut.

6 Here's a photo of the finished product. Secure the top of the shock with a set of locking pliers so you can tighten and affix the top locking nut (inset). Only use new locking hardware—don't reuse the old hardware here. Add the Z3 reinforcement plates to the rear shock mounts (green arrow). They are very cheap insurance against tearing your sheet metal.

E36 Performance Suspension/ Lowering Your BMW

Shocks and springs

The PSS performance suspension kit from Bilstein is the one of the top performing kits available for the E36 3 Series. The system includes two front coil-over spring/shock setups, two high-performance rear shocks, and a set of rear springs that integrate with adjustable spring perches. Both the front and rear springs are easily adjustable for tweaking the exact ride height you desire. The kit is a bolt-in replacement available for all non-M3 E36 cars manufactured since June 1992 and can be fitted to all earlier E36 models (including the M3) with a few minor suspension retrofits. The kit comes in two varieties: The PSS kit incorporates adjustable spring perches for both front and rear height adjustment. The PSS 9 kit is identical to the PSS kit, with the added feature that the four shock absorbers are easily adjustable.

Installation of either kit is no more difficult than installing stock shock absorbers and new springs (see Projects 60 and 61). The installation of the rear spring is a little different, as it incorporates an adjustable spring perch (see Photos 4 through 6 for installation).

After you've installed the PSS kit, have the car realigned. Due to the design of the front suspension, the alignment specs will change when you lower the car from the stock height (see Project 58). In addition, the PSS kits are lower at their highest spring perch setting than the stock struts, which

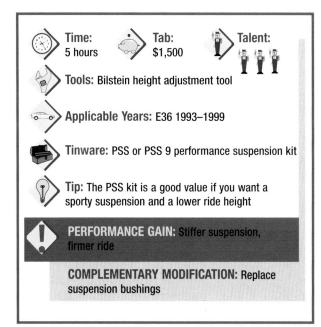

Time: 5 hours

Tab: $1,500

Talent: 🥜🥜🥜

Tools: Bilstein height adjustment tool

Applicable Years: E36 1993–1999

Tinware: PSS or PSS 9 performance suspension kit

Tip: The PSS kit is a good value if you want a sporty suspension and a lower ride height

PERFORMANCE GAIN: Stiffer suspension, firmer ride

COMPLEMENTARY MODIFICATION: Replace suspension bushings

can cause issues with clearance of wider wheels and tires. Before you test the suspension to the max, check your tire and wheel clearances. See Project 61 for a tip on raising the rear of your car if you encounter any tire clearance issues.

SUSPENSION

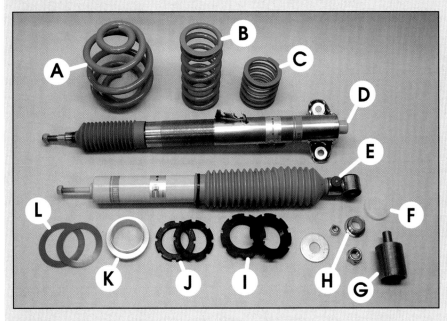

1 This is half of the Bilstein PSS 9 kit. **A:** Rear spring. **B:** Front upper spring. **C:** Front lower spring. **D:** Adjustment knob for front shock. **E:** Adjustment knob for rear shock. **F:** Rear spring perch support cover. **G:** Rear spring perch support. **H:** Rear trailing arm bushing. **I:** Front/rear spring perches. **J:** Spring perch retaining ring. **K:** Upper/lower front spring retainer. **L:** Slip inserts for front spring retainer.

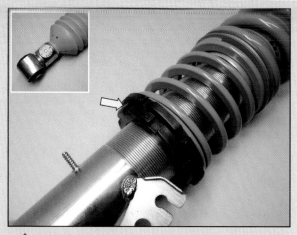

2 Shown here is a close-up of the front PSS 9 shock. The upper and lower springs are separated by the spring retainer and two blue plastic slip inserts (inset photo, upper right). The adjustment knob is located at the bottom of the shock for easy adjustment (inset, lower right). Turn the knob to nine for a softer ride, or one for a stiffer performance feel.

3 To adjust ride height, rotate the spring perch and retainer (yellow arrow) up or down the length of the shock. The rear shock adjustment knob is located off to the side of the shock (inset).

4 In the rear assembly, the rear spring perch support bolts into the rear trailing arm. Ride height adjustment is similar to the front—rotate the spring perch and retainer up or down on the threaded perch support.

5 With the rear spring removed, insert the rear trailing arm bushing into the mounting hole from the bottom of the trailing arm (inset). Then attach the threaded rear spring perch support to the trailing arm with the large nut included. Install the white plastic cover into the top of the perch support.

Sway bars

The M3 uses a different sway bar mounting setup than other E36 models. On E36 M3s, the sway bar mounts to the strut instead of the control arm (see Photo 7). Mounting the sway bar on top of the strut allows the sway bar to be more effective than the stock mounting location. The actual geometry and mounting configuration of the M3 roll bar and the regular E36 roll bar are nearly identical; the main difference is in this drop link setup. Most aftermarket manufacturers only offer sway bars for the M3 models, but they will also fit other E36s. However, due to the change in this drop link orientation, sway bars have varying degrees of effectiveness, depending upon whether they're installed on an M3 or an E36.

This is important for a variety of reasons. Installing a sway bar designed for an M3 into a stock E36 setup will work fine; however, it will not give the exact effect the manufacturer originally designed it to have. If you wish to upgrade your sway bars, choose an aftermarket M3 set that will produce a measured increase in anti-roll stiffness while balancing

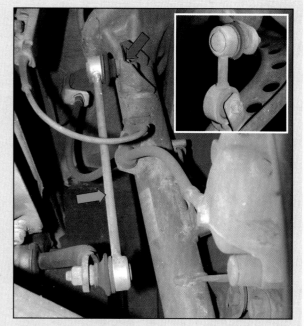

6 The completed rear spring assembly is shown here. Unfortunately, it's difficult to get into the trailing arm cup and adjust the height of the rear suspension, and you'll have to make a few adjustments after installation.

7 The sway bar drop link on the M3 (green arrow) attaches directly to the strut (red arrow). The PSS kit can be made to work with the M3, but it requires that you replace the strut-mounted sway bar drop link with the one used on the standard E36 suspension (inset). This drop link attaches to the control arm.

the changes with upgraded springs and stiffer shocks. To demonstrate this difference in sway bar effectiveness, compare the various sizes of stock sway bars:

Model	Front bar	Rear bar
Stock 95 M3	22.5 millimeters	19 millimeters
Stock 96+ M3	23 millimeters	20 millimeters
Stock 328i	24 millimeters	15 millimeters
Stock 328i Sport	25.5 millimeters	18 millimeters

The front sway bar for the M3 is thinner than the stock sway bar for the 328 because the sway bar drop linkage on the M3 is more effective and doesn't require a heavier, thicker bar.

If you select the PSS suspension system for your M3, first convert the sway bar drop links to the stock E36 setup. You will lose some of your effective anti-roll capabilities because of the shorter drop link configuration used on the stock cars. Counter this by installing a beefier sway bar at the same time. The conversion to the stock drop links is easy and requires only about $40 worth of parts. Here are the part numbers required for this conversion:

Quantity	Part number	Description
2	31-35-1-091-764	Drop link
2	31-35-1-127-263	Control arm bracket
2	07-11-9-912-506	Hex screw
2	07-12-9-922-716	Brass nut
2	07-12-9-964-672	Nut
2	31-11-1-114-348	Washer

Unbolt the drop link from the sway bar and strut, and attach the new drop link and U-bracket to the control arm. There should be a mounting hole pre-drilled in the control arm. E36 cars manufactured before November 1991 also have this strut-mounted sway bar setup and may require this conversion in order to use performance shocks and springs designed for late-model E36s.

If you own an E36 manufactured prior to June 1992, you may have noticed that most performance suspension kits are only available for later-model cars. This is because BMW changed the front strut mount in June 1992 (for the 1993 models). Fortunately, the early cars can be retrofitted with these later-style components in order to use the same shocks, springs, and performance kits as the later cars. Simply swap the late-model parts with the ones on the top of your struts, and you will be able to use any late-model suspension setup. Total cost for this retrofit is about $175.

Quantity	Part number	Description
2	31-33-1-092-885	Upper strut mount
2	31-33-1-135-580	Upper spring plate
2	31-33-1-128-523	Upper spring pad
2	31-31-1-139-453	Top covering cap
2	31-32-1-139-422	Self-locking nut
2	33-31-1-125-916	Flat washer
2	31-33-1-094-288	Gasket
2	31-33-1-110-196	Sealing ring
2	31-33-1-116-983	Flat washer

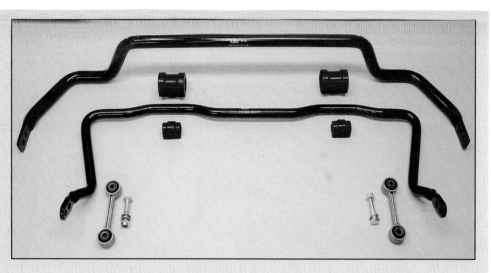

8 This aftermarket front and rear sway bar kit from Eibach is specifically designed to work with non-M3 E36 cars and includes new bushings and drop links. The bar has two adjustment settings. Bolting the drop links to the outer holes produces a softer ride, whereas using the inner holes results in a stiffer suspension.

PROJECT 64
http://www.101projects.com/BMW/64.htm
Installing a Strut Tower Brace

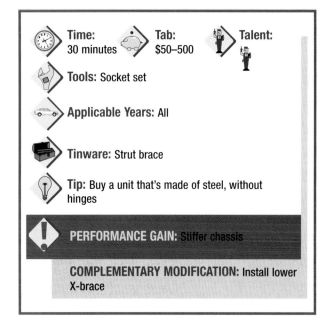

Time: 30 minutes   **Tab:** $50–500   **Talent:** 🎯

Tools: Socket set

Applicable Years: All

Tinware: Strut brace

Tip: Buy a unit that's made of steel, without hinges

PERFORMANCE GAIN: Stiffer chassis

COMPLEMENTARY MODIFICATION: Install lower X-brace

The BMW 3 Series cars are well known for their agility and superb handling. However, because of the chassis design, there is a weakness in the 3 Series cars. The front shock towers are not well supported in the 3 Series chassis. In fact, they are somewhat isolated and unsupported. As a result, the towers can bend and flex under heavy cornering. This flexing can cause detrimental changes in the handling of your car, because, in general, the stiffer the chassis, the better the handling of the car. Camber strut braces are designed to maintain the distance between the shocks under heavy cornering. A bar linking the top of the shock towers ensures the towers do not bend when the chassis is flexing.

Well, that's what the marketers say when selling these bars. The strut bars are yet another controversial product that many people feel the need to install on their BMWs. On some cars (the early Porsche 911s, for example), the installation of the strut bar is an important chassis stiffening device. Because of the Porsches' rear-engine design, the front chassis can be decidedly weak, particularly when rust has started to affect chassis stiffness. But the BMW chassis is different. It's supported by a much more rigid frame that includes a very strong engine mount bar that runs the width of the car under the engine.

Which strut bars are most effective? I have little faith in the aluminum strut bars. Aluminum is not a very strong metal—you can often bend aluminum pipes with your hands. Add to this the fact that most strut bars are angled to fit neatly around the engine and under the hood, since there's no straight shot across the engine bay. This combination creates a very weak support when you consider the forces you're trying to counteract. In my opinion, an aluminum strut brace is merely window dressing for the engine compartment.

I'm also not fond of bars with hinges built into the strut mounts. If they move at all, the shock towers are likely to see movement that would place the strut brace under compression and tension. A stiff connection between the strut towers is vital to proper strut bar operation. Any time you place a fastener in the assembly, you introduce backlash and slop in at least one direction. Thus, the bar becomes ineffective in either compression or tension.

The best strut tower braces are one-piece units manufactured out of thick, welded steel pipe. These braces offer the best protection against chassis flex when installed between the two strut towers. The strut braces manufactured by Ireland Engineering for the E30 cars fit this description

1 I bought this strut brace from a major manufacturer and was very disappointed when it arrived. The camber strut brace attaches to the top of the shock towers with the three nuts that also hold the top shock mount. This polished aluminum model is made to fit the 318is. I do not recommend this type of strut bar as a performance improvement. Aluminum is not very strong, the mounts on the top of the strut allow for too much slop, and the angle of the bar makes it look like I could bend it with my own two hands. I consider bars like these mostly for show.

2 Shown on this M3 is a strut tower brace from Dinan. This beautiful product has carbon-fiber inlays and anodized caps for the top of the strut towers and really spruces up the engine compartment. However, I question how much structural support it actually provides, considering its relatively thin aluminum construction and its bowed construction.

3 Although not as attractive, this brace is probably the most effective. The thick, large-diameter steel pipe directly reinforces the shock towers and requires significant forces to deflect and bend. Despite the two rather large angles in the brace, the strength of the steel pipe should compensate for the reduced rigidity. This is the type of bar I'd recommend if you want to install one in your car.

perfectly. Their strut bars are some of the beefiest designs on the market.

If you ask die-hard racers who drive their 3 Series cars on the track, most of them don't run with a strut brace and can't feel the difference even when pulling significant side loads (1.4 g's) out of the corners. For dedicated track cars, the strut towers are often reinforced with steel pipe welded diagonally across the engine, connected to the front of the firewall.

The bottom line? If you believe a strut bar will benefit you, or if you are looking to spruce up the engine compartment, adding one to your car is a relatively simply task–simply bolt it on top of your strut towers. If your goal is increased performance, I recommend the bar only for a very stiffly sprung, dedicated track car. Make sure it's a high-quality unit that's designed properly: close-fitting on the struts, manufactured out of steel, a minimal amount of angles in the bar itself, and no hinges. A better upgrade, and one that should be installed first, is the BMW E36 convertible lower X-brace that stiffens the lower part of the chassis (see Project 66).

SUSPENSION

Steering Wheel Replacement

⏱ **Time:** 1 hour

Tab: $150–250

Talent: ♟♟

🔧 **Tools:** Torx driver set

🚗 **Applicable Years:** All

🧰 **Tinware:** Steering wheel and hub adapter

💡 **Tip:** Use the 1984–1991 hub cap emblem for the center horn button

⚠ **PERFORMANCE GAIN:** Great improvement in driving feel

COMPLEMENTARY MODIFICATION: Aftermarket shift knob, replace steering column switches

1 This is one of my favorite aftermarket steering wheels from MOMO. The Jet wheel comes with a standard MOMO horn button. Also available is a small hubcap sticker from the older 3 Series cars that fits perfectly on the center horn button, giving it that performance OEM look (part number 36-13-1-181-082).

Adding an aftermarket steering wheel is one of the most exciting and rewarding projects you can perform on your BMW. There are a wide variety of wheels to choose from, and let's face it—the stock BMW wheel is not too exciting. Even the stock M3 wheels are a little dull.

All later-model BMWs came from the factory equipped with driver's side air bags. Air bags are important pieces of safety equipment, and I fully recommend keeping them in place. That said, you cannot install an aftermarket steering wheel and also keep your air bag in place. With this in mind, I recommend you install an aftermarket wheel only if your car originally didn't come with an air bag (like the older E30 cars), or if you're converting your car into a club racer or weekend track car. If you choose to install an aftermarket steering wheel in your street car, be forewarned: Air bags are probably the best protection you will have in a crash. Also, state and local regulations may restrict what you can do with your air bag. For the purpose of this project, I'll assume that the aftermarket wheel is going to be installed on a track car.

First, disconnect the battery and wait at least 30 minutes (see Project 84). The air bag is a dangerously explosive package and can be set off accidentally by a variety of triggers. The air bag control system is designed to remain operational for up to 15 minutes after the battery has been disconnected.

Remove the lower plastic cover under the steering wheel and disconnect the orange air bag connector. Then, remove the air bag from the steering wheel by disconnecting the two Torx screws that attach it to the front of the wheel (see insets, Photo 3). The air bag should be loose from the wheel. Disconnect the small harness, remove it, and place it aside.

Next, remove the wheel itself. If you don't own an impact wrench, here's a neat trick for removing the steering wheel: First, take one of those obnoxiously large, red steering wheel locks and clamp it onto the steering wheel. The long handle on the lock provides a significant amount of leverage on the wheel. Then, insert a deep socket onto the nut. Compressing together the steering wheel lock handle and the long handle attached to the socket will enable you to loosen up the steering wheel nut. Under no circumstances should you ever turn the steering wheel all the way to the end of the rack and use the end stop to hold the wheel while you remove the nut. The steering wheel has a lot of leverage, and you can easily damage your rack and pinion if you apply too much torque to the wheel.

Once you have the nut off of the wheel, simply pull the wheel off the steering column. If the wheel is stuck on the splines and doesn't want to come off, take a rubber mallet and gently tap the rear of the wheel until it begins to move. Install the new wheel onto the included steering wheel hub and then onto the car. Hook up the horn and test it before you tighten the wheel down again.

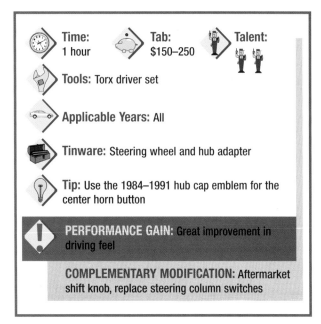

SUSPENSION

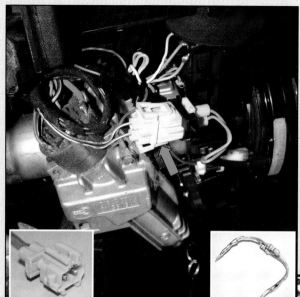

2 After you remove the lower plastic cover, you can see the collection of wires underneath. Unplug and unclip the neon orange air bag connector prior to removing the steering wheel. If you remove the air bag permanently, you need to trick the air bag computer into thinking that it's still connected. Place a 3.3 ohm resistor across the two terminals of the connector to trick the computer into thinking that the air bag is still in place, instead of triggering the air bag lamp. This should allow the system to continue to properly control and operate the passenger's side air bag.

Removal of the steering wheel itself is pretty easy. Remove the two screws on **3** either side (blue and green arrows) of the steering wheel with a T-25 Torx driver. These screws are somewhat hidden from view and have tiny access holes in the back side of the steering wheel. With the two screws loosened, the air bag should pop out of the center of the wheel. Disconnect the wire harness for the air bag (red arrow shows the connector; purple shows where it plugs into the air bag), and place it aside.

4 I developed this trick for removing steering wheels: Lock the wheel with a steering wheel locking device such as "The Club." Don't allow the steering wheel to lock against the mechanism in the lock cylinder, and don't let it bottom out against the steering rack. Using a breaker bar and The Club in this fashion, you can easily remove the steering center nut.

5 Although you lose the safety of the air bag, the new steering wheel really spices up the interior of the car and gives your BMW that motorsport feel.

Installing the Lower Crossbrace

Time: 2 hours

Tab: $150

Talent: 👔👔

Tools: Drill, Allen wrench, GearWrench reversible ratcheting wrench

Applicable Years: E36 (All)

Tinware: Crossbrace, four nutserts, four bolts with washers

Tip: Use the procedure below to install the nutserts—no need for expensive tools

PERFORMANCE GAIN: Stiffer chassis

COMPLEMENTARY MODIFICATION: Oil change

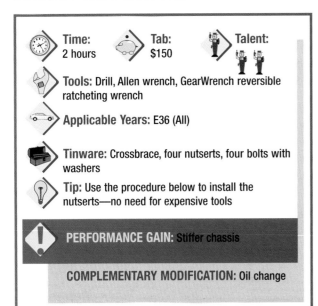

1 The factory lower support brace stiffens the chassis and provides undercarriage protection, especially for cars that have been lowered.

2 The E36 convertibles all have this brace installed as stock equipment from the factory. The crossbrace replaces the single cross bar installed as standard equipment on nonconvertible E36 models. The crossbar mounting points are shown with yellow arrows. The new nutserts need to be installed into the front axle support bar in the locations indicated by the blue arrows. As you can see, the crossbrace installed in this car has done its job—the bottom is scratched with scars from battles with the pavement. The bar also protects the bottom engine sump.

Many E36 owners upgrade their chassis with the factory crossbrace that mounts underneath the engine. This crossbrace was installed as stock equipment on all convertibles and the 1995 LTW, a lightweight version of the M3. The convertibles received this bar to stiffen up the chassis since their chassis are naturally less stiff than coupes or sedans because they have no roof. Installing the crossbrace on a standard E36 coupe or sedan serves a dual purpose: The crossbrace stiffens up the chassis and also protects the engine sump from road hazards. Here's what you need:

Quantity	Part number	Description
1	51 71 8 410 212	Crossbrace
4	07 11 9 915 093	M8X20-Z1 Allen bolt with washer
4	51 71 8 175 003	M8 blind rivet nut (nutsert)

Installing a crossbrace is quite easy; the only difficult part is installing the inserts that attach the crossbrace to the front axle support bar. M3 cars manufactured after October 1994 already have these inserts installed. For all other cars, the holes are predrilled in the front axle support bar, but you will need to install the inserts.

The inserts corresponding to the crossbrace are called "blind rivet nuts," or "nutserts." The nutserts are installed into the front axle support bar and are compressed against the sheet metal so they don't turn. They support loads from the attachment bolts.

First, jack up the front of the car and support it on jack stands (see Project 1). Identify the four holes in the front axle support bar and remove any dirt or debris that may have

gathered in them. Test-fit the nutserts into the holes. If they don't fit, chase the holes with a ⁷⁄₁₆-inch or 11-millimeter drill.

Now, install the four nutserts into the holes. Use the procedure outlined in Photo 3. Check to make sure the nutserts are installed tightly and do not rotate in their bores. If they do rotate, pop out the insert and try again with a new one.

With the inserts installed, remove the support bar that runs just behind the rear of the engine sump. The crossbrace

SUSPENSION

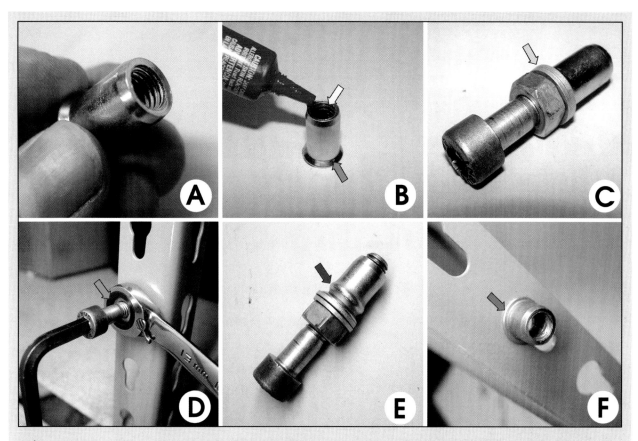

3 Installing the nutsert is the most confusing part of this relatively simple project. This photo sequence shows exactly how they work and how to install them without special tools. **A:** Here's a close-up shot of the nutsert. The outer end of the nutsert contains threads. These threads will be used to install the nutsert and serve as the mating threads for the mounting hardware for the crossbrace. The lip on the other end butts up against the sheet metal in the front axle support bar. **B:** Apply red Loctite in two places on the nutsert—on the inside threads (yellow arrow) and along the bottom lip (green arrow). This will keep the bolt secure in the nutsert, and the Loctite on the lip will help keep the nutsert from turning in its hole. Note: Only apply Loctite on the lip of the nutsert right before you are ready to insert it into the front axle support bar. **C:** With the Loctite still wet, place a nut and two washers onto the hex bolt and then insert the assembly into the nutsert, making sure that at least some of the threads protrude out the end (see Frame E). Lubricate both sides of the washers with WD-40 or other penetrating lubricant prior to installing them on the nutsert (orange arrow). Be sure not to get any oil on the area where you apply the Loctite. Let the entire assembly sit for a few minutes as the Loctite hardens. Only use high-quality bolts and washers for this installation. Do not use a bolt and nut more than twice to install each fastener; after that, they may yield and break off under the force of installation. **D:** Insert the nutsert into the hole in the front axle support bar. For the purpose of demonstration, I installed this nutsert into a spare hole on some shelving in my garage. Use an Allen wrench to keep the bolt from turning, and use a wrench to turn the nut clockwise. I prefer the GearWrench ratcheting wrenches with the reversible switch because they have a lip that secures the nut while you tighten it (blue arrow). When you start turning the wrench, it will require a lot of force as the nutsert begins to deform. After a short while, it will get easier. When you can't tighten anymore, simply back off the nut and then unscrew the hex bolt. The nutsert should be tightly installed. **E:** You normally can't see this when installing the nutsert. The nutsert will deform (red arrow) as you pull the outer threads closer to the lip. This will create a small sandwich of metal material, and the nutsert will eventually be very tightly compressed around the sheetmetal hole. **F:** Shown here is the back side of the nutsert. You normally cannot see this because it is hidden in the recesses of the front axle support bar. The metal has been deformed so there is now a lip on both sides, effectively sandwiching the nutsert between the sheet metal (purple arrow).

replaces this bar. Bolt in the new crossbrace and apply blue Loctite Threadlocker on the threads of the bolts as you install them. Tighten the larger rear bolts to 70 N-m (51.5 ft-lbs) and the smaller ones that mate with the nutserts to 27 N-m (19.9 ft-lbs).

There's been some talk in BMW circles about the benefits of welding the crossbrace in place. This is **not** a good idea, as it would require you to cut out the crossbrace if you needed to drop the oil pan to replace a seal or your rod bearings.

Body/
Interior Trim

You spend a large amount of time inside the car, so why not have it look good on the inside as well the outside? A great-looking interior improves the overall appearance of your BMW, and also makes it more fun to drive. Along these lines, a few moments spent on grooming exterior items can sweep away the effects of aging on your car. This particular section is a grab bag of projects dealing with everything from headlamp upgrades to door equipment repair. Whether you're planning on replacing your hood shocks or installing a rear spoiler on your car, the projects in this section will help you improve the overall look and performance of your BMW.

PROJECT 67
Door Panels and Lock Troubleshooting

Time: 1–5 hours

Tab: None

Talent: 👤👤👤

Tools: Torx driver set

Applicable Years: All

Tinware: Door handle, door stay, mirror switch, speaker, etc.

Tip: Use 3M weatherstrip glue to reattach the plastic door pockets

PERFORMANCE GAIN: Working door equipment

COMPLEMENTARY MODIFICATION: Repair your window regulator

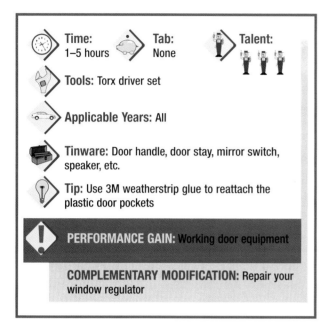

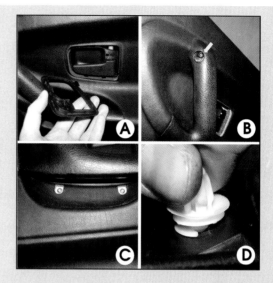

1 Shown here is the sequence for removing the door panel. **A:** Slide the outer door handle trim piece toward the front of the car to remove it. **B:** On this convertible, there's an additional hidden screw on the passenger-side door handle underneath a small plastic plug. The location and quantity of screws varied slightly over the years. **C:** Below the handle, two small plastic plugs cover two screws that secure the handle of the door panel to the door frame. **D:** Eleven of these small plastic clips secure the outer edges of the door panel to the door frame. Carefully pry each of these out of their mating holes to remove the door panel from the door.

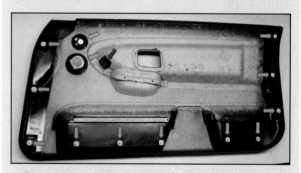

2 Shown here is the back side of the left (driver side) door panel from an E36 convertible. There are 11 plastic clips that attach the panel to the door. You need to pry each of these clips from the door prior to removing the door panel. It will feel like you're breaking the door panel, but you will need to apply significant force to pull off each of the plastic clips. Use a stiff plastic spatula to wedge the door panel out without scratching the paint on the door. The blue arrows show the back sides of the two door speakers, and the red arrow shows the side mirror switch.

If you are not the original owner of your BMW, chances are there are quite a few things amiss with your car, and you are left wondering how they got broken. There probably isn't a place on the car with more gadgets and devices that break than the door. Not only do you have window glass and potentially leaky seals, but you have door handles, mirror switches, window regulators, door stays, and door panels—all of which are very susceptible to breakage or damage. Even if you only work on your car from time to time, there is a very good chance you will need to dive into the door to fix something that has broken. This project specifically targets the replacement of the door lock assembly, but because there are so many moving parts on the door, I'll discuss just about everything else as well.

The first step in working on your car door is removing the door panel. (An important note: If you're looking to remove your outside mirror, you do not need to remove the door panel; see Project 76.) Photos 1 and 2 detail the process of door panel removal. The toughest part is pulling the panel out from the door—it is attached with 11 plastic clips that can be difficult to snap out of their frames. Also, the door panel often separates as you pull it away from the frame, leaving the plastic door pockets attached. Never fear, though, these are easily glued back on at reassembly time with some 3M Super Weatherstrip glue.

With the door panel removed, you should see a foam covering glued onto the back side of the door. A black, sticky goo attaches this to the door, which can be removed and reused again if the material is still pliable. Be careful not to tear the foam covering when you remove it, though.

BODY/INTERIOR TRIM

199

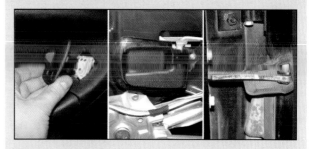

4 The mirror switch simply pops out of the door panel (left). If you need to replace this switch, pry it up out of the door and unplug it. If you're removing the door panel, then remove this switch. The plastic door handle is a part that can wear out and break (center). With the door panel removed, replacement is a snap. Simply unbolt the door handle, detach it from the actuator rod, and install the new one in its place. While you have access, you might want to replace your door stay if it's worn out (right). Simply unbolt it and remove the pin from the body.

3 With the door panel removed, you should see the foam covering (top). This material has a plastic back to keep moisture out of the door and a foam front to help reduce noise in the interior. Carefully remove the foam barrier by peeling it back. It's attached to the door with a gooey, black adhesive. Be careful not to tear the piece as you remove it. The bottom photo shows the door with the foam barrier removed. The purple arrows point to the four rivets that need to be drilled out if you are removing the window regulator. The blue arrow shows the Allen bolt that holds the end of the window regulator to the door. In the inset photo, you can see the back sides of the two door speakers. These speakers need to be disconnected prior to removing the door panel. Reach around the top of the door panel and disconnect the wire harnesses by pulling on them carefully.

With the panel removed, you will have access to a number of items inside the door. The door stay can simply be unbolted from the door frame and removed. The plastic door handle can easily be swapped out. The window regulator can be removed or repaired (see Project 70). Any door seals or channel guides that need renewing are accessible to you as well. If any door-mounted speakers are broken, don't forget to replace them while you have the chance. The E36 speakers have a thin outer lip on their housing that often cracks as people bang on the door panel with their feet and knees. Unfortunately, this small lip is an integrated part of the speaker, and you must replace the entire speaker with a new one if you want to fix the broken lip.

One common failure point of the E36 BMWs is the small switch located inside the power lock assembly. These switches get a lot of use, and when they wear out, they can cause all sorts of problems. Switches that are stuck open tell the car the door is ajar all the time. The dashboard chime may ring continuously, or the gauge cluster may experience some erratic behavior. If the switch is stuck closed, then coupe and convertible owners may have a heck of a time opening and closing their doors because the window won't roll down that ¼-inch or so to allow you to pull it away from the car. The replacement of the lock assembly is detailed in the sequence in Photo 5.

On my 1993 E36, I had a really tough time chasing down a fault with the alarm system and door locks. I thought for sure it was related to the door switches, but in the end, the problem was related to faulty wiring in the trunk. (See Photo 2 of Project 82 for more details on this failure.)

Closing up the door panel is straightforward. I always like to use new plastic door panel clips because not only are the new ones cheap, the old ones get brittle and may break in the very near future, causing an annoying rattle. Don't forget to install the foam covering. It's very common to accidentally leave this on your workbench, only to discover it later on when you're putting your tools away!

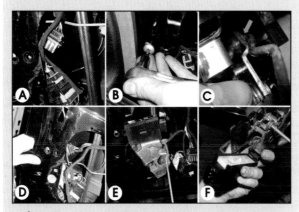

5 This photo sequence shows the procedure for replacing the lock actuator and switch assembly. **A:** Start by disconnecting the wire harness that attaches to the lock actuator. **B:** Remove the Torx bolts that hold the entire latch assembly to the door. Don't forget the bolt that is on the side of the door. **C:** Loosen and/or disconnect the actuator rod (green arrow) from the door lock assembly. **D:** Maneuver the assembly out of the door with your hand. **E:** Pull the entire assembly out of the door so you can access the black plastic actuator on the top of the latch assembly. **F:** Remove the actuator from the top of the latch assembly, and replace it with your new one.

Installing an Aftermarket Shift Knob

One of the most popular and easiest upgrades for your car is the addition of an aftermarket shift knob. Let's face it, the steering wheel, gauges, and shift knob are the three main items on the car that you have a personal interaction with each time you drive your car. Why not spruce them up a bit?

I personally find the BMW OEM shift knob to be quite boring. The shift knob chosen for this article was the MOMO chrome sphere. Installation literally takes about 15 minutes, and the kit includes all of the tools you will need for the install. The only caveat to this project is with the M3 shift knobs, which have an internal light. You need to disconnect this and stash the harness out of the way if you are installing a nonlighted aftermarket knob. When you replace your knob, it's also a good time to replace your leather shift boot. Original BMW ones are about $60 or so and simply snap out of their retainer in the center console. Some people who prefer a color-coordinated interior choose to replace their steering wheel and shift knob at the same time, using matching equipment from the same manufacturer.

Time: 30 minutes
Tab: $50–85
Talent: 👤

Tools: None

Applicable Years: All

Tinware: Shift knob kit

Tip: Be careful not to smack yourself in the face removing the old knob

PERFORMANCE GAIN: Cooler shifts

COMPLEMENTARY MODIFICATION: Aftermarket steering wheel, replace leather shift boot

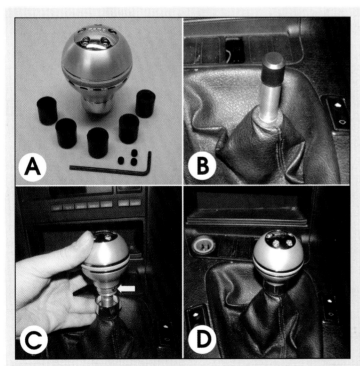

1 This photo shows the assembly sequence for installing a new aftermarket shift knob on your manual transmission. **A:** This shows the MOMO chrome sphere shift knob, complete with all the parts included in the installation kit. **B:** Remove your old knob by simply pulling upward on it—be careful not to accidentally smack yourself in the face! Install the small rubber boot on the shaft. **C:** Place the collar on the shaft, then place the knob over the rubber boot. Tighten the setscrews in place (you should only need the short ones that were included with the kit). **D:** The finished product—way cooler than that ugly stock OEM knob!

Wish you had a way to get that manual trans look, but without having to give up your automatic? JJL Customs offers a unique new product for automatic transmission owners. This shift knob works the same as your old pistol or T-handle shift knob. Instead of squeezing the trigger, you simply pull up on the spring-loaded knob to move the shifter through the gear detents. A simple leather boot covers the mechanism beneath. **2**

Replacing Hood Shocks

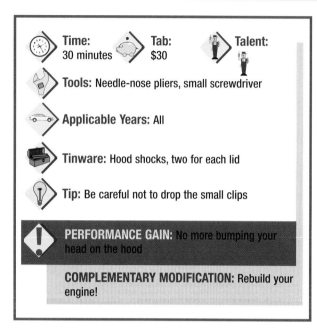

Time: 30 minutes	**Tab:** $30	**Talent:**

Tools: Needle-nose pliers, small screwdriver

Applicable Years: All

Tinware: Hood shocks, two for each lid

Tip: Be careful not to drop the small clips

! PERFORMANCE GAIN: No more bumping your head on the hood

COMPLEMENTARY MODIFICATION: Rebuild your engine!

1 Each shock is held in place by a small pin and clip to keep it in position. Be sure not to lose the clip or the pin into the recesses of your engine compartment or trunk. The new shocks should last several years before they begin to wear out again.

Are you getting tired of having your front or rear trunk lids drop on your head? Then it's probably time to replace your hood shocks. These are among the most disposable of parts on the BMW. They will fail, it's just a matter of when. Replacing them is an easy task, one made even easier for those with small hands who can manipulate tiny pieces. With a little bit of patience, you can replace your hood and trunk lid shocks in about 30 minutes.

The front hood uses two gas-pressurized shocks to hold up its weight. Start by lifting up the front hood and propping it open using a long stick or a baseball bat. Make sure this support is securely affixed, as the hood will hurt you if it falls upon your head. Starting with the right side, remove the small clip on the pin that connects the hood shock to the hood itself.

Remove the same pin from the mount that connects the shock to the lower mount in the engine compartment.

Install the new shock in the same place and orientation as the old one. Refasten the clips to the pins and make sure they are secure. Repeat the procedure for the left side. It is very easy to drop both the pin and the clip down into the recesses of the engine compartment, so work carefully and don't rush.

The rear trunk shocks are very similar in their replacement process. There's a small clip that holds in a plastic retainer on the E36 models—simply use a small screwdriver to pry up the clip, and then pull off the plastic retainer clip.

While you're in this area, you will probably want to check out your trunk's wire harness. See Photo 2 of Project 82 for more details.

Replacing the Window Regulator and Motor

Are you tired of having to open your door and get out at the drive-through restaurant to retrieve your burger? Does your window constantly reverse itself when you're trying to raise it? Perhaps it's time to replace or clean your window regulator, or install a new power window motor. The difficulty of this project varies depending upon which year car you have, but the results are immediate and quite rewarding. Not much is better than driving in your BMW with the sunroof open and the windows down on a nice, sunny day. Having a broken window regulator can surely put a damper

on that. Or worse if you own a convertible, a broken window regulator will keep you from putting the top down.

The first step in replacing either the regulator or the power window motor is to remove the door panel. Make sure you eliminate the power window switch as a potential problem, however, before you start tearing into your door. Double-check all the fuses that control the power windows, and swap out the relays to make sure there isn't a problem with one of them. If one window now works and the other doesn't, chances are it's the window motor or the window switch. The

BODY/INTERIOR TRIM

202

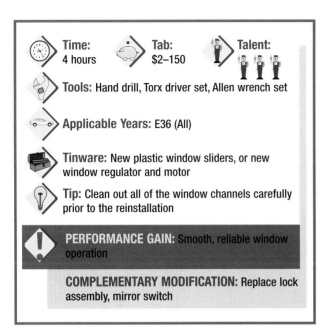

Time: 4 hours

Tab: $2–150

Talent: 👤👤👤

Tools: Hand drill, Torx driver set, Allen wrench set

Applicable Years: E36 (All)

Tinware: New plastic window sliders, or new window regulator and motor

Tip: Clean out all of the window channels carefully prior to the reinstallation

PERFORMANCE GAIN: Smooth, reliable window operation

COMPLEMENTARY MODIFICATION: Replace lock assembly, mirror switch

switches themselves are often faulty, which can sometimes make this an easy fix. Test the switch by removing it from the center console, and swap it with one that is working. If there is any noise coming from the door (such as clicks or whines) but the window isn't moving, then it's quite obvious the motor is fine, but the regulator needs to be repaired.

For details on removing the door panel, see Project 67. When you have the door panel removed, you can access the regulator. With your fingers clearly out of the way, roll down the window until it's about 75 percent of the way down. Take a look at the white, square plastic sliders that attach the bottom of the regulator to the window. If they are worn (and they're almost always worn), replace them using the procedure documented in Photo 3.

If your window doesn't respond at all and you've eliminated the possibility that it might be a broken window switch, then you'll need to remove the window regulator.

Unfortunately, the window regulator is attached to the door frame with rivets. You will need to drill out these rivets in order to remove the regulator from the door. (See Photos 2 and 3 for details on removing the regulator.)

With the regulator detached from the door frame and the window, you should test the motor prior to disconnecting the electrical connection. With your hands out of the way of the regulator, carefully press lightly on the window switch and see if the regulator moves. If the window was stuck previously, but now it moves, it means that the tracks of the regulator and the window are sticky and need lubrication. Photo 4 and Photo 5 show the process for greasing the regulator tracks prior to reinstallation. If the motor doesn't move at all, it is probably worn out (assuming you've checked the window switch).

Before you reinstall the regulator, I recommend you inspect and replace the front window channel guide too, if it's worn. This is the channel that guides the front of the window as it is raised and lowered by the regulator. Also worth replacing are the window slot seals. These inner and outer window scrapers keep water from dripping down into the recesses of the door. You should grease each and every moving part of the regulator: the slides, the motor, the gears, and the large-toothed section of the regulator.

Before you close everything up inside your door, it's a wise idea to test the proper operation of the window. Hook up the power connections to the window motor, and try to raise and lower the window. Also verify the stop positions of the window once you have reinstalled the regulator. There are screws located inside the door that control these stop positions. Once you're satisfied everything is running smoothly, reseal the door panels and you're on your way again.

1 Before you start tearing apart your door to fix your window, check the window switch first. Pull up on the trim around the switch, and the assembly should pull out of the center console. Swap around connectors and test the nonfunctional window with another switch to see if the problem lies with a faulty switch.

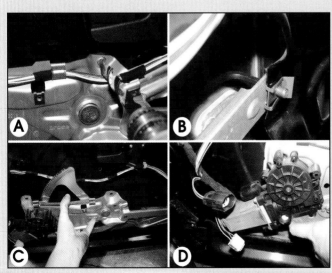

2 This photo shows the sequence for removing the window regulator. **A:** The regulator is riveted to the door frame; the rivets must be drilled out by a large drill bit. **B:** An Allen bolt at the rear of the door holds the regulator in place. I've seen several different mounting places for this bolt over the range of model years. **C:** With the rivets gone and the Allen bolt removed, the regulator should be loose from the door frame. **D:** Disconnect the wires to the motor assembly, and you should be able to remove the regulator from the car.

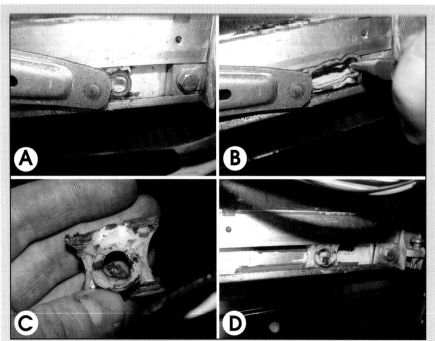

3 This photo sequence shows the detachment of the window regulator from the bottom window channels. **A:** The window regulator is attached to the metal rails at the bottom of the window by small, square, plastic sliders, which are held in by small spring clips (part number 51-32-1-938-884). **B:** Using a pair of pliers, pull on the clips and remove them from the plastic sliders. **C:** These sliders are the most common failure point in the window regulator. The grease in the window channel often becomes gooey and doesn't allow the sliders to move easily in the channel. They often deteriorate and break after many years of service. Tip for installing new sliders: Insert the slider into the channel with the metal retaining clip already installed into its final resting place, then press on and snap in the ends of the regulator. **D:** The channels the sliders ride in also become caked with dried-out grease. These channels need to be fully cleaned prior to installing the new sliders.

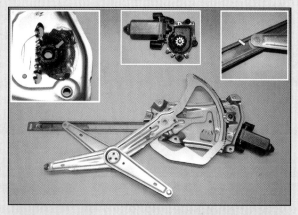

5 Shown here is a photo of the regulator removed from the car. The entire regulator is available as an assembly without the motor. The upper left shows the small black plastic bushing that centers the motor in the regulator. This bushing can sometimes wear out, preventing the gear from fully engaging the tooth on the regulator. The center photo shows the motor assembly. This assembly has a built-in motion sensor that prevents the window from rolling up if it encounters resistance (say, if someone's arm is stuck in the window). As the assembly ages, this sensor can malfunction, causing the window to occasionally stop and back up in the middle of rolling it up. In the upper right is shown the center channel for the window regulator. This channel needs to be lubricated liberally with grease prior to reinstallation.

4 The rear of the window rides in a metal channel that runs up and down the inside of the door. Often, the original grease installed at the factory becomes gooey and impedes the window's sliding action. I recommend spraying WD-40 into this channel (with the window raised). The WD-40 will help clean out some of the old grease, while lubricating the channel. When you install the new plastic regulator sliders (inset), liberally coat them with white lithium grease. Also, lubricate the aluminum channel the sliders ride in.

Replacing Lenses and Bulbs

There are few projects that are as easy, yet so dramatically improve your car's appearance as lens replacement. Replacing old, faded lenses not only improves the overall look of your car, it increases its safety as well. Faded lenses tend to be harder to see and block much more light than brand-new lenses. On the front of the E36, the corner lenses can be removed simply by sliding them forward; a plastic snap tab holds them in place. Don't use too much force, though, or you may break this small tab. On the E30, the small turn signal lenses can easily be removed with a few small screws.

The third brake light is also accessible from the rear of the trunk. Simply pop off the cover on the top of the trunk, and you should have easy access to the bulb.

A word of caution: Make sure you replace your old bulbs with the same exact style and wattage as the originals. Swapping in higher-wattage bulbs could damage your wiring and possibly melt your lens and bulb holder.

Time: 30 minutes

Tab: $15–250

Talent: 👤👤

Tools: None

Applicable Years: All

Tinware: New lenses, bulbs

Tip: Don't tug heavily on the lenses when removing them or they may break

PERFORMANCE GAIN: Better-looking exterior, clearer lamps

COMPLEMENTARY MODIFICATION: Upgrade to clear corners and clear rear lenses

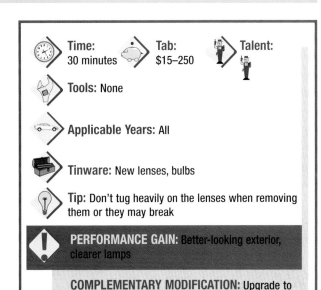

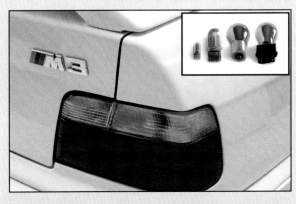

1. On a white car, clear lenses really look their best. For some reason, OEM amber lenses just don't cut it. In order to maintain legal standards, though, you must run orange bulbs inside the lenses. This can cause the lens to take on an orange hue. I recommend a product called Stealth Bulbs (inset), available online at PelicanParts.com. These bulbs are silver-coated on the outside but glow bright orange when electricity is applied. They look clear when installed in the clear lenses but retain the orange illumination required for U.S. roads.

3. The front clear corners look great on white cars as well. Here you can see the Stealth Bulbs installed with no orange glow. To remove the lens, simply pull on it toward the front of the car. It rides in a slot in the frame, so don't try to pry it out from the side. The bulb on the inside simply clips into the lens. The inset photo shows the back side of the corner lens.

2. Removal of the rear tail lamp is easy. Simply use an 8-millimeter socket and driver to remove the four nuts that hold on the rear assembly. Then push out the assembly and pull from the opposite side (lower right). If all you need to do is change bulbs, simply twist them out of their sockets and pull (lower left).

BODY/INTERIOR TRIM

205

Time: 6 hours	**Tab:** $50	**Talent:** 👤👤👤

Tools: Torx set, socket set

Applicable Years: E36 (All)

Tinware: New headliner material, Permatex adhesive

Tip: New headliner pieces are $220 from BMW

⚠ PERFORMANCE GAIN: Neater-looking interior

COMPLEMENTARY MODIFICATION: Repair sunroof

If you own an E36 BMW, be assured that replacing your headliner is a much easier task than it appears. Although it may at first seem daunting to remove the large top panel from your car, it's actually one of the easier projects to work on. Unfortunately, for E30 owners, replacing the headliner requires removing nearly all the car's windows. In addition, the E30 headliner fabric must be carefully cut, glued in place, and tightened all at the same time. I tried this once, and although the results looked pretty good, it's not a task I would ever want to do again (see www.101Projects.com for tips on replacing the E30 headliner).

The good news for E36 owners is that newer technology has made the headliner replacement project a snap. The headliner material is made of a sponge/fabric composite glued to a fiberglass/cardboard pre-formed panel. The procedure involves dropping this panel, removing the old material, gluing on the new material, and reinstalling it.

The first step is the removal process. Refer to Photo 1 for detailed instructions on what to remove and where it's

1 This photo shows all the various items and objects that need attention in order to remove the headliner:
A: Start with the rearmost pillars of the car (C-pillar). The interior lamp can be simply pulled out of the rear pillar and unplugged. Then, using your fingers, gently pry out the fabric-covered side panel—it should simply snap out. Pull up on it, as it will be stuck in place at the bottom by the rear seat back. Be careful not to disturb the mess of wires underneath the panel as you remove it. Some people have told me they had to remove the rear seat panel and lower side panels to get at the C-pillar headliner, but I didn't have to with my two-door coupe. **B:** Now turn your attention to the front of the car. Pull down on the small center panel and unplug the sunroof switch. The front light assembly can be simply pried out of its home and unplugged as well. **C:** The sun visor is attached at two points that have electrical connections integrated into the mounts. Remove the mounts and unplug the wires. Pull out the vanity mirror lamp from the headliner and unplug it. **D:** For each of the upper grab handles in the car, remove the small plastic covers that hide the mounting screws. These small covers

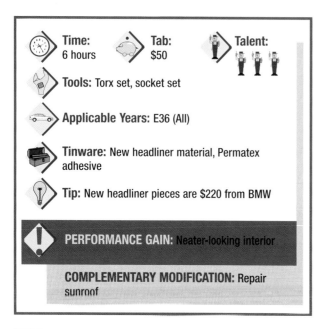
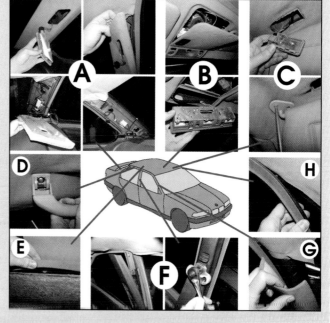

have tiny plastic posts that can easily be broken if not removed with care. Remove the screws from both sides of the handle, and it should simply fall off. **E:** Pull back the headliner material around the edges of the sunroof opening. The sunroof is still attached to the car; you need to push the seal off all the way around the sunroof opening. **F:** The side B-pillar covering needs to be removed on at least one side of the car in order to gain enough maneuvering room to remove the headliner. Pull off the upper seatbelt cover and remove the bolt. This should allow you to remove the plastic cover and drop down the edge of the headliner. **G:** The front A-pillars near the windshield should simply pop off when you pull on them. They are gently wedged at their bottom into a slot in the top side of the dash. Finally, the upper portion of the door seal covers the edges of the frame. Gently pull back on the door seal to release it from the edges of the headliner.

located—there are about 10 different parts connected to the roof that help hold up the headliner. Once you have the headliner released from the roof, you will have to maneuver it carefully to remove it from the car (see Photo 2). Wear gloves when handling the roof panel or you may end up with some nasty fiberglass splinters in your hands—nearly invisible, but no less painful. (If this happens, a removal trick I recommend is to wrap duct tape all over your hands and then strip it off like you're tearing off a bandage. This will remove most of the fibers from your hands.)

With the headliner removed from the car, move it to a spot in your garage where it's safe to make a mess. Pull the old fabric off the panel. Using a dry rag or a tire scrub brush, simply brush off of the old foam; it shouldn't take too much effort to remove the old, weakly attached foam from the fiberglass/cardboard panel. You can cut the material first and then glue it onto the panel, or glue it first and then cut it. I prefer to glue first, as it minimizes the risk of a cutting mistake. Use fine-tipped hobby knifes for this step, and make sure you have a whole bunch of new blades on hand as they tend to dull very quickly when cutting the foam—you don't want your new headliner material to rip.

The glue I recommend for this procedure is Permatex headliner and carpet adhesive (which comes in an orange can with blue top). Other people have tried other adhesives with mixed results; the Permatex product is the only one that seems to have garnered no complaints. I'd hate for you to spend all this time replacing your headliner only to have the hot sun melt the adhesive in your headliner. One can should suffice, although I always like to have an extra can on hand in case I run out.

Reinstallation is pretty much the reverse of removal. (For instructions on removing and recovering the sunroof center panel, see Project 78.)

2 Success! With all the small pieces that hold up the headliner removed, it should simply drop down onto the seats (inset, upper right). If it doesn't drop down, it may be slightly glued to the roof of the car at the top of the windshield. Pull very carefully, as the fiberglass/cardboard panel is very fragile and can easily be bent and damaged. For coupe and sedan cars, slide both front seats all the way forward and then tilt them all the way back. This should give you enough clearance to get the headliner out the door. Again, be careful with the panel—it is very thin and can be easily damaged as you're removing it from the car. New headliner material is cheap and looks great. The photo inset in the upper left shows brand-new foam headliner material that is essentially a spongy bottom coated with a black cloth-like upper layer. Total cost for a roll to cover the headliner was about $25.

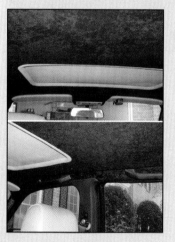

4 Shown here is a particularly nice headliner installation using a faux-suede fabric that has become increasingly popular in recent years. The inner panel of the sunroof is impossible to remove without removing the entire sunroof, so most people leave it the same color as it previously was (see Project 78 on sunroof repair). In this case, the visors and the sunroof were kept the original color, which in my opinion gives a nice accent to the interior. Also, the black headliner typically looks better when you swap out and use black door seals and black pull handles (available from BMW). Beware, though—headliners have always been traditionally light colors so that light inside the car at night reflects off of the lighter fabric and illuminates better. You may be surprised at how dark your car feels at night if you install a black headliner. *Rob Canova*

3 If you don't want to recover your own headliner, you can purchase a BMW headliner piece from PelicanParts.com that is factory original and ready to install. The cost is about $220 and it eliminates the hassle and work of cutting and gluing a new piece, making this a pretty good solution for anyone who is time conscious. The down side is you won't be able to install any exotic colors or materials. This photo shows the dramatic difference between the old headliner and the new one.

Installing a Rear Spoiler

One neat addition to the profile of any 3 Series car is a rear spoiler. Although they really have very little functional aerodynamic purpose, they certainly look cool on the back of the car.

There are many different styles available today; some even include an integrated third brake light. Fortunately, installation for most styles is very easy; simply follow the procedure for marking and wiring the lamp in Photos 1 and 2.

Before installing the spoiler, though, be sure to have it painted to perfectly color-match your car. The best way to ensure this is to remove your gas flap and take it along with your spoiler, and then have them match the paint to the flap. When completing the installation, make sure you place a small amount of rubber sealing compound on the spoiler so water doesn't leak into your trunk from the holes drilled in the trunk lid.

Time: 1 hour	**Tab:** $200	**Talent:**

Tools: Drill, marker, tape measure

Applicable Years: All

Tinware: Spoiler and mounting hardware

Tip: Paint to match your gas flap

PERFORMANCE GAIN: Sporty-looking body

COMPLEMENTARY MODIFICATION: Replace rear lenses

1 Shown here is one of my favorite aftermarket spoilers for E36 cars. This one spans the length of the trunk and includes an integrated center-mount brake lamp. The lamp is wired into the brake lamp circuit by tapping into the wires that power the left rear brake lamp assembly.

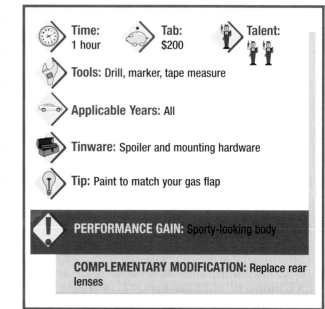

3 If your rear spoiler has an integrated third brake light, snake the cable down the trunk hinge alongside the main trunk lock cable. Tap it into one of the wires that feeds your brake lights. You'll have to get a multimeter and test the wires at the connectors while an assistant steps on the brake pedal to see which ones turn on the brake lights, as they've varied throughout the years. Run the red wire to the brake light lead, and ground the other wire to the chassis.

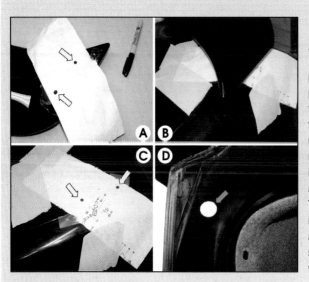

2 This photo sequence shows one of the methods I recommend for installing the spoiler. **A:** Start by taping a piece of paper to the spoiler itself using scotch tape. Using a permanent marker that will seep through the paper, feel with your finger and mark the holes in the spoiler with the marker. **B:** Place the spoiler on the car in the exact place where you want it to be. Once you have it positioned, then tape down the paper to the car using masking tape. **C:** Remove the spoiler and the paper should indicate exactly where to drill the holes. Take some measurements and confirm that these are in the proper spot prior to drilling. **D:** The trunk frame on the E36 is too thick and angled to have a bolt run all the way through. Using a very small hole saw, cut a small access hole (green arrow) so you can insert the bolt and a swivel-socket driver. When done drilling, coat the edges of all the holes with some paint to prevent the bare metal from rusting.

BODY/INTERIOR TRIM

Convertible Top Adjustment and Repair

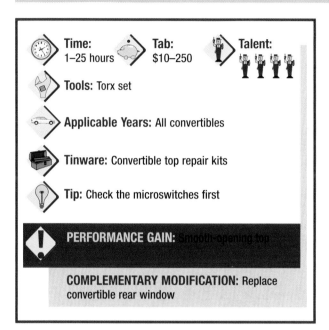

⏱ **Time:** 1–25 hours	🐷 **Tab:** $10–250	🧑 **Talent:** 🔧🔧🔧🔧

🔧 **Tools:** Torx set

🚗 **Applicable Years:** All convertibles

🧰 **Tinware:** Convertible top repair kits

💡 **Tip:** Check the microswitches first

> ⚠ **PERFORMANCE GAIN:** Smooth-opening top

COMPLEMENTARY MODIFICATION: Replace convertible rear window

The BMW convertible top is one of the most complicated systems on the car. A lot of people have problems with their convertible tops. Some problems are easy to fix, while others are much more complicated. The E36 convertible top contains a plethora of switches and sensors that tell the convertible top controller when and how to lower the top. If any of these sensors stop working, it can render your entire top inoperable.

One of these sensors checks the position and operation of the window. If your window is stuck in the up position, you won't be able to lower your top (see Project 70). Another annoying problem that often occurs is with the trunk. The lock on the trunk is connected to the top system, and when it fails, you'll find that you can't lower the top when the trunk is open, or you can't open the trunk if the top is not fully closed. If you have any problems with your trunk wiring (see Project 82), they can stop the top from lowering. In a similar manner, sometimes the headliner can get caught when you close the roof and keep the convertible top cover from closing all the way. This may prevent one of the convertible top microswitches from closing, which in turn will prevent you from opening the trunk. If you can't get into your trunk when your roof is down, try pushing down on the convertible top cover, and it should trigger the switch.

BMW makes at least seven different repair kits that can be used to fix parts of the roof that may have worn out or become broken. Photo 1 shows six of these seven kits and what they aim to repair.

FYI, the parts system for BMW cars (known as "ETK") is very unclear when it comes to what is included in these kits, so I ordered all of them just to see what came with each kit. All

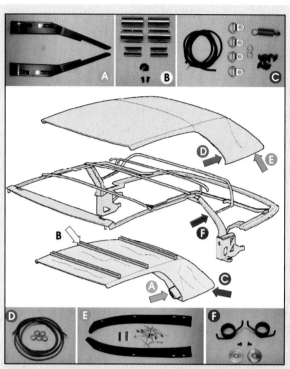

1 Shown here is a sampling of the repair kits described in the main text.

2 This photo shows the convertible motor linkage, which is located under the large, hinged convertible top cover. You can access this area by pressing the top-down switch and letting the cover rise up all the way. The blue arrow points to the cam that drives the bottom part of the convertible top. This is the part that lifts up so the convertible top cover can be raised. If the convertible top cover hits the edge of the top when the roof is being lowered, you can adjust the linkage to push the bottom part of the cover back further (green arrow). While you're in this area, check to make sure your convertible top motor screws are tight (they were loose on my car when I checked them; yellow arrows).

209

3 The left side of this photo shows the right-side latching mechanism for the convertible top cover. The yellow arrow shows one of the springs that often wear out after many years of use—unfortunately, it's not a part you can order separately, so head to a good hardware store for a replacement. The green arrow points to one of the infamous microswitches, which should be checked first if you have unexplained problems raising or lowering your top, or opening your trunk. On the right are two areas commonly repaired using the kits in Photo 1. The Column C inserts are shown with the red arrow, and one of the bow tension springs is shown with the blue arrow.

5 This is the handle of last resort. Many convertible owners don't know this, but there is an emergency roof release handle located underneath the rear seat. Usually, you can fish around and pull out the red strap, but if you can't, simply pull up on the rear seat, and it will pop right out. Pull on the handle to disconnect the roof mechanism and cables from the two motors. You should then be able to manually raise the roof with your hands. Don't lower the roof if the cables are disconnected—the convertible roof top cover can catch the wind and fly open while you're driving!

4 With the convertible top cover raised, you can also see the bow mechanism located toward the front of the car. The yellow arrow shows one of the finicky microswitches that should be tested first when having unexplained problems. If the roof is not lowering or raising the proper amount, you can adjust it by turning the adjustment turnbuckle shown by the green arrow.

6 One of my favorite options for convertible owners is the color-matched hardtop. This top fits on your car with the top down and turns it as close to a coupe as you can get. The top is perfect for people who love convertibles but have to drive a significant number of miles in cold and inclement weather where top-down motoring just isn't practical. The tops are quite heavy and not that easy to install on the car, so plan on using two people and spending several minutes getting it installed. New tops are about $2,300 from BMW (color-matched to your car), but you can usually find a used one if you look around. If your car didn't come with one originally, you'll need the factory installation kit (part number 54-21-8-163-061).

are now available from PelicanParts.com. They are displayed in Photo 1, and a brief description follows:

A: Column C Ceiling Insert Repair Kit (part number 54-31-8-211-902). Contains: Column C inserts and crimp rings. This kit contains both a left and right insert to repair the delicate piece that folds out of the way when the top is lowered. The red arrow in Photo 3 shows this plastic piece that folds into the headliner material. The small tabs on the insert piece often get caught and break off, such that the top must be lowered in steps to avoid having the headliner catch on the frame. Replacement of these pieces requires you rethread some of the rope in the top assembly.

B: Internal Headliner Repair Kit (part number 54-31-8-227-354). Contains: Screws and reinforcement clips. My

own car needed this kit to repair a tear in the headliner. In Photo 1, you can see the three long, plastic rails that snap the headliner onto the convertible top. The headliner and rails can break, letting the headliner sag. These metal clips grab onto the existing plastic rails and use screws to reattach the headliner so it won't sag anymore. One kit should cover the entire headliner. (See BMW technical bulletin 54 04 96 (091).)

C: Column C Ceiling Tension Rope Repair Kit (part number 54-31-8-189-989). Contains: Tension rope, Torx bolt, tension spring, brackets, and lead seal. This kit contains the parts necessary to repair the inner rope on one side of the Column C insert. This rope can be viewed in Photo 3, and I recommend replacing the inserts as well (repair kit A).

D: Column C Cover Tension Rope Repair Kit (part number 54-31-9-068-572). Contains 1,000 millimeters tension rope and five aluminum links. This is replacement rope for tension ropes located in the C column of the convertible roof. Follow the instructions included with the kit to repair the ropes, and be sure to melt each end of the rope to avoid fraying.

E: Repair Kit Column C Cover Insert (part number 54-31-8-209-781). Contains: Column C insert, reinforcement angle, two different sizes of rivets, blind rivet adapter. This kit is used to repair separation of the canvas top from the frame, around the outer edges. The repair is pretty straightforward and documented in the included instructions. (See BMW technical bulletin 54 01 95 (891).)

F: Repair Kit for Corner Bow Tension Spring (part number 54-34-8-201-077). Contains: Two tension springs, washers, Torx screws. This kit contains the parts needed to replace the tension springs shown by the light blue arrow in Photo 3. If these springs break or weaken, it can affect the ability of the roof to raise and lower itself properly. If renewing your roof, you should replace these springs.

PROJECT 75   http://www.101projects.com/BMW/75.htm
Convertible Rear Window Replacement

Time: 3 hours

Tab: $150–400

Talent: 🤵🤵🤵

Tools: Awl, plastic knife

Applicable Years: All convertibles

Tinware: Rear window replacement kit

Tip: Trial and error with window placement is the only way to install these

PERFORMANCE GAIN: Easier to see through the rear window

COMPLEMENTARY MODIFICATION: Repair convertible top

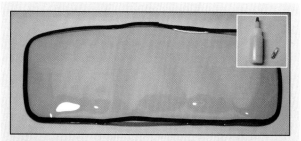

1. Shown here is a brand-new aftermarket window replacement kit. The kit includes the pre-sewn window, a bottle of contact cement, and a starter zipper. Both aftermarket and OEM replacement windows may not fit as tight as the originals, depending upon the age and condition of your convertible roof.

2. Begin the process by popping open the roof to relieve tension on the rear window.

One of the most common complaints of convertible owners is the condition of the rear window. It's manufactured out of a clear plastic, and as such, it does not have the longevity of a clear glass window. With time and exposure to the elements, the window can become scratched, damaged, or faded.

The good news is the rear window is zipped into place and is relatively easy to replace. I say "relatively" with a note of caution: Although it may seem like a simple process of zipping the window in and out of the convertible top, the actual process is much more difficult and takes quite a bit of patience. The procedure for replacing the window is documented in the sequence of photos accompanying this project.

With your new window in place, you'll want to keep it pristine and unscratched. To minimize creases and scratches when the top is down, use some terry cloth towels to cover the window whenever the roof is lowered. BMW also has a factory rear window cover you can use to protect the window at all times. For cleaning the rear window, I recommend 3M Plastic Polish or the poly/glass rear window cleaner from Porsche (recommended for the Boxsters).

BMW has its own brand of cleaner (BMW part number 81-22-9-407-666), and BMW factory literature recommends Meguiar's plastic cleaner #17 (BMW part number 82-14-1-467-128) and Meguiar's plastic polish #10 (BMW part number 82-14-1-467-129) for heavier cleaning. All of these cleaners will do a good job of keeping your window clean and clear.

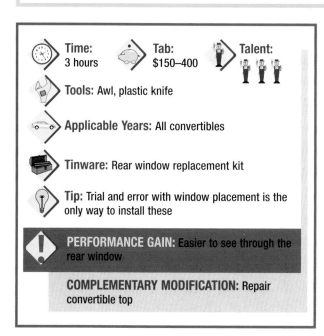

BODY/INTERIOR TRIM

211

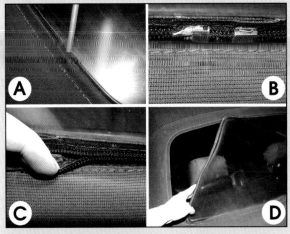

A   B
C   D

3 Removal of the rear window is straightforward. **A:** Using a plastic butter knife, or a plastic mechanical pencil, gently separate the roof fabric from the rubber trim. This rubber trim is sewn to the window and will be removed when the window is taken out of the car. **B:** From the inside of the car, locate and remove the zipper ties from the bottom center of the window. These two were added by an aftermarket installer and don't necessarily reflect the original factory installation. Carefully pry back the tabs on these clips, and remove them from the window. **C:** Using your finger, gently separate the window zipper. **D:** Pull gently on the window, and the zipper should separate, allowing you to remove it from the car.

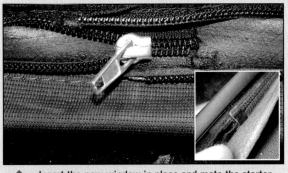

4 Insert the new window in place and mate the starter zipper. This is by far the most difficult part of the process. There are no end caps on the zipper teeth, so you may have to use a pair of needle-nose pliers to help get the starter zipper started. Begin by lining up and installing the starter zipper onto the two ends of the zipper teeth that point toward the left, if you're sitting inside the car facing the rear. The starter zipper should easily make its way clockwise (from the inside of the car) around the edge of the window, using minimal effort (make sure that the fabric and/or window material doesn't interfere with the starter zipper). The BMW factory manuals say that these teeth should be offset by no more than one in either direction, but in reality you may have to vary them by several teeth in one direction. If the zipper snags or is difficult to move, you may have to realign the zipper teeth on the start one or two teeth in the opposite direction. This was the most time-consuming part of the installation. I ended up varying the zipper teeth about seven teeth to the right in order to install the window with no wrinkles. When you are happy that the window fits properly, use the factory clamps (inset photo) to constrain and lock the zipper (BMW part numbers 54-31-8-134-598 and 54-31-8-134-599)

5 I found the most frustrating part of the whole process to be the actual zipping in of the window. You have to use a trial-and-error approach to get the window installed properly (it took about 35 tries for me). If the window isn't lined up perfectly, you will get diagonal creases in the window when the top is up (shown here). To eliminate these, you need to release the zipper, then increase or decrease the zipper teeth offset. Moving in one direction or another will allow you to observe if the creases are getting worse or better. If the zipper won't close without separating, you're probably way off of the mark—the zipper should very easily make its way around the entire window.

6 As added protection against the zipper separating, I used two factory clamping plates to sandwich both zippers together. In this regard, I think that the BMW single-clamp design is not sufficiently strong to prevent the zipper from separating. Place one clamp on the outside and one on the inside, and tie them together with thin wire that you can push through the thread surrounding the zipper teeth. With the window properly zipped and installed, peel back the roof fabric and apply a thin bead of contact cement. Wait about five minutes for the cement to harden slightly—and be especially careful not to spill this on your newly installed window. Using a small awl, run it around the inside of the rubber seal, fitting the cloth fabric inside. Press down on the cloth to adhere it to the contact adhesive. The cement is very easy to clean up with a paper towel after it starts to become gooey.

Installing M3-style mirrors is one of those neat projects that can really add some spice to the look of your car without taking up too much of your time. The total install time for a pair of mirrors should be less than two hours.

The mirrors are attached to the door with three bolts hidden from view by a small plastic panel that is easily popped off the door. Once the panel is popped off, you can unbolt the old mirrors and bolt in your new ones.

The toughest part of the job is actually finding a set of mirrors that will match your body color. If your car is white or black, there are usually aftermarket mirrors available in those two colors. Any other color will need to be custom-painted to match your body paint. There are many different mirrors out there, and they vary in quality. I prefer the German OEM mirrors from BMW, but they can be quite expensive (about $200 each from PelicanParts.com).

Some aftermarket mirrors are manufactured with an additional lamp in the side. This can be wired to either to your parking lamps or your turn-signal lamps. Either one requires additional wiring to be threaded through the door, so I usually don't recommend this approach. Most of the cars I've seen with lamps in the side of the mirrors don't actually have them connected—they're just for show.

Time: 2 hours

Tab: $150–300

Talent: 👔👔

Tools: Screwdriver, 10-millimeter socket and driver

Applicable Years: E36 (All)

Tinware: M3 mirror set

Tip: Replica mirrors are about half the price of originals

PERFORMANCE GAIN: Cooler-looking mirrors

COMPLEMENTARY MODIFICATION: Fix other problems inside your door frame

---

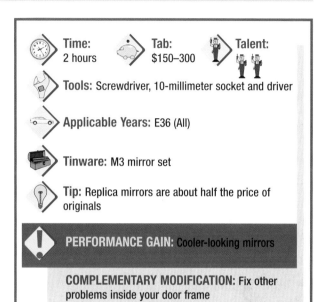

2 Shown here are the M3-style mirrors installed. This particular mirror set contains an extra lamp inside the mirror, a neat feature but one that requires you to run extra wires through the door harness—generally, more trouble than it's worth.

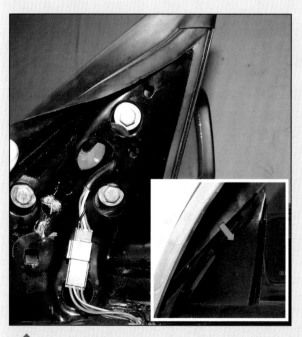

1 You don't need to remove the door panel to access the mirror mounting points. Simply pry off the top plastic piece (inset photo) and slide it upward to remove it. Underneath, you will see the three bolts that hold the mirror to the door. Disconnect the wire harness, remove the bolts, and the mirror should fall right off the door. Make sure you grab the mirror while removing the last bolt or it will fall and scratch your paint.

BODY/INTERIOR TRIM

213

Replacing Emblems

One of the easiest ways to quickly improve the external appearance of your BMW is to replace old, worn-out hood and trunk emblems. They are relatively cheap and can be installed in less than 15 minutes. The removal procedure for hood emblems is documented in the sequence in Photo 1.

The replacement procedure for the emblem on the trunk is very similar. If you wish to replace the numbers on the back of the car, these are typically attached using heavy-duty double-sided tape. Simply use a hobby knife to cut around the old tape, weakening it. Then gently pry the emblem off the metal. Use some rubbing alcohol or adhesive remover to carefully clean off the old tape residue, and then reapply the new emblem.

In addition to replacing your emblems, swapping out your old, tarnished front and rear lenses can really do wonders for improving the external appearance of your BMW. See Project 71 for more details, or visit the message boards on PelicanParts.com where motor enthusiasts swap ideas and offer suggestions for upgrading their cars.

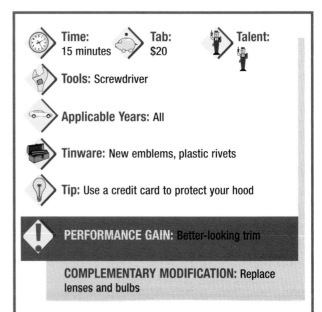

Time: 15 minutes
Tab: $20
Talent:

Tools: Screwdriver

Applicable Years: All

Tinware: New emblems, plastic rivets

Tip: Use a credit card to protect your hood

PERFORMANCE GAIN: Better-looking trim

COMPLEMENTARY MODIFICATION: Replace lenses and bulbs

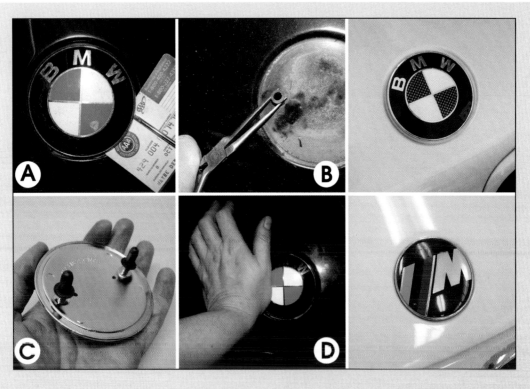

1 This photo sequence shows the proper procedure for replacing the Roundel emblem on the front hood. **A:** Using a small screwdriver and a credit card as an insulator, carefully pry the emblem off of the hood. Work from side to side to pry it up, but don't use too much force—you don't want to damage your hood. **B:** Remove the old rubber grommets with a pair of needle-nose pliers. **C:** Install new rubber grommets onto the back of the emblem. **D:** Carefully press down on the emblem and install it into place on the hood. If you want to differentiate your car from the rest of the pack, try installing a nontraditional emblem on the front hood (right).

Sunroof Removal and Repair

Time: 6 hours

Tab: $10–150

Talent: 👨👨👨👨

Tools: Torx set, 4-millimeter Allen wrench

Applicable Years: E36 (All)

Tinware: Sunroof repair kits, depending on what is broken

Tip: Try removing the metal panel first to see if that gains you enough access

PERFORMANCE GAIN: More sun, more fun!

COMPLEMENTARY MODIFICATION: Replace headliner

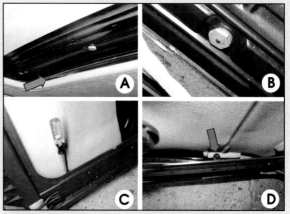

This photo sequence shows how to remove the top metal sunroof panel from your car without taking out the entire assembly. **A:** With the sunroof closed, begin by tapping your sunroof switch just a little bit to have it drop down 2 to 4 millimeters and open slightly. With clean hands (or gloves), carefully slide back the headliner piece toward the back of the car (green arrow). It should require some moderate force to move it, but not the iron grip of death. Now close the sunroof. **Important:** Do not open the sunroof with the headliner piece pushed in the back; you could damage the mechanism. **B:** Unfasten the three large adjustment nuts in the rear of the sunroof. These will release the rear of the sunroof from the frame, allowing you to push up on the rear from the inside and raise the rear of the roof to give you more access to the front screws. When reinstalling the roof, these nuts adjust the height of the rear of the roof. **C and D:** Using a Torx driver, remove the attachment screws hidden in the inside of the frame (purple arrow). When these have been removed, you should be able to lift up on the entire metal roof panel and detach it from the car.

BMW sunroofs can be very confusing if you've never worked on one before. With so much of the mechanism hidden away, it's often difficult to figure out what is wrong with the roof. A certain hesitancy to disturb the headliner, combined with a lack of widespread knowledge about making repairs, has left many owners' sunroofs inoperable.

In reality, the sunroof is relatively easy to repair—what's harder is getting your hands on some of the items that need to be replaced. The sunroof motor drives two cables that move the roof forward and backward in a track, mounted to a fiberglass frame, attached to the roof of the car. The primary problems with the sunroof involve the small track guide pieces breaking or the roof leaking. This project will go over the details associated with complete sunroof removal and renewal of these pieces.

Sunroof removal

The sunroof assembly (also called the "sunroof cassette") can be removed as an entire unit, but you will need to lower and remove the fiberglass headliner piece first (see Project 72). You should remove the assembly if you already have the headliner out, and you are going to be making major repairs to the sunroof mechanism. However, if you're just trying to fix a small sunroof problem, and you don't want to remove the headliner, you may try just removing the top metal roof portion first, and then see if you can replace the broken parts with your sunroof cassette frame still installed in the car. (See Photo 1 for the metal panel removal instructions; also, BMW Tech Bulletin 54-12-100 is quite helpful if you have access to a copy.)

If you need more access and need to remove the entire assembly, then refer to Photo 2 for instructions. I recommend you grab yourself a helper, as it's easy to damage your interior trim if you try to remove the entire sunroof assembly yourself.

Sunroof repair

With the sunroof panel off of the car, or the sunroof assembly removed from the car, you can start to inspect the roof to determine which parts need replacing. In order to figure out what is wrong with your roof, slowly move the roof through its normal motion by manually turning the motor with a 4-millimeter hex socket (see Photo 6). You can open and close the roof frame manually, regardless of whether you chose to remove the entire assembly or not. **Important:** If you slide back your sunroof headliner piece when you go to remove the metal panel, you

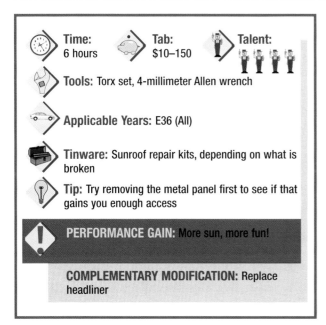

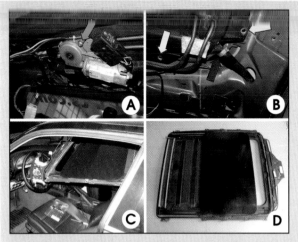

2 This photo sequence shows how to remove the entire sunroof assembly from the car. The first step is to completely remove the headliner (see Project 72). After you get the headliner out of the car, you will be able to see the fiberglass frame of the sunroof assembly, or cassette, which is attached to the roof of the car. **A:** Start by removing the center bolt that also helps attach the sunroof motor (green arrow). **B:** Next, disconnect the four rainwater drain tubes connected to the assembly at each of the four corners (red arrow). Then remove the perimeter Torx bolts (yellow arrows), leaving the bolts at the rear of the car in place. With all the front and side bolts removed, remove the rearmost bolts. These bolts are attached to a spring clip and allow for forward/rearward adjustment of the entire assembly when you reinstall it. Remove these rearmost bolts, and you should be able to drop the assembly down once it's free from the rearmost clips. **C:** Toss some towels or moving blankets over the tops of your seats to protect them from damage as you let the assembly down. There's a large tab in the front of the assembly that fits into a slot in the metal frame of the car—this will hold up the front part of the roof as you lower it. If you recline your seats all the way back, you should be able to maneuver the assembly out of the car. I managed to lower the assembly and remove it myself, but I was working on a project car and didn't care too much about the upholstery. I recommend that you have the help of an assistant if you don't want the sunroof assembly to scratch your interior. **D:** This is what the entire assembly looks like after it has been removed from the car. To make the job easier, you can remove the metal panel from the assembly prior to removing it (see Photo 1).

This photo shows the steps required to remove the sunroof headliner panel. **A:** The panel is held in place with Torx

3 screws that must be removed in order to release the panel from the sunroof assembly (green arrow). **B:** The red arrow shows one of the plastic guide pieces for the headliner panel that has been completely bent and destroyed. This happens when the roof is opened with the headliner panel already pushed back toward the rear of the car. **C:** With all the screws removed, simply lift up and remove the headliner panel (blue arrow). **D:** As you can tell from this photo, the panel needs some serious attention. When you replace the headliner on the panel, be sure to use a relatively thin fabric, as the panel needs to easily slide in and out of the rearmost section of the sunroof assembly.

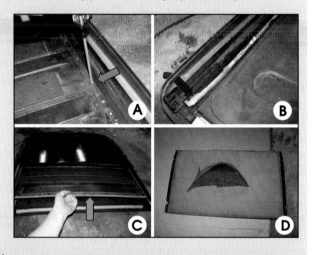

4 Here's a collection of photos of various parts that can break inside your sunroof assembly. Every sunroof malfunction is different—you really need to just open up the assembly and see what's broken in there. Manually operate the sunroof by turning the motor (see Photo 6), and take a look at what is going wrong with the mechanism. With this sunroof, there were quite a few different items that were broken. **A and B:** This photo shows the metal lifting piece (yellow arrow) for the rear of the sunroof. When I removed this particular assembly from the car, this piece fell out (not a good sign). It's held in place with various plastic pieces that can become brittle and break. Inspect this piece carefully, and replace any broken support pieces. Also inspect the lifting cam/guide, which pushes this lever upward as the cable moves back (green arrow). **C:** The attachment point for the control rail on my sunroof was broken in two. Fortunately, this failure was fairly easy to spot, and

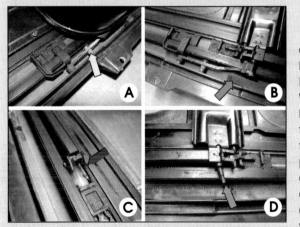

replacement/repair kits are available for these pieces. Even with this breakage, the sunroof was surprisingly operational, using the opposite side rail to do all of the lifting work. **D:** On the opposite side from Frame B, the lever that attaches to the metal lifting piece (yellow arrow, Frame A) has been clearly bent and damaged. This is probably what led to the lifting piece falling out when I removed the assembly.

5 Before you reinstall your assembly, be sure to clean it thoroughly. Carefully clean out each of the tracks with isopropyl alcohol and cotton swabs. Also spread some white lithium grease on all of the tracks and moveable parts. Verify that all dirt and debris has been cleaned from the assembly before you reinstall it.

6 The sunroof motor has a built-in switch to stop the motor when the roof is completely closed, which prevents it from popping open at the rear. This completely closed position is called the "zero setting," or "zero position." If you need to remove the sunroof motor from the car, be aware that you need to reinstall the motor with its position set to the zero setting. Start by setting the sunroof panel and assembly at the fully closed position. For sunroof motors prior to mid-1994, the zero position on the sunroof motor is when the shaft center points of the motor, notch, and pin all line up (yellow arrow). For motors in cars manufactured from mid-1994, the zero setting is no longer visible to the naked eye. Instead, set the motor to the zero setting by plugging it in and pressing the switch until it stops by itself. When you have the motor electrically unplugged from the car, you can move it quite easily by placing a 4-millimeter hex socket into the back of the motor gear and turning it slowly (inset). This is useful for troubleshooting the assembly when it is out of the car, with the motor still attached.

7 When you remove the sunroof motor, you can see the cables that run inside the copper channels. These cables (called "Bowden cables" by BMW) can break as they get old. If you do have to replace the cables, get some long pipe cleaners and brush out the inside of the copper channels prior to installing the new ones. The gear of the motor meshes with the opening on the left—the right-side opening is not used. Install the motor only when it's at zero position and the roof is completely closed (see Photo 6). I don't recommend removing the motor unless you feel you really need to. The two sunroof cables are aligned with respect to each other, and you will have to verify that all of the lifting pieces are correctly aligned again before reinstalling the motor.

cannot open the roof all the way—use caution when manually moving the roof open or closed.

There are many items on the sunroof that break, and even more that have been redesigned and superseded by BMW. I've highlighted in Photo 4 some of the components that break and need replacing most often. The basic process of repairing your sunroof involves removing it, inspecting the parts to see what is broken, cleaning the tracks, then reinstalling and adjusting the roof. See the remaining photos in this project for more details.

Seat Removal and Sport Seat Installation

Time: 4 hours

Tab: $0–1,000

Talent: ▮▮

Tools: Socket set

Applicable Years: All

Tinware: Seats, adapter brackets

Tip: Talk to people who have previously installed a particular brand of seat

PERFORMANCE GAIN: Sportier, firmer-hugging seats

COMPLEMENTARY MODIFICATION: Fix air bag faults

The stock seats installed in the BMW 3 Series have never been bad, but they certainly are nothing to rave about to your friends at parties. Most BMW owners who perform seat upgrades opt to replace their stock seats with stock M3 seats. There are a few reasons for this. The M3 seats are an easy, bolt-in replacement for the stock seats, and there's no need to mess with seat rails or fit issues. In addition, the belt buckle and latching mechanisms are the same, so replacing them will not result in problems or warnings from the air bag system.

If you do decide to go with an aftermarket seat, I have a few suggestions. First, you'll want to make sure the brand and style of seat you choose will fit well in your car. I suggest you purchase the seat from a reputable dealer that sells many of them and has sold that particular seat for your model of 3 Series BMW. Seats are very difficult to fit, and if you don't have the proper brackets, and haven't tested the configuration, you may be stuck with an undesirable installation. The seat may ride too high, or it may interfere with the center console; a host of problems can occur. One of the best things you can do is head to one of the Internet chat boards (like the one at PelicanParts.com) and ask other BMW owners which aftermarket seats they installed in their cars. I would list some combinations here, but manufacturers change styles and configurations so often that the information would soon be outdated. The best bet is to perform your own research.

If you do install aftermarket seats, I suggest you try your best to keep the stock BMW seatbelt mechanisms in place. These systems are integrated with the air bag controller, and keeping them will reduce the difficulty involved in modifying the air bag system to accept a new belt system. If you

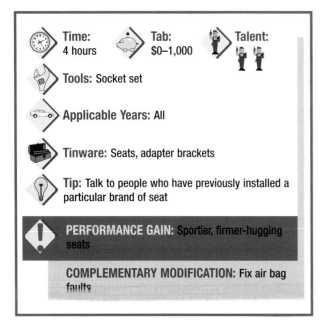

1 I couldn't resist snapping a photo of this interior at a recent show. The sport seats installed here, coupled with the custom-matched interior, really add a great look to the car. The seats are tastefully trimmed with matching red leather on the bolsters. Be careful, though—an interior with too much red can really make you yearn for dark sunglasses. However, it's important to note that the harness in this case is attached to a harness bar, extending across the length of the car. This is not the best method of running the harness. Although the bar is attached to the two very strong seatbelt attachment points in the car, these points are not typically designed to withstand the bending and torque that may be placed upon them with a harness bar. The preferred solution is to mount the harness to the floor or rear subframe of the car and run it up over the harness bar. If you install a roll cage in your car, the strength of the cage is typically not an issue, and you can mount belts directly to the cage.

2 This is a photo of a seat setup I hadn't seen before. The owner of this M3 convertible apparently purchased a set of Sparco sport seats, then removed all of the cloth fabric and had them recovered in leather to match the rest of the car. I thought this was a clever solution to the age-old problem of how to install sport seats in your car without making it look like a track car. To the untrained eye, these seats look like they were a factory option!

remove the stock seatbelts, you will need to have resistors installed across the seatbelt receptacles and also the passenger-side seat sensor (see Project 80). This will help eliminate any errors from the airbag system that may result because of the missing components.

BODY/INTERIOR TRIM

218

PROJECT 80
Power Seat Repair

Surprisingly, seats are some of the most complicated components on any car. When you start adding bells and whistles to them (like heaters, occupancy sensors, power motors, and air bag sensors), you end up with a complicated device that gets a lot of use and often needs some attention. This project covers three basic repair procedures involving the E36 power seats: seatbelt receptacle replacement, seat occupancy sensor replacement, and power seat switch replacement.

The first step is to remove the front seat, which is a pretty easy task. Unbolt the seat from the chassis floor according to Photo 1. Then disconnect any electrical connections that may be located underneath the seat (Photo 2). Because each seat weighs between 60 and 80 pounds, I suggest that you have a helper assist you in lifting and carrying the seat from your car. You'd hate to lose your balance while lifting and bang your seat against the side of your car.

With the seat removed, you will have relatively easy access to the remainder of the seat components. The belt buckle receptacle can easily be replaced once the seat is removed from the car (see Photo 1). The electrical switch inside this receptacle often fails, resulting in air bag warning lamp error messages (see Project 83). Replacement is as simple as unbolting the old unit, attaching the new unit, and running the wire harness through the seat.

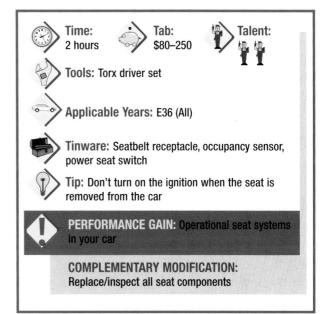

Time: 2 hours

Tab: $80–250

Talent:

Tools: Torx driver set

Applicable Years: E36 (All)

Tinware: Seatbelt receptacle, occupancy sensor, power seat switch

Tip: Don't turn on the ignition when the seat is removed from the car

PERFORMANCE GAIN: Operational seat systems in your car

COMPLEMENTARY MODIFICATION: Replace/inspect all seat components

The passenger seat occupancy sensor is used to tell the air bag computer whether or not there is a person sitting in the passenger seat. This avoids a potentially costly deployment of the passenger-side air bag if there isn't anyone sitting there.

1 Removing the seat is easy. Simply slide the seat all the way back, and remove the nut that attaches the seat to the floor (under the black plastic cap). Next, slide the seat all the way forward, and remove the bolts at the rear. The seat should then be able to be tipped upward so you can disconnect any of the electrical connections that attach to it from underneath.

BODY/INTERIOR TRIM

2 With the seat unbolted from the car, simply disconnect the wire harnesses from underneath. Your particular seat may have a few more or a few less harnesses than the one shown here. The green arrow shows the power connector; the yellow arrow shows the seatbelt receptacle sensor plug; the orange arrow shows the air bag occupancy sensor plug.

4 On the bottom of the seat, you will see the complicated mess that controls all of the seat functions. In order to gain access to the electric seat switches or the passenger seat occupancy sensor, you need to first remove the top cushion. The cushion is held on at four points—on some cars, using four plastic clips; on others, a combination of screws and clips. This particular seat has both. The plastic clips need to be clipped off (blue arrows), and the screws that hold the front of the pad to the seat need to be removed using a Torx driver (yellow arrows).

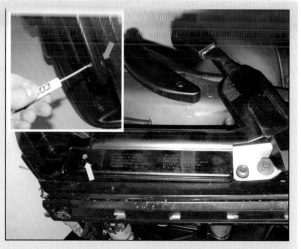

3 The first thing to do when you get your seat onto your workbench is disable the seatbelt pyrotechnic receptacle. This seatbelt device activates in conjunction with the air bags in an accident, and it can accidentally go off while you're working on it. Using a small screwdriver, turn the small green lever (yellow arrow) until the indicator on the side of the unit turns to red (blue arrow). In this photo, you can also see the nuts that attach this seatbelt assembly to the seat (use a Torx driver). If your assembly has activated accidentally, you can easily replace it now. Remember to turn the seatbelt mechanism back on when you install the seat back into the car.

This sensor gets lots of use and is responsible for a significant portion of air bag lamp faults. Once you have determined that this sensor is the cause of the problem, replacement is fairly straightforward and costs about $85.

To access the sensor, you need to remove the lower seat pad. This pad is attached at four points, sometimes with screws and sometimes with plastic clips (see Photo 2 for removal instructions). With the pad removed, the sensor becomes visible. It is simply tacked down to the lower seat cup by double-sided tape that comes pre-attached to the sensor. To replace the sensor, simply pull off the old one and stick on the new one. Reroute the wire harness for the sensor underneath the seat. Before buttoning up the seat completely, I would carefully carry it over to your car and plug it into the wire harness to see if the air bag computer still gives an error message (for this, you will need an air bag reset/code reading tool like the one described in Project 83). It's better to find out now if there is a problem with the assembly than after you have reinstalled the seat.

A note of caution. Do not put the key into the ignition with the seat removed if you are not having trouble with your air bag. If you put the key into the ignition and turn it on with the seat disconnected, the air bag computer will register a fault, and the light will go on. Then you will not be able to reset the light without a code reset tool.

The power seat switch assembly is a complicated electrical piece that often fails after many years of use. To replace

5 With the top cushion removed, you can now see the seat occupancy sensor in place. This sensor is a thin, complicated-looking film attached to the top of the seat cup using double-sided tape. A brand-new replacement sensor is shown in the inset photo. Replacement is as easy as peeling back the old sensor and attaching the new one. Also shown here are the Torx bolts that attach the seat cup to the rest of the seat assembly (green arrows). Removal of these bolts is necessary in order to gain access to replace the electrical seat switches.

6 Shown here are the electrical seat switches. With the lower seat cup removed from the rest of the frame, you can remove the three or four small Torx screws that attach the seat switch retainer to the seat frame. Once this retainer is free, you can easily remove the switch. Begin by prying off the switch knobs with a small screwdriver. Then remove the one Phillips-head screw that attaches the switch to the retainer (red arrow). The switch should then be able to be snapped out of the plastic retainer.

7 This photo shows the electric seat switch assembly. Remove it from the seat wire harness by pulling back on both ends of the connector retainer (yellow arrows). Pull away from the connector in the direction of the blue arrow, and you should be able to pull the switch assembly from the connector. The front face of a brand-new electrical switch assembly is shown in the photo inset.

the switch, simply remove the bolts that attach the lower seat cup to the assembly (Photo 3). Then flip the seat around and remove the switch retainer from the seat assembly (Photo 4). Finally, the switch should pop out of its connector, once the retaining ring is released (Photo 5).

You may want to check the seat springs before you reinstall. Coating them with some light oil will prevent them from squeaking in the future. Reassembly of the seat is indeed the opposite of assembly. The seats weigh roughly 70 pounds, so you might want to have a helper assist you with the final installation process.

Gauges and Electrical Systems

This section covers a wide variety of projects aimed at reducing the number of electrical and gauge-related problems in your car. In addition, I've also tossed in several projects that focus on upgrades and improvements to your BMW. Whether your vehicle has a broken odometer or trouble turning over the starter, the projects in this section will help you troubleshoot and repair nagging problems.

Headlamp Switch Replacement

It's not uncommon to experience a failure of your headlamp switch. Years of repeated use and abuse have a tendency to take their toll on the switch. Some symptoms of a faulty switch include headlamps that won't turn on, inoperable fog lamps, and strange chimes coming from the dashboard, just to name a few. In addition, there's a small light bulb that's contained within the switch itself that often burns out.

Replacement is very easy and only requires about 30 minutes of your time. See Photo 1 for the breakdown of the replacement procedure. The only tricky part for some people may be removing the plastic nut that fastens the switch to the vent housing. If you have a 22-millimeter deep socket, you can simply place this socket on the nut and turn it by hand. If you don't have access to a deep socket this size, you may have to resort to a pair of needle-nose pliers to remove the nut.

The part number for the replacement switch is 61-31-1-393-395. The part number for the mini-light bulb contained within the switch is 61-13-8-360-844.

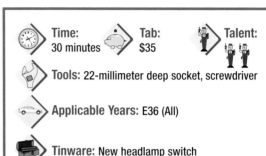

Time: 30 minutes

Tab: $35

Talent: 👨👨

Tools: 22-millimeter deep socket, screwdriver

Applicable Years: E36 (All)

Tinware: New headlamp switch

Tip: Replace mini bulb inside switch as well

PERFORMANCE GAIN: Ability to drive at night again

COMPLEMENTARY MODIFICATION: Replace bulbs in gauges

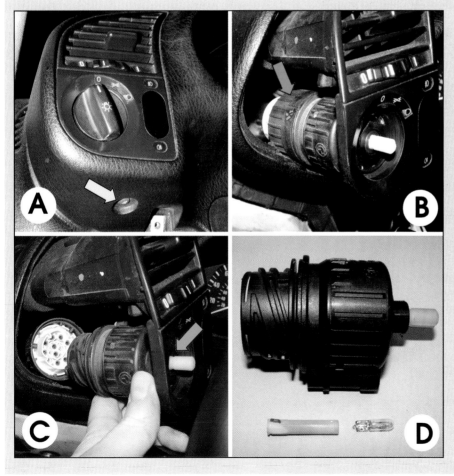

1 This photo shows the sequence for removal of the headlamp switch on the E36. **A:** The switch and vent are attached to the dashboard via one screw (yellow arrow) and a clip behind the dash. Remove this screw, and the vent/switch assembly should simply pull out. **B:** This photo shows the switch after the vent has been pulled out. Remove the wire harness connector (green arrow) by turning the retainer counterclockwise. The knob simply pulls off of the switch. **C:** With the connector disconnected from the wire harness, the entire assembly should be able to be pulled out. The blue arrow points to the 22-millimeter plastic nut that secures the switch to the vent housing. **D:** Shown here is a replacement switch, along with a new mini-light bulb. Most owners don't even realize the switch is supposed to light up when it's turned on.

Troubleshooting Electrical Problems

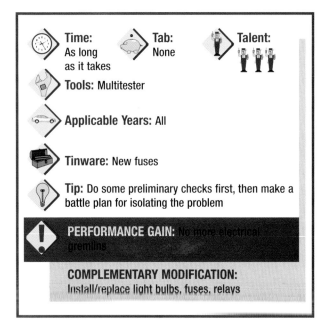

Time: As long as it takes

Tab: None

Talent: ★★★

Tools: Multitester

Applicable Years: All

Tinware: New fuses

Tip: Do some preliminary checks first, then make a battle plan for isolating the problem

PERFORMANCE GAIN: No more electrical gremlins

COMPLEMENTARY MODIFICATION: Install/replace light bulbs, fuses, relays

GAUGES AND ELECTRICAL SYSTEMS

One of the most annoying problems with older cars can be an intermittent electrical problem. Example: A dashboard light goes on when you hit the brake, but only when the rear defogger is on; or the radio only works when you are in reverse. As bizarre as it sounds, electrical problems like these have become more and more common as cars have become increasingly complex. Unfortunately, they can be quite difficult to fix.

What typically goes wrong with the wiring on these cars? Several things can happen. First and foremost, every time the car is sold, there is a big chance the new owner will do some modification to the wiring that only he or she will know about. Installing a new stereo, European headlamps, a radar detector, or—worst of all, an aftermarket alarm system—can seriously mess up your wiring configuration if not installed correctly. You're left holding the mess, armed with only a few sporadic clues as to what is causing the problem. Troubleshooting electrical problems is a tough chore and one most automotive repair shops will not perform without telling you they charge an $80-an-hour diagnostic fee.

This project will give you some tips for troubleshooting your electrical system, but it's not meant to be a step-by-step guide for fixing all of your problems. That would take almost as many pages as are contained in this book!

The first step in troubleshooting is to make sure you are armed with all the latest and greatest information available for your car. Obviously, the most important item you need is a copy of the electrical diagrams for your model year. At the time of this writing, these diagrams are only available from a few sources. BMW has published books with extensive elec-

trical diagrams in the past, but these can be difficult to find. Bentley Publishers prints manuals for most BMW 3 Series cars with summarized electrical diagrams in the back; these are available at PelicanParts.com. They are definitely a good starting point for troubleshooting.

One of the most persistent of these nagging problems is a continuous drain on the battery. Say you leave the car sitting for a week or two, and when you come back, you find the battery completely drained. This means that something is on inside the car, bleeding the battery of power. Start your troubleshooting process by disconnecting your battery ground (see Project 84) and connecting an ammeter between the battery negative and the chassis. The ammeter will show the amount of current that your electrical system is draining from the battery. When you hook the meter up, it will most likely show that there is some small current flowing through the system. Warning: Don't start the car or turn on any electrical accessories, because this might blow up your meter.

First, disconnect the trunk (E36) and engine compartment (E30) light before beginning any testing. Now, move to the fuse box in the front engine compartment, and start removing fuses. Carefully watch the ammeter to see if the current drops to zero when a particular fuse is pulled. If it does, you have successfully isolated the problematic electrical circuit. You are more than halfway to solving your problem. Look at the electrical diagrams, and see if you can tell what components are located on that circuit. Try disconnecting each one while watching the ammeter, and you should find the culprit. If pulling fuses doesn't reveal anything, however, try pulling out the various relays. Sometimes a relay will be powered on, but the device it controls will be disconnected. This may also lead to a gradual battery drain.

Another common electrical problem is the device that just won't work. If you look carefully at the electrical diagrams, you will notice that there are actually six points of failure for most electrical devices. For lack of a better example, we'll use the horn to explain and demonstrate the electrical troubleshooting process.

Starting from the rear of the electrical chain, the first point to be concerned about is the actual device itself. You can start the troubleshooting process by testing the horn. Unplug it, and apply 12 volts DC to the horn to see if it will make a sound. It if doesn't, then you have a problem with your horn.

While the horn is unplugged, another excellent test to perform is to check the electricity in the wires leading to the horn. If you press the horn button on the steering wheel and there is no power going to the wires that power the horn, then the problem lies somewhere else.

The next spot to check would be the relay for the horn. Consult the electrical diagrams to determine which one is the

1 The fusebox is at the heart of your BMW's electrical system. Located on the rear, left side of the engine compartment, the relays and fuses inside are sometimes vulnerable to corrosion and failure. Typically, when I encounter an odd electrical problem, I check the fuses and the relays first, since they are the easiest and cheapest potential solution to fix annoying electrical gremlins.

2 Some cars have wiring issues that show up as strange electrical problems. One prime example of this is the faulty trunk wiring on the E36 3 Series. If your BMW's alarm system repeatedly refuses to arm the car—instead, giving you the signal that a door is open or ajar—there may be a problem with your trunk wiring. Open the trunk, and peel back the black insulation that connects the wire harness to the trunk lid. As shown in the main image, repeatedly opening and closing the trunk makes the wires and insulation brittle and causes them to break. Solder the two broken wires together, and cover any missing insulation with tape, as shown in the photo inset.

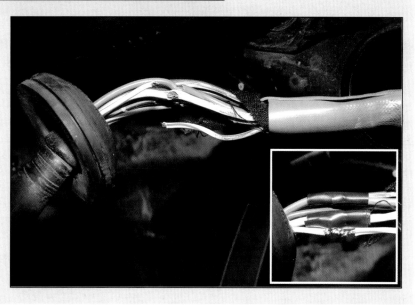

correct relay. When the horn button is pressed, the relay should make a slight clicking noise, on and off. Swapping out relays with one that is known to work is a good method of checking the proper operation of the relay as well.

If the relay checks out, you want to make sure that the fuse is still good. Identify the proper fuse that powers the horn circuit, and make sure it has not blown. Also, keep in mind that the spade-type fuses that BMW uses are sometimes affected by corrosion building up on the terminals. Make sure the fuses are clean and securely seated. If necessary, check the continuity across the two points that hold and mount the fuse.

Many electrical components on the car are also switched through the ignition, enabling them to be turned on and off when you start your car. If a device such as a window motor doesn't work, along with a host of other equipment, you might have a faulty ignition switch. One clear symptom of this can be seen when the dashboard lights and other equipment turn on

and off as you jiggle the key back and forth. Additionally the switch for the device itself may be faulty. In the case of the horn, the switch is mounted in the center of the steering wheel. Remove the wheel, and check the switch with a continuity tester to make sure it is working properly.

Finally, if all the other tests fail to locate the problem, the wiring itself may be at fault. Especially on older cars, the connecting wires tend to become brittle and sometimes break, even if the outer insulation is intact (see Photo 2). Using a continuity tester, check each of the wires in the harness that powers the blower motor to see if any have lost continuity.

If none of these steps succeed in helping you pinpoint the problem, then you may have made a mistake somewhere along the line—or there might be a short circuit hiding somewhere in the switch or the wiring of the car. In that case, you'll need to continue with more painstaking tests using a continuity tester in order to locate the source of the problem once and for all.

GAUGES AND ELECTRICAL SYSTEMS

Resetting the Air Bag Warning Lamp (SRS)

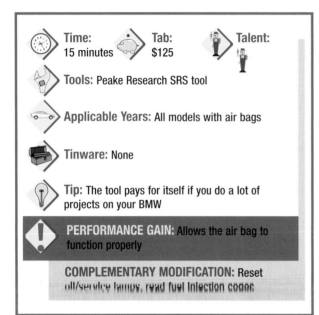

Time: 15 minutes

Tab: $125

Talent:

Tools: Peake Research SRS tool

Applicable Years: All models with air bags

Tinware: None

Tip: The tool pays for itself if you do a lot of projects on your BMW

PERFORMANCE GAIN: Allows the air bag to function properly

COMPLEMENTARY MODIFICATION: Reset oil/service lamps, read fuel injection codes

One of the newer problems associated with the late-model E36 BMWs is the somewhat troublesome air bag warning lamp. This warning lamp has dogged do-it-yourselfers for years. The lamp is like a little gremlin—there's no apparent how or why to its activation—and any number of seemingly harmless actions can set it off. The air bag lamps on all three of my E36 BMWs have been on at one time or another. Sometimes the light will stay lit and then go out after about three minutes of driving. Sometimes it will blink and stay lit. Sometimes it will stay on continuously from the time I start the car. Either way, each of these occurrences indicates the air bag computer (also known as the SRS, or supplemental restraint system) has had a problem in the past.

The SRS warning lamp is often triggered for relatively minor reasons that do not require any maintenance on the system. Any number of harmless acts can trigger the SRS lamp: Driving the car through a large puddle, or being exposed to lots of rain; swapping steering wheels; removing the gauge cluster to replace light bulbs; aggressive and/or track driving; accidentally disconnecting an SRS component while hooking up electrical accessories, such as an alarm or stereo; pulling a fuse for the SRS system while performing electrical troubleshooting; or a bad seatbelt sensor in the belt receptacle (common failure).

You can't clear the lamp by disconnecting the battery—it will stay on. You can take the car to your BMW dealer, but they will charge you anywhere from $80 to $300 just to diagnose the system and reset the lamp. However, there is a new tool available for the home mechanic that allows you to troubleshoot and diagnose air bag problems. The R5/SRS

scan and reset tool from Peake Research is very similar to the fuel injection code reader featured in Project 28. The tool plugs into the same socket and allows you to diagnose the problem with your air bag and also to reset that annoying lamp. The instructions are very simple: Just plug it in, read the codes, and then reset the lamp.

Most of the time, the air bag error code will be relatively minor, particularly if you know what caused the error. For example, the air bag light went on after I removed the gauges from my E36 and turned the ignition on in order to move the steering wheel out of the way so they could be reinstalled.

Many people have told me the air bags will not deploy when the air bag lamp is illuminated. This remains an area of much controversy, as I have also been told by more than a few people that their air bags have, in fact, deployed when the light was on. From this unscientific evidence, I would hazard a guess that the air bag system does indeed continue working when the light is on—as long as the actual fault in the system is minor. However, the light is obviously there to warn of a potential fault in the system, so you should check it out immediately if it does happen to light up.

There are quite a few BMW technical bulletins available on the design and maintenance of the SRS system. Bulletin 72.01.85 details the SRS system; bulletin 71.01.93 discusses the later-model central activation module; and bulletin 61.02.00 describes the procedures for installing various SRS sensor wire harness repair kits.

1 The SRS reset tool plugs into the same diagnostic socket as the fuel injection scan tool (green arrow). Operation is exactly the same, except this tool can only read and diagnose SRS codes. Some early 1992 and 1993 E36 cars have finicky air bag computers that may cause problems with communication between the tool and the car.

Starter Replacement

Time: 6 hours

Tab: $155

Talent: ★★★★

Tools: Torx socket set, extensions

Applicable Years: All

Tinware: New starter

Tip: Save money with a rebuilt starter

PERFORMANCE GAIN: Reliable starting

COMPLEMENTARY MODIFICATION: Replace battery

There are some projects that seem like they should be relatively routine—and are very easy to perform on other cars—but are a huge pain on the BMW 3 Series cars. Replacing the starter is one of them. Most other cars I've worked on have had relatively accessible starters. If you are quick with the tools, you can have the starter replaced within 15 minutes on some engines. Not so with the 3 Series. The only way to replace the starter is to remove the intake manifold (Project 12) or remove the transmission (Project 43).

The first and most critical step in the removal process is to disconnect the battery from the car (Photo 1). This is very important, as live current is connected to the starter at all times. You can seriously injure yourself and damage your electrical system if you accidentally ground the large red wire connected to the starter.

To disconnect the battery, disconnect the negative, or ground lead from the battery. Always disconnect the negative or ground lead first—if you disconnect the positive/hot lead, there is a chance that your tool may touch the metal chassis. This could result in a short circuit, which would not bode well for you. The worst-case scenario might be if your wrench hit the chassis and was instantly welded there by the current, then the battery overheated and exploded because you couldn't break the connection. In other words, don't risk it—be sure to disconnect the ground first.

If your car has the original radio in it, be aware you will need the radio code if you disconnect the battery. The BMW dealer can look this up for you if you don't have it, but that

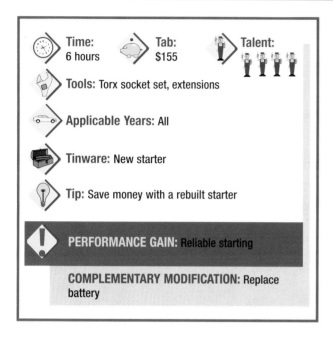

1 The battery is located in the engine compartment on E30 cars, and in the rear trunk on E36 cars. Shown in this photo is a special BMW battery designed for the convertible (it's larger and intended to withstand increased vibration). Always disconnect the black negative, or ground, connection first (green arrow). If you are not planning to remove the battery, this connection is all you need to disconnect—there is no need to disconnect the positive/hot lead to the battery. When you disconnect the ground from the battery, make sure you place or tape the ground lead aside. You don't want it accidentally falling on the terminal of the battery while you're working and accidentally connecting up the battery again. A handy device I like to install on all my cars is a battery cutoff switch (lower inset). Installation of this switch on the battery ground allows you to remove the green knob and shut off all power to the car. An added tip: Connect a small inline fuse from one end to the other, and a small amount of current will continue to flow, keeping your radio presets from being cleared out when the battery is disconnected. The E30 battery is shown in the upper inset.

GAUGES AND ELECTRICAL SYSTEMS

2 Here is the view from the top of the E36 engine compartment with the intake manifold removed. The starter is relatively easy to access at this point (the starter's solenoid shown by orange arrow); however, there are some hoses and cables that will still get in your way. The red arrow shows where the battery cable is connected to the wire harness. Danger: This wire is connected straight to the battery and is live unless the battery is disconnected. The blue arrow points to the starter control harness, and the green arrow points to one of the nuts that hold the starter to the transmission.

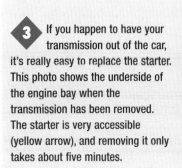

3 If you happen to have your transmission out of the car, it's really easy to replace the starter. This photo shows the underside of the engine bay when the transmission has been removed. The starter is very accessible (yellow arrow), and removing it only takes about five minutes.

can be a huge pain, and most dealers will charge you for the service. Disconnecting the battery may also erase fault codes stored in your DME. To be on the safe side, I recommend you read your fuel injection fault codes prior to disconnecting the battery (see Projects 28 and 29).

You'll need to remove either the manifold or transmission to access the starter. Once you have the manifold or transmission removed, the actual process of replacing the starter is not too difficult. Verify again that the battery is disconnected, and then unbolt the large, thick red wire harness that connects to the starter. Also disconnect the much smaller wire harness that plugs into the terminals on the back of the starter solenoid.

The starter is attached to the transmission case with two Torx bolts. Remove these bolts (see Project 43), and you should be able to lift the starter out of the engine compartment (if you removed the manifold first), or out the back of the engine (if the transmission was removed). Verify that your old starter looks the same as the new starter and has the same number of electrical connections on the back.

As indicated in Project 43, the nuts that hold the starter in place may be very difficult to hold when tightening up the bolts. This is definitely a job made easier with an assistant on hand. Have your assistant hold the nuts in the engine compartment while you tighten the bolts from underneath.

Starter System Troubleshooting

🕐	**Time:** As long as it takes	🐁	**Tab:** None	🎅	**Talent:** 🎅🎅🎅

🔧 **Tools:** None

🚗 **Applicable Years:** All

🧰 **Tinware:** None

💡 **Tip:** Check your drivetrain ground strap if you're having starting problems

⚠️ **PERFORMANCE GAIN:** Reliable starting

COMPLEMENTARY MODIFICATION: Replace starter

At one time or another, most BMW owners will come to experience a problem of some sort while starting their cars. The first place to look for trouble in your starting system is your battery. The battery is perhaps the most important electrical component on the car, and due to its design and nature, is perhaps one of the most troublesome. Before doing anything drastic like replacing your starter, you should make sure your battery is in good condition.

Begin by using a voltmeter to check the voltage at the battery posts. Be sure to place the meter's probes on the posts of the battery, not the clamps. This will give the most accurate indication of the voltage in the battery. A normal battery should register slightly above 12 volts with the car sitting still and no electrical devices on. (The small trunk light in the trunk or hood shouldn't make a difference in the voltage reading.) A typical reading would be in the 12.6-volt range when the battery is fully charged. If the reading is 12 volts or less, the battery needs charging or needs to be replaced with a new one. To be certain, you can take your battery to an auto parts store for testing.

I recently had an OEM BMW battery fail on me in my BMW 5 Series. The car was running perfectly fine. I had just driven about 350 miles the previous day, so it should have been well charged. The next morning, I got in the car and it started right up. I drove about three miles and stopped to pick something up. I shut off the car and left it for three minutes at the most. When I got back, the battery was almost completely dead. There wasn't even enough juice left to open the power door locks. It turned out to be complete battery failure. I was surprised, because I'd never had a battery fail like this before; they always seemed to give out slowly. Some of the research I've done since then, however, indicates the

GAUGES AND ELECTRICAL SYSTEMS

1 The infamous drivetrain ground strap is one of the easiest parts on the car to overlook, yet it can cause many electrical troubles. Since the transmission and engine are insulated by rubber mounts, the ground strap is the only significant ground to the engine. If the ground strap is disconnected or missing, the current that turns the starter must travel through the engine harness or other small points of contact. Needless to say, this situation usually doesn't provide enough current to start the car. The location of the ground strap has varied over the years; this photo shows three common locations. On the left, the yellow arrow points to a typical E36 ground strap, which is attached to the right-side engine mount. The center shows a ground strap from an E30 318 attached to the lower valve cover. It is very easy to forget this attachment when performing a valve adjustment. The right side shows a ground strap from a 1987 325e, which is attached to the lower part of the power steering pump.

newer technology used in these batteries occasionally tends to lead to this type of sudden failure.

When the car is running, the alternator should output anywhere from about 12.5 volts to about 14.5 volts. If you don't see any significant change in the voltage after you start up the car, your alternator or voltage regulator could be faulty. If the voltage is high at the battery (around 17 volts or higher), then the regulator is most likely faulty and needs to be replaced. Warning: Overcharging the battery at these higher levels may cause it to overflow and leak acid all over the inside of your car. For most cars, the voltage regulator is attached to the rear of the alternator and is replaceable. Typical cost is around $35.

Once you have determined your battery is fine, you should make sure your engine ground strap is properly installed. The engine and transmission are mounted to the chassis using rubber mounts. While great for the suspension, the rubber mounts make lousy electrical conductors. To compensate for this, there is an engine ground strap that electrically connects the transmission and engine assembly to the chassis. To accurately assess the condition of the ground strap, you need to crawl underneath the car after it's been jacked up and take a look at the bottom of the engine. If the strap is corroded or damaged, it might be best to install a new one. Make sure you clean both ends of the strap and the areas it mounts to on the chassis. With all electrical connections, it's a good idea to clean the mounting area with rubbing alcohol and sand it lightly with fine-grit sandpaper or emery cloth. Doing so will remove any dirt, grime, surface rust, or other corrosion that may interfere with creating a good electrical connection. While you're at it, clean up the battery terminals in a similar manner.

Another problem area for starting is the starter, of course. The starter is a somewhat complex device for what would seem to be a simple task. A solenoid on the starter both actuates the small gear that turns the flywheel and switches on the main starter motor. It is important to throw in a note of caution here: The starter motor is, at all times, connected directly to the positive terminal of the battery. If you accidentally touch the terminals of the starter with a metal object that is grounded, you will quickly generate heat, sparks, and enough current to fry your alternator and a large chunk of your electrical system! I have heard two separate reports of how a person was working on his car, and his watch accidentally touched the terminals of the starter and the chassis ground. This literally caused the watch to become welded to the chassis of the car! Exercise extreme caution in this area. Don't wear any jewelry when working on the car, and always disconnect the negative terminal from the battery prior to working near the starter.

Another potential problem is the starter teeth on the flywheel or ring gear. If the starter seems to engage and spin up with a high-pitched whirring sound, then it is likely that the starter is not fully engaging the flywheel. This is especially prevalent with intermittent problems, in which sometimes the starter will work fine and then other times it will spin

freely. The fix for this is to inspect the flywheel teeth and to replace the flywheel when the engine is out of the car. A bad solenoid can also cause similar problems.

When BMWs have trouble turning the engine over with the starter motor, it is often because there isn't enough current to fully trigger the solenoid on the starter. You'll get a "click-click-click" sound when trying to start it up. A number of factors can cause this. One common cause is old wiring. As the car ages, the wiring tends to lose some of its electrical conductivity. This can be triggered by the wires getting bent or crimped, or by the constant heating and cooling of the wires. This tempering of the metal within the wires can directly affect their conductivity. With age often comes corrosion, and as we can see simply by looking at the Statue of Liberty, copper corrodes quite easily, leaving a light-green layer that doesn't conduct very well.

The solution, then, is to methodically track down the problem in the wiring and fix it. Very often, tracing back the electrical connections from the starter and carefully cleaning all the contacts will improve the situation significantly. While this can be a time-consuming process, it's really the only way to track down these electrical gremlins. Chances are, if you are having wiring conductivity problems with your starting system, it's probably affecting other electrical systems as well.

The primary method of tracking down bad connections is to test them with an electrical multimeter. Test the resistance across lengths of wires and connections in your car, and look for any that are significantly higher than others. Chances are, with a little cleaning of both the wires and the contacts, the system will improve.

The electrical portion of the ignition switch is another source of trouble. This small part often wears out and fails after many years. One symptom of this problem is an ignition switch that requires a lot of force to start the car. Another symptom is headlamps or other accessories that flicker on and off when you wiggle the key.

If you cannot find the problem causing your starting woes, there is a potential solution called a "hot start relay kit" (typically installed only on older cars). While this solution will work by bypassing some of the faulty wiring, it is a proverbial bandage for a much bigger problem. The hot start relay kit takes the power from the starter cable connected to the battery and uses it to activate the solenoid. The relay is powered by the electricity that travels through the faulty wiring. Since the hot start relay only requires a few milliamps of electrical current to operate, it often fixes the problem of starting the car. However, as mentioned previously, if you have electrical starting problems, you probably have additional electrical problems elsewhere. These are best tracked down and fixed, instead of glossed over.

Finally, if you have determined that the problem lies with your starter, you should replace it. The starter is not easy to replace on these cars. See Project 84, for a more in-depth look at the process of removing your starter.

Brake Switch Replacement

Time: 30 minutes

Tab: $20–50

Talent: 👨👨

Tools: Screwdriver

Applicable Years: All

Tinware: New brake-lamp pedal switch

Tip: Break the old switch to remove it

! PERFORMANCE GAIN: Working brake lamps

COMPLEMENTARY MODIFICATION: Install aftermarket pedals

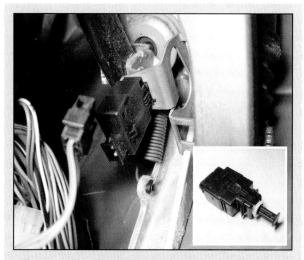

1. After you remove the knee panel above the pedal cluster, you should be able to view the brake pedal switch. Unplug the harness by squeezing on the sides of the connector. A new replacement switch is shown in the photo inset.

2. You may have to twist and break the old switch in order to remove it from its bracket. Use a pair of pliers to get a better grip on the switch if you have trouble removing it by hand.

There may come a time when someone on the road motions to you about your brake lights not coming on, or your onboard computer indicates a brake light system failure. The brake pedal switch in both the E30 and E36 BMW gets a lot of use and has a tendency to fail once in a while. Replacement is really easy, and should take only about 30 minutes.

The first step is to verify that your brake lamps are not working. If you're by yourself, wait until nightfall and back up against a brick wall. You should see the reflection off the wall when you step on the brakes—if you don't, your switch is probably shot. It's important to note that, at least on some model years, the BMW warning system that tells you when a lamp is out will not tell you if the switch is broken; you may have to figure it out for yourself.

The first step is to gain access to the switch. Remove the panel directly above the driver-side footwell; a few screws and snaps secure this panel. In addition, you may have an electrical speaker unit attached to the panel. Disconnect the harness and pull the panel down.

The brake switch is shown in Photo 1. It's the rather large switch assembly that moves in conjunction with the brake pedal. Remove the harness from the brake switch and yank the switch out of its bracket. I found that I had to break the plastic housing of the switch in order to actually remove it (Photo 2). That's perfectly okay, since you will be replacing it with a new one very soon anyway.

To finish the job, simply install the new switch into place, and reconnect the wire harness. Test the brake lights to make sure they are working properly, and then reinstall the knee panel.

DME Swap/Repair

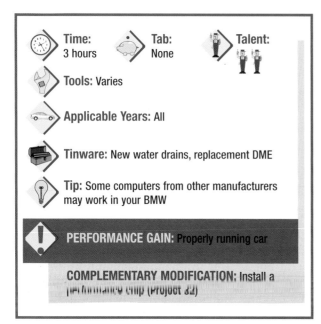

Time: 3 hours

Tab: None

Talent: ★★

Tools: Varies

Applicable Years: All

Tinware: New water drains, replacement DME

Tip: Some computers from other manufacturers may work in your BMW

PERFORMANCE GAIN: Properly running car

COMPLEMENTARY MODIFICATION: Install a performance chip (Project 32)

GAUGES AND ELECTRICAL SYSTEMS

The Bosch Motronic engine management system is what controls and monitors the ignition, timing, and emissions controls of the later-model 3 Series cars. As such, it can be considered the brain of the car. The ECU (electronic control unit, sometimes called the DME) of this system will cause the engine to run poorly or to stop running altogether if it becomes damaged. In this project, we'll talk a little about the DME and how to troubleshoot its problems, prevent damage to the unit, and repair or replace the unit.

First, if you are having problems with your car, you should check to see if the computer is giving out any fault codes (see Projects 28 and 29). If the code readers are having trouble connecting to the unit, you need to look further.

Many people I've spoken to have had problems with the relay that controls the DME computer itself. It's not uncommon for the main relay to have its contacts become corroded and fail to work 100 percent of the time. Even if the relay is intermittent, it might show up as the engine running rough, or stalling, or any number of other failures. One of the first steps I would take is to identify this relay. On E36 BMWs, it's relay number two, the white one, next to the fuel pump. Try swapping it out with a known good one if you have one, or swap it with another one on the board (like the one for the fog lamps). Then try starting the car. If you see an improvement, you might have found the problem. Start with the relay since it is the easiest and cheapest item to replace.

On E36 BMWs manufactured prior to July 1994, there is a design problem with the car that causes a number of problems with the main DME computer. The water relief channels of the car are not beefy enough to withstand a significant influx of water onto the car, especially around the windshield. While perfectly adequate for anything that nature may throw at the car, the channels are woefully inadequate for a simple car wash. If too much water is used, or if the water channels are clogged with leaves or debris, the water will overflow and leak into the compartment where the DME is stored (see Project 32 for the location of the DME in the engine compartment). I have heard stories of owners who have opened this compartment, only to have a gallon of water or more come flowing out. Needless to say, having the main computer for the car submerged in water is not a good thing.

How exactly does the water get into the box? The DME compartment is located right next to the intake plenum cowl for the heating and air conditioning system. This cowl is open to the environment, and thus becomes an unwitting receptacle for rainwater. There are drains at the bottom designed to drain out this rainwater. However, if the volume of water is too great, or if the channels become clogged with leaves or other debris, this plenum will overflow directly into the DME compartment. If enough water fills this chamber, it may also leak into the passenger-side footwell—although this often goes unnoticed, as the water will leak under the passenger floor mat. Creating further problems, the cowling below the windshield can become brittle and break, resulting in a hole that lets water down into that area.

BMW has issued a service bulletin that details a relatively inexpensive fix for the problem. The fix is to install a third drain and use an improved style of drainage hose. The BMW factory bulletin that describes this repair is 41 03 93 (3914), dated July 1994. Begin by removing the plastic screen covering the plenum and the portion of the plenum that covers the firewall; then move the wiring harness out of the way on the left side of the engine compartment. Remove the cylinder head valve cover (see Project 9)—you will need to do this to gain clearance to work. Cover the top of the engine with a drop cloth or plastic garbage bag to prevent anything else from falling in.

Now, pull back the insulation on the firewall. Remove and throw away the right-side plenum drain hose at this time. Behind the insulation material is a circular area pre-stamped in the firewall just above and to the right of the original drain location. You will need to drill out this hole and install the new drain hose there. BMW specifically recommends that you not use a hole saw, because metal shavings are too likely to contaminate either the engine or the plenum area. Instead, start with a 0.375-inch pilot hole and use a ½-inch conduit punch. Then, use a ¾-inch conduit punch and enlarge the hole to 28.2 millimeters (1.11 inches). File off the edges, paint with a small bit of primer, and then reinstall the firewall insulation. Drill a corresponding hole in the insulation,

1 This photo shows the area of concern for the water channel fix. The cylinder head has been removed in this photo, but you can perform the fix even if you only remove the valve cover. The old-style water channel hose is indicated by the green arrow. The yellow arrow shows where the third, additional water outlet hose will be installed. Water can also enter into the DME compartment when your lower windshield trim piece is damaged and broken (inset photo). I haven't seen a 3 Series yet that doesn't have at least some cracking and missing edges there (red arrows). If yours is exposing the edge of the glass, be sure to replace it.

2 Cracked solder joints occur when an electrical circuit board is exposed to heat cycles and vibration cycles over extended periods of time. As these cars age, more and more electronic components such as the DME will begin to fail due to cracked solder joints. The solution is to reflow the solder around the joints most likely to exhibit failure. These are often attached to components that put out the most heat—typically the transistors with large heat sinks attached to the circuit board.

and install your two new drain hoses (part number BW-51-73-8-144-152), slightly angled 30 degrees toward the center of the car. That's the BMW fix described for this problem. Photo 1 shows the area where you need to drill (yellow arrow), and also points to the water drain hose (green arrow) that should be pulled out and replaced.

If you are not fortunate enough to have read this article before your DME got wet, you may still have a chance to revive it. Open the DME compartment and remove the DME unit (see Project 32). Even if your DME is covered and soaked with water, you may be able to save it. Take the unit apart and expose the two circuit boards. Although I have not used it myself in this particular fashion, I have had several Pelican Parts customers tell me that spraying the board with WD-40 helps to dispel any water, dries the board, and sometimes works. The board is already soaked in water at this point, what could it hurt? Take the DME boards and place them in an oven set at about 100 degrees Fahrenheit, and let them sit for a few hours. This should help evaporate any remaining water that may have made it into the unit. Reassemble the unit, and plug it back into your car to see if the problem still exists. If it does, you will probably have to replace the unit with another one.

Some DMEs stop working for reasons that don't seem as obvious as being submerged in water. If you borrow a DME

computer from a friend and your car works perfectly, then you have indeed isolated the problem to the DME circuit board. It is possible to sometimes inspect and repair these units. The most common failure associated with old electronic units is cracked solder joints. Have you ever had a Walkman-type stereo that had a broken head phone plug? If you wiggled the plug one way, you could hear, but if you let go of the plug it would stop working properly and the sound would cut out? This is a symptom of a cracked solder joint, and it can occur in your DME as well. When I worked at Hughes Space and Communications building satellites, one of their primary concerns was the potential for cracked solder joints shaken loose by the vibration from the launch cycle. Turns out it's a very common problem among all electronic equipment.

If you take a close look at your board, you may be able to spot a cracked solder joint. Some broken joints are not easily seen with the naked eye though. To repair a cracked solder joint, simply get out your solder arm and reflow the solder. If I am repairing a circuit board, I usually like to reflow the solder on all the joints that are pretty large, and particularly the ones that look like they are attached to heat sinks. The heat causes the crack to enlarge and then separate, causing an intermittent failure. The same thing can happen if the DME rattles when driving or is exposed to excess vibration.

If you've tried all the approaches outlined above and your DME unit still doesn't work, you will probably have to replace it. A little-known secret is that many of the DME units are exactly the same across different automotive manufacturers. The only difference lies with the programming chip contained within the unit. If the DME unit is the same version of Motronic, has the same connector on the unit, and has a removable chip, chances are it can be a good replacement for your failed unit. This means a $10 DME from a Volkswagen in a junkyard may work in place of the $650 one

that a BMW used parts dealer wants to sell you. A few of my customers have experimented with this by swapping BMW DME computers with the ones used on the Porsche 944 and 911 and have experienced good results. Some units won't work (it's a matter of trial and error), but many will. The main thing to remember is that you must have the same software version of Motronic, the connector must be the same, and you must swap the chip from your DME to the new one. For further reference, see the 101Projects.com website for a complete table of interchangeable DME computers.

PROJECT 88   http://www.101projects.com/BMW/88.htm

Radio Head Unit Installation

Time: 3 hours

Tab: $300

Talent: ★★★

Tools: Radio removal tool

Applicable Years: All

Tinware: Radio, antenna adapter, wire harness adapter

Tip: Get the correct adapters for your car, so you don't have to cut any wires

PERFORMANCE GAIN: Great-sounding tunes!

COMPLEMENTARY MODIFICATION: Upgrade your speakers

One of the first projects new BMW owners tend to perform on their cars is to remove and replace their stereo head unit. If I buy a car that has a weak stereo, it's one of the first things to go. The factory BMW head units (manufactured by Alpine) are best described as barely adequate—the technology is at least 10 years old in most cases, and the units seem to have a rather high failure rate after many years of use.

The good news is the replacement process is relatively easy, provided you have the right information and the right parts. First, disconnect the battery (see Project 84). The radio harness has constant voltage supplied to it, and you don't want to accidentally blow any fuses or damage any electrical components. Begin by flipping open the small flaps on the sides of the OEM head unit. Underneath, you will find a funky five-sided bolt on the inside. I guess BMW thought it would be more difficult to remove the stereo if the bolt it was mounted with was a nonstandard one. Well, my standard Allen wrench fit right in there, and I was able to remove it with no significant effort involved. If your bolts are more

1 Removing the OEM radio head unit is relatively easy. Flip up the flaps on each side of the unit (yellow arrow). Underneath you will find the five-sided screw (red arrow). I found that a small SAE Allen wrench fit well into the screw and was able to release it quite easily (green arrow). Once the screws are released, the unit should simply pull out.

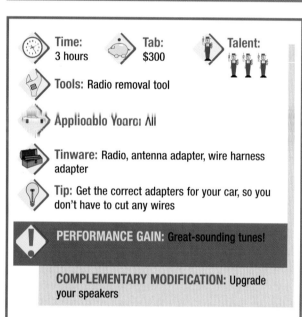

2 Shown here is the new radio ready for installation. The green arrow shows the antenna adapter installed. The bracket is installed in the center dashboard, ready for the radio (red arrow). The factory harness is connected to the adapter (yellow arrow), and the connector for the radio is plugged into the back of the new head unit (blue arrow). It's normal to have one or two wires that are not used (purple arrow). In this case, the wires correspond to external antenna and external amplifier control. In this photo, I plugged in all of the connections and then turned on the ignition to test the proper operation of the radio. I recommend testing prior to the final installation, as these radios are designed to be difficult to remove.

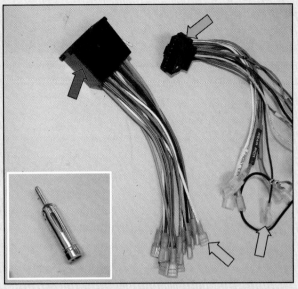

3 The BMW harness adapter is shown on the left (red arrow), and the harness that came with the new radio is shown on the right (green arrow). I used simple spade connectors (blue arrows) to link the two together. In general, I do not recommend cutting wires in your car—it becomes very difficult to fix and/or restore the electrical system back to stock if anything goes wrong. In the photo inset is the antenna adapter I used to convert the plug on my new head unit to the connector on the antenna harness in the car.

securely tightened, you may need a specific five-sided tool for the task. After the bolts are loose, you should be able to simply pull the unit out by hand.

On the back of the unit, there is a large black connector and a smaller antenna connector. Remove the antenna connector by simply tugging on it. The large black connector has a retaining strap that needs to be released prior to pulling it out of the radio. Don't force the connector, or you may break it.

In order to install your new radio, you will need a BMW cable adapter. This adapter plugs into the factory connector and has leads on it you can connect to the leads or connector on your new radio. You can cut the OEM connector off and tap directly into the factory harness, but I strongly caution against this—it's best to use the adapter cable (costs about $10). I put some spade connectors on the ends of the harness adapter and the connector that plugged into my new radio.

In general, most wire harnesses are configured according to an industry standard shown in the following table:

Blue	Power antenna
Orange	Illumination
Black	Chassis ground
Red	12-volt switched power
Yellow	12-volt constant power
Green	Left rear speaker positive

Green/Black	Left rear speaker negative
Violet	Right rear speaker positive
Violet/Black	Right rear speaker negative
White	Left front speaker positive
White/Black	Left front speaker negative
Gray	Right front speaker positive
Gray/Black	Right front speaker negative

Plug the harness adapter into the factory connector, and then plug the harness into the back of the head unit and connect all of the spade connectors.

On this particular head unit, I found the antenna jack on the back of the unit was not compatible with the one in the factory harness, so I needed an antenna adapter ($7) as well. Plug the adapter into the back of the unit, and you should be able to plug the antenna cable into the unit.

Once the new head unit is wired up, reconnect the battery, and turn it on to test it. If all of the speakers, radio, and lights work, install the radio bracket into the center dashboard. This is the bracket that comes with your new unit and typically has tabs you bend into place once you position the bracket.

When the bracket is secure, simply slide the radio into its spot in the center dashboard. Be careful, though, most of these units are designed to be easy to install but very difficult to remove, so make sure that everything works before inserting it into the dashboard.

Alternator Troubleshooting and Replacement

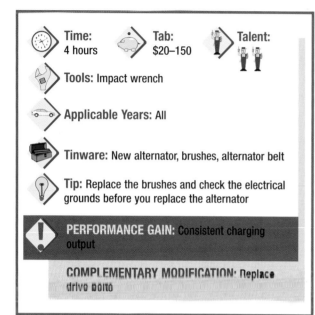

Time: 4 hours

Tab: $20–150

Talent: ★★

Tools: Impact wrench

Applicable Years: All

Tinware: New alternator, brushes, alternator belt

Tip: Replace the brushes and check the electrical grounds before you replace the alternator

PERFORMANCE GAIN: Consistent charging output

COMPLEMENTARY MODIFICATION: Replace drive belts

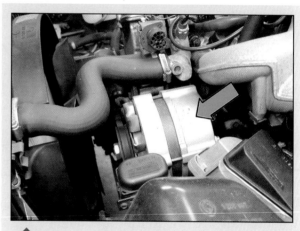

1 Here is an alternator nestled into the engine compartment on an E30 318i. It's relatively easy to reach, although on some models, you may have to remove the air cleaner and some hoses to completely pull it out.

GAUGES AND ELECTRICAL SYSTEMS

One of the nice things about the configuration of the BMW engine is the relative ease with which you can replace the alternator. The alternator is nestled neatly on the left side of the engine compartment and is easily accessible. The replacement and repair process is straightforward and should take you about an afternoon to complete.

First, make sure your alternator is indeed the cause of the problems with your charging system. Sometimes bizarre electrical problems can be caused by a number of faults other than the alternator. It's important to troubleshoot the system prior to replacing your alternator.

The first component to check is the belt that drives the alternator. Is it tight and amply turning the fan? If not, tighten it according to the procedures outlined in Project 5. Modern belts seldom break, but they do get brittle and glazed with age, and can slip on their pulleys. Replace it with a new one if it looks cracked or brittle.

The next item to check is the voltage at the battery. This should read a little more than 12 volts with the engine off. When the car is running, the voltage should read at in the range of 13 to 14.5 volts with the engine at 2,000 rpm. If your battery appears to be leaking, your voltage regulator has probably failed. The battery will usually only leak acid if it has been overcharged at a much higher voltage. If the voltage measured at the battery is more than 16 or 17 volts when the engine is running, the regulator is probably bad. If your battery has boiled over and has acid flowing out the top, clean it up immediately. Dousing the area with a water-and-baking-soda solution should help considerably to neutralize the acid and prevent it from eating away at the metal.

An important item to check on your car is the engine ground strap. The engine is electrically isolated from the chassis by rubber motor mounts. If the engine ground strap is missing or disconnected, you might have a whole bunch of problems, including electrical system malfunctions and difficultly turning over the starter. (See Project 85 for the exact location of this ground strap.) Also, some BMW alternators have an external ground that may get disconnected accidentally.

Almost all the 3 Series cars have a replaceable voltage regulator/brush assembly. If you've determined the regulator to be working properly, then you should probably remove the alternator for testing and inspection. Before starting any work, make sure you disconnect the battery. The positive battery terminal is directly connected to the alternator, and it can be dangerous to work on if it's live (see Project 85).

The first step in removing the alternator is to remove the belt that drives it. (See Project 5 for detailed instructions on belt removal.) Removing the alternator from its bracket is a very easy process. On the early 3 Series, the alternator is affixed to the car via a pivot bolt, and a rack-and-pinion assembly is used to adjust the belt tension. Disconnect the rack-and-pinion assembly if your car has one (see Photo 2), and unbolt the alternator from its bottom pivot bolt. For the later E36 cars, the alternator is fixed in place, and the multifunction belt is tightened on the alternator with a spring-loaded tensioner pulley (see Project 5 for details and photos). Simply unbolt the alternator from where it's attached to the engine after removing the belt. Depending upon which engine you have, you may need to remove some

2 Shown here is the rack-and-pinion system used to apply tension to the belt on early cars. Loosen the bolt at the rear of this bracket before you try to turn the front toothed bolt. If you don't, you will break off teeth on the rack and thus make it very difficult to tighten the alternator belt. This particular bracket has been abused and has suffered the loss of one tightening tooth (red arrow).

3 I've never seen a new or rebuilt alternator supplied with the pulleys attached, so you'll need to transfer them from your old unit. Removing the pulley can be tricky if you don't have an impact wrench (a good reason to buy an electric one). Also useful may be a strap wrench, which is a handle with a rubber strap on it that can secure and tighten around a pulley. These four frames show the removal and reinstallation of the pulley on an E30 318i alternator. Be sure to take notes as you disassemble the alternator pulley assembly—it must be reassembled in exactly the same manner on the replacement alternator.

Nearly all 3 Series alternators have a brush/regulator assembly in the rear that can be easily removed and replaced (blue arrow). Remove the brushes and inspect them carefully if your alternator is not working well. If the contacts are short in length, they are worn and need to be replaced. If they are long (as shown in the photo), you probably have some other internal problem with the alternator that's causing it to malfunction. Replacing this regulator assembly is a good step to take prior to spending money on a rebuilt alternator.

4

equipment such as the air cleaner and cool air guide located above the alternator. See Project 12 for details on removing components that are in the way.

With the alternator unbolted, disconnect the electrical connections from the rear. I recommend taking a digital photo of the connections, because many people mix them up when reinstalling the alternator. If you make a mistake and hook them up incorrectly, it's possible to do some significant damage to your electrical system. Reminder: Do not touch any of these connections while the battery is still hooked up! (Review Project 85 for additional details.)

With the alternator out of the car, remove and inspect the regulator/brush assembly (see Photo 4). If you are replacing the alternator completely, transfer the old pulley assembly to the newly rebuilt alternator (see Photo 3). Installing the new alternator is now simply the reverse of removal. Make sure you reconnect all the wires to their proper terminals when you are done.

Replacing Gauge Cluster Light Bulbs

GAUGES AND ELECTRICAL SYSTEMS

Time: 1 hour

Tab: $2

Talent: ♦♦

Tools: Stubby Phillips screwdriver

Applicable Years: E36 (All)

Tinware: Replacement gauge light bulbs

Tip: Disconnect the battery first

PERFORMANCE GAIN: Ability to see all your warning lamps

COMPLEMENTARY MODIFICATION: Install colored gauge faces

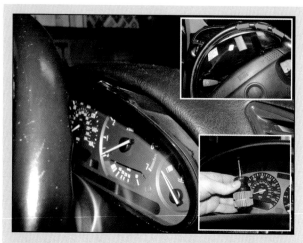

It's inevitable—one day, one of the lamps will burn out in your gauge cluster. Most people just tolerate this because, in their minds, the bulbs are difficult to reach and nobody knows how to get to them anyway. In reality, it's quite easy if you know the procedure for safely pulling out and removing the gauge cluster.

The first step is to write down which bulbs are burned out, and then disconnect the battery (see Project 84). I really can't stress this enough, for reasons I'll explain later in the text. Make sure you have the proper radio code required to reset your radio if you do disconnect the battery. Nothing is more frustrating than realizing your radio is dead and you don't have the code (although it is available from the BMW dealer).

With the battery disconnected, use a small stubby screwdriver to remove the two screws that fasten the gauge clusters to the top of the dashboard. On some later cars, these screws may require a stubby Torx driver—or you might be able to get away with using a small flat-head screwdriver in the top of the Torx head.

With the two screws removed, you should be able to pull the cluster out of its home in the molded dash. This, of course, is easier said than done. There isn't a big grab handle to pull the cluster out with. The best method is to grab the top of the cluster with your fingernails and pull it down. Using a soft plastic wedge, such as an old credit card, can help, and it won't damage the delicate plastic assembly.

With the gauges pulled out from the dash, you now need to reach behind and disconnect the wire harnesses from the rear. For each harness, you need to push a small tab on the rear of the connector, which then allows the white retaining lever

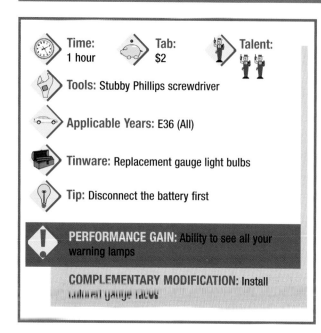

1 On the E36, the gauge cluster is secured to the dash by two screws. Remove these screws with a small, stubby screwdriver (lower right). Pulling out the gauges themselves requires some effort, and it helps if you have long fingernails. Using a small pick, you can pull at the gauge cluster tabs that the screws mount into. Once the gauge cluster is pulled out far enough, disconnect the wire harnesses in the rear of the cluster (see Photo 3). With the harnesses disconnected, the cluster can be removed if you pull it all the way out; then rotate the steering wheel to the side (inset photo, upper right).

to be lifted up. Don't use too much force, or you will break the delicate retaining levers; then the connectors will never be secure. (See Photo 2 for details.)

With the harnesses disconnected, you can now maneuver the gauge cluster out from the car. Be careful not to scratch the front of the gauge cluster on your steering wheel column. The removal process will require you to turn the steering wheel. Insert the key into the ignition and turn it so you can rotate the steering wheel. Verify that your battery is disconnected—if you turn on the ignition with the gauge cluster disconnected, the air bag computer will sense a fault and will trigger the air bag warning lamp. The air bag warning lamp can only be reset by using a special reset tool (see Project 83). If you don't have one, you'll be taking an expensive trip to the dealer.

With the gauge cluster removed, you can use a small screwdriver to replace the bulbs. There are three large green ones; they illuminate the analog gauges (3-watt bulb, part number 07 11 9 978 372). There are two medium-sized white/tan ones that illuminate the odometer display (1.5-watt bulb, part number 62 11 1 391 260). Finally, the small black ones are for illuminating the warning lamps (1.2-watt

2 Be especially careful with the delicate retaining levers that attach the wire harness to the rear of the gauge cluster. The left photo shows one connector plugged into the rear of the cluster. The green arrow points to the small tab that must be pressed down in order to release

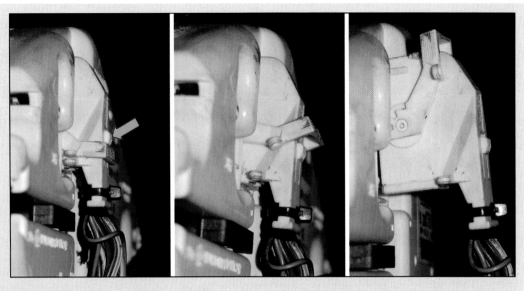

the retaining lever. The middle photo shows the retaining lever being pulled back. Finally, in the right photo, the retaining lever has been pulled all the way up to the top, and the connector snaps out of the plug.

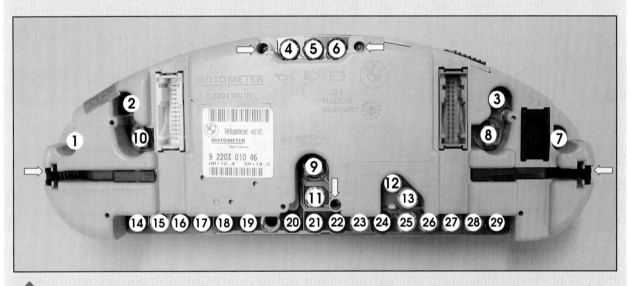

3 Here is a photo of the rear of the E36 gauge cluster. Each one of the plastic tabs is the back side of an instrument bulb. The black ones indicate individual lamps (like the ABS warning lamp), whereas the green ones are used for backlighting the gauges. The tan ones are used to illuminate the LCD/odometer display. Be sure to make a note of which bulbs are burned out before you pull the gauge cluster. The yellow arrows point to the five screws that must be removed to access the inside of the gauge cluster (see Project 91). **1:** Temperature warning. **2:** Right turn signal. **3:** Left turn signal. **4:** Oil pressure warning. **5:** High-beam indicator. **6:** Battery-charging indicator. **7:** Low-fuel-level warning. **8/9/10:** Gauge cluster illumination. **11:** AST warning. **12/13:** LCD/odometer illumination. **14:** Air bag warning. **15:** Catalytic converter warning. **16:** Parking brake indicator. **17:** Brake fluid warning. **18:** Brake pad wear warning. **19:** ABS warning. **20:** Seatbelt warning. **21:** System check control. **22:** Automatic transmission warning. **23:** Not enabled. **24:** Check-engine warning. **25:** Convertible anti-roll warning. **26:** Washer. **27:** Heater. **28:** Rear fog lamp. **29:** Front fog lamp.

bulb, part number 62 13 1 383 311). I recommend replacing all three of the large green ones, the two white/tan ones, and the two turn-signal lamps, as they are lit the longest and tend to burn out more often than the others.

When you are ready to reinstall the gauge cluster, make sure that the small retaining levers on the wire harnesses are

pointed upward. Don't force them, as they are fragile and can break.

So what can go wrong with instrument clusters? Well, there are a lot of strange problems that can be attributed to faulty clusters and/or faulty wiring. The cruise control computer acquires speed information from the cluster, so when

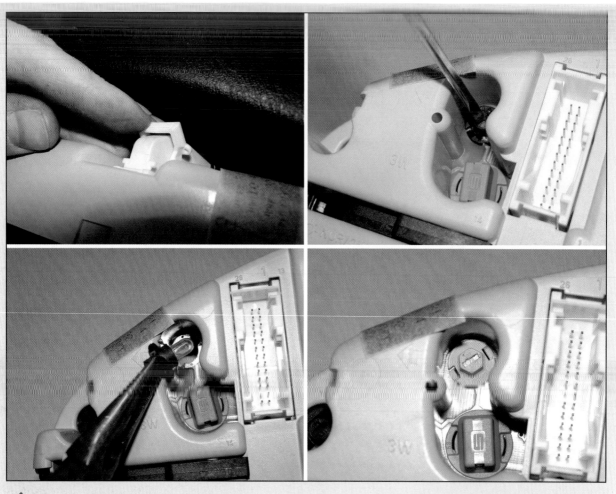

4 This photo shows the sequence for removing and replacing bulbs. In the upper left, you need to pull out the gauge cluster and disconnect the wire harness prior to removal. The upper right shows the process of removing one of the bulbs. Simply use a small screwdriver to turn the bulb counterclockwise. Use a pair of needle-nose pliers to pluck the bulb out of the assembly, as shown in the lower left. Finally, the new bulb is installed and twisted into place by the screwdriver, as shown by the photo on the lower right.

the cluster is having problems, the cruise control often shuts off. Radio volume on OEM radios is integrated with the gauge cluster output, so problems with the gauges often cause the radio volume to be lowered as well. Also adding to gauge problems may be a faulty door switch (see Project 67) or faulty wiring in the trunk (Project 82). Sometimes, when you install a short shift kit (Project 42), the installation may accidentally pinch some wires in the tunnel, so double-check your work if you have recently installed one of these kits.

Also problematic are the harness plugs on the back of the gauges. Previous owners may not have been as careful with them and may have broken the connector-securing brackets. It's possible for these to vibrate loose after many miles.

A neat feature of the gauge cluster is the self-test function. This is used by the BMW dealers to diagnose various problems with the cluster, and also to test the various instrument modules. To activate the diagnostic mode, press and hold the odometer button. Then turn the ignition switch to

the radio position, which is the first position on the ignition switch. The display should read "tESt 01." Once you see that message, let go of the odometer button. The instrument cluster will then cycle through some test cycles and display some numbers. Here is what they mean:

First display: BMW part number (six digits)
Second display: code number (five digits)—the internal coding plug
Third display: K number (four digits)
Fourth display: chassis number (five digits) part of your BMW's VIN
Fifth display: software version (three digits)
Sixth display: revision index (two digits)—hardware number

After all of the information is displayed, a set of tests of the analog gauges will be performed. You can also use this test/diagnostic mode to reset your odometer. See www.101Projects.com/BMW/95.htm for more details on this procedure.

Installing Colored Gauge Faces

Time: 4 hours

Tab: $50

Talent: ♟♟♟

Tools: Torx driver set

Applicable Years: E30/E36 (All)

Tinware: Colored gauge kit

Tip: Use a household fork to remove the needles

PERFORMANCE GAIN: Cooler-looking gauges by day and night

COMPLEMENTARY MODIFICATION: Replace burned-out bulbs in the cluster

One of the coolest upgrades you can do to your BMW is installing white gauge faces. One notch even higher on the cool scale is the addition of indiglo faces. These faces are manufactured out of a material that glows when electricity runs through it. You can alter the brightness and even change the color with the controller that comes with it. Installation is a bit above the beginner level, but the end result is definitely worth it.

Begin by removing the gauge cluster from your car (see Project 90). When the gauge cluster is removed, bring it over to your workbench. Photo 3 of Project 90 shows the five Torx screws that must be removed to separate the two cluster halves (shown by the yellow arrows). Pull the cluster apart after carefully peeling back the BMW certification sticker. With the cluster open, the gauge halves should resemble what is shown in Photo 1. Now separate the actual gauges from the clear plastic housing by rotating the white part of the locking mechanism about 180 degrees. You will probably need a pair of pliers or a small screwdriver for this task. Once these are rotated out of the way, the gauges should be able to be pulled from the housing.

With the gauge cluster removed (Photo 2), pull out the miles-per-gallon (mpg) gauge from the back of the cluster (inset of Photo 1). Each of the needles on all five gauges needs to be removed in order to perform the face swap. Take a small soft pencil or light marker and mark on each of the white faces where the fuel and temp needles lay prior to removing them. The mpg, rpm, and mph needles do not need to be marked because they rest against the stops when they're off. The needles themselves are easily removed by using two screwdrivers to wedge them off (Photo 2). A common household fork works as an excellent pry tool as well. Be aware that

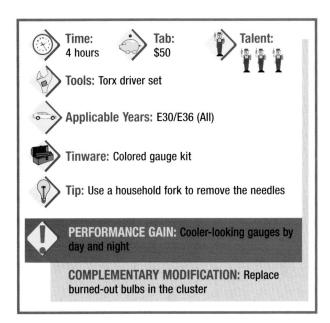

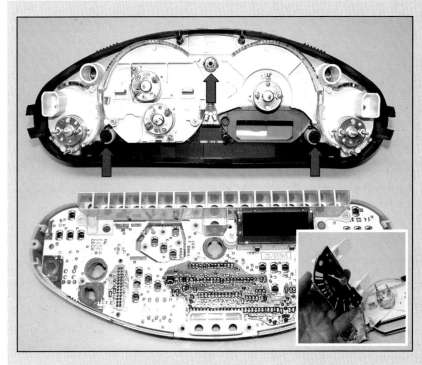

1 Shown here is the gauge cluster, after being removed and separated. The top part shows the actual gauges and actuators; the bottom is the circuit board that drives the gauges. The red arrows point to the three plastic fasteners that hold the gauge cluster to the clear plastic housing. To separate the gauge cluster from the housing, carefully rotate the white plastic holder on the fastener post so that it no longer holds the gauges in place. A close look at these fasteners will instantly reveal in clearer detail how they work. The mpg mini-gauge is snapped into place on the back of the cluster. Carefully pry back the tabs, and the mini-gauge should pop out (inset photo).

GAUGES AND ELECTRICAL SYSTEMS

2 Shown here is the original gauge cluster removed from its housing. The trickiest part of this process is the removal and reinstallation of the needles. Some may require more effort than others. Use two small screwdrivers on either side of the needle to apply pressure evenly, back and forth. The needle is mounted on a fragile metal post that can easily be bent, so be careful during this removal step. While you're installing the new faces, you may also be interested in adding chrome outer gauge rings (inset, lower left).

3 With the needles removed, place the gauge faces on top of the old faces. There should be some circular-cut double-sided sticky tape included with the kit. Carefully remove the tape and apply it to the old gauge faces. The new faces should lie down on top perfectly, but test-fit them first to make sure. Since your stock needles are white, you won't be able to see them with white gauge faces. I chose to use some Testors neon orange paint to apply some color to the needles. (As you can see from Photo 5, the results were fantastic!)

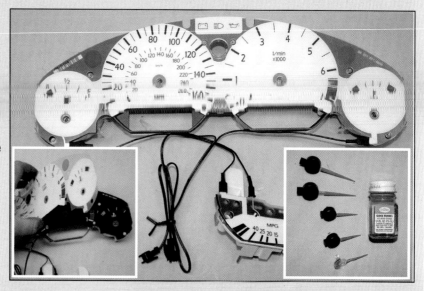

the needle may suddenly fly off, so make sure you know where it goes when it flies through the air (safety goggles are a good idea here, too). At this point, you will probably want to paint the needles, as shown in the inset of Photo 3.

With all the needles removed, install the gauge faces on top of the old ones. There should be some double-sided-tape templates included with the kit. Cut these, and place them on the back of the new gauge faces. It's important that the new face overlays do not start to unstick and back off of the original faces, as the new face overlay will then push up against the backs of the needles and make them stick. This is actually a common problem with the original black face overlays, which can also delaminate and make the needles stick.

Begin the needle replacement by pushing on the fuel and temp needles first. Line them up with the marks you made previously, and push them on gently, leaving a small gap between them and the new face overlay. For the mph, mpg, and rpm needles, place them on the gauges so they are just touching the resting stop. Do not wind them back so they are

4 Route the cable inside the cluster so it doesn't interfere with any of the gauges or the clear areas that pass light through. To route the cable outside of the cluster, I cut a small notch all the way on the side of the cluster with a pair of clippers (yellow). Place your notch far off to the side so that it won't interfere with the other light-blue half of the gauge cluster when reassembled.

preloaded on the resting stop—they should simply rest against the needle. Push the needle down, leaving a small gap between the needle and the overlay. When all of the needles have been installed, carefully swing them through their range of motion to make sure they won't get stuck on some high point of the gauge overlay.

Reinstall the mpg gauge, and insert the gauges back into the clear plastic housing. Route the cable as shown in Photo 4. Here's a tip: I clipped a small piece of plastic out of the housing so the wires could be routed out the bottom of the cluster. This spot should give you enough clearance to reinstall the cluster into the car. If you have problems with the wires getting pinched, you can route them through the back of the cluster by running them through an unused bulb holder. However, to accomplish this, you need to clip off and resolder the connectors to the harness.

Now close up the housing (replacing any burned out bulbs you may have along the way), and reinstall the cluster into the car.

The electrical wiring for indiglo gauges varies significantly according to which car you have. The main wire harness that powers the unit requires a 12-volt supply that is live when the ignition switch is turned on. You can usually tap into the dimmer switch wires or the headlamp switch; use a multimeter and some trial and error to figure out which wire is hot when the ignition is on. Or, if you know which wire powers the radio circuit, you can tap into that as well. The indiglo gauges have an adjuster that can be placed on the dashboard or just behind it. Most people adjust their gauges once or twice and never mess with it again.

5 Shown here is the finished product. The top shows how the gauges look in daylight. White backgrounds with the orange needles really stand out a lot more than the standard black-and-white of the stock gauges. The bottom photos show the gauges at night. Since the actual gauge material lights up, the illumination is even and very clear. On this set of indiglo gauge faces, you could adjust the brightness level and also change the color of the illuminated faces from blue to green. After driving with these for one day, you'll think all other gauge clusters are boring!

PROJECT 92
BMW Alarm Systems

http://www.101projects.com/BMW/92.htm

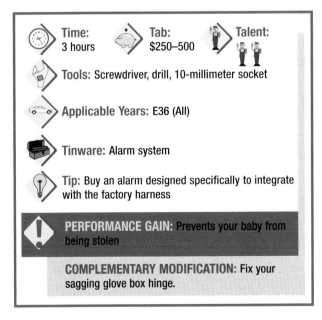

Time: 3 hours

Tab: $250–500

Talent: 👤👤

Tools: Screwdriver, drill, 10-millimeter socket

Applicable Years: E36 (All)

Tinware: Alarm system

Tip: Buy an alarm designed specifically to integrate with the factory harness

! PERFORMANCE GAIN: Prevents your baby from being stolen

COMPLEMENTARY MODIFICATION: Fix your sagging glove box hinge.

Nothing is worse than having your BMW stolen or messed with. Although many BMWs came from the factory with a keyless alarm system, many did not. The good news is you can easily install either a factory alarm unit or an aftermarket one in your car in a short amount of time. BMW designed the car to accept an alarm and pre-wired all the connections for the alarm to communicate with the rest of the car's systems. Installation is a snap—basically, plug in the unit and it will integrate automatically with the ignition cutoff, the doors, the trunk, and the windows. Good aftermarket alarm units, such as those manufactured by Stellar, are an excellent choice in place of the factory unit. The Stellar units start at about $250 and add a host of additional features like a microwave proximity sensor, integrated window control, shock sensitivity, and/or remote starting. The unit I chose for my 325ic convertible was the basic unit with window control and a microwave sensor. The microwave sensor is very important for convertibles, as it sounds the alarm if anyone goes near the interior of your car with top down.

243

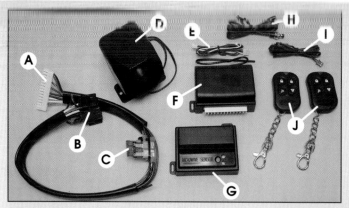

1 This photo shows the complete alarm kit for a 325ic, manufactured by Stellar alarms. This kit is ideal for installation into your BMW because it tightly integrates with the BMW factory harness and all of the internal controls. Installation consists of basically just plugging it in. **A:** Connector that plugs into the Stellar alarm unit. **B:** Connector that plugs into the BMW factory alarm harness. **C:** Two fuses that protect the factory wiring and the alarm unit. **D:** Siren. **E:** Wire harness for microwave unit. **F:** Stellar alarm unit. **G:** Microwave proximity sensor. **H:** Valet button/configuration switch. **I:** Status LED. **J:** Two key chain alarm controllers.

2 Shown here is the glove box on an E36 (convertible). Removal is a snap—simply remove the six screws indicated by the yellow arrows. The lower screws can be a bit tough to remove using a normal or even a stubby screwdriver. I employed a right-angle driver for this process (right inset). With the screws removed, pop out the glove box lamp (left inset). With the lamp removed, you should be able to remove the 10-millimeter bolt that attaches the glove box to the frame of the car (green arrow).

The installation procedure is very easy. Simply remove the glove box from your car (see Photo 2). Then locate the factory alarm plug (see Photo 3). Plug in the unit and route it along the side of the electronics compartment. At this point, you can plug in all of the components and test to see if the system is working. If everything tests okay, pop out the center onboard computer (OBC), the unit that displays the time, date, etc. It simply pops out if you place a credit card in between the seam on the upper part of the unit. With the OBC out of the way, you can pull up on the lower console piece that contains the cigarette lighter. It should also pop right out. Drill a small hole for the alarm LED indicator, and mount the microwave sensor underneath as well.

The microwave sensor will have at least two sensor adjustments on the unit that you may need to play with for quite a while to get the sensitivity just right. The ideal location for the microwave sensor is in the center of the car, as long as it's not obstructed by metal. Microwaves will go through fabric, plastic, wood, and glass, but they won't travel through metal. Start the adjustment process by putting the top and windows down. Start walking toward the car. If the alarm goes off before you get to the car, then you need to reduce the sensitivity. It will take many tries before you get the settings just right so that if someone waves their hand inside your convertible, the alarm will activate. The microwave sensor can also be used on non-

convertible cars, but since they are locked most of the time, it is usually not necessary.

Route all the wires for the LED and the microwave sensor down the side of the center console and into the glove box. Use some nylon zip ties to constrain the wires to the frame of the car. Drill a small hole in the bottom of the kick panel, and install the valet button; you need to be able to press this button while turning the ignition on in the car.

Installation of the siren is also very easy. If you're not using a factory siren, then simply tap into the two existing siren wires with some electrical wiretaps. Mount the siren in the engine bay, toward the front right side of the car (see Photo 5).

Synchronizing remotes with an existing factory system

More often than you might think, pre-owned BMWs are sold without the factory remotes that control the alarm system. Since the BMW factory alarm doesn't arm itself automatically, you don't need one of the remotes to use the car on a daily basis. Many times a car is sold and the new owner doesn't even know that there's a factory alarm system installed. If you pop open your glove box and discover a factory unit plugged into the wire harness, that's excellent news—all you need now is a remote control and some time to reprogram it. Remote controls can be found for about $100 or so at the dealer, or

3 Shown here is the electrical "spaghetti" that controls a lot of the car's functions. In this photo, the Stellar alarm unit is shown installed on the right side of the compartment (blue arrow). The wire harness from the alarm unit is routed across the top of the compartment (green arrow). The 12-pin BMW alarm connector is very difficult to see, as it's hidden in the back of the compartment (purple arrow).

4 After you pull out the onboard computer (OBC), you should be able to pull upward on the lower console to gain access for the installation of the LED alarm indicator (green arrow). Also shown here is the glass breakage (GB) sensor, which is part of the factory alarm system, indicated by the yellow arrow.

5 This photo shows the BMW factory alarm siren installed in the front right corner of the engine compartment (blue arrow). The yellow arrow shows the wire harness—if using an aftermarket alarm system, you may have to tap into this harness. The red arrow shows the factory siren mounting bracket.

6 Shown here is the BMW factory keyless alarm unit installed on cars up through August 1995. This controller works with the three-button remote shown in the left inset photo. The alarm controller is programmed to work with a specific remote by synchronizing the small chip in the remote to the alarm unit. Open up the alarm remote, and carefully remove the small chip (red arrow, lower right inset). Then pull out the alarm unit from your car, leaving the main wire harness attached. Insert the chip from the remote into the connector in the unit (blue arrow). Then turn on the ignition, and press the reset button for at least 10 seconds (green arrow). The red alarm indicator on your center console should flash, indicating that the codes have been read and accepted. Turn off the ignition, reinstall the chip in your remote, and test it—it should work! The later-style two-button remote used from September 1995 (upper right inset) uses a different synchronization method described in the main text.

you can typically pick up a used remote for much less at swap meets or Internet auction sites.

On the E36 models (and many other BMW models), the factory installed two different alarm types. The early type is designated by the three-button rectangular remote and was installed in cars up to August 1995. Starting in September of that year, BMW began installing an updated system distinguished by a two-button, round remote control. Both of these systems can be programmed to be used with new or replacement remote controls. The three-button remote reprogramming involves swapping chips into your factory control unit; see Photo 6 for the exact procedure.

The two-button remote can be reprogrammed without having to take apart the glove box. Simply perform the following procedure:

Prepare the car
1. Close all the doors, the trunk, and front hood.
2. The alarm must be placed into disarm mode (not armed and not activated). If this reprogramming procedure doesn't work after attempting it a few times, you may have to pull out the glove box and disconnect the harness to the alarm unit (or pull the fuse) to reset it and put it into disarm mode.
3. Remove the key from the ignition.

Start code-learning mode
4. Open the rear trunk, and leave it raised and open.
5. Open the driver's door and sit down in the driver's seat.
6. While sitting in the driver's seat, close the driver's door.
7. Turn the ignition switch on, then off, five times. Do not

start the engine. Simply turn the switch to the on position each time so all the dash warning lamps illuminate. Important: All five cycles of the ignition switch must be performed within 10 seconds.

The entire sequence of steps (one through seven) must be performed within 45 seconds. When the steps are performed properly, the red alarm LED will illuminate continuously, and the alarm siren will sound a single chirp. This indicates that the code-learning mode has been started. Do **not** start the engine at this time.

Register remote ID codes
8. While remaining in the driver's seat, open the driver's door.
9. Close the driver's door.
10. Press and release any button on the remote control unit you wish to register with the alarm unit. The alarm LED indicator will turn off momentarily to indicate that the ID code has been registered with the system.
11. For additional remotes (up to a total of four), repeat steps 8 through 10.
Exit the code-learning mode
12. Open the driver's door, and get out of the car, but leave the door open.
13. Close the rear trunk.
14. Close the driver's door. The alarm status LED will turn off, and the siren will sound a chirp twice.
15. The registration process should be complete and you should be able to use all the remotes that you registered with the system.

PROJECT 93
Installing an HID Lighting System
http://www.101projects.com/BMW/93.htm

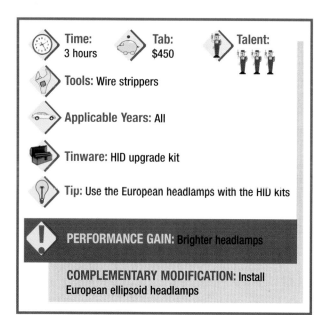

Time: 3 hours

Tab: $450

Talent: ♟♟♟

Tools: Wire strippers

Applicable Years: All

Tinware: HID upgrade kit

Tip: Use the European headlamps with the HID kits

PERFORMANCE GAIN: Brighter headlamps

COMPLEMENTARY MODIFICATION: Install European ellipsoid headlamps

One of the more exciting upgrades you can perform on your BMW is installing and upgrading your lamps to a high-intensity discharge (HID) system. This type of lighting system uses xenon bulbs, or, under the Bosch brand name, Litronic bulbs. The lamps use electric current that runs through a xenon gas mixture to create light, not unlike the operation of an ordinary fluorescent light bulb. In order to get the lamps working, however, the gas mixture must be subjected to an initial voltage of about 28,000 volts. Two small ballast units create this high voltage when starting the lamps and then taper it down to about 40 volts to keep the light on. The Hella units used in this particular project have a built-in safety circuit to prevent the 28,000 volts from being discharged if there are any disruptions or anomalies in the circuit.

Replacement bulbs tend to be very expensive, at about $100 each. I expect the cost to decrease, though, as more and more cars come equipped with this technology as stock equipment. The good news is that, unlike traditional halogen bulbs, the HID bulbs do not often burn out since they have

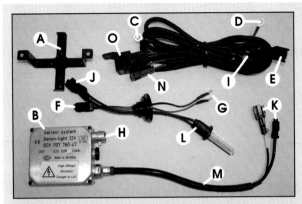

1 Shown here is a typical HID conversion kit for European ellipsoid headlamps. **A:** Bracket for mounting the ballast. **B:** Hella-manufactured ballast unit. **C:** Battery ground connection. **D:** Battery positive lead connection. **E/F:** H4 connector (taps into the car's original lamp harness and reroutes power to the relay). **G:** Plugs that tap into the original lamp connector. **H/I:** Plug to provide power to the ballast unit. **J/K:** High-voltage wires that supply the bulb. **L:** HID bulb. **M:** High-voltage wire harness. **N:** Inline fuse. **O:** Relay.

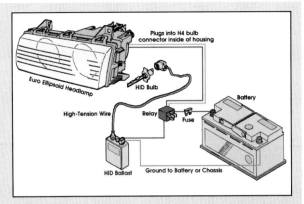

2 Most of the HID kits I have seen include hard-to-read wiring diagrams, so I created this easy-to-follow schematic. The voltage from the battery supplies the HID ballast unit, and its on/off function is controlled by the relay integrated into the harness. This connection is also protected by an inline fuse. The relay that triggers power flow to the ballast is powered by the voltage from the original H4 plug located inside the headlamp housing. Because of this wiring arrangement, the relay is powered on (and turns on the HID system) when voltage is applied to the plug where the old H4 bulb was located.

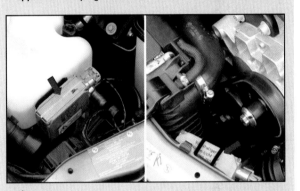

3 Shown here are two potential mounting places for the HID ballast units. Although not ideal, attaching it with Velcro to the washer bottle does allow easy access. I would follow up with long zip ties to secure the unit to the bottle. The right-hand-side ballast is attached underneath the front support bar with zip ties and Velcro.

no internal mechanical components and actually run very cool (like a normal fluorescent light bulb).

The lamp kits typically use 35-watt bulbs, which means that they draw about 2 to 3 amps of current after the initial startup. It's not uncommon for the ballast units to draw about 15 amps for less than a second as they are starting up the bulbs. The actual startup phase is typically less than a second—barely a noticeable difference from the stock configuration. With a halogen lamp system, a large portion of the energy spent in the system goes toward excess heat given off by the bulb. The HID systems are much more efficient. For example, a typical HID 35-watt bulb is about three times as bright as a 100-watt halogen bulb.

Thankfully, the installation is not difficult. It simply requires that you mount the ballast, integrate the bulbs into your housing, and wire up the system. HID systems only work well with the European ellipsoid headlamp housings (see Project 94). As of yet, I have never seen an HID kit installed in stock U.S.-spec headlamps. I'm sure it's possible, but the European headlamps make the task much simpler and will also disperse the light from the bulb in the proper fashion.

The European headlamps have large plastic covers on the rear that need to be slightly modified. Most of the HID kits available have a wire harness that has a large grommet on it. You need to take a small holesaw or Dremel tool and cut a hole in the rear of your plastic housing for the grommet to fit. Two wires are connected to the HID bulb; the other two tap into the connections for the old halogen bulb and power the relay located in the wire harness.

The HID system uses electrical current drawn off the battery and is controlled by a relay. The harness included with the HID kit powers the relay with the current that formerly powered the original bulb. (See Photo 2 for a schematic of the system for further details.)

Mounting of the ballast can be a bit tricky. Just find a safe, secure spot near your headlamps and use the double-sided sticky tape or mounting brackets included with the HID kits (see Photo 3). You can also install an HID kit for your low beams, high beams, and even fog lamps.

When you're finished with the installation, be sure to align your headlamps so that the beams are not pointing into oncoming traffic. In most states, the use of nonfactory HID kits is designated for off-road use only. Keep in mind that if you don't have a street-legal headlamp system, you may invite tickets from law enforcement.

Euro Ellipsoid/Angel Eyes Installation

Time: 3 hours

Tab: $300

Talent: ★★★

Tools: 8-millimeter socket with long extension, soldering iron, wire strippers

Applicable Years: All

Tinware: Euro ellipsoid headlamps and wiring kit

Tip: Order a set with angel eyes for that BMW 5 Series look

PERFORMANCE GAIN: Brighter lighting, sporty look

COMPLEMENTARY MODIFICATION: HID lamp kit installation

1 Shown here is a European ellipsoid headlamp kit manufactured by Inpro. The headlamps in this kit contain the standard European high-beam/low beam lenses with the addition of the angel eye rings on the outside. In order to make this kit plug into the U.S.-spec cars, you will need a harness connector, four small harness pins, four standard wire taps, and a rubber boot.

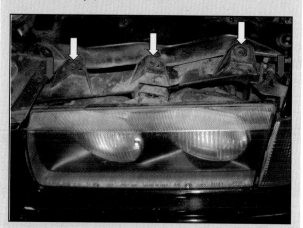

2 Removal of the headlamp is an easy job. Depending on which year car you have, you may have to remove the front plastic piece that covers the radiator (see Photo 1 of Project 34). Unplug the two harness connectors from the back of the lamps, and remove the side marker lens (see Project 71). Then remove the five screws that attach the lamp to the chassis. The ones on top (yellow arrows) have small plastic adjusters that may spin as you try to remove the headlamp—use a 19-millimeter wrench to secure them in place. The two screws at the bottom of the assembly will need a ratchet and an extension to remove (red arrows point toward them; see also Photo 3). With the screws removed, you should be able to pull the headlamp out.

GAUGES AND ELECTRICAL SYSTEMS

One of the most popular and sporty upgrades for both the E30 and E36 cars is installing the European ellipsoid headlamps. The U.S.-spec headlamps are a sealed-beam unit that is inferior to the European version. The low beams on the European lamps have an ellipsoid lens that focuses the beam of light in a more direct pattern and also uses brighter bulbs. The difference between the U.S.- and Euro-spec headlamps can be dramatic, particularly for people who drive at night on very dark roads. The Euro headlamp upgrade is popular with both the E36 and E30 cars, although this particular project will specifically cover the E36 install. (The E30 installation is similar in scope.)

Although these lamps are supposed to be used for off-road use only, there are thousands of people who drive with them on the road every day. Back in the early part of this century, the U.S. government decided sealed-beam headlamps should be required on cars and trucks. This was to prevent moisture from entering into the headlamp and corroding the reflector, creating a dim lamp. The regulation has stuck until this day; thus, most of the cars sold in the United States have different headlamp systems than their European counterparts. Many people incorrectly think that the law limits the wattage of the lamp, but it really dictates the sealed-beam enclosure. On the flip side, it's also true that European headlamps do corrode and become dim much faster than the U.S.-spec lamps.

In addition to the installation of the Euro-spec headlamps, many BMW owners use the opportunity to add a unit that has built-in angel eyes. Sometimes also called "demon daylight eyes," these are circular light rings that surround the

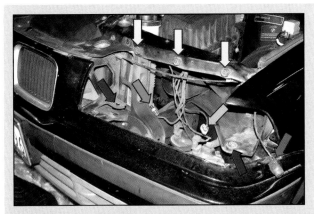

3 It's a somewhat scary sight with the headlamp removed. Shown here are the three headlamp adjusters from the previous photo (yellow arrows). Note the spot where the lower two screws mount to the chassis (red arrows). The high-beam harness is indicated by the green arrow; the low-beam is shown by the orange arrow. The purple arrow points to the side-marker lamp harness.

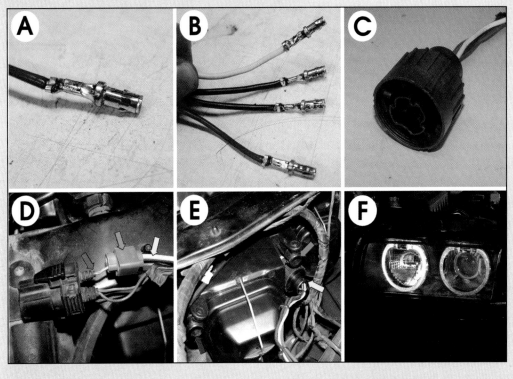

4 Here's a step-by-step photo array of the harness assembly. **A:** Begin by stripping the wire and crimping it onto the connector. For added security, solder the connection in place with a soldering iron. **B:** Crimp and solder all four wires, using 16-gauge wire (and different colors) for each one. Create the left and right harness at the same time. **C:** Insert the connector into the back of the headlamp to determine which pin fits where. Wire the pins according to the instructions included in the wiring table in the main text. **D:** Shown here is the wiretap (blue arrow) installed on the parking lamp wire harness. The purple arrow points to the parking lamp wire, which is on when you first pull the headlamp switch. The yellow wire connects to the angel eye bulbs in the new headlamp assembly. **E:** The main wire harness is shown by the yellow arrow. Don't forget to slide on the protective rubber boot before you start tapping into your chassis harness. The red and green arrows show the adjuster screws for the low and high beams. **F:** The finished product is very cool. The angel eyes look just like the factory ones on the late BMW E39 5 Series cars.

lamp and are hooked into the parking lamp circuit. They give off a unique glow and give the car a distinct, aggressive look. BMW first used these light rings on the late-model E39 5 Series cars. You used to have to purchase a separate kit with the rings and install them in the European headlamps, but now it's very easy to purchase the whole assembly with them pre-installed.

Installing Euro-spec headlamps is really very easy—all you need to do is swap in the new headlamps and tap into the wiring. The European headlamps use a different harness than the U.S.-spec lamps, so you need to order a few harness components in order to install the headlamps. Table 1 and Photo 1 both show the parts that you need to install the E36 Euro-spec headlamps in a U.S.-spec car.

Assemble the wire harness according to Photo 4 and Table 2. Use simple wiretaps (available at almost all hardware stores) to connect the new harness to your existing wire harness. The new lamps are simply bolted into the same place as the U.S.-spec lamps and are identical in size and shape. Test your new units before you reinstall the screws and fasteners.

With the new headlamps installed, you will have to adjust the beams to light the road properly. There are two adjusters on the back of each assembly that adjust horizontal and vertical leveling of the lamp (see part E of Photo 4). The adjuster in the middle accounts for vertical height of the beams; the adjuster on the edge of the lamps controls the horizontal positioning. Move these adjusters carefully, as they are made of plastic and can break if you overtighten them.

Take your car to a parking lot and park it about 15 feet from a wall. Aim the headlamps at the wall. For left-hand-drive cars, the left lamp should be aimed slightly off to the right and down a bit from level to reduce the glare that falls into oncoming traffic. The right-side beam should be pointed straight ahead. Use both the adjusters on the headlamps themselves and the adjusters that the mounting screws feed into (yellow arrow, Photo 2). These can be turned in and out to change the level of the headlamps. Fine-tuning of the beam can be accomplished using the adjusters on the headlamps themselves.

Table 1

Quantity	Description	Part number
2	Euro lamp connector	61-13-1-392-222
2	Connector boot	12-52-1-707-302
8	Connector pins	61-13-1-376-202
8	Wire taps	hardware store

Table 2

My harness color	Connector position	Controls lamps	Chassis harness color, left side	Chassis harness color, right side
Black	Top	Ground	Brown	Brown
Yellow	Right	Parking lamps	Grey/Purple	Grey/Yellow
Blue	Bottom	Low beams	Yellow/Green	Yellow/Blue
Red	Left	High beams	White/Green	White/Blue

PROJECT 95
Installing a CD Changer

http://www.101projects.com/BMW/95.htm

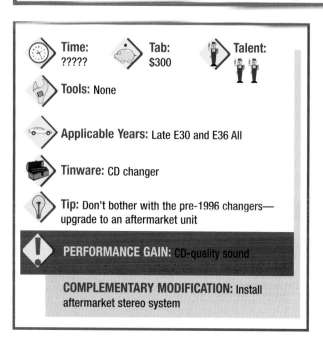

Time: ?????

Tab: $300

Talent:

Tools: None

Applicable Years: Late E30 and E36 All

Tinware: CD changer

Tip: Don't bother with the pre-1996 changers—upgrade to an aftermarket unit

PERFORMANCE GAIN: CD-quality sound

COMPLEMENTARY MODIFICATION: Install aftermarket stereo system

When I bought one of my first E36 BMWs, I noticed it didn't come with a CD changer installed. Knowing that all E36s are pre-wired from the factory for easy installation, I soon set out to find a unit that would work with my car and operate reliably. This proved to be a much more difficult task than I ever imagined. I gathered the information in this project from a host of confusing Internet sources. I believe it to be mostly accurate; however, some information directly contradicts other sources. At the same time, I have attempted to compile the latest information available from original BMW part numbers and documentation. To the best of my knowledge, the information here

is accurate, but be forewarned—the BMW CD-changer saga is very confusing.

In order to figure out what type of CD changer will work with your stock stereo, you will need to find out which stereo head unit you have. With the radio turned on, press down the "PROG" button along with the "MODE" or "Tuner" (-) button. The radio will then print out on its display the manufacturer name, and what version of the radio it is. The two original manufacturers of BMW radio head units were Pioneer and Alpine, so it will be one or the other. The number following the manufacturer typically corresponds to the model year of the car that the radio was made for.

For example, the 1995 radio might say "ALPINE 5" when the buttons are pressed. (There are a few exceptions to this rule. For example, the 318 from 1992 through 1996 all appear to have used the PIO2 head unit.)

The 1989–1991 cars were fitted with a radio head unit that used a 13-pin plug. The Pioneer head units (ke-83zbm) could control the aftermarket Pioneer CD changer, CDX-M30, without the use of an adapter cable. The Alpine radio head units (CM5908) could control the Alpine six-disc or 12-disc changers (Alpine part number TR-1600 and TR 1008). Attempting to use the Pioneer changer with an Alpine unit (or vice versa), however, can result in damage to the units. Although the plugs on these units are identical, they do not use the same interface. Attempting to plug them together may result in short circuits and blown fuses.

The 1991–1994 radios were outfitted with a 14-pin round data cable that is terminated in the rear trunk. The aftermarket Pioneer unit CDX-M30 can be installed in these vehicles with the addition of the BMWPIO/M adapter cable. With the adapter cable, these units can control any of

Radio model	Manufacturer	Display name	Year/Application	CD changer	Adapter
CM5908 (Infrared slot-type unit)	Alpine		1989–1993 E30	Alpine BMW OEM only (13-pin units)	
KE83zbm	Pioneer	KE83zbm	1989–1993 E30	CDX-M30 (or M Series)	None required
CM5901	Alpine	Alpine Alpine 2 Alpine 3	1991 to early 1994 (all)	Alpine BMW OEM or Pioneer BMW OEM or CDX-M30	BMWPIO for M-series
KE91zbm	Pioneer	PIO PIO1	1991 to early 1994 (all)	Alpine BMW OEM or Pioneer BMW OEM or CDX-M30	BMWPIO for M-series
KE91zbm v4	Pioneer	PIONEER 4	Late 1994 to 1995 E36	Factory OEM Only (Alpine or Pioneer CDX-M91ZBM)	
CM5903L	Alpine	Alpine 4 Alpine 5	Late 1994 to 1995 E36	Factory OEM Only (Alpine or Pioneer CDX-M91ZBM)	
KE93zbm	Pioneer	PIO2 PIO3 PIO4	Late 1994 to 1995 E36	Factory OEM Only (Alpine or Pioneer CDX-M91ZBM)	

the Alpine changers within this era and also the factory and aftermarket Pioneer units.

In late 1994, the price of the BMW factory Pioneer changer unit was about $700 (Pioneer model CDX-M91ZBM), whereas the aftermarket units were about half that price (Pioneer model CDX-M30). It was much cheaper to forgo the factory unit and instead install the same Pioneer unit (with an BMWPIO/M adapter cable), than it was to purchase the option from the BMW dealer. So BMW changed the electronics interface in 1994/1995 so that the only changers that would work with the head unit were available exclusively from

the dealer. As a result, if you have an "ALPINE 5" or a "PIONEER 4" head unit, it won't work with the aftermarket Pioneer CD changers. Above is a summary of the radios and changers available from 1989–1995.

In 1996, BMW again changed the interface used to control the CD changers. This later-style interface is called "IBUS," whereas the earlier interface was known as "MBUS." The IBUS and MBUS cars have different plugs and wires for the CD changers. The IBUS system is designed to connect the CD changer, the navigation system, MP3 players, etc. It's fully expandable, and there's even a group of loyal followers on

1 This photo shows a BMW OEM Alpine CD changer installed in a 1995 325ic. This convertible has the CD changer installed in a small compartment located in the front part of the rear trunk. A handle on the outside of the compartment allows you to lift it open and access the CD player. In the photo inset is a Pioneer CDX-M30 CD changer. Although this particular unit is an aftermarket unit, it looks nearly identical to the OEM unit.

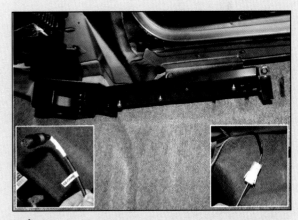

2 This photo shows the mounting brackets installed for the Alpine CD changer on a 1993 325is. The lower left inset photos show the pre-wired 14-pin round connector, typically located in the taillight housing. The lower right inset photo shows the power connector that attaches to the rear of the Alpine CD changer and is typically located in the right rear quarter panel, underneath the carpet.

3 In order to determine which radio head unit you have installed in your BMW, press the "MODE" or "Tuner" (-) button and the "PROG" button at the same time. The manufacturer and radio year code will be displayed, allowing you to determine which CD changer will work with your radio.

Yahoo.com that have hacked the IBUS and written software so commands could be read by a laptop computer! In addition, there are interface adapter cables available that will convert IBUS, allowing you to install and use inexpensive and versatile aftermarket changers and MP3 players.

When referring to the aftermarket Pioneer CD changers, it is also important to note that any "M" series changer will work. The Pioneer CDX-M30 is the last of the M series, and probably the most reliable unit available.

There was also a Pioneer 12-disc unit that could be recognized and controlled by the early factory head units. You could cycle through each of the 12 discs by holding down each of the six buttons on the factory unit (holding down button number one loaded up disc seven). This aftermarket unit was never officially offered through BMW, but if you have a 1992 or 1993 Pioneer radio head unit, it should be compatible.

It's important to note that BMW OEM Alpine CD changers all used an interface that was specific to BMW cars. None of the aftermarket Alpine units worked with BMW factory radios.

Where is the pre-wired cable for the CD changer located? It seems the cable ends have been left all over the place, apparently depending upon the mood of the assembler in Germany at the time. They may be located under the back seat, near the rear speakers in the trunk, or all the way back in the taillight area. The power cable is a separate connector and is usually located underneath the carpet, near the right rear of the trunk area. Hunt around in this area—it will be located somewhere within the right rear quarter panel. The end is terminated with a three-pronged white plastic connector that should have only a red and brown wire attached. Some early production E36 sedans (four-door model) did not have the factory CD changer wiring preinstalled. In this case, the only way to get the CD changers to work properly would be to purchase the wire harness and install it yourself (not easy and not cheap, either).

In those days, the CD changers were mounted on the upper right side of the trunk, just above the battery. There should be studs there that accept the factory mounting brackets. The CD changer for the E36 convertibles was mounted in the forward right part of the trunk, in a compartment that has a handle and rocks forward when opened.

Depending upon which changer you have, and which year your car is, there appears to be a large assortment of brackets available. It's best to try to pick up the brackets along with the changer if you purchase a used one.

If you install your CD changer according to these guidelines and the head unit is not recognizing the changer, you may want to check the connections on the back of the head unit. Although the cars were supposed to be pre-wired from the factory, many times the CD changer data cable was not securely fastened to the rear of the radio head unit. Remove the head unit (see Project 88), and check the connections.

If you can find one of the original OEM-style units that works with the factory radio head units, that's only half the battle. I've spoken with many people, including some at stereo repair shops, who have had very negative experiences with some of the OEM units, in particular those manufactured by Alpine. For the pre-1996 cars, the newest of these units are more than 10 years old and often show their age. They break easily and are generally deemed unreliable. I've had three go bad in my cars over the years. Ailments range from refusing to give up the six-disc CD carrier to just plain refusing to acknowledge that there's any power applied to the unit. From informal surveys, I have found the older Alpine units are not as reliable as the Pioneer units, many of which are still in operation today.

My recommendations? If you have a 1996 or later BMW, there's good news for you. The CD changers on the market for these cars are plentiful, and they are pretty reliable as well. New units are very easy to find that will simply plug in to the harness, will read burned discs, and will work flawlessly with the stock factory radio head unit (at a cost of about $250 or so). In addition, units from almost all other cars in the 1996–2004 BMW line will be interchangeable (3/5/7 Series, X5, Mini Cooper, etc.), which means a robust market exists for changers that were abandoned when owners upgraded their stereo systems.

The only exceptions to this rule are the cars with in-dash navigation systems (NAV) and the 1996 318ti. In addition, there are new products out now from a company called Blitzsafe that plug directly into MP3 players such as the Apple iPod and allow you to tap the iPod directly into the head unit, as if it's a CD changer.

So what about the 1995 and earlier cars? Interestingly enough, at the time of this writing, the original Alpine and Pioneer CD changer kits appear to still be available from BMW (part number 82-11-1-468-014 and part number 82-11-1-467-700), although their price runs around $500 and $750, respectively. However, after messing around with CD players and changers in all my BMWs, I can honestly recommend that you ditch the OEM equipment and upgrade to a newer stereo and CD changer. A knowledgeable stereo storeowner who worked on these BMW systems all the time gave me this advice when I first started kicking around with trying to install the factory CD changers. I can say now that, after dealing with the older CD players breaking, and dealing with the problems installing and matching up the OEM units, I would take his advice and start over with the newest and best technology.

Miscellaneous

This section contains an assortment of projects that didn't quite fit into any of the other categories. Take a look at Project 96 for my pick of the most interesting and unique additions BMW owners have made to their cars. An eclectic mix of car bras, bolt removal, wheel selection, and car care are also detailed in this section. Read on and enjoy!

As principle photographer and owner of the Internet-based BMW parts company PelicanParts.com, I've had the opportunity to photograph a lot of different modifications people have done to their BMWs over the years. While not all of them improve the looks of the car in my own opinion, it can certainly be said that BMW owners like to modify their cars more than most people.

Whether it's the addition of GTR flares and body panels, or the installation of carbon-fiber panels—if you can think of it, it's likely that some passionate BMW owner has spent hundreds of hours and thousands of dollars to do it. This gallery of images is designed to give you some ideas for your own BMW projects.

 Time: Infinite   **Tab:** $1–10,000   **Talent:**

 Tools: Unlimited

 Applicable Years: All

 Tinware: Just about everything in the catalog

 Tip: Keep an eye out at local swap meets, magazines, and shows for cool additions that can add value to your BMW

! **PERFORMANCE GAIN:** The sky is the limit

COMPLEMENTARY MODIFICATION: Wash your car

1 This photo shows the front of a modified E36 M3. Among the styling touches are clear corner lenses, a lower skirt on the M3 spoiler, a blacked-out chrome grille, European headlamps with angel eyes, and eyelids above the lenses. When you see this baby coming, you can't help but think it's badass.

2 A sporty and popular addition to your car may be the BMW Motorsport front and rear decals. These are available in many different colors, and give your car the sporty look—just like the BMW Motorsport E36 M3 lightweight. The front and rear decal set can be found in original tricolor (blue-purple-red) and also a handful of solid colors (white, black, silver) for use on nonwhite cars.

3 Here are two clever paint jobs on two four-cylinder M3s, reflecting the traditional BMW Motorsport colors.

4 These days, nothing says cool like carbon fiber. This car has an entire hood manufactured out of it, complete with matching Roundel emblem (see Photo 1 of Project 77). Also shown here are the E36 eyelids that cover the top part of the headlamp for that sleepy, sporty, low-down look.

6 It's common to put on a new exhaust for your BMW. Even more common are chrome exhaust tips that can spruce up the exterior of your car. These have the small head of a cat actually cut into the pipes themselves.

8 This is one of the most unusual cars I've seen in a long time. It's an E46 pseudo-GTR clone with Lamborghini-style doors. Definitely very bling and very unusual. The owner of this car apparently decided that money was no object in creating one of the most unique BMWs on the road today.

5 Simple stylish touches can accent your interior. Shown here is an AC Schnitzer emergency brake handle—a vast visual improvement over the stock unit.

7 Engine compartments have so much potential for detailing, and this one does not disappoint. Check out how this E30 M3's valve covers and intake air box have been painted in the traditional BMW Motorsport color scheme. A lot of detail went into making this look just perfect, so kudos to the owner!

9 Pedal upgrades are another common accessory for BMW owners. A word of caution: Make sure you get a set that isn't slippery. These pedals may be great looking, but they're a little too

slippery for my tastes—particularly if I'm wearing leather-soled shoes. I recommend sets that have integrated anti-slip rubber inserts in them.

Check out my choice for "Best in Show" from the 2003 BimmerFest—this 1995 E36 M3 club racer built by Evosport. It has a normally aspirated S54 race-spec engine with an AEM Race EMS engine management system. But it also has a Brembo race-spec system with an RRT brake cooling kit, Advance Design custom-valved DA true coil-overs, H&R race springs, Ground Control adjustable camber plates, TC Kline adjustable rear lower control arms, and RRT front control arms and bushings. The interior sports a Sparco seat, harness, steering wheel, and fire system. The body is mostly carbon fiber by MA Shaw. The wheels are CCW competition wheels running 18x10 in the front and 18x12 in the rear, equipped with Dunlap racing slicks (280/650-18 in the front and 315/680-18 in the rear). Sweet!

11 More carbon fiber—this one with a unique twist. The left and right side of the hood have been painted, along with the front grille, to match the rest of the car. The wheels on this particular car are the somewhat-uncommon M3 Motorsport wheels from 1995.

12 When you see one of these installed in a car, you know the driver means business. The small blue box that has replaced the gauges is a System 2 compact dashboard display. When used in conjunction with the Pi Club Expert software, the system becomes a data logger perfect for club racing events. The dash displays speed and user-definable alarms for rpm, two temperatures (typically oil and water), two pressures (typically oil and fuel), and two user channels. The floor pedals, gear shift knob, and steering wheel with quick-release hub are part of a matching set from Sparco.

Here's one of the most popular upgrades these days, the European ellipsoid headlamps with built-in angel eye rings. **13** These lamps, sometimes called "daylight demon eyes," are modeled after the BMW factory angel eye lamps used on the late-model BMW E39 5 Series models. See Project 94 for installation instructions.

14 This car is one of my favorites. One look at it and you can tell it definitely means business. The dominant features on this car are the large GTR-style flares on the front and rear. If you look closely, both the rear quarter panels, the skirts, and the doors themselves need to be highly modified to fit the huge rear Kinesis wheels. The front flares (inset) are a bit easier to install. The aluminum racing-style gas cap is a clever addition to a car that needs no excuses on the road.

15 To many people, there's no such thing as too much carbon fiber. Originally created as a next-generation high-strength fiberglass replacement, carbon fiber has emerged as a cool, though expensive, way to decorate your car. Nearly all of the carbon fiber I've seen installed is only for show, but it certainly looks great when used in the engine compartment.

16 Here's a highly modified E30 M3. The owners of these cars usually take one of two paths. Either the cars are bone stock or completely decked out with the latest bling. This particular E30 M3 has an aftermarket spoiler, a carbon-fiber hood, blacked-out grille, matching blue-tint driving lamps, European ellipsoid lenses, and, if you look closely, you'll see there's a salute to the E46 M3 with the small grilles on the side.

17 One of the smallest detail touches you can place on your car are BMW valve stem caps for your wheels. These are really neat, factory OEM valve caps (part number 36-11-0-009-840) and a set typically runs about $20 at PelicanParts.com.

Time: 1 hour

Tab: $25–750

Talent:

Tools: Air conditioning pressure gauge, specialized A/C equipment

Applicable Years: All

Tinware: R134a recharge kit, or BMW R12 upgrade kit

Tip: Don't use off-the-shelf drop-in solutions

PERFORMANCE GAIN: Better cooling during the summer months

COMPLEMENTARY MODIFICATION: Replace A/C bolt

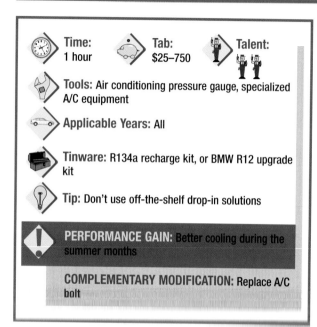

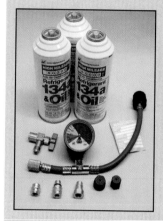
1 This great starter A/C kit from Interdynamics contains three cans of R134a refrigerant and oil and is specifically designed to replenish older cars that may have a few small leaks in the O-rings of the air conditioning system. The kit is available for about $35 at most general automotive stores and has everything you need to recharge your R134a air conditioning system. It includes a can adapter valve, an in-line pressure gauge, and several adapters used for converting old R12 systems to the newer R134a fittings.

On any car, the A/C system is a complicated beast. This project is not intended to be a repair manual for your A/C system, but should serve more as a guide to how the system works and offer key points about the maintenance involved with its upkeep.

Air conditioning systems work using the theory of thermodynamics, whereby heat flows from a warmer surface to a colder one. Heat from inside the car is transferred to the cold metal fins of the evaporator. The refrigerant in the system picks up the heat from the evaporator and takes it to the compressor. The gas is then pressurized, which concentrates the heat by raising the temperature of the refrigerant gas. The gas is then sent to the condenser. The condenser cools the refrigerant and turns the gas back into a liquid. The liquid is then sent to the receiver-dryer, where any water vapor that may have formed in the system is removed. The receiver-dryer also acts as a storage container for unused fluid. From the receiver-dryer, the liquid flows into the expansion valve, which meters it into the evaporator located inside the car. Here the liquid absorbs heat and becomes a low-pressure gas. This evaporation, or boiling of the refrigerant, absorbs heat just as a boiling pot of water absorbs heat from the stove. As heat is absorbed, the evaporator is cooled. A fan blows air through the evaporator and into the cockpit of the car, providing the cooling effect. The compressor then pumps the refrigerant through the entire system. An electromagnetic clutch on the compressor turns the A/C system on and off. In addition to cooling the car, the system also removes water vapor from the ambient air. It is not uncommon to find a small puddle of water underneath your car from the condensation of the air

conditioning system. A thermostat control on the evaporator keeps the condensation in the evaporator from freezing and damaging the unit.

So what can you do to maintain and protect the system from deterioration? First and foremost, operate the air conditioning system at least once a week if the outside temperature is below 50 degrees Fahrenheit. Doing this will circulate the refrigerant in the system and help keep the seals from drying out. Most failures are caused by refrigerant leaking out of the system, which you can prevent simply by making sure that you run the system more frequently.

A belt that runs off the main crankshaft operates the A/C compressor. On cars with a manual adjustment, make sure you don't tighten this belt too tightly, or you may place undue pressure on the bearings inside the compressor. If you suspect you might be having problems with the compressor, check the belt first. Turn on the system, and verify that the electromagnetic clutch is engaging. If it is not, you may need to replace it. Check the power connection to make sure it is live before replacing the clutch.

The original Freon used in the older-style R12 air-conditioned cars is no longer being manufactured. In the early 1990s, auto manufacturers started phasing out Freon-based A/C systems and started implementing the newer R134a systems (BMW appears to have started installing R134a systems with the 1993 models). The cost of the replacement R12 Freon is skyrocketing as the current supplies disappear. This Freon, which was once sold to the public in do-it-yourself kits, can only be legally purchased now by dealers who are trained in recharging these systems.

MISCELLANEOUS

258

If your A/C system needs a major overhaul, it's wise to upgrade your system to R134a, although the R134a refrigerant is not as efficient, is slightly more prone to leak out, and cools slightly less than the original R12. You can purchase R134a inexpensively at your local auto parts stores, and retrofit kits are easy to install (as I will explain a little later). You can determine which type of refrigerant you have in your car from the shape of the connectors and/or the sticker on the front right side of the engine compartment.

Refilling A/C systems

The biggest problem with A/C systems is a loss of refrigerant. Luckily, replacing and topping off refrigerant is a relatively easy process, particularly if you have an R134a system already installed. Interdynamics manufactures the kit I used to refill the car in this project (see Photo 1).Outside your garage, start the car, turn on the A/C system and fan to full blast, and let the car run for about three minutes. Following the instructions included with the kit, connect a new can of refrigerant to the hose/gauge assembly. Be sure you shake the can for about 30 seconds and turn it upside down when you connect it to the gauge assembly. Connect the gauge assembly to the low-side port of your A/C system (see Photo 2). Be sure to wear eye protection and heavy leather gloves when handling the coolant and gauge assembly! If coolant leaks out at any time, it can literally freeze a small patch of your skin quite easily and give you frostbite.

With the car running and the A/C system turned on full blast, take a reading on the pressure gauge. A properly charged system should read between 25 and 45 psi. If the pressure is low, turn the valve on the can to release more refrigerant into the system. Be aware that the pressure gauge reading will automatically elevate as you add more coolant, so periodically close the valve on the can to check if the pressure is rising in the system. If the pressure doesn't increase after adding one complete can, you most likely have a major leak in your system and should seek the help of a professional A/C system mechanic.

With the system properly filled and measured with your gauge, head to the passenger compartment and check the temperature of the air exiting the vents. On a system that is operating really well, the temperature will be in the mid-30s Fahrenheit. For older systems or ones retrofitted to work with R134a, the temperature readings will most likely be higher. Also keep in mind that if your system is cooling air in the 30 degrees Fahrenheit range, the compressor will tend to turn itself on and off, causing the temperature to go up and down slightly. This is not a defect of the system; the system turns itself off as the evaporator nears the freezing temperature of water. This prevents the evaporator from becoming frozen and clogged with icy buildup.

Retrofitting R12 systems

What are your options if your system uses R12 and is currently not working properly? Many drop-in replacements for R12 are out there, but it's unwise simply to place them into your system without performing a valid R134a retrofit. Why? When mechanics at an A/C service station work on your car, they will need to vacuum out and reclaim the refrigerant in your system. If the system contains R12 or R134a, they can combine it with their existing stock. However, if your system contains some aftermarket additive, most A/C service stations will refuse to work on your car (their sensors can determine whether the system is running R12, R134a, or something else). Needless to say, placing these additives into your system limits your options. The best thing to do is either stick with R12 (expensive) or perform a qualified upgrade to R134a.

What are the downsides to upgrading to R134a? The refrigerant doesn't cool as efficiently as R12, meaning your system will perform marginally less than with the R12 Freon. In most cases, however, you won't be able to tell the difference between the two. In addition, the R134a molecule is a little bit smaller than the R12 molecule, meaning an R134a system is more prone to leaks. However, if your system's seals and O-rings are in good condition, this should not be a concern. Some of the Bosch compressors used on the older cars are not compatible with R134a, so you may need to replace your compressor to convert to R134a. All of the E36 cars should have R134a-compatible compressors. An E36 conversion kit is available for the early cars that ran R12 instead of R134a (P/N 82-31-9-067-403, about $200). This kit contains a new receiver drier, new O-rings, a capacity label, and a set of R134a valve adapters. You will also need some PAG compressor oil (P/N 82-11-1-468-042).

The E30 cars are a little more difficult, as almost all of them were fitted with R12 systems. A detailed BMW Tech Bulletin covers the R12 to R134a conversion (BMW Document # 64 05 96). The E30 cars with compressors that are not compatible with R134a include the 318i (July 1985–August 1985); the 325e, 325i, and 325iC (July 1987–October 1988); the 325iX; and the M3. You should check the part number on your compressor prior to the upgrade to make sure that it is compatible with R134a.The following table shows a list of compressors that are not compatible with R134a. You should replace these compressors with part number 64-52-8-363-550.

64 52 1 377 944	64 52 1 377 947
64 52 1 385 416	64 52 1 385 930
64 52 1 386 411	64 52 1 377 940*
64 52 1 377 941*	64 52 1 377 943*
64 52 1 377 946*	

*Requires clutch wiring adapter P/N 64-52-1-386-224

If your E30 has an R134a-compatible compressor, or if you purchase the upgraded one, all you need is the E30 R134a retrofit kit. Like the E36 kit, it contains a new receiver drier, new O-rings, a capacity label, and a set of R134a valve adapters (part number 82-31-9-067-394). If your compressor is low on oil, you will also need PAG compressor oil (part number 82-11-1-468-042).

2 This photo shows the location and orientation of the A/C ports on the 1993 and later E36 cars. (Earlier E36 cars may have R12-based or other systems.) The A/C ports normally have black plastic covers that simply screw off (inset). The low side (the side where you attach the gauge and refrigerant) has the smaller port adapter and is attached to the larger pipe (yellow arrow). The high side (used primarily for checking the compressor during diagnostic testing) has the larger adapter (green arrow) and a smaller diameter pipe.

3 With the engine running, connect the gauge to the low-pressure port on the A/C system. The high side has a larger adapter, so you can't accidentally attach the gauge to the wrong port. With the gauge attached, you can now turn the valve to add more refrigerant to the system. In the photo inset, you can see the pressure for this A/C system is exactly where it should be—in the middle of the white range. Remember to use heavy-duty leather gloves and eye protection when working around A/C components. It's possible that a fitting or a valve may break or otherwise leak refrigerant on your hands.

The process of installing retrofit kits typically requires specialized equipment available only at an A/C service shop, but I'll give an overview of the process. First, have a shop mechanic remove and recycle any old R12 you have left in your system (don't vent it to the atmosphere). Then, swap out the compressor if you are replacing it. Be sure to use new O-rings on all the connections that are opened in the system while you are working on it. Install the new pressure switch (included in the kit) on the receiver/drier. Install the new receiver drier in the car, replacing all O-rings in the process (they are included in the retrofit kit as well). Splice the new switches into the chassis wire harness according to the instructions in the factory retrofit bulletin. Install the R134a adapters on both the high and low side of the system. Then, pull a vacuum on the system for a minimum of 40 minutes and fill with R134a according to the instructions detailed above. Remember to add compressor lubricant if you haven't replaced your compressor. Finally, check the system for leaks using an R134a leak detector, and check the temperature of the air in the passenger cabin.

As you can tell, you need a serious selection of specialized equipment to perform a proper retrofit of your A/C system. The bottom line is that giving your A/C system a major overhaul can be a difficult and time-consuming process. Clearly, the magnitude of repairing and replacing most A/C components is beyond the scope of the average weekend mechanic. Seek professional assistance if your system needs any major work beyond a simple refill.

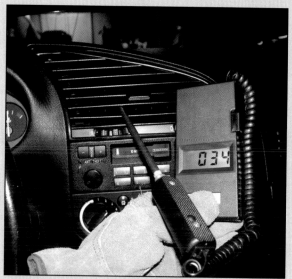

4 Your hand is a pretty poor indicator of relative temperature. Use a digital thermometer and probe, like the one here, to get an accurate reading. A number of factors can affect the final temperature performance of your A/C system—age, quantity of refrigerant, the condition of the compressor or associated components, and whether the system was designed to use R134a, as was this 1995 325ic. During this reading, the outside temperature was probably around 65 degrees Fahrenheit. If you achieve temperatures in the mid-30s, your A/C system is working in top condition!

MISCELLANEOUS

Stubborn Bolt/Stud Removal

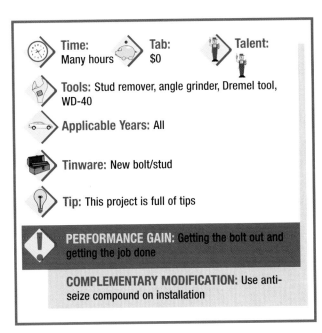

Time: Many hours

Tab: $0

Talent:

Tools: Stud remover, angle grinder, Dremel tool, WD-40

Applicable Years: All

Tinware: New bolt/stud

Tip: This project is full of tips

PERFORMANCE GAIN: Getting the bolt out and getting the job done

COMPLEMENTARY MODIFICATION: Use anti-seize compound on installation

If you are planning to restore a car that is even a few years old, you will undoubtedly come across the odd nut, bolt, or stud that is rusted solid and won't come off. This project will expose you to some of the methods used by several of the "experts" in the field.

The first step in getting rusty or stuck fasteners off is to perform a preemptive strike. It is often the case that you find a nut or stud will not come off after you have already stripped or damaged it. If you think a nut might give you problems, it's far better to tackle the removal process carefully rather than destroy one of your precious parts.

If you are planning to remove an old rusty bolt in a day or two, soak the area with a good penetrating lubricant like WD-40 or liquid wrench. The lubricant will seep down and penetrate the joint, making it easier to remove and break apart. This seeping process takes time, however. At the very least, soak the bolt the night before you attempt to remove it. This will place you a step ahead in the battle.

When removing these old bolts, you must have the right tools for the job. A properly fitting wrench is essential. People often use the wrong tool for the wrong bolt. The female Torx bolts are an excellent example. A simple hex socket tool will sometimes fit onto the bolts, and you may be able to remove some of them, but chances are one of the bolts will become stripped. Using the right-sized tool to remove a fastener means you are increasing the odds it will come off easily.

For pulling studs, Snap-On offers an excellent collet-based stud-removal tool that does the job very well without damaging the stud. This tool incorporates a collet that latches onto and compresses the threads of the stud, squeezing them

tight. Then the tool and the stud can be removed. If you are removing studs from an engine case, an extra vise-grip or two might be useful as well to get more torque on the studs.

Exhaust studs are sometimes difficult to remove from the heads, as they rust and corrode very easily. Make sure you lubricate the area heavily before even attempting to remove a rusty exhaust manifold. Unfortunately, if a stud snaps off, there really isn't too much you can do. Since the studs are heated by the exhaust, they often become very brittle over time. The only way to remove a broken head stud is to have it drilled out or removed using an EDM process.

A common propane torch or, even better, an oxy-acetylene torch may help you out when you need to remove bolts. These torches are available at most hardware stores and are useful beyond belief. A torch can give you an extra advantage in removal, particularly on bolts and studs that have had red Loctite 271 used on them.

With the torch, heat the metal surrounding the stud. This will help melt any Loctite on the threads and will also help expand the metal that is surrounding the stud. Use caution, though; do not apply heat directly to the stud, as this will heat the stud, and it will become even more stuck in the hole. If you are removing a stud from an engine case or a cylinder head, you will find it takes a surprisingly long time to heat up the case. Aluminum and steel conduct heat very well, so focus the torch on the case for a while before you try to remove any studs. Also, be sure to use the torch only in a well-ventilated area.

On the opposite side of the equation, you can sometimes use coolant to help remove a stuck bolt. One of the best-kept secrets is the "compressed air in a can" your local office supply store sells for blowing dust out of old computer equipment. If you hold the can upside down, the gas inside (which is not actually ordinary air) will drip out as a very cold liquid. You can drip this liquid onto bolts and into areas you might be having trouble with. Be careful, though. The cold will have a tendency to make the metal increasingly brittle and prone to breaking. Always use eye and skin protection when using coolants, as they can be deceptively dangerous.

The application of heat and cold together can be a powerful combination. As the joint heats up and then cools again, rust and Loctite may break free from the rapid expansion and contraction. There is no exact science for this, so trial and error is the rule of thumb.

Another important point is to make sure that the nut or bolt you are trying to remove can actually be removed. Often someone will try to remove an embedded stud or a nut that has been welded on, only to find that this is an impossible task. Before you dig out the angle grinder, check and double-check to make sure you aren't missing something obvious.

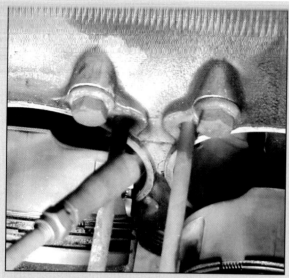

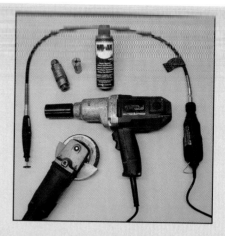

1 The propane or oxy/acetylene torch is one of my personal favorite tools. Make sure you heat the case and not the stud. You may notice it takes a long time for the case to warm up. Keep the torch focused on the area and don't let it stray onto the stud. The white inner portion of the flame is the hottest, the blue part indicates a cooler region. Make sure you only use the torch in a well-ventilated area, as the propane will create harmful carbon monoxide gases.

2 The tools of destruction and mayhem are shown here. The Dremel rotary tool (right) with flexible attachment is best suited for cutting off small nuts, bolts, or studs. This tool will solve about 95 percent of your problems. The angle grinder (lower left) is for more serious tasks where you must completely grind down rusted nuts. WD-40 is an excellent penetrant for removing rusted and stuck bolts. The Snap-on stud remover (upper left) is a hard-to-find tool, yet very useful for removing those troublesome studs. Finally, the pneumatic impact wrench (center) is good for removing nuts that have been mounted with a lot of torque.

Sometimes it makes sense to weld a nut onto a stud that is stuck and immovable. Doing this will allow you to place a wrench on the nut and, hopefully, remove the stud. Before you attempt to weld, make sure that you clean off all of the rust, debris, oil, and anything else that might be on the stud. Sometimes the stud will be old and brittle and may not take well to welding, as is often the case with exhaust studs. Also, you can only effectively weld most studs if they are made of steel. Some alloy studs you cannot weld—the nuts just break off as soon as you try to turn them.

The impact wrench is another useful tool and is most helpful when you are trying to remove a nut that rotates on a bearing (for example, the steering wheel nut) or one that is attached with a great amount of force. The impact wrench "hits" the nut with repeated blows, knocking it loose, which will save you plenty of time when you need to remove specialty bolts. There are two types of impact wrenches available—ones that run on compressed air and simple electric ones that plug into a standard household socket. I recommend the electric style if you don't have an air compressor.

My weapon of choice when all else fails is the Dremel tool or its big brother, the angle grinder. These two tools of destruction really don't stop at anything when it comes to cutting through metal. The Dremel tool is my personal favorite because it is so small and you can place it in so many different positions. Adding to its versatility is the fact that you can add a flexible shaft to the tool that allows you to put the rotating blade just about anywhere you can reach.

The Dremel, or rotary, tool spins at about 50,000 rpm and uses small ceramic-like discs to cut and grind through steel. There are other small fiber-reinforced discs available that are more expensive than the regular discs, but they last longer, and are more effective at cutting through steel quicker. I recommend using these discs, particularly if you can buy a large bag of them at a swap meet or other venue. Make sure you don't ever use the Dremel tool without eye protection.

The angle grinder makes no apologics for being the most destructive of all the tools in my collection. The grinding wheel can grind, wear, cut, and melt away steel much faster than any other tool I own. It's especially useful for grinding off nuts and studs that are so badly rusted there is no way to get a grip on them. Make sure you use appropriate eye, ear, and nose/throat protection when using the grinder, as this tool kicks up a lot of small metal particles.

When all else fails, you can sometimes use a hand drill to bore out an embedded or broken stud. While not the prettiest solution, the hand drill is still an effective method of removal. For greater success with a drill, start out with a very small drill bit and gradually increase the diameter. Also, use plenty of lubricant. When the hole you are drilling gets to be about the size of the stud, try to remove the remains of the stud using a pick. Be careful not to damage the threads of the hole by drilling too large of a hole. When you are finished, chase a tap down the hole to clear out the threads, or if it's damaged, thread the hole to a larger diameter.

MISCELLANEOUS

Using Car Bras and Car Film

Time: 15 minutes

Tab: $125

Talent: ▮▮

Tools: None

Applicable Years: All

Tinware: Front car bra, mirror bras

Tip: Make sure the bra is tight—flapping bras can do more damage to your paint than rocks from the road

PERFORMANCE GAIN: Protects your car's paint job and resale value

COMPLEMENTARY MODIFICATION: Mirror bras

On just about every road in the world, many hazards exist that threaten your car. None can be as damaging to your BMW's paint, however, as the gravel, rocks, and other debris kicked up by the other cars in front of you. Many people don't realize the amount of paint damage that can occur until it's too late. Protecting your car from damage while it is still in good condition will help it hold its resale value. Without a doubt, the most effective method of protection is a vinyl front cover, comically named a "car bra." Many people feel that the look of the car bra detracts from the overall lines of the car. However, not much else is available to protect the front surface of your car. Most bras are made out of a stretchy type of black vinyl that has a leathery feel to it. The bra is attached to the front of the car and protects the bumper, hood, and sides of the fenders from rocks and gravel. The inside of the bra is lined with a felt-like material. Not only does the bra protect your car from scratches, but it can also reduce the amount of damage inflicted from flying rocks. You can minimize expensive and damaging paint chips by using a front mounted bra.

Most BMW bras are two-piece units that cover the fenders and hood separately. This allows you to open the hood when the bra is attached. All the bras must be ordered specifically by model year. Bras typically have openings for the U.S. fog lamps, if your car has them as an option. Most bras can be specially tailored toward your specific car. For example, you can eliminate the license plate opening, front bumper guard openings, or fog lamp openings, or you can add holes for headlamp washers. Either way, it's smart to get a bra that fits your car well.

1 When installing a bra on your BMW, make sure it's tight and properly attached. Poorly installed bras can do more damage than rocks kicked up from the road. There are a few different types of bras depending upon the year and model of your 3 Series. Some allow you to open the hood easily, while others fit better by using the hood as an attachment point.

Without a doubt, bras can be unwieldy and cumbersome, and it's wise to follow a few rules of thumb when using one. First, never leave the bra on the car when it's wet. Doing this will allow condensation to build up underneath the bra. The resulting water vapor can seriously damage the paint—whether by cracking the clear coat or altering the color. Thus, you should get in the habit of removing the bra immediately whenever it gets wet. You would hate to have to put the bra on the car just to cover up damage it was supposed to prevent!

Second, watch the seams of the bra. One tip is to use soft felt squares on any point where there is a seam touching metal. Routine driving may cause the chassis to flex enough

MISCELLANEOUS

263

2 An interesting alternative to the traditional cloth bra is plastic film. While traditional car bras are much thicker and will deflect larger objects, clear plastic film applied to the front of your car can do wonders to protect the paint from nasty rock chips. The film works well, although it is fairly difficult to install and is not inexpensive. In general, installing the film is not a do-it-yourself project, as you can easily make a mistake and ruin the film. I recommend seeking professional installation if you decide to go this route.

to cause substantial rubbing, especially on the hood. Adding these felt squares reduces the likelihood of damage.

Finally, the most important thing to do is keep the bra clean. It won't help your car if there is dirt trapped between the bra and the paint. Routine driving with a dirty bra will only result in scratches to your paint. It's also generally not a wise idea to purchase a used bra for your car, because it will probably be too dirty to amply protect your car from damage. They are really tough to get completely clean—so when in doubt, throw it out!

http://www.101projects.com/BMW/100.htm

PROJECT 100
Tire and Wheel Sizing

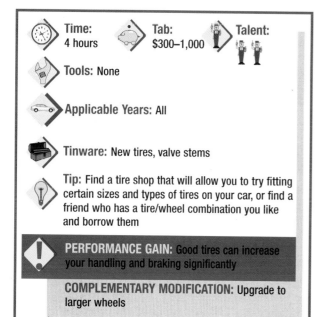

Time: 4 hours

Tab: $300–1,000

Talent: ▮▮▮

Tools: None

Applicable Years: All

Tinware: New tires, valve stems

Tip: Find a tire shop that will allow you to try fitting certain sizes and types of tires on your car, or find a friend who has a tire/wheel combination you like and borrow them

PERFORMANCE GAIN: Good tires can increase your handling and braking significantly

COMPLEMENTARY MODIFICATION: Upgrade to larger wheels

For this project, I polled a number of people on Internet chat boards to figure out the best and most popular combinations of tire and wheel sizes for the various models of the BMW 3 Series. I confirmed what I believed to be inherently true about almost all hardcore BMW owners: They love to modify and tweak their cars. Out of all the responses, no two were exactly alike. I've compiled and summarized the feedback here so that you can make an educated decision when equipping your BMW.

Let's talk for a few moments about tires in general. Although you can write volumes on tire sizing and design, we'll try to cover only the basics here. Tires are sized using a system that takes into effect the tire's aspect ratio. This aspect ratio is a function of the tire's width with respect to its height. An example of a common European tire size is 195/65R15. The first number, 195, refers to the width of the tire in millimeters. The second number, 65, refers to the height of the tire as a percentage of the width. Therefore 65 percent of 195 would give a tire height of about 127 mm. The "R" following the width and length denotes radial construction. The next

1 The typical fender-rolling tool allows you to tuck the inside edge of the fender inward and also lets you push the entire fender outward if you so desire. When using a rented fender-rolling tool, be sure to warm the paint with a heat gun. Doing this will prevent cracking. Roll slowly back and forth a bit, tighten, and then repeat. You may have to readjust the roller head periodically in order to keep it flush. Also, if the fender is not very concentric with the wheel well, you may not be able to roll the entire fender in one complete stroke—you may have to roll one side at a time and then reposition the tool.

number is the tire's inner diameter, in this case 15 inches. Finally, the number followed by a letter is the load rating, and the letter is the tire's maximum speed safety ratings. Speed ratings are as follows:

Q=99 mph, 160km/h	V=149 mph, 240km/h
S=112 mph, 180km/h	W=168 mph, 270km/h
T=118 mph, 190km/h	Y=186 mph, 300km/h
U=124 mph, 200km/h	Z=149+ mph, 240km/h and over
H=130 mph, 210km/h	

There is an exception to all this: If a tire is Z-rated, the "Z" is noted immediately after the height and before the "radial" denotation. If our example above were Z-rated, it would be 195/65ZR15. A good Z-rated tire should be more than adequate for non-suicidal driving! Tread is another important consideration in selecting a tire. You should select your tire based on what type of driving you plan to do. With the BMW 3 Series, it can be a bit more complicated, because some people don't drive them in all types of weather. For example, an all-weather tire seems like a natural choice for a family sedan located in a snowy environment. However, many BMW owners do not drive their cars in the snow or the rain.

In an ideal setting, such as on the racetrack, flat-surfaced tires called "racing slicks" are best because a maximum amount of tire rubber is laid down on the road surface. However, slicks have almost no traction in wet weather. The water

has a tendency to get underneath the tire and cause the car to hydroplane by elevating the wheel onto a wedge of water.

The full array of choices for tire treads is way beyond the scope of this project. One rule of thumb, though, is to make sure you purchase a tire appropriate for your climate. Using a snow tire or an all-weather tire on a BMW that is rarely driven in the snow will significantly reduce the tire's contact patch area and also reduce cornering performance on dry roads. However, failing to equip your car for bad weather can result in disastrous effects if an unforeseen storm catches you unprepared. If you drive your car only during the dry summer months, look for a conventional performance tire with a maximum contact patch area.

Another important consideration is tread wear versus traction. Tread wear refers to the average number of miles that the tires can handle before they need to be replaced. A tread wear indicator of 100 means that the tires should last about 30,000 miles. An indicator mark of 80 means that the tires will last 20 percent less, or 24,000 miles. Wear will be different for each car and vary according to each driver's personal driving habits, but the various ratings are good for comparisons among different brands and types of tires. Traction relates to the type of materials used in the tire. The harder the rubber used in the tire, the longer the tires will last. However, hard rubber provides much less traction. An "A" rating for traction is best. These tires will grip the road well, but will generally wear out faster than the "B" or "C" tires.

It is also important to consider longevity when selecting a tire. Most tires have a limited shelf life based on the rubber's natural process of breaking down and becoming brittle. It doesn't pay to purchase a 30,000-mile tire if you are only going to be putting 3,000 miles a year on your car. After ten years, the rubber may be cracked and deteriorated beyond safe use, even if there is plenty of tread left. This is also an important consideration if you are purchasing a BMW that has been in storage or sparsely driven for many years. Although the tires may have plenty of tread on them, they actually may be dried out and ready to fail. If tires develop cracks in their sidewalls from aging, they can blow out when heated up from driving. A blowout is a very bad situation and can cause you to lose control of your car very quickly.

So, which tires and wheels can you fit on your BMW 3 Series? It all depends upon the wheel design, offset, and type of tires you prefer to run on your car. With so many different combinations out there, it's impossible to document them fully in a mere few pages. I did create a wheel collage (opposite page) you can use for generating ideas about which wheels to mount on your car. This array contains photos of BMWs I took at various meets and club events over a period of three years. Expanding the pool of options, you can also use spacers to accommodate different wheels that weren't originally designed for your car. When going this route, I recommend the use of BMW-specific hub-centric spacers, which are located on the hub by a machined center hole, as opposed to lug-centric spacers located by the position of the lug nuts alone.

2 No matter which wheels you buy, you're going to want to protect your investment with a set of wheel locks. The factory wheel locks available from BMW look very nice and match the appearance of the factory lugs.

Rolling the fender involves using a special tool to fold in the inside of your fenders so you can fit wider tires (see Photo 1). Many people perform this modification in order to get bigger wheels or clear tire fit. However, there are those who don't like the look of rolled fenders, so this could adversely affect the resale value of the car. If you give the suspension a bit of negative camber (angling the top of the wheel inwards), you can also make the larger rims fit on your car.

With many of the older cars, tire sizes that fit often depend upon the condition of the car. Sometimes the chassis

3 Many factory wheels have a center hubcap secured by plastic snaps. To remove this hubcap, you can use the removal tool located in the factory tool kit found in your trunk. If this tool is missing, however, you may use a pair of larger channel locks instead. You should verify that your factory tool is still located in your tool kit, as otherwise it may be very difficult to remove the hubcaps from wheels when you're stuck on the side of the road with a flat tire. When reinstalling the hubcap, line up the small arrow with the line cast into the wheel (green arrow).

is perfectly balanced from left to right, and sometimes it is slightly off from being in an accident or simply from body sag. It's best to find a tire shop that will allow you to try out several tires to find the best fit. Go in during the afternoon on a slow day and talk with your tire salesman to see if he will let you size the tires on your car. If he won't, go to a different shop—there are plenty of them out there willing to cater to you, especially if you are going to shell out some significant money for high-performance tires.

If you want to go with larger wheels on the E36, the best combination for 18-inch wheels would probably be 225/40R18 in the front and 245/35/R18 in the rear. For more tire patch on the rear, you can probably fit a 255/35R18, but the best handling comes from having the same sized tires and wheels on all four corners. If you are willing to roll the fenders on your car and run spacers, the number of wheel options increases for you. With wider wheels, tire options grow exponentially. Again, rolling the fender can help accommodate a wider wheel and tire. The type of offset used on the wheel and the tire size will affect whether it will fit or not. The offset of a wheel is the distance of the center of the wheel from the edge of the mounting flange on the hub. Different wheels with varying offsets will affect tire sizing considerably, so make sure you know which types of wheel and offset you have before you attempt to mount tires.

So after reading this project, are you still a little bit confused? You should be, and rightly so. It would appear that there is a never-ending set of options for tire sizing on the various BMW models. The best way to figure out what type of tires to place on your car is to ask around. Check on the Internet—and check into the chat room of one or more technical bulletin boards—like the one at PelicanParts.com. I'm also fond of the TireRack.com website; it has useful tools for determining the right wheel/tire combinations to fit your car. Regardless of what the "pros" think, you will find that the majority of BMW owners have an opinion to share about a wheel/tire option they have tried on their car.

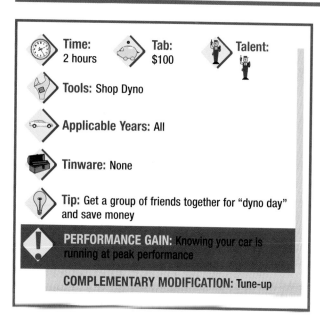

Time: 2 hours

Tab: $100

Talent: 🕴

Tools: Shop Dyno

Applicable Years: All

Tinware: None

Tip: Get a group of friends together for "dyno day" and save money

PERFORMANCE GAIN: Knowing your car is running at peak performance

COMPLEMENTARY MODIFICATION: Tune-up

1 This photo shows Chris Bethel's 1995 M3 on a rolling dynamometer. Engine modifications include large bore throttle body, cold air intake, Jim Conforti chip, Stromung exhaust, lightweight aluminum flywheel, 3.2L M3 clutch package, Schrick 256/264 camshafts, and 24 lb. Ford Motorsport fuel injectors. For this test, the car was driven slowly through its full rpm range on the dyno while carefully recording all of the applicable data. Fans and air temperature/humidity measurement devices ensured that the environment remained constant between dyno runs.

What performance project book would be complete without a section on dynamometer testing? One of the neatest trips you can make is to your local "dyno" shop. For about $100, you can make a few runs on the dyno and actually measure the horsepower generated by your engine. The whole process is somewhat complicated, with varying degrees of detail and accuracy, but for the sake of this section, we'll just cover the basics.

What is a dyno? Short for "dynamometer," the dyno measures the horsepower output of your engine. There are two basic types of dynos: one that you bolt the engine up to and run, and one that measures horsepower at the rear wheels of your car. This is also called RWHP (rear-wheel horsepower). Most modern dyno testing is performed on a rolling dyno that measures the power output at the wheels. You drive your car onto big rollers and accelerate at full throttle until you reach your rev limit. Then, you let the clutch out and let the rollers spin down freely. Large fans and environmental controls aim to keep the test environment at a steady state so you can compare dyno runs. The dyno works by placing a load on the car, similar to air friction as you drive down the road at high speeds. By measuring this load, combined with the total rpm of the vehicle, a graph of the power output by the car can be derived.

Torque/horsepower

The dyno actually measures the torque output by your rear wheels. Torque is a measurement of rotational force and is related to the overall power output by your engine. The horsepower output by your engine is equivalent to the following formula, derived from an early English standard:

$$\text{Horsepower} = \text{torque} \times \text{rpm}/5252$$

This translates into a power relationship that horsepower is defined as 33,000 ft-lb (force) per minute. This is also referred to as the "horsepower definition," as defined by the Society of Automotive Engineers (SAE Horsepower).

You may have also seen other values for power and wondered what they meant. European documentation often gives power numbers in kilowatts. For reference, one horsepower equals 0.746 kilowatts. BMW's ratings are often listed in the European standard of DIN HP or kilowatts (kW). One DIN horsepower is rated as the power required to raise 450,000 kilograms one centimeter in one minute (or about .73 kW). The values of SAE and DIN horsepower are very similar, with 1 SAE HP being equal to .98629 DIN HP. For all practical purposes, you can think of them as about the same.

You may also have heard the term "brake horsepower" (BHP). Brake horsepower is measured at the flywheel of the engine with no load from the chassis, without any electrical or mechanical accessories attached, under ideal fuel and timing conditions. In modern terms, the brake horsepower figure would be mostly associated with what is now called gross horsepower.

Air/fuel measurement

In addition to measuring output torque and RPM, some dynos can also monitor your air/fuel mixture. This will allow you to adjust the mixture tables on an engine management system (Project 23) to match the power output correctly. In other words, if you find that your engine is running lean at 4500 rpm, you can adjust the fuel injection mixture to richen

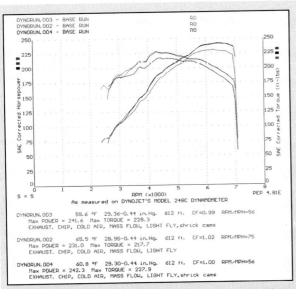

```
DYNORUN.003 - BASE RUN                    RO
DYNORUN.002 - BASE RUN                    RO
DYNORUN.004 - BASE RUN                    RO
```

DYNORUN.003   59.6 °F   29.36-0.44 in.Hg.   612 ft.   CF=0.99   RPM/MPH=56
   Max POWER = 241.6 Max TORQUE = 228.3
   EXHAUST, CHIP, COLD AIR, MASS FLOW, LIGHT FLY,shrick cams

DYNORUN.002   65.5 °F   28.95-0.44 in.Hg.   612 ft.   CF=1.02   RPM/MPH=75
   Max POWER = 231.0 Max TORQUE = 217.7
   EXHAUST, CHIP, COLD AIR, MASS FLOW, LIGHT FLY

DYNORUN.004   60.8 °F   29.30-0.44 in.Hg.   612 ft.   CF=1.00   RPM/MPH=56
   Max POWER = 242.3 Max TORQUE = 227.9
   EXHAUST, CHIP, COLD AIR, MASS FLOW, LIGHT FLY,shrick cams

2 Shown here is a typical dyno graph for the car in Photo 1. The graph shows rear wheel peak horsepower of about 242 hp. The rating for this engine in its stock configuration is 215 at the rear wheels. Note that per the relationship between torque and horsepower, they are equal when the rpm has reached 5252.

it up and produce more ideal combustion. This translates to more horsepower output from the engine.

Dyno results

The dyno will generate a graph of horsepower versus rpm for the engine being tested. With this graph, you will be able to determine the engine's peak horsepower and peak torque. The graph will also show you the peak horsepower output from the engine. On a modified six-cylinder M3 engine, this will typically be at the higher end of the rpm range, near 6,000 rpm. The engine will peak in horsepower and then fall off dramatically as the rev-limiter in the engine cuts off the ignition system.

Comparing results

An unfortunate downside to dyno tests is that they often cannot be compared to one another accurately. For one thing, large dynos cannot be calibrated easily. As a result, tests from the same dyno with the same car on different days may produce different results. Even the manufacturers of some dynamometers admit that their dyno at one location may test 5 to 10 percent differently than the same model at another location. When you consider the discrepancies may become bigger when you include dynos from different manufacturers, the ability to accurately compare results becomes significantly less useful.

Another important issue with respect to dyno figures is that environmental conditions heavily influence the test. This includes temperature, humidity, and altitude, to name a few. Since conditions may change from day to day, dyno runs that span multiple days may produce different results.

Engine optimization

As previously mentioned, dyno testing can be very subjective. Other than bragging rights, pure dyno numbers are not very useful. The true benefit of the dyno test comes when you are able to use it to optimize your engine. Particularly with engine management systems like the TEC-3 (Project 23), you really need extensive dyno testing in order to determine what your optimum operating parameters are on the fuel ratio and ignition timing maps. The factory used the same type of procedure to optimize and program the Motronic factory chips the stock engine management system uses.

In order to gain the most horsepower from your engine, you need to perform several dyno runs while varying different engine parameters (timing, mixture, advance curve, etc.). Don't forget the scientific method: Only change one variable at a time, or you won't know which change made the difference. Only after carefully analyzing the data can you determine what the best values are for your engine management system map. Measuring the power output of the engine will allow you to optimize your engine and get the peace of mind of knowing you are extracting the maximum horsepower out of your engine.

Driveline losses

Since dyno testing is performed using rollers under your car's drive wheels, some forces will reduce the power between the flywheel and the rear wheels. These driveline losses include friction from the transmission, losses from brake discs dragging slightly, and friction in the wheel bearings. On the E36 BMW, typical driveline loss estimates are often about 15 percent, although modifications to the chassis can raise or lower that value. Through a complicated process of calculations computed by the dynamometer, you can determine your driveline losses by counting the time it takes the dyno rollers to stop when you let out the clutch. Using these calculations, you can then estimate what your horsepower output is at the flywheel.

Transmission gearing

One of the benefits of dyno testing is the ability to design your transmission ratios to meet the exact power characteristics of your engine. Depending on where you want optimum performance, you can install taller or shorter gears into any of the five speeds on your transmission. The results of a dyno test will give you specific horsepower numbers for each rpm range and allow you to tailor your transmission gearing to suit your desires.

Software dynos

This software is what I call the poor man's dyno. It plugs into your BMW's OBD-II port and estimates power and torque based upon a variety of factors. The AutoEnginuity software that you use to monitor OBD-II functions also has a very good dyno emulator built in. With preprogrammed profiles for almost all BMWs, it has proven itself to be extremely accurate in predicting engine performance. (See Project 29 for more details.)

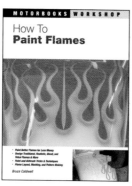

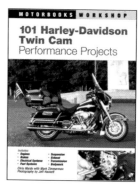